Mathematics In Our World

Second Edition

Grade 3

Robert E. Eicholz

Phares G. O'Daffer

Charles R. Fleenor

▲ **Addison-Wesley Publishing Company**

Menlo Park, California · Reading, Massachusetts · London · Amsterdam · Don Mills, Ontario · Sydney

Photograph Acknowledgments

The Astrodome, Houston, Texas: 32–33

Richard Crone*: 342 bottom left

William R. Curtsinger/U.S. Navy: 342 top right

George B. Fry III*: 1 top left and bottom right,
2 top, 12 top, 13 top right and bottom right, 14–15,
16, 17, 19, 20 top, 29, 30, 36 both, 48 top left,
center left and bottom left, 55 top left, bottom left
and bottom right, 56, 65 bottom left, 66, 78, 86
both, 87, 88, 92, 98, 100 top, 111 top left, bottom
center and bottom right, 112 top, 114, 115, 116,
119, 124 bottom, 128–129 both, 130–131 both,
132–133 center, 136, 144–145, 147, 160, 166 top, 175
top, center left, bottom center and center right, 176
all, 182–183, 186, 190, 191 all, 208–209, 212, 214,
216 all, 220 all, 233 top left and bottom left, 238,
240, 245, 248, 250 both, 251, 259, 262–263,
270 all, 271, 276, 282, 286 all, 287, 288, 293 top left,
top right and bottom left, 298 top, 304, 314, 316,
317 all, 326, 328, 329 both, 334 top, 338 top and top
center, 339, 342 top left, center left and center right

Burt Glinn/Magnum Photos: 138–139 top center

George Hall*: 149 bottom

Pamela Johnson Meyer*: 4–5

Bil Plummer*: 82–83, 342 bottom right

Burk Uzzle/Magnum Photos: 139 bottom right

Nikolay Zurek*: cover

*Photographs provided expressly for the publisher.

All other illustrations and photographs by
Addison-Wesley staff.

Illustration Acknowledgments

Artworks: 111, 140, 141, 152, 153, 154, 155, 156, 157
175, 180, 181, 192, 193, 198, 202, 203, 204, 205, 221,
252, 253, 260, 261, 312

Robert Bausch: 185, 194, 195, 206, 207, 278, 279

Dick Cole: 6, 7, 22, 23, 24, 25, 26, 27, 34, 35, 62, 68,
69, 81

Susan Jaekel: 272, 273, 274, 350B, 351B, 352A, 352B

Heather King: 236, 237

Pat Marshall: 8, 9, 37, 118, 337, 353D

Masami Miyamoto: 178, 179, 188, 189

Wayne and Teresa Snyder: 38, 78, 79, 120, 121, 126,
127, 150, 151, 168, 169

Ed Tabor: 85, 142, 143

Bill Yenne: 72, 94, 95

ISBN 0-201-16050-1

BCDEFGHIJKL-KR-854321

Contents

Level 23

Numeration
Adding Whole Numbers
Subtracting Whole Numbers
Using Your Skills
Points, Lines, and Angles

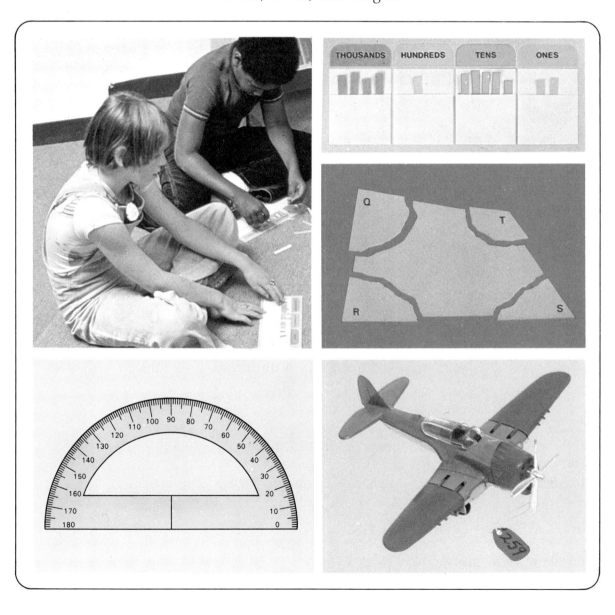

Numeration

Getting started

The colored strips in the pocket chart show the number *one thousand four hundred twenty-three.*

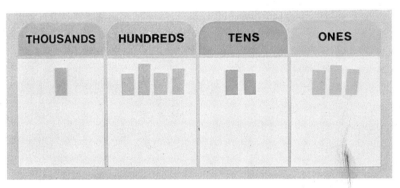

| 1 thousand | 4 hundreds | 2 tens | 3 ones |

1 4 2 3

What number is shown on this pocket chart?

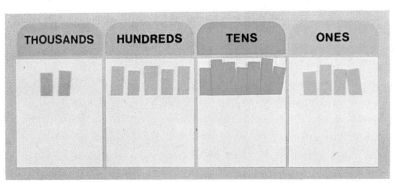

How would you show 5148 on a pocket chart?

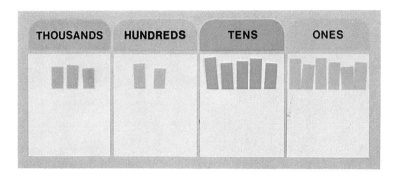

$$3000 \quad + \quad 200 \quad + \quad 50 \quad + \quad 6 \quad \leftarrow \text{ expanded numeral}$$

$$3\ 2\ 5\ 6 \qquad\qquad \leftarrow \text{ standard numeral}$$

Give the expanded numeral and the standard numeral for each pocket chart.

1.

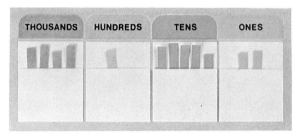

2.

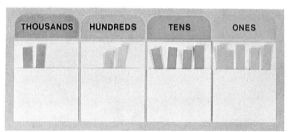

3.

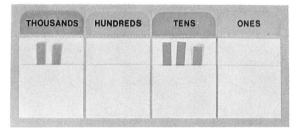

4.

Write each of the following as a standard numeral.

5. 7000 + 200 + 10 + 9

6. 8000 + 700 + 30 + 6

7. 9000 + 400 + 70 + 1

8. 5000 + 600 + 20 + 7

9. 2000 + 100 + 60 + 8

10. 9000 + 400 + 8

11. 4000 + 600 + 20 + 9

12. 300 + 70 + 5

13. 3000 + 50 + 6

14. 9000 + 400 + 30 + 7

Thousands

A record crowd of 141 670
persons attended a rodeo.

hundred thousands	ten thousands	thousands	hundreds	tens	ones
1	4	1	6	7	0

We see:

We write: 141 670
We say: one hundred forty-one thousand,
               six hundred seventy

Read each numeral.
Tell what each red digit means.
Example: 747 623

> seven hundred forty-seven thousand,
> six hundred twenty-three. The four
> means four ten thousands or forty thousand.

1. 122 047	2. 538 717	3. 24 953	4. 307 481	5. 725 461
6. 168 162	7. 27 359	8. 743 286	9. 417 358	10. 80 392
11. 241 536	12. 503 829	13. 12 685	14. 648 365	15. 105 297
16. 357 035	17. 92 814	18. 710 982	19. 64 375	20. 962 148

Write the <u>expanded numeral</u> for each number.

Example: 3158 = 3000 + 100 + 50 + 8

21. 2493	22. 6344	23. 975	24. 349	25. 1170
26. 2346	27. 1257	28. 3074	29. 26 447	30. 83 589
31. 7995	32. 38 576	33. 129 844	34. 178 625	35. 653 019

Write each numeral.

1. forty-six thousand, eight hundred nineteen
2. fifty-nine thousand, six hundred twenty-seven
3. two hundred fourteen thousand, nine hundred five
4. six hundred thousand
5. one hundred twenty thousand, one hundred twenty

This abacus shows the number 562 342.

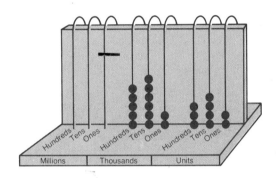

Give the number shown by each abacus.

6.
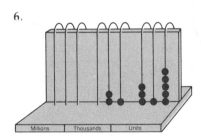

7.
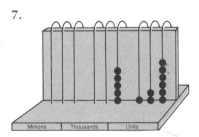

8.
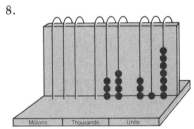

9.
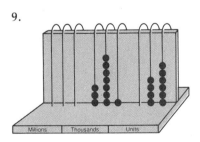

10.
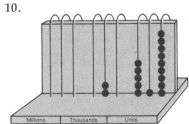

11.
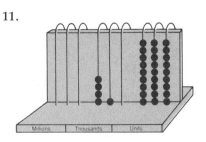

An astronaut on a trip
to the planet Mars might
be 54 172 389 km
from Earth.

Each group of three digits is separated into **periods.**
Periods are separated by spaces.

Millions			Thousands			Units		
hundred millions	ten millions	millions	hundred thousands	ten thousands	thousands	hundreds	tens	ones
	5	4	1	7	2	3	8	9

We say: fifty-four million, one hundred seventy-two thousand,
        three hundred eighty-nine
We write: 54 172 389

Read each numeral. Tell what each red digit means.

1. 5 103 286

2. 36 258 342

3. 127 240 316

4. 306 526 319

5. 80 000 275

6. 100 000

7. 7 629 037

8. 65 070 002

9. 23 796

10. 127 240 316

11. 17 623 409

12. 14 014

13. 296 748 842

14. 709 806 111

15. 17 000 000

The Skylab I space station traveled about 18 674 500 kilometers.

For this numeral, give the digit that is in each of the following places.

1. ten thousands
2. ones
3. hundred thousands
4. millions
5. hundreds
6. thousands
7. ten millions
8. tens

Write the standard numeral for each.

9. eighty-four million, sixty-seven thousand, three hundred seventy-five

10. four hundred seventy-nine million, eight thousand, twenty-three

Write the numeral for the number in each sentence.

11. The first manned satellite traveled forty thousand, eight hundred sixty-eight kilometers.

12. The first woman astronaut (Valentina Tereshkova) traveled one million, nine hundred seventy-one thousand kilometers.

13. The Apollo XIII astronauts were four hundred thousand, one hundred one kilometers from Earth on their moon flight.

☆ 14. Find the distance from Earth to a planet that is interesting to you.

I have nine digits and no more. All are zeros except one 4.

Who am I?

Rounding numbers

We often **round numbers** to the
nearest ten, hundred, or thousand.
The bag contains 392 grams.

What is 392 rounded to the **nearest ten?**

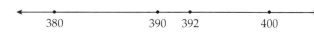

392 is closer to 390 than to 400.
392 rounded to the nearest ten is 390.

What is 392 rounded to the **nearest hundred?**

392 is closer to 400 than to 300.
392 rounded to the nearest hundred is 400.

What is 350 rounded to the **nearest hundred?**
350 is halfway between 300 and 400.
350 is rounded up to 400.

75 rounded to the **nearest ten** is 80.
2534 rounded to the **nearest thousand** is 3000.

Round to the nearest ten.	Round to the nearest hundred.	Round to the nearest thousand.
1. 319	7. 642	13. 2347
2. 124	8. 2776	14. 7944
3. 86	9. 519	15. 6007
4. 547	10. 3844	16. 5129
5. 1275	11. 7550	17. 1978
6. 3368	12. 9193	18. 8296

Round the number of grams to the nearest ten.

1.

274 g

2.

168 g

3.

336 g

Round the number of grams to the nearest hundred.

4.

448 g

5.

343 g

6.

896 g

Round the number of grams to the nearest thousand.

7.

2240 g

8.

1814 g

9.

4480 g

Answers for Self-check 1. 6382 2. 7508 3. 1645 4. 9000 + 100 + 20 + 5 5. 8000 + 10 + 3
6. 3000 + 900 + 70 + 1 7. five thousand 8. thirty thousand 9. six million 10. nine hundred
thousand 11. 6749 12. 432 251 13. 805 920 14. 6000 15. 8000 16. 9200 17. 3500

Self-check

Write as a standard numeral.

1. $6000 + 300 + 80 + 2$ 2. $7000 + 500 + 8$ 3. $1000 + 600 + 40 + 5$

Write as an expanded numeral.   Tell what each red digit means.

4. 9125   5. 8013   6. 3971   7. 35 128   8. 437 029
                                      9. 6 413 572   10. 917 638

Write the standard numerals.

11. six thousand, seven hundred forty-nine
12. four hundred thirty-two thousand, two hundred fifty-one
13. eight hundred five thousand, nine hundred twenty

Round to the nearest thousand.   Round to the nearest hundred.

14. 6392   15. 7682   16. 9176   17. 3506

Answers for Self-check—page 9

Test

Write as a standard numeral.

1. $8000 + 400 + 50 + 7$ 2. $6000 + 300 + 8$ 3. $5000 + 700 + 30 + 2$

Write as an expanded numeral.   Tell what each red digit means.

4. 6351   5. 5076   6. 9282   7. 159 264   8. 28 038
                                          9. 7 328 604   10. 631 429

Write the standard numerals.

11. fifty-six thousand, two hundred seven
12. nine hundred forty-one thousand, three hundred sixty-eight
13. seven thousand, twenty-three

Round to the nearest thousand.   Round to the nearest hundred.

14. 3628   15. 1859   16. 5238   17. 8479

Ancient Egyptian Numerals

The ancient Egyptians used pictures called *hieroglyphs* to represent numbers and words. They did not use place value, but simply added the value of each symbol to get the number.

Egyptian Hieroglyphic Numerals						
Stroke	Arch	Coiled Rope	Lotus Flower	Pointed Finger	Tadpole	Astonished Man
1	10	100	1000	10 000	100 000	1 000 000

∩ | | | | = 14   ⌐⌐∩∩∩ | | | | = 235

⌐⌐⌐∩∩∩∩ | | | | | = 1336

What numbers do these Egyptian numerals show?

1. ∩∩∩∩ | | | | | 2. ⌐⌐∩ | | | 3. ⌐⌐⌐∩ | |

4. ⌐⌐⌐∩∩∩∩∩ | | 5. ⌐∩∩∩∩∩∩∩∩⌐⌐⌐∩ | | |

Write Egyptian numerals for these numbers.

6. your age   7. the year you were born   8. this year

More practice, page 358, Set A

Adding

Getting started

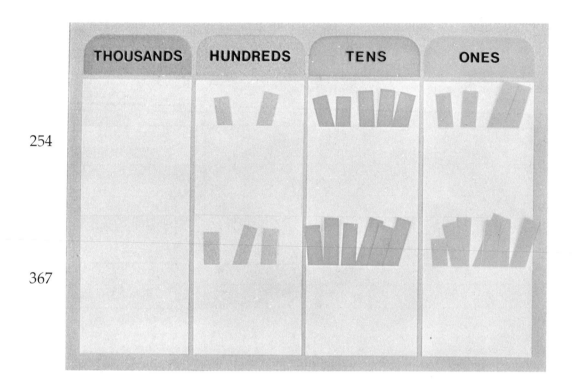

Two numbers, 254 and 367, are shown on this pocket chart.

How would you show the sum of these
two numbers on a pocket chart?

Trade 10 ones for 1 ten
when you can.

Trade 10 tens for 1 hundred
when you can.

Give the sum of each pair of numbers shown on the charts.

1.

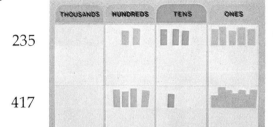

235

417

2.

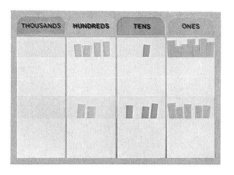

417

235

Associative Principle:
changing the grouping
235 + 417 = 600 + 40 + 12
              = 600 + 40 + (10 + 2)
              = 600 + (40 + 10) + 2
              = 600 + 50 + 2
              = n

Commutative Principle:
changing the order
417 + 235 = 235 + 417
417 + 235 = n

3.

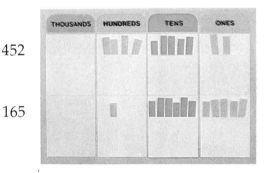

452

165

4.

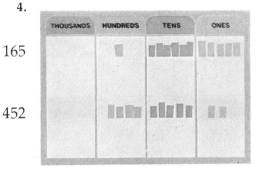

165

452

Associative Principle
452 + 165 = 500 + 110 + 7
              = 500 + (100 + 10) + 7
              = (500 + 100) + 10 + 7
              = 600 + 10 + 7
              = n

Commutative Principle
165 + 452 = 452 + 165
165 + 452 = n

More practice, page 356A

Adding with regrouping

Randy has 477 United States stamps.
He also has 158 stamps from other
countries. How many stamps does
he have?

Finding the answer

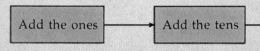

| Add the ones | → | Add the tens | → | Add the hundreds |

```
   1                1 1              1 1
  158              158              158
+ 477            + 477            + 477
─────            ─────            ─────
    5               35              635
```

Randy has 635 stamps.

Other examples

```
   1              1 1              1 1              1 1
  35             574              735             6237
+ 48            + 89             +478            +5184
────            ─────            ─────            ──────
  83             663             1213            11421
```

Find the sums.

1.   35
    + 26

2.   57
    + 19

3.   39
    + 67

4.   58
    + 72

5.   62
    + 79

6.   627
    + 184

7.   566
    + 249

8.   809
    + 78

9.   173
    + 284

Find the sums.

1. 327
    + 649

2. 872
    + 328

3. 663
    + 564

4. 279
    + 153

5. 408
    + 307

6. 846
    + 385

7. 299
    + 507

8. 738
    + 528

9.   43
    + 578

10. 633
    + 772

11. 743
    + 78

12. 369
    + 129

13. 903
    + 437

14.   79
    + 89

15. 698
    + 303

16. 466
    + 538

17. 6927
    + 4845

18. 1308
    + 8659

19. 2594
    + 7086

20. 5665
    + 8798

21. Margaret had 289 stamps.
    She collected 35 more.
    How many does she have now?

22. Saul had 457 stamps.
    He bought 83 more. How
    many does he have now?

Start with 1. Add 2, add 3, add 4,
and so on. How many numbers must
you add to get to 100? How many must
you add to get to 1000?

More practice, page 359

Column addition

Pam and Rosa made a game of turning over number cards to form 2-digit numbers. The low score for the sum of three numbers wins. Pam's score was 101. What was Rosa's score?

	1st number	2nd number	3rd number	score
Pam	58	19	24	101
Rosa	37	16	28	

Finding the answer

Add the ones	→	Add all the tens

$$
\begin{array}{r}
\overset{2}{3}7 \\
16 \\
+28 \\
\hline
1
\end{array}
\qquad
\begin{array}{r}
\overset{2}{3}7 \\
16 \\
+28 \\
\hline
81
\end{array}
$$

Rosa's score was 81.

Other examples

$$
\begin{array}{r}
\overset{2}{5}8 \\
19 \\
+24 \\
\hline
101
\end{array}
\qquad
\begin{array}{r}
\overset{2}{2}\overset{2}{7}9 \\
388 \\
+577 \\
\hline
1244
\end{array}
\qquad
\begin{array}{r}
\overset{1}{3}\overset{1}{1}\overset{2}{4}4 \\
1217 \\
+1799 \\
\hline
6160
\end{array}
\qquad
\begin{array}{r}
\overset{1}{8}\overset{2}{4}\overset{2}{3}5 \\
7286 \\
189 \\
+5577 \\
\hline
21487
\end{array}
$$

Find the sums.

1.
$$
\begin{array}{r}
16 \\
23 \\
+19 \\
\hline
\end{array}
$$

2.
$$
\begin{array}{r}
42 \\
37 \\
+86 \\
\hline
\end{array}
$$

3.
$$
\begin{array}{r}
56 \\
28 \\
+44 \\
\hline
\end{array}
$$

4.
$$
\begin{array}{r}
634 \\
318 \\
+177 \\
\hline
\end{array}
$$

5.
$$
\begin{array}{r}
271 \\
328 \\
+415 \\
\hline
\end{array}
$$

Add.

1.	348 692 + 843	**2.**	784 65 + 892	**3.**	743 806 + 59	**4.**	984 376 + 977	**5.**	856 972 + 800
6.	9283 7651 8420 + 9165	**7.**	9037 8066 579 + 7432	**8.**	8651 784 97 + 8465	**9.**	982 7655 8 + 93	**10.**	7836 965 1749 + 88

Find the sums.

11. 6784 + 932 + 89 + 7864

12. 6528 + 9328 + 657 + 9827

13. 5748 + 297 + 3608 + 94

14. 3427 + 15 348 + 19 + 384

Find the total scores.

15.

	1st number	2nd number	3rd number
Kurt	29	67	80
Brian	42	38	59

16.

	1st number	2nd number	3rd number
Vicki	69	38	14
Diane	35	17	60

17.

	1st number	2nd number	3rd number
Carla	45	13	89
Bert	27	60	35

☆ **18.** Play the number game with a classmate.

Think!

Each ▥ in this problem covers the same digit. What is it?

```
  3 ▥ 5 2
  1 0 7 ▥
  5 4 ▥ 2
+ ▥ 7 3 ▥
─────────
1 ▥ 9 2 ▥
```

Self-check

Add.

1. 21 + 34	2. 65 + 19	3. 437 + 129	4. 628 + 793	5. 884 + 595
6. 26 38 + 54	7. 52 75 + 18	8. 36 47 + 95	9. 237 584 + 606	10. 286 739 + 415
11. 452 197 368 + 546	12. 633 827 481 + 726	13. 2137 5649 6053 + 8214	14. 7477 169 89 + 3476	15. 8288 7644 5909 + 6832

Answers for Self-check—page 17

Test

Add.

1. 66 + 15	2. 49 + 33	3. 166 + 258	4. 749 + 626	5. 893 + 769
6. 47 23 + 56	7. 82 16 + 75	8. 94 27 + 85	9. 129 336 + 415	10. 483 127 + 746
11. 714 269 543 + 975	12. 482 136 281 + 765	13. 5123 7484 2809 + 6637	14. 8346 7487 3229 + 1776	15. 3749 689 95 + 8

Number Hunt

Copy the chart. Then find and ring the names for all the whole numbers from zero to fourteen. The names may be backward, forward, up, down, or diagonal.

T	E	V	L	E	W	T	N
E	H	O	N	E	V	E	S
N	N	I	N	E	E	O	E
F	T	O	R	T	W	T	L
E	O	H	R	T	O	H	E
V	S	U	G	E	E	R	V
I	O	I	R	I	Z	E	E
F	R	Z	X	Q	E	E	N

Subtracting

Getting started

These two charts show the same number.

Before a trade

After a trade

THOUSANDS	HUNDREDS	TENS	ONES

4 hundreds   2 tens   5 ones

THOUSANDS	HUNDREDS	TENS	ONES

3 hundreds   12 tens   5 ones

Give the missing numbers after each trade.

Before the trade	Trade	After the trade
73	1 ten for 10 ones	▦ tens ▦ ones
348	1 hundred for 10 tens	▦ hundreds ▦ tens ▦ ones
4652	1 thousand for 10 hundreds	▦ thousands ▦ hundreds ▦ tens ▦ ones

1. Are any trades needed to subtract 32 from the number shown on the chart?

2. How would the chart look after subtracting 32?

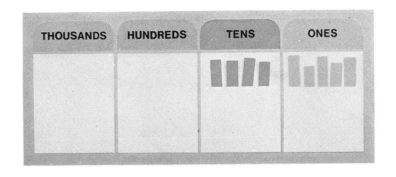

3. To find 53 − 27, what trade would you need to make?

4. How would the chart look after subtracting 27?

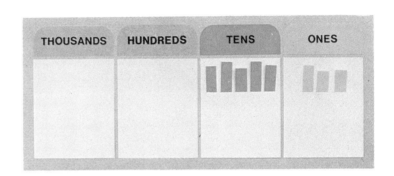

5. What trades would be needed to subtract 162 from the number on the chart?

6. How would the chart look after subtracting 162?

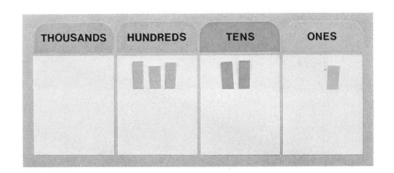

7. To find 3455 − 1832, what trade would you need to make?

8. How would the chart look after subtracting 1832?

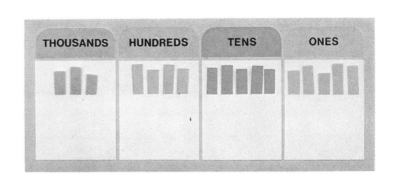

More practice, page 356B

Subtracting with regrouping

Marsha's heart beats 58 times per minute. After she has jumped rope, it beats 97 times per minute. How many more times per minute does her heart beat after she has jumped rope?

Finding the answer

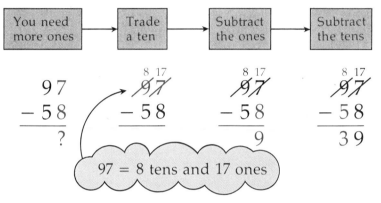

You need more ones	→	Trade a ten	→	Subtract the ones	→	Subtract the tens

$$\begin{array}{r} 97 \\ -58 \\ \hline ? \end{array} \qquad \begin{array}{r} {}^{8\ 17}\\ \cancel{97} \\ -58 \\ \hline \end{array} \qquad \begin{array}{r} {}^{8\ 17}\\ \cancel{97} \\ -58 \\ \hline 9 \end{array} \qquad \begin{array}{r} {}^{8\ 17}\\ \cancel{97} \\ -58 \\ \hline 39 \end{array}$$

97 = 8 tens and 17 ones

Marsha's heart beats 39 times more per minute after she has jumped rope.

Other examples

$$\begin{array}{r} {}^{7\ 13}\\ \cancel{83} \\ -37 \\ \hline 46 \end{array} \qquad \begin{array}{r} {}^{6\ 10}\\ \cancel{70} \\ -45 \\ \hline 25 \end{array} \qquad \begin{array}{r} {}^{5\ 12}\\ 1\cancel{62} \\ -\ \ 27 \\ \hline 135 \end{array} \qquad \begin{array}{r} {}^{1\ 13}\\ \cancel{238} \\ -\ \ 96 \\ \hline 142 \end{array}$$

Find the differences.

1. $\begin{array}{r} 83 \\ -29 \\ \hline \end{array}$
2. $\begin{array}{r} 27 \\ -18 \\ \hline \end{array}$
3. $\begin{array}{r} 67 \\ -54 \\ \hline \end{array}$
4. $\begin{array}{r} 95 \\ -75 \\ \hline \end{array}$
5. $\begin{array}{r} 72 \\ -34 \\ \hline \end{array}$
6. $\begin{array}{r} 64 \\ -28 \\ \hline \end{array}$

7. $\begin{array}{r} 62 \\ -21 \\ \hline \end{array}$
8. $\begin{array}{r} 93 \\ -66 \\ \hline \end{array}$
9. $\begin{array}{r} 80 \\ -56 \\ \hline \end{array}$
10. $\begin{array}{r} 47 \\ -29 \\ \hline \end{array}$
11. $\begin{array}{r} 91 \\ -38 \\ \hline \end{array}$
12. $\begin{array}{r} 60 \\ -28 \\ \hline \end{array}$

Subtract.

1. 75 − 36	**2.** 80 − 59	**3.** 33 − 18	**4.** 54 − 37
5. 68 − 26	**6.** 183 − 46	**7.** 185 − 58	**8.** 244 − 63
9. 160 − 53	**10.** 267 − 95	**11.** 129 − 55	**12.** 143 − 81
13. 169 − 85	**14.** 133 − 98	**15.** 156 − 79	**16.** 92 − 78
17. 169 − 87	**18.** 178 − 36	**19.** 151 − 77	**20.** 134 − 56
21. 150 − 78	**22.** 139 − 46	**23.** 141 − 94	**24.** 272 − 58

25. Dave's heart beats 72 times per minute. After he has run to school, it beats 110 times per minute. How many more beats per minute is this?

☆ 26. Find the number of times your heart beats in one minute while you are resting. Find the number of times it beats in one minute after you have been exercising 5 minutes. Find the difference.

Can you find the digits for the letters in the subtraction problem?

cba
− ed
fcb

Part of the code is given.

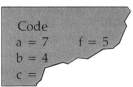

Code
a = 7   f = 5
b = 4
c =

More practice, page 361, Set A

Subtracting larger numbers

Scott lives 385 km from Toronto. He lives 651 km from Chicago. How much closer does he live to Toronto than to Chicago?

Finding the answer

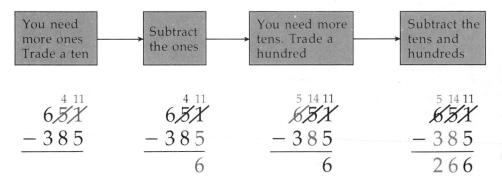

You need more ones Trade a ten	Subtract the ones	You need more tens. Trade a hundred	Subtract the tens and hundreds

$$\begin{array}{r} \overset{4\ 11}{6\cancel{5}\cancel{1}} \\ -385 \\ \hline \end{array}$$

$$\begin{array}{r} \overset{4\ 11}{6\cancel{5}\cancel{1}} \\ -385 \\ \hline 6 \end{array}$$

$$\begin{array}{r} \overset{5\ 14\ 11}{\cancel{6}\cancel{5}\cancel{1}} \\ -385 \\ \hline 6 \end{array}$$

$$\begin{array}{r} \overset{5\ 14\ 11}{\cancel{6}\cancel{5}\cancel{1}} \\ -385 \\ \hline 266 \end{array}$$

Scott lives 266 km closer to Toronto.

Other examples

$$\begin{array}{r} \overset{4\ 12\ 14}{\cancel{5}\cancel{3}\cancel{4}} \\ -266 \\ \hline 268 \end{array} \qquad \begin{array}{r} \overset{6\ 13\ 10}{\cancel{7}\cancel{4}\cancel{0}} \\ -176 \\ \hline 564 \end{array} \qquad \begin{array}{r} \overset{7\ 13\ 12}{1\cancel{8}\cancel{4}\cancel{2}} \\ -\ 966 \\ \hline 876 \end{array} \qquad \begin{array}{r} \overset{3\ 14\ 13}{\cancel{4}\cancel{5}\cancel{3}7} \\ -2864 \\ \hline 1673 \end{array}$$

Subtract.

1.	434 − 166	**2.**	750 − 282	**3.**	652 − 317	**4.**	555 − 267	**5.**	841 − 375
6.	263 − 138	**7.**	944 − 259	**8.**	830 − 362	**9.**	713 − 564	**10.**	425 − 178
11.	641 − 146	**12.**	528 − 269	**13.**	720 − 153	**14.**	942 − 529	**15.**	461 − 188

Find the differences.

1. 725 − 268

2. 524 − 296

3. 782 − 391

4. 458 − 269

5. 340 − 27

6. 723 − 327

7. 643 − 156

8. 827 − 287

9. 650 − 193

10. 714 − 328

11. 573 − 284

12. 212 − 187

13. 633 − 566

14. 815 − 556

15. 729 − 333

16. 8427 − 6583

17. 6513 − 2465

18. 4627 − 1651

19. 7214 − 3888

20. 9131 − 5884

21. 5549 − 3478

22. 7632 − 1475

23. 6621 − 3746

24. 8192 − 7848

25. 4474 − 1975

26. Dallas to Atlanta: 1160 km
Dallas to New Orleans: 712 km
How much farther to Atlanta?

27. San Francisco to Vancouver: 1635 km
San Francisco to Los Angeles: 648 km
How much farther to Vancouver?

☆ 28. Find the distances from your home to two cities. Find the difference in the distances.

Can you find the next number in the pattern?

2 8 5 6 7 1 9
2 9 5 6 8 1 9
3 0 5 6 9 1 9
3 1 5 7 0 1 9

Zeros in subtraction

How much longer is the
condor's wingspan than the
bald eagle's?

California Condor
Wingspan 302 cm

Finding the answer

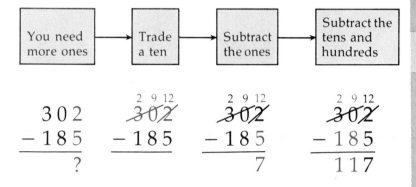

| You need more ones | → | Trade a ten | → | Subtract the ones | → | Subtract the tens and hundreds |

$$
\begin{array}{r} 302 \\ -185 \\ \hline ? \end{array}
\qquad
\begin{array}{r} {\scriptstyle 2\ 9\ 12} \\ \cancel{302} \\ -185 \\ \hline \end{array}
\qquad
\begin{array}{r} {\scriptstyle 2\ 9\ 12} \\ \cancel{302} \\ -185 \\ \hline 7 \end{array}
\qquad
\begin{array}{r} {\scriptstyle 2\ 9\ 12} \\ \cancel{302} \\ -185 \\ \hline 117 \end{array}
$$

The condor's wingspan is 117 cm longer.

Bald Eagle
Wingspan 185 cm

Other examples

$$
\begin{array}{r} {\scriptstyle 6\ 9\ 11} \\ \cancel{701} \\ -356 \\ \hline 345 \end{array}
\qquad
\begin{array}{r} {\scriptstyle 2\ 9\ 10} \\ \cancel{300} \\ -127 \\ \hline 173 \end{array}
\qquad
\begin{array}{r} {\scriptstyle 6\ 9\ 9\ 14} \\ \cancel{7004} \\ -3786 \\ \hline 3218 \end{array}
\qquad
\begin{array}{r} {\scriptstyle 4\ 9\ 9\ 10} \\ \cancel{5000} \\ -1754 \\ \hline 3246 \end{array}
$$

Find the differences.

1. $\begin{array}{r} 704 \\ -276 \\ \hline \end{array}$
2. $\begin{array}{r} 207 \\ -138 \\ \hline \end{array}$
3. $\begin{array}{r} 502 \\ -277 \\ \hline \end{array}$
4. $\begin{array}{r} 801 \\ -349 \\ \hline \end{array}$
5. $\begin{array}{r} 306 \\ -158 \\ \hline \end{array}$

6. $\begin{array}{r} 106 \\ -77 \\ \hline \end{array}$
7. $\begin{array}{r} 401 \\ -135 \\ \hline \end{array}$
8. $\begin{array}{r} 602 \\ -88 \\ \hline \end{array}$
9. $\begin{array}{r} 907 \\ -655 \\ \hline \end{array}$
10. $\begin{array}{r} 807 \\ -708 \\ \hline \end{array}$

11. $\begin{array}{r} 703 \\ -416 \\ \hline \end{array}$
12. $\begin{array}{r} 505 \\ -158 \\ \hline \end{array}$
13. $\begin{array}{r} 206 \\ -139 \\ \hline \end{array}$
14. $\begin{array}{r} 708 \\ -389 \\ \hline \end{array}$
15. $\begin{array}{r} 400 \\ -193 \\ \hline \end{array}$

Subtract.

1. 5001 − 3679	**2.** 6004 − 2845	**3.** 3007 − 1228	**4.** 7005 − 4186	**5.** 2001 − 1257

6. 8006 − 1739	**7.** 9002 − 5277	**8.** 4003 − 2654	**9.** 8000 − 1672	**10.** 1007 − 329

11. 6004 − 1556	**12.** 5005 − 1877	**13.** 6205 − 1984	**14.** 7062 − 1728	**15.** 8602 − 3479

16. 7026 − 1550	**17.** 6034 − 1655	**18.** 3003 − 1888	**19.** 6000 − 2774	**20.** 5013 − 2766

21. 2000 − 1647	**22.** 9304 − 5077	**23.** 7206 − 3958	**24.** 6200 − 3715	**25.** 6007 − 1359

26. The condor is about 140 cm long. The bald eagle is about 76 cm long. How much longer is the condor?

27. There are about 3500 bald eagles left in the U.S. and about 40 condors. How many more bald eagles?

A palindrome is a numeral that is the same whether read from left to right or right to left. You can make a palindrome by adding. Sometimes this takes many steps.

What are the palindromes for these numbers?

1. 87   2. 678   3. 3279   4. 125698

76	start
+ 67	reverse
143	sum
+ 341	reverse
484	palindrome

Answers for Self-check 1. 71 2. 21 3. 47 4. 53 5. 146 6. 369 7. 568 8. 348 9. 678 10. 1236
11. 25 12. 434 13. 2158 14. 3573 15. 2869 16. 1447 17. 2019 18. 2544 19. 1534 20. 657

Self-check

Subtract.

1.	83 − 12	**2.**	60 − 39	**3.**	73 − 26	**4.**	126 − 73	**5.**	341 − 195
6.	621 − 252	**7.**	944 − 376	**8.**	753 − 405	**9.**	2325 − 1647	**10.**	3214 − 1978
11.	209 − 184	**12.**	802 − 368	**13.**	6032 − 3874	**14.**	9001 − 5428	**15.**	5800 − 2931
16.	4125 − 2678	**17.**	9206 − 7187	**18.**	5811 − 3267	**19.**	7002 − 5468	**20.**	1516 − 859

Answers for Self-check—page 27

Test

Subtract.

1.	56 − 13	**2.**	81 − 24	**3.**	42 − 25	**4.**	95 − 68	**5.**	72 − 35
6.	389 − 197	**7.**	546 − 285	**8.**	931 − 468	**9.**	3187 − 1869	**10.**	6495 − 3786
11.	502 − 156	**12.**	703 − 458	**13.**	8041 − 4596	**14.**	6002 − 3475	**15.**	7200 − 5368
16.	3479 − 1658	**17.**	8012 − 5394	**18.**	9235 − 4467	**19.**	5001 − 2870	**20.**	2568 − 1299

The 20 Game

Rules: Start with 20 marks.

At your turn, erase 1, 2, or 3 marks.
The player who erases the last mark
loses the game.

Try this game with a classmate.
Does it make a difference which player starts the game?
Can you always win if you start first?

Using Your Skills

Getting started

Can Drive

	Number of children	Cans 1st week	Cans 2nd week
Room 4	25	132	121
Room 5	31	145	160
Room 6	26	72	151
Room 7	28	139	84
Room 8	25	164	152

1. How many cans did the children collect in the first week?
2. How many more cans did Room 8 collect than Room 7?
3. What other problems can you solve?

Sometimes you are given more facts than you need.

Sometimes facts are given in a table.

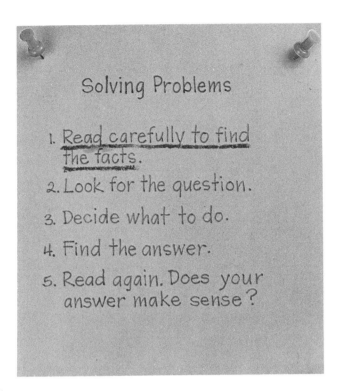

Solving Problems

1. Read carefully to find the facts.
2. Look for the question.
3. Decide what to do.
4. Find the answer.
5. Read again. Does your answer make sense?

Tell which facts are needed to solve each problem.

1. Four children were absent from Room 5 during the can drive. In the first week Room 5 collected 145 cans. In the second week they collected 160 cans. How many cans was this in all?

2. Use the table on page 30. How many cans did Room 7 and Room 8 collect altogether?

3. There were 135 children in the 5 classes that joined in the can drive. In the first week 652 cans were collected. In the second week 668 cans were collected. How many more cans were collected in the second week?

4. Use the table on page 30. Which room collected the most cans during the two week drive?

Sports stadiums

Have you ever been in a large sports stadium? There are many large stadiums built to seat thousands of people for football, baseball, and other events. Stadiums cost many millions of dollars to build.

1. A stadium will seat 65 000 for football. It will seat 56 371 for baseball. How many more will it seat for football?

2. The attendance for three baseball games was 32 794 the first game, 35 669 the second, and 49 708 the third. How many people in all attended these games?

3. Sometimes as many as 65 000 people attend a football game. The attendance for three football games was 64 372 for a Dolphins game, 62 973 for a Rams game, and 63 726 for a Jets game. How many people attended these three games?

4. The distance from home plate to the right field wall in a stadium is 100 meters. The height of the roof is 37 meters less than this. What is the roof height?

Find the differences in the number of seats.

1. Rose Bowl, Pasadena, California:
   101 025 seats
   Cotton Bowl, Dallas, Texas:
   73 032 seats

2. Superdome, New Orleans, Louisiana:
   97 365 seats
   Astrodome, Houston, Texas:
   66 000 seats

3. Orange Bowl, Miami, Florida:
   80 500 seats
   Gator Bowl, Jacksonville, Florida:
   74 813 seats

4. University of Michigan Stadium,
   Ann Arbor, Michigan: 100 001 seats
   Soldier Field, Chicago, Illinois:
   99 670 seats

5. Stanford Stadium, Palo Alto, California:
   90 000 seats
   Ohio State University Stadium
   Columbus, Ohio: 81 455 seats

6. John F. Kennedy Stadium,
   Philadelphia, Pennsylvania: 105 000 seats
   Memorial Coliseum, Los Angeles, California:
   93 791 seats

7. Riverfront Stadium, Cincinnati, Ohio:
   51 726 seats
   Jarry Park, Montreal, Canada:
   28 000 seats

8. Shea Stadium, New York, New York:
   55 300 seats
   Yankee Stadium, New York, New York:
   65 010 seats

National parks

The map shows
approximate road
distances between
some national
parks in the
United States.

WASHINGTON

Glacier

1017 km

OREGON

613 km

MONTANA

Crater
Lake

Yellowstone

IDAHO

997 km

WYOMING

UTAH

882 km

NEVADA

Rocky
Mountain

903 km

666 km

Yosemite

Canyonlands

COLORADO

CALIFORNIA

Grand
Canyon

1256 km

ARIZONA

Use the facts on
the map to answer
the questions.

What are the
distances between
the following parks?

1. Yosemite and Canyonlands
2. Yellowstone and Crater Lake
3. Grand Canyon and Rocky Mountain

Which distance is greater? How much greater?

4. From Grand Canyon to Yosemite or from
   Yellowstone to Glacier
5. From Crater Lake to Glacier or from
   Crater Lake to Yosemite
6. From Yellowstone to Rocky Mountain or from
   Grand Canyon to Canyonlands
☆ 7. Think of a trip starting at Yosemite, traveling
   through all the parks, and returning to Yosemite.
   What would be the road distance of this
   trip as given on the map?

Tall trees

The table below gives the heights, names, and locations of some of the tallest trees that have ever lived.

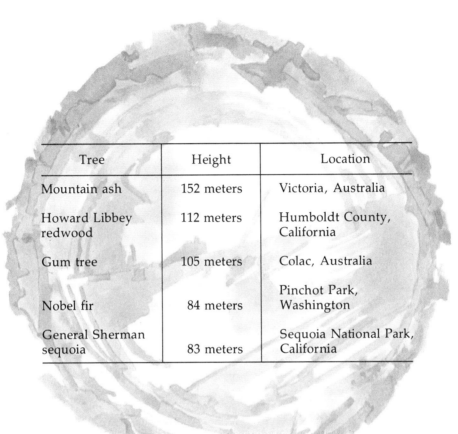

Tree	Height	Location
Mountain ash	152 meters	Victoria, Australia
Howard Libbey redwood	112 meters	Humboldt County, California
Gum tree	105 meters	Colac, Australia
Nobel fir	84 meters	Pinchot Park, Washington
General Sherman sequoia	83 meters	Sequoia National Park, California

1. How much taller is the Howard Libbey redwood tree than the General Sherman sequoia?

2. How many meters taller is the Australian mountain ash than the gum tree?

3. Find the difference between the heights of the Howard Libbey redwood and the Nobel fir.

4. The total height of the five trees in the table is only 93 meters more than the height of the Sears Tower building in Chicago. How tall is the Sears Tower?

5. The oldest living tree is a bristlecone pine tree on Wheeler Peak, Nevada. It is about 4900 years old. The General Sherman sequoia is about 3500 years old. How much older is the bristlecone pine?

Adding and subtracting money

What is the total cost of the two models?

Line up the dollars and cents	Add	Give the answer in dollars and cents

$$\begin{array}{r} \$\ 2.5\,9 \\ +\ 1.9\,8 \\ \hline \end{array}$$
$$\begin{array}{r} {\scriptstyle 1\ 1} \\ \$\ 2.5\,9 \\ +\ 1.9\,8 \\ \hline 4\,5\,7 \end{array}$$
$$\begin{array}{r} {\scriptstyle 1\ 1} \\ \$\ 2.5\,9 \\ +\ 1.9\,8 \\ \hline \$\ 4.57 \end{array}$$

The models cost $4.57.

How much more does the airplane cost than the rocket?

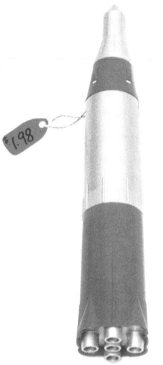

Line up the dollars and cents	Subtract	Give the answer in dollars and cents

$$\begin{array}{r} \$\ 2.5\,9 \\ -\ 1.9\,8 \\ \hline \end{array}$$
$$\begin{array}{r} {\scriptstyle 1\ 15} \\ \$\ \cancel{2}.\cancel{5}\,9 \\ -\ 1.9\,8 \\ \hline 6\,1 \end{array}$$
$$\begin{array}{r} {\scriptstyle 1\ 15} \\ \$\ \cancel{2}.\cancel{5}\,9 \\ -\ 1.9\,8 \\ \hline \$\ 0.61 \end{array}$$

The airplane costs 61 cents more.

Find the total amounts.

1. $ 7.45	2. $ 5.67	3. $ 3.27	4. $ 9.23	5. $ 2.39
+ 1.68	+ 0.85	+ 4.68	+ 6.58	+ 6.98

Find the differences in amounts.

6. $ 7.98	7. $ 6.19	8. $ 10.00	9. $ 29.95	10. $ 54.50
− 2.74	− 1.25	− 3.69	− 6.78	− 2.98

Find the total amounts or differences.

1. $ 24.40
+ 57.95

2. $ 66.98
+ 19.37

3. $ 4.26
+ 3.78

4. $ 9.07
+ 8.58

5. $ 125.75
+247.88

6. $ 23.75
− 8.44

7. $ 19.80
− 12.66

8. $ 6.19
− 1.25

9. $ 29.95
− 6.75

10. $ 10.00
− 3.69

11. $ 4.26
3.78
+ 4.65

12. $0.79
0.69
+ 0.39

13. $ 10.11
8.53
+ 12.44

14. $ 22.35
15.75
+ 3.45

15. $ 53.58
42.80
+ 17.90

16. $ 60.04
− 37.16

17. $ 57.05
− 16.66

18. $ 30.22
− 17.37

19. $ 20.00
− 7.35

20. $ 16.09
− 9.53

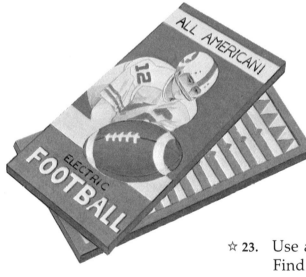

21. Skateboard: $19.94
Air jet hockey table: $39.84
How much more for the hockey table?

22. Electric football game: $9.87
Basketball game: $14.97
How much for the two games?

☆ 23. Use a catalog or advertisement.
Find the total cost of three things
you would like to buy.

Which is greater: the sum
of all the even numbers
that are less than 100 or
the sum of all the odd numbers
that are less than 100?

More practice, page 362, Set B

Estimating sums and differences

When you do not need an exact answer, you can **estimate** the answer.

Estimate the total cost of the skateboard and light.

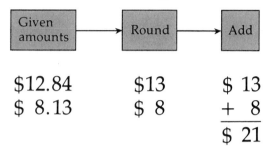

Given amounts	→	Round	→	Add

$12.84 $13 $ 13
$ 8.13 $ 8   + 8
                ――――
              $ 21

The total cost is about $21.

Estimate the difference in cost between the skateboard and the light.

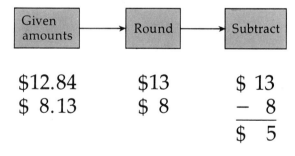

Given amounts	→	Round	→	Subtract

$12.84 $13 $ 13
$ 8.13 $ 8   – 8
                ――――
              $ 5

The skateboard costs about $5 more than the light.

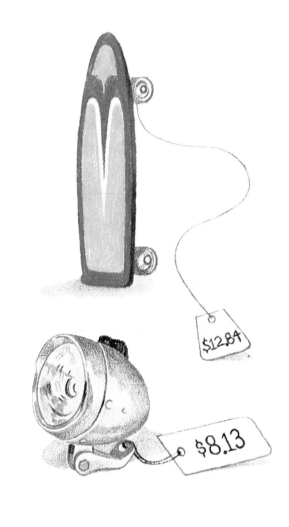

$12.84

$8.13

Estimate the total cost of each pair of items.

1. Book: $5.75
   Weaving set: $8.95

2. Tennis racket: $14.95
   Tennis balls: $2.95

3. Paint-by-number set: $7.10
   Baseball glove: $9.45

4. Shirt: $4.08
   Pants: $9.25

Estimate the total amounts.

1. $6.95	2. $23.88	3. $18.09	4. $ 8.33	5. $14.66
$7.77	$ 9.99	$ 6.10	$11.95	$13.85

6. $1.20	7. $3.09	8. $9.95	9. $10.22	10. $5.35
$3.79	$4.18	$3.25	$ 8.14	$0.85
$1.15	$5.75	$6.75	$ 5.97	$1.79

Estimate the difference in cost for each pair of items.

11. Music book: $5.95
    Art tablet: $2.78

12. Photograph poster: $2.79
    Art poster: $3.65

13. Hiking boots: $11.12
    Backpack: $5.98

14. Stamp album: $4.08
    Photo album: $2.50

Estimate the difference in amounts.

15. $8.32	16. $12.75	17. $49.95	18. $11.15	19. $8.09
$1.99	$ 3.95	$29.98	$ 6.89	$6.83

20. A jacket costs $19.98.
    Slacks cost $14.95.
    Estimate the total cost.

21. Blue jeans cost $11.88.
    A shirt costs $8.15.
    Estimate the difference
    in cost.

☆ 22. Choose some things you would
    like to buy. Estimate the total
    cost. How much difference is
    there between your estimate
    and the exact cost?

Start with a 3-digit number.	471
Reverse the digits and subtract.	− 174
	297
Reverse and add.	+ 792
	1089

Try this with other 3-digit
numbers. What do you discover?

Answers for Self-check   1. $11.10   2. $36.40   3. $7.99   4. $34.45   5. $28.79   6. $5.63   7. $6.05
8. $6.53   9. $8.58   10. $8.78   11. $16   12. $2   13. 8845   14. 2628

Self-check

Find the total amounts.

1. $ 2.96
   + 8.14

2. $ 17.45
   + 18.95

3. $ 1.88
   2.97
   + 3.14

4. $ 6.23
   18.45
   + 9.77

5. $ 12.02
   9.99
   + 6.78

Find the difference in amounts.

6. $ 12.50
   − 6.87

7. $ 20.00
   − 13.95

8. $ 10.00
   − 3.47

9. $ 72.14
   − 63.56

10. $ 17.95
    − 9.17

11. Estimate the total amount.
    $7.85 $3.99 $4.12

12. Estimate the difference.
    $8.01 $5.99

13. Attendance at a soccer game was 9142. 297 people got in free. The rest paid. How many people paid to see the game?

14. A stadium parking lot will hold 8000 cars. 5372 cars were parked. How many more cars could be parked?

Answers for Self-check—page 39

Test

Find the total amounts.

1. $ 6.27
   + 9.55

2. $ 18.25
   + 16.75

3. $ 2.56
   1.79
   + 1.49

4. $ 12.42
   8.16
   + 6.29

5. $ 7.42
   3.56
   + 9.78

Find the difference in amounts.

6. $ 18.50
   − 7.77

7. $ 5.00
   − 3.44

8. $ 32.95
   − 18.66

9. $ 50.00
   − 27.88

10. $ 25.00
    − 16.86

11. Estimate the total amount.
    $5.98 $6.75 $3.27

12. Estimate the difference.
    $19.78 $7.95

13. Find the total distance driven.
    Monday: 586 km
    Tuesday: 475 km
    Wednesday: 519 km

14. The distance around a large redwood tree is 31 meters. The distance around a large cypress tree is 18 meters more. What is the distance around the cypress?

Look-alikes

Which two figures are exactly alike?

A   B   C   D

E   F   G   H

I   J   K   L

Points, Lines, and Angles

Getting started

Fold a sheet of paper any way you wish.

Fold again so the fold line folds on itself.

The fold lines should make square corners.

Use this method of folding to make a rectangle with the fold lines.

A **line** is named by
two of its points.

We say: line *RS*
We write: $\overleftrightarrow{RS}$

Line *AB* and line *AD*
intersect at point *A*.

Tell where each of these pairs
of lines intersect.

1. $\overleftrightarrow{AB}$ and $\overleftrightarrow{BC}$
2. $\overleftrightarrow{DC}$ and $\overleftrightarrow{AD}$
3. $\overleftrightarrow{DC}$ and $\overleftrightarrow{BC}$

4. Lines *AB* and *DC* are **parallel** lines.
    They do not intersect. What other
    lines are parallel?

5. The two lines that intersect at
    each corner of the rectangle are
    perpendicular lines. Line *AD*
    and line *DC* are perpendicular
    at point *D*. Which two lines are
    perpendicular at point *B*?

6. Which two lines are perpendicular at
    point *C*?

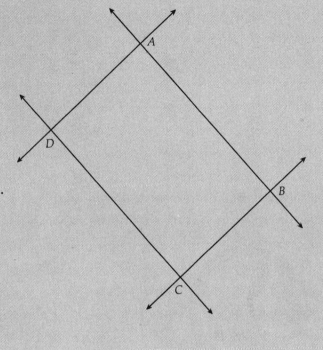

What objects can you see in your classroom
that remind you of the following?

7. parallel lines

8. perpendicular lines

9. intersecting lines

Angles

The two hands of the clock suggest an **angle.**

An **angle** is formed by two rays from one point.

We say: angle ABC

We write: $\angle ABC$

Vertex B Rays

A

C

The middle letter names the vertex of the angle.

Write the name for each angle.

1.

R

S

T

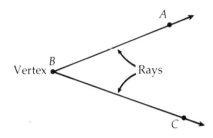

2.

M

O

N

3.

F

E D

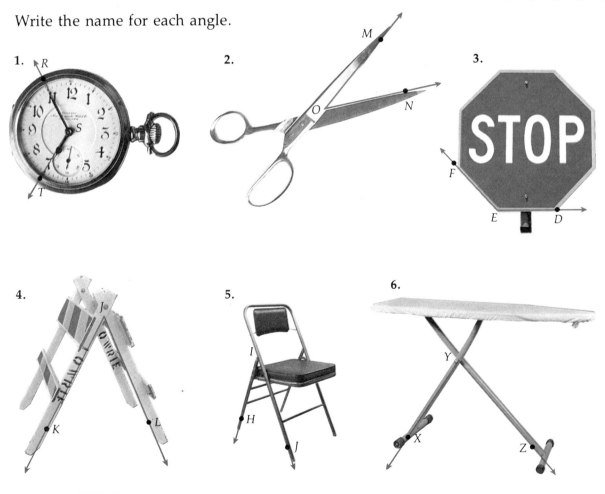

4.

J

K L

5.

I

H

J

6.

Y

X

Z

The hands of the clocks suggest different kinds of angles.

right angle	obtuse angle	acute angle

	larger than a right angle	smaller than a right angle

Tell whether the angle is right, obtuse, or acute.

1.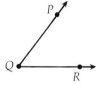

2.

3.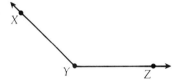

4.

5.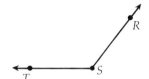

6.

Practicing your skills

1. $\begin{array}{r} 737 \\ + 629 \\ \hline \end{array}$

2. $\begin{array}{r} 1287 \\ + 3976 \\ \hline \end{array}$

3. $\begin{array}{r} 228 \\ 799 \\ + 149 \\ \hline \end{array}$

4. $\begin{array}{r} 846 \\ 395 \\ + 142 \\ \hline \end{array}$

5. $\begin{array}{r} 204 \\ 547 \\ + 618 \\ \hline \end{array}$

6. $\begin{array}{r} 519 \\ - 344 \\ \hline \end{array}$

7. $\begin{array}{r} 826 \\ - 507 \\ \hline \end{array}$

8. $\begin{array}{r} 304 \\ - 195 \\ \hline \end{array}$

9. $\begin{array}{r} 871 \\ - 354 \\ \hline \end{array}$

10. $\begin{array}{r} 422 \\ - 148 \\ \hline \end{array}$

11. $\begin{array}{r} 2288 \\ 7391 \\ 6429 \\ + 8153 \\ \hline \end{array}$

12. $\begin{array}{r} 9635 \\ - 7147 \\ \hline \end{array}$

13. $\begin{array}{r} 57 \\ 96 \\ 38 \\ + 47 \\ \hline \end{array}$

14. $\begin{array}{r} 3740 \\ - 1828 \\ \hline \end{array}$

15. $\begin{array}{r} 955 \\ 747 \\ 628 \\ + 153 \\ \hline \end{array}$

Measuring angles

A protractor is an instrument
used to measure angles. The
unit for measuring angles
is the **degree**.

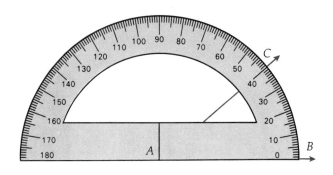

The measure of ∠CAB is 40 degrees.
For 40 degrees we write: 40°

Give the measure of each angle.

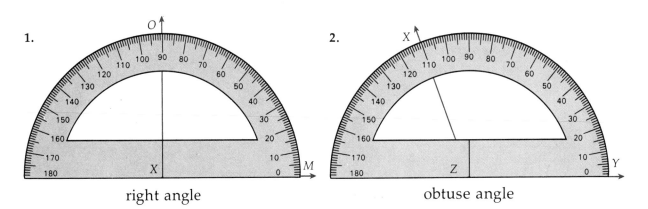

1.

right angle

2.

obtuse angle

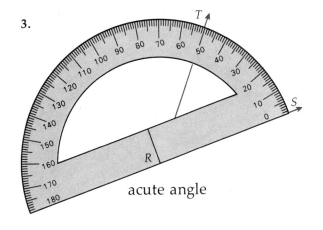

3.

acute angle

4.

obtuse angle

Complete each sentence.
5. The measure of a right angle is ▓ degrees.
6. An obtuse angle has a measure greater than ▓ degrees.
7. An acute angle has a measure less than ▓ degrees.

Congruent angles have the same measure.

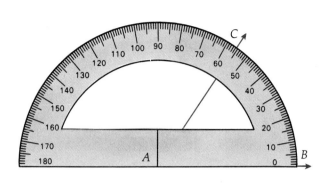

$\angle CAB$ and $\angle DEF$ each have a measure of 55°.
$\angle CAB$ is **congruent** to $\angle DEF$.
We write: $\angle CAB \cong \angle DEF$.

Find the measure of each angle.

1.

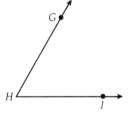

2.

3.

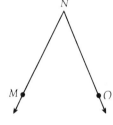

4.

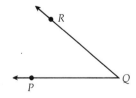

5.

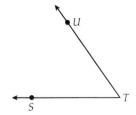

6.

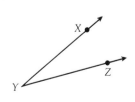

7. Which pairs of angles above are congruent angles?

✪ Angles of triangles

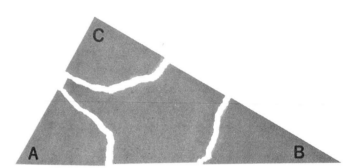

Cut out a triangle.

Tear off the three corners.

Fit the three corners along
one side of a line.

Try this with some other triangles.

Do the corners always fit along one side of a line?

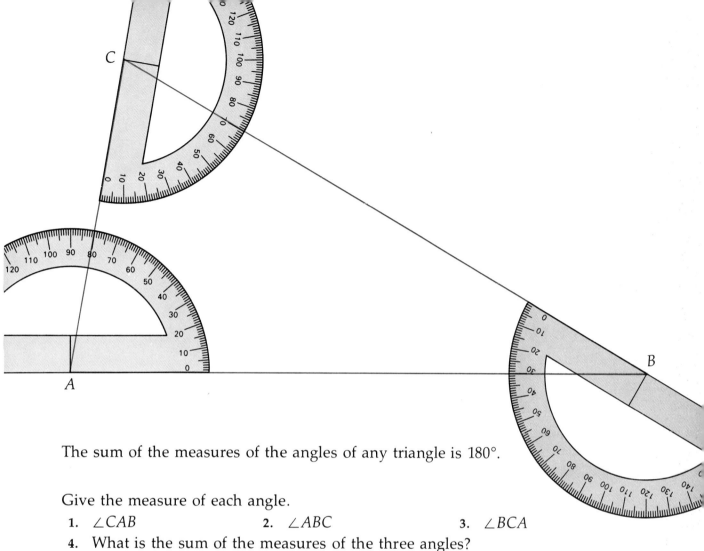

The sum of the measures of the angles of any triangle is 180°.

Give the measure of each angle.

1. ∠CAB   2. ∠ABC   3. ∠BCA

4. What is the sum of the measures of the three angles?

In each triangle, find the measure of the third angle.

5.
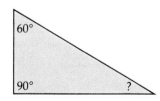

Example: The sum of the measures
of all the angles is 180°.

90°	180°	The measure of the
+ 60°	− 150°	third angle is 30°.
150°	30°	

6.
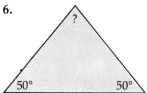

7.
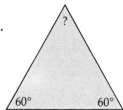

8.

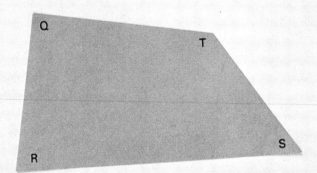

Cut out a
quadrilateral.

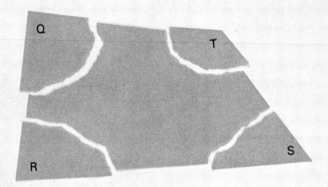

Tear off the
four corners.

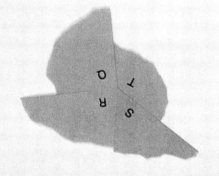

Fit the four corners
together around a point.

Try this with some other quadrilaterals.
Do the four corners always fit together around a point?

The sum of the measures
of the angles of a
quadrilateral is 360°.

90°
134°
56°
+ 80°
‾‾‾‾‾
360°

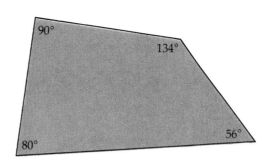

Find the measure of the fourth angle.

1.
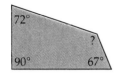

Example: The sum of the four angle
measures is 360°.

72°   360°   The measure of the
90°   − 229°   fourth angle is 131°.
+ 67°   ‾‾‾‾‾
‾‾‾‾‾   131°
229°

2.

3.    **4.**    **5.**    **6.**

7. 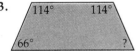   **8.**    **9.**    **10.**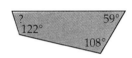

Practicing your skills

1. $ 12.95	**2.** $ 18.50	**3.** $ 125.00	**4.** $ 58.53	**5.** $ 1.17
23.74	37.25	77.46	64.66	5.49
+ 16.48	+ 66.75	+ 84.55	17.75	6.28
			+ 52.95	+ 9.56

6. $ 37.75	**7.** $ 70.49	**8.** $ 193.39	**9.** $ 20.00	**10.** $ 517.08
− 28.44	− 42.37	− 75.66	− 15.64	− 268.17

Answers for Self-check 1. parallel 2. obtuse 3. 70° 4. 92° 5. 85° 6. 60° 7. ∠DEF ≅ ∠GHI

Self-check

1.

Lines *AB* and *CD* are _____?_____.
(parallel, perpendicular)

2.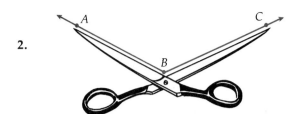

∠*ABC* is _____?_____.
(right, acute, obtuse)

Find the missing measure.

☆ 3.

☆ 4.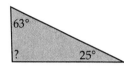

☆ 5.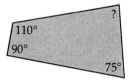

☆ 6.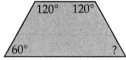

☆ 7. Which two of these angles are congruent?

Answers for Self-check—page 51

Test

1.

Lines *RS* and *XY* are _____?_____.
(parallel, perpendicular)

2.

∠*PQR* is _____?_____.
(right, acute, or obtuse)

Give the missing measure.

☆ 3.

☆ 4.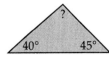

☆ 5.

☆ 6.

☆ 7. Which two of these angles are congruent?

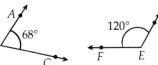 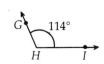

A 3 in 1 Puzzle

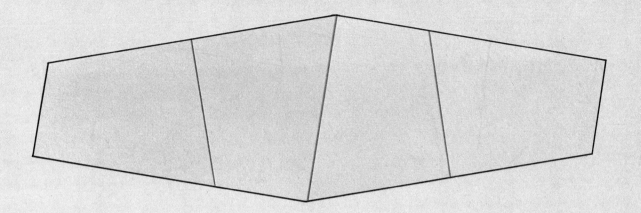

Trace this figure and cut out the four pieces on the solid lines.

Try to solve these puzzles.

1. Make a square with the four pieces.

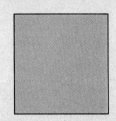

2. Make a parallelogram with the four pieces.

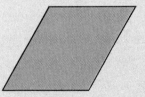

3. Make a square hole in a square with the four pieces.

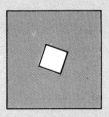

Level 23 review

Write each numeral.
1. six hundred forty-five thousand, nine hundred eighty-two
2. seven hundred three thousand, six hundred seventy-one
3. twenty thousand
4. seven million
5. ninety million, five hundred one thousand, four hundred seventeen

Add.

6.	7.	8.	9.	10.
396	802	147	826	905
721	725	721	521	428
+ 456	+ 638	+ 649	+ 375	+ 693

11. $ 8.01	12. $ 11.46	13. $ 3.50	14. $ 6.19	15. $ 5.99
+ 2.25	+ 9.37	+ 7.68	+ 7.89	+ 2.85

Subtract.

16.	17.	18.	19.	20.
542	701	4195	8806	9387
− 367	− 433	− 2087	− 5928	− 4698

21. $ 9.72	22. $ 2.18	23. $ 10.00	24. $ 8.10	25. $ 7.28
− 5.46	− 0.99	− 6.75	− 4.97	− 3.97

26. Estimate the total cost.
Swim fins: $6.89
Goggles: $4.25

27. Estimate the difference
in the amounts.
Jewelry box: $12.75
Desk lamp: $11.09

28. Three records: $2.47
Two long-playing records: $7.98
How much in all?

29. Bird cage: $22.50
Singing canary: $42.90
How much more for the canary?

Level **24**

Decimals
Adding and Subtracting with Decimals
Using Your Skills
Length
Polygons

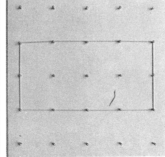

Decimals

Getting started

This picture shows 2 ones and 3 tenths.
We say: two and three tenths

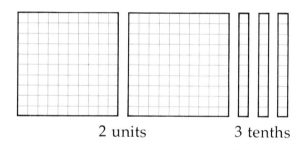

2 units   3 tenths

Which numbers below could you show
if you had these pieces?

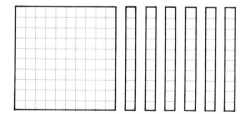

1. one and four tenths   2. five tenths   3. two and three tenths

4. one tenth   5. one and six tenths   6. one and nine tenths

7. eight tenths   8. one and three tenths   9. two and zero tenths

We often write **decimals** to name units and parts of units.

We see: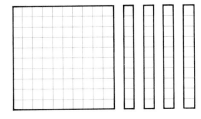

We write: 1.4
We say: one and four tenths

We see: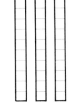

We write: 0.3
We say: three tenths

Write a decimal for each picture.

1.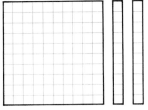

one and two tenths

2.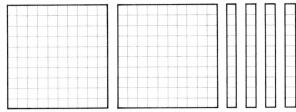

two and four tenths

3.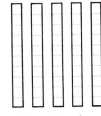

five tenths

4.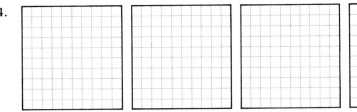

three and one tenth

Write a decimal for each number.

5. eight tenths

6. one and two tenths

7. four and nine tenths

8. two and seven tenths

9. eight and five tenths

10. one tenth

11. twenty-three and six tenths

12. ninety-nine and nine tenths

Hundredths

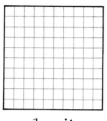  □

     1 **unit**   1 **tenth**   1 **hundredth**

2 tenths and 4 hundredths
is the same as 24 hundredths.

We write: 0.24
We say: twenty-four hundredths

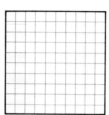

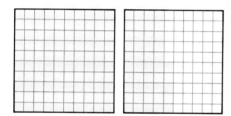

ones	tenths	hundredths
1	4	5

We write: 1.45
We say: one and forty-five hundredths

ones	tenths	hundredths
1	0	6

We write: 1.06
We say: one and six hundredths

How much is shaded? Write a decimal for the answer.

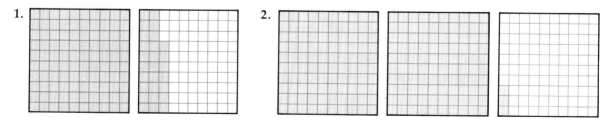

1.

one and twenty-seven hundredths

2.

two and three hundredths

Write the decimal for each picture.

1.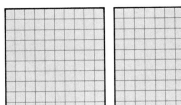

2.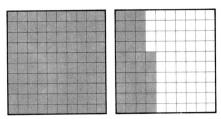

3.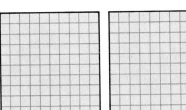

4.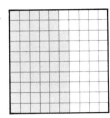

5.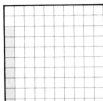

6.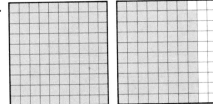

Give the missing numbers.

7.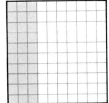

    |||| tenths are shaded.
    |||| hundredths are shaded.

8.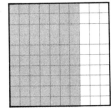

    |||| tenths are shaded.
    |||| hundredths are shaded.

Write the decimal.

9. four and seven tenths

10. eight and fifty-two hundredths

11. three and twenty-one hundredths

12. seven and nine tenths

13. twelve and six hundredths

14. five and thirty-one hundredths

15. one and twelve hundredths

16. ten and five tenths

Thousandths

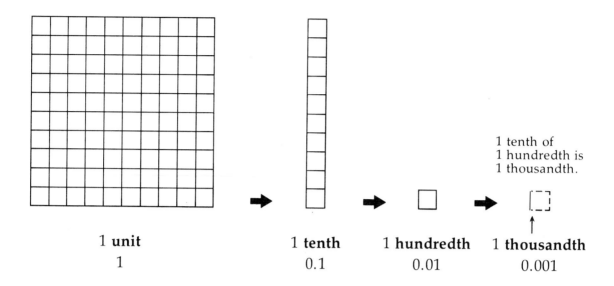

1 unit
1

1 tenth
0.1

1 hundredth
0.01

1 thousandth
0.001

1 tenth of
1 hundredth is
1 thousandth.

A place-value chart can help you read decimals.

	ones	tenths	hundredths	thousandths	
	1	6	3	8	

We write: 1.638
We say: one and six hundred thirty-eight thousandths

Read each decimal.

1. 7.351
2. 0.642
3. 23.149
4. 0.017

5. 8.518
6. 23.667
7. 2.577
8. 6.425

9. 3.003
10. 18.67
11. 0.953
12. 0.004

13. 15.799
14. 0.001
15. 0.087
16. 1.234

17. 101.01
18. 2.05
19. 3.191
20. 0.704

21. 54.157
22. 60.05
23. 0.041
24. 10.105

Tell what each red digit means.

Example: 6.384   Answer: 8 hundredths

1. 2.764
2. 0.183
3. 10.503
4. 36.724
5. 19.025
6. 59.185
7. 2.963
8. 703.2
9. 0.471
10. 53.06
11. 0.268
12. 94.152

Write a decimal for each number.

13. three and two hundred seventy-six thousandths

14. one hundred thirty-seven thousandths

15. thirty-four thousandths

16. ninety-seven and forty-four hundredths

17. sixty-two and three hundred two thousandths

18. eight and thirty-seven hundredths

19. six hundred fifty-nine thousandths

20. one hundred fifty-three and five tenths

21. eight and one hundred twenty-five thousandths

22. twelve and twelve thousandths

Donna started at city **A**. She drove through each of the other cities once and returned to city **A**. Her trip was exactly 415 km. What path could she have taken?

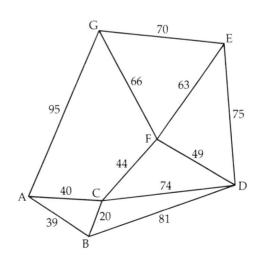

Comparing decimals

Pat and Bill have odometers
on their bicycles that show
how far they have ridden.
The last digit shows tenths.

Pat 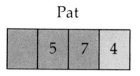   Bill

Which odometer shows the
greater distance?

Finding the answer

Compare the tens	Compare the ones	Compare the tenths

57.4	57.4	57.4
57.9	57.9	57.9
same	same	9 is greater than 4

$57.9 > 57.4$ 57.9 is greater than 57.4

or

$57.4 < 57.9$ 57.4 is less than 57.9

Bill's odometer shows the greater distance.

Other examples

$3.6 < 3.9$ $9.27 > 9.23$ $7.491 > 7.465$

Give the correct symbol ($>$ or $<$) for each 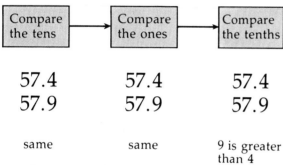.

1. 5.4 ● 5.9   2. 1.44 ● 1.54   3. 8.06 ● 8.01   4. 0.743 ● 0.749

5. 26.84 ● 25.84   6. 9.75 ● 9.62   7. 13.63 ● 13.64   8. 0.77 ● 0.88

9. 3.074 ● 3.047   10. 0.547 ● 0.543   11. 6.90 ● 6.89   12. 1.781 ● 1.771

The number line can help you compare decimals.

0 0.1 0.2 0.3 0.4 0.5 0.6 0.7 0.8 0.9 1.0 1.1 1.2 1.3 1.4 1.5 1.6 1.7 1.8 1.9 2.0

0.2 < 0.5　　　　　0.9 > 0.5　　　　　0.8 < 1.2

Give the correct symbol (> or <) for each ◉.

1. 0.4 ◉ 0.7　**2.** 0.6 ◉ 0.1　**3.** 1.2 ◉ 1.3　**4.** 0.5 ◉ 1.5　**5.** 0.9 ◉ 0.5

6. 1.0 ◉ 2.0　**7.** 1.9 ◉ 0.7　**8.** 0.1 ◉ 1.0　**9.** 1.6 ◉ 1.2　**10.** 0.9 ◉ 1.0

Give the number that is **one tenth** more.

11. 0.4　　**12.** 0.7　　**13.** 0.9　　**14.** 0.1　　**15.** 1.3
Answer: 0.5

16. 1.9　　**17.** 2.6　　**18.** 2.9　　**19.** 3.0　　**20.** 4.6

Give the number that is **one hundredth** more.

21. 1.11　　**22.** 0.25　　**23.** 0.73　　**24.** 5.39　　**25.** 12.44
Answer: 1.12

26. 0.09　　**27.** 6.30　　**28.** 5.99　　**29.** 0.01　　**30.** 3.77

31. How many different decimals
can you form using 4 slips
of paper like these?

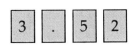

The decimal point must
always be between two
digits.

What is the number for the
point halfway between 1.994
and 2.004?

1.994　　　　?　　　　2.004

Answers for Self-check　1. 0.19　2. 0.33　3. 6.9　4. 69.43　5. 0.24　6. 0.547　7. >　8. <　9. <

Self-check

How much is shaded? Write a decimal for the answer.

1.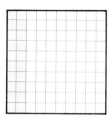

2.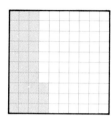

Write the decimal.

3. six and nine tenths

4. sixty-nine and forty-three hundredths

5. twenty-four hundredths

6. five hundred forty-seven thousandths

Give the correct sign (> or <) for each ⫶.

7. 0.6 ⫶ 0.4

8. 0.37 ⫶ 0.47

9. 2.137 ⫶ 2.138

Answers for Self-check—page 63

Test

How much is shaded? Write a decimal for the answer.

1.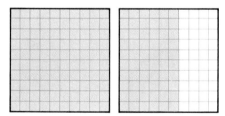

2.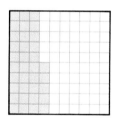

Write the decimal.

3. seven and fifty-three hundredths

4. ninety-two and thirty-one hundredths

5. five tenths

6. two hundred sixty-five thousandths

Give the correct sign (> or <) for each ⫶.

7. 2.95 ⫶ 2.91

8. 0.317 ⫶ 0.713

9. 6.148 ⫶ 7.148

The Four-Square Puzzle

Draw, number, and cut out
16 shapes like these.

Try this puzzle:

Put the sixteen pieces on the
grid so each **row** ↔, **column** ↕,
and long **diagonal** ↘ ↗ has
exactly one of each shape and
one of each number.

If you can do this you will have
a magic square whose magic
sum is 10.

Adding and Subtracting with Decimals

Getting started

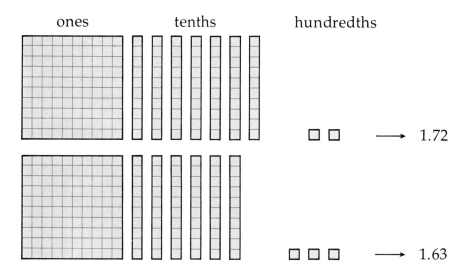

ones	tenths	hundredths

1.72

1.63

How much of the unit squares could be covered
with both sets of pieces?

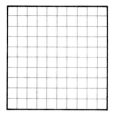 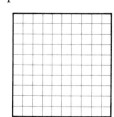 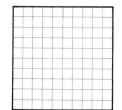 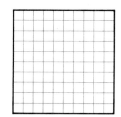

Give the missing numbers.

1.

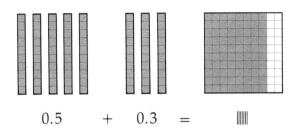

    0.5   +   0.3   = ||||||

2.

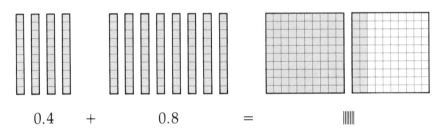

    0.4   +   0.8   = ||||||

3.

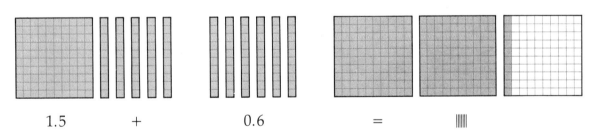

    1.5   +   0.6   = ||||||

4.

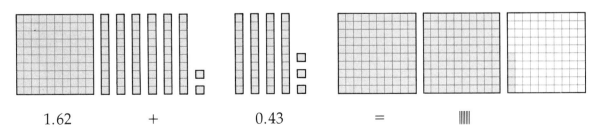

    1.62   +   0.43   = ||||||

Adding with decimals

Miki hiked 7.3 km on Monday. She hiked 8.9 km on Tuesday. How far did she hike in all?

Finding the answer

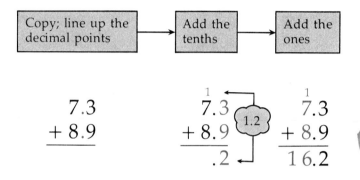

Copy; line up the decimal points	Add the tenths	Add the ones

$$\begin{array}{r} 7.3 \\ +\ 8.9 \\ \hline \end{array}$$

$$\begin{array}{r} {}^{1}\,7.3 \\ +\ 8.9 \\ \hline .2 \end{array} \quad 1.2$$

$$\begin{array}{r} {}^{1}\,7.3 \\ +\ 8.9 \\ \hline 16.2 \end{array}$$

Miki hiked 16.2 km.

Other examples

$$\begin{array}{r} {}^{1}\,12.6 \\ +\ 23.9 \\ \hline 36.5 \end{array} \qquad \begin{array}{r} {}^{1\ 1}\,3.67 \\ +\ 9.48 \\ \hline 13.15 \end{array} \qquad \begin{array}{r} {}^{1}\,6.9 \\ +\ 8.34 \\ \hline 15.24 \end{array} \qquad \begin{array}{r} {}^{2\ 1}\,0.672 \\ 3.58 \\ +\ 1.9 \\ \hline 6.152 \end{array}$$

Find the sums.

1. $\begin{array}{r}3.6\\+1.5\end{array}$	2. $\begin{array}{r}0.9\\+0.6\end{array}$	3. $\begin{array}{r}7.4\\+8.1\end{array}$	4. $\begin{array}{r}8.5\\+9.5\end{array}$	5. $\begin{array}{r}11.7\\+34.9\end{array}$	6. $\begin{array}{r}20.4\\+13.6\end{array}$
7. $\begin{array}{r}3.8\\+0.8\end{array}$	8. $\begin{array}{r}256.4\\+139.8\end{array}$	9. $\begin{array}{r}0.4\\0.7\\+0.8\end{array}$	10. $\begin{array}{r}1.3\\1.9\\+2.6\end{array}$	11. $\begin{array}{r}12.4\\15.3\\+19.7\end{array}$	12. $\begin{array}{r}37.9\\42.8\\+56.7\end{array}$

Find the sums.

1. 6.18 + 3.77	**2.** 0.95 + 1.23	**3.** 8.44 + 9.65	**4.** 12.48 + 19.75
5. 37.46 + 19.2	**6.** 3.115 + 7.448	**7.** 8.2 + 7.68	**8.** 23.7 + 19.84
9. 64.73 + 12.08	**10.** 5.19 + 4.582	**11.** 3.625 + 42.09	**12.** 81.772 + 65.931
13. 26.7 18.4 + 25.5	**14.** 129.32 74.88 + 86.77	**15.** 1.796 2.077 + 3.548	**16.** 2.638 0.75 + 0.9
17. 54.48 27.09 36.42 + 18.71	**18.** 1.663 2.704 5.918 + 4.773	**19.** 18.4 2.59 6.437 + 23.75	**20.** 124.7 642.8 376.5 + 290.1

21. 8.123 + 7.466 + 8.017   **22.** 1.774 + 25.85 + 2.98

23. 12.37 + 8.5 + 9.45   **24.** 66.7 + 88.3 + 112.4

25. Monday: 9.4 km
Tuesday: 6.8 km
Wednesday: 7.7 km
How far in all?

26. Friday: 55 km
Saturday: 12.6 km
Sunday: 25.8 km
How far in all?

Put decimal points in the addends
so the sums will be correct.

	Addends	Sum
1.	258 + 16 =	4.18
2.	258 + 16 =	41.8
3.	258 + 16 =	27.4
4.	258 + 16 =	2.74
5.	258 + 16 =	258.16
6.	258 + 16 =	16.258
7.	258 + 16 =	0.418
8.	258 + 16 =	259.6

More practice, page 363, Set A

Subtracting with decimals

Bowling ball: 7.27 kg
Bowling pin: 1.58 kg
How much heavier is the
bowling ball than the
bowling pin?

Finding the answer

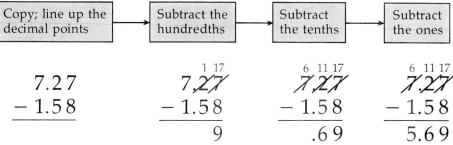

Copy; line up the decimal points	→	Subtract the hundredths	→	Subtract the tenths	→	Subtract the ones

$$
\begin{array}{r} 7.27 \\ -1.58 \\ \hline \end{array}
\qquad
\begin{array}{r} {}^{1\;17}7.\cancel{2}\cancel{7} \\ -1.58 \\ \hline 9 \end{array}
\qquad
\begin{array}{r} {}^{6\;\;11\;17}\cancel{7}.\cancel{2}\cancel{7} \\ -1.58 \\ \hline .69 \end{array}
\qquad
\begin{array}{r} {}^{6\;\;11\;17}\cancel{7}.\cancel{2}\cancel{7} \\ -1.58 \\ \hline 5.69 \end{array}
$$

The bowling ball is 5.69 kg heavier than the bowling pin.

Other examples

$$
\begin{array}{r} {}^{2\;\;14}\cancel{3}.\cancel{4} \\ -1.8 \\ \hline 1.6 \end{array}
\qquad
\begin{array}{r} {}^{7\;\;10}3\cancel{8}.\cancel{0} \\ -15.3 \\ \hline 22.7 \end{array}
\qquad
\begin{array}{r} {}^{7\;9\;17}0.\cancel{8}\cancel{0}\cancel{7} \\ -0.369 \\ \hline 0.438 \end{array}
$$

Subtract.

1. $\begin{array}{r}5.1\\-2.7\\\hline\end{array}$	**2.** $\begin{array}{r}11.4\\-\;6.5\\\hline\end{array}$	**3.** $\begin{array}{r}27.0\\-13.9\\\hline\end{array}$	**4.** $\begin{array}{r}0.9\\-0.2\\\hline\end{array}$	**5.** $\begin{array}{r}10.0\\-\;8.3\\\hline\end{array}$

6. $\begin{array}{r}8.43\\-2.27\\\hline\end{array}$	**7.** $\begin{array}{r}23.81\\-19.44\\\hline\end{array}$	**8.** $\begin{array}{r}6.783\\-2.535\\\hline\end{array}$	**9.** $\begin{array}{r}11.27\\-\;9.42\\\hline\end{array}$	**10.** $\begin{array}{r}39.33\\-18.44\\\hline\end{array}$

Sometimes you must annex zeros when subtracting.

Example:
$$\begin{array}{r} 45.6 \\ -22.14 \\ \hline \end{array}$$
Rewrite 45.6 as 45.60
$$\begin{array}{r} \overset{\text{5 10}}{45.\cancel{6}\cancel{0}} \\ -22.14 \\ \hline 23.46 \end{array}$$

Subtract.

1. $\begin{array}{r} 0.92 \\ -0.65 \\ \hline \end{array}$
2. $\begin{array}{r} 0.83 \\ -0.26 \\ \hline \end{array}$
3. $\begin{array}{r} 6.95 \\ -3.47 \\ \hline \end{array}$
4. $\begin{array}{r} 8.81 \\ -2.54 \\ \hline \end{array}$
5. $\begin{array}{r} 7.41 \\ -5.07 \\ \hline \end{array}$

6. $\begin{array}{r} 6.9 \\ -2.98 \\ \hline \end{array}$
7. $\begin{array}{r} 8.07 \\ -1.58 \\ \hline \end{array}$
8. $\begin{array}{r} 0.93 \\ -0.307 \\ \hline \end{array}$
9. $\begin{array}{r} 7.064 \\ -1.255 \\ \hline \end{array}$

10. $\begin{array}{r} 7.602 \\ -0.009 \\ \hline \end{array}$
11. $\begin{array}{r} 7.8 \\ -3.99 \\ \hline \end{array}$
12. $\begin{array}{r} 0.832 \\ -0.076 \\ \hline \end{array}$
13. $\begin{array}{r} 3.77 \\ -1.88 \\ \hline \end{array}$

14. $\begin{array}{r} 35.9 \\ -27.32 \\ \hline \end{array}$
15. $\begin{array}{r} 0.181 \\ -0.136 \\ \hline \end{array}$
16. $\begin{array}{r} 10.00 \\ -2.75 \\ \hline \end{array}$

17. $2.3 - 0.9$
18. $3.74 - 1.687$
19. $5.83 - 3.96$

20. $0.444 - 0.175$
21. $91.06 - 3.2$
22. $8.04 - 5.1$

23. Tennis ball: 58.1 grams
Golf ball: 46.8 grams
How much heavier is the tennis ball?

☆ 24. Find 2 kinds of balls used in sports. Find the mass of each ball. Find the difference of their masses.

Complete this square so that it is a magic addition square. Each row, column and diagonal must have the same sum.

5.3		
	4.1	4.9
		2.9

Adding and subtracting practice

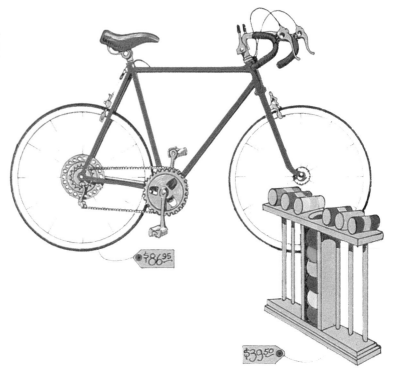

What is the total cost?

$$\begin{array}{r} \$\ 86.95 \\ +\ 39.50 \\ \hline \$126.45 \end{array}$$

How much more does the bike cost?

$$\begin{array}{r} \$\ 86.95 \\ -\ 39.50 \\ \hline \$47.45 \end{array}$$

Find the total amounts.

1. $\begin{array}{r} \$\ 6.59 \\ +\ 8.23 \\ \hline \end{array}$	2. $\begin{array}{r} \$\ 3.65 \\ +\ 6.25 \\ \hline \end{array}$	3. $\begin{array}{r} \$\ 4.87 \\ +\ 7.38 \\ \hline \end{array}$	4. $\begin{array}{r} \$\ 12.27 \\ +\ \ \ 9.44 \\ \hline \end{array}$	5. $\begin{array}{r} \$\ 32.75 \\ +\ \ \ 1.68 \\ \hline \end{array}$
6. $\begin{array}{r} \$\ 18.95 \\ +\ 14.27 \\ \hline \end{array}$	7. $\begin{array}{r} \$\ 52.84 \\ +\ 76.99 \\ \hline \end{array}$	8. $\begin{array}{r} \$\ 25.00 \\ +\ 17.76 \\ \hline \end{array}$	9. $\begin{array}{r} \$\ 1.09 \\ +\ 3.98 \\ \hline \end{array}$	10. $\begin{array}{r} \$\ 44.75 \\ +\ 23.25 \\ \hline \end{array}$

11. $15.42 + $18.77 12. $26.99 + $33.72 13. $18.01 + $16.98

14. $123.47 + $52.66 15. $829.73 + $84.58 16. $63.38 + $36.62

Find the difference in amounts.

17. $\begin{array}{r} \$\ 3.75 \\ -\ 1.84 \\ \hline \end{array}$	18. $\begin{array}{r} \$\ 7.42 \\ -\ 6.88 \\ \hline \end{array}$	19. $\begin{array}{r} \$\ 14.09 \\ -\ \ \ 9.50 \\ \hline \end{array}$	20. $\begin{array}{r} \$\ 5.95 \\ -\ 3.49 \\ \hline \end{array}$	21. $\begin{array}{r} \$\ 20.83 \\ -\ 13.75 \\ \hline \end{array}$
22. $\begin{array}{r} \$\ 42.66 \\ -\ 39.57 \\ \hline \end{array}$	23. $\begin{array}{r} \$\ 113.23 \\ -\ \ \ 75.15 \\ \hline \end{array}$	24. $\begin{array}{r} \$\ 227.38 \\ -\ 129.55 \\ \hline \end{array}$	25. $\begin{array}{r} \$\ 12.00 \\ -\ \ \ 8.95 \\ \hline \end{array}$	26. $\begin{array}{r} \$\ 728.47 \\ -\ 375.50 \\ \hline \end{array}$

27. $9.72 − $6.84 28. $29.50 − $6.75 29. $51.84 − $39.27

Find the sums or differences.

1. $8.53
  + 4.27
	2. $0.96
	  + 4.34
		3. $10.90
		  + 5.38
			4. $34.59
			  + 86.79
				5. $ 7.16
				  + 18.09

6. $9.67
  − 4.83
	7. $6.75
	  − 0.86
		8. $10.00
		  − 3.67
			9. $50.00
			  − 46.72
				10. $12.02
				  − 5.85

11. 8.38
  + 6.75
	12. 0.927
	  + 0.846
		13. 32.8
		  + 65.4
			14. 9.762
			  + 8.431
				15. 64.35
				  + 74.69

16. 72.80
  + 97.54
	17. 8.346
	  + 7.52
		18. 92.6
		  + 87.59
			19. 600.4
			  + 738.7
				20. 92.65
				  + 34.71

21. 87.4 + 65.2 + 93.1   22. 4.58 + 7.6 + 25.8   23. 64.3 + 2.74 + 84.5

24. 0.832 + 5.26 + 39.1   25. 52.74 + 6.5 + 23.88   26. 9.642 + 376 + 84.75

27. 6.4
  − 2.8
	28. 2.3
	  − 0.9
		29. 8.6
		  − 1.9
			30. 0.92
			  − 0.65
				31. 0.83
				  − 0.26

32. 0.76
  − 0.09
	33. 6.82
	  − 0.63
		34. 7.41
		  − 5.07
			35. 6.95
			  − 2.97
				36. 0.930
				  − 0.307

37. 8.07
  − 1.58
	38. 7.064
	  − 1.255
		39. 7.602
		  − 3.009
			40. 12.726
			  − 9.377
				41. 8.317
				  − 2.669

42. Radio:
Regular price $24.99
Sale price $19.97
How much less is the
sale price?

43. Jeans: $8.99
Shirt: $5.97
How much altogether?

☆ 44. Choose two articles you would
like to buy. Find the total cost.
Find the difference in cost.

Answers for Self-check 1. 22.1 2. 9.4 3. 10.29 4. 14.6 5. 33.04 6. 5.8 7. 7.8 8. 6.6 9. 0.143
10. 3.362 11. 29.81 12. 50.71 13. 3.62 14. 28.83 15. 11.29 16. 8.853 17. $29.58 18. $35.99
19. $4.21 20. $10.99

Self-check

Add.

1. 12.4
   + 9.7

2. 0.9
   + 8.5

3. 3.47
   + 6.82

4. 9.5
   1.7
   + 3.4

5. 18.42
   3.87
   + 10.75

Subtract.

6. 8.3
   − 2.5

7. 11.4
   − 3.6

8. 25.0
   − 18.4

9. 0.315
   − 0.172

10. 9.817
    − 6.455

Find the sums or differences.

11. 3.26 + 21.85 + 4.7

12. 16.05 + 9.2 + 25.46

13. 1.09 + 0.35 + 2.18

14. 12.42 + 8.46 + 7.95

15. 25.01 − 13.72

16. 9.04 − 0.187

Find the total amounts or differences.

17. $ 12.75
    + 16.83

18. $ 26.42
    + 9.57

19. $ 8.00
    − 3.79

20. $ 16.98
    − 5.99

Answers for Self-check—page 73

Test

Add.

1. 0.7
   + 1.8

2. 12.4
   + 3.9

3. 0.413
   + 0.746

4. 1.9
   7.4
   + 6.9

5. 3.46
   7.70
   + 5.87

Subtract.

6. 9.4
   − 6.8

7. 12.6
   − 8.2

8. 23.1
   − 19.8

9. 0.715
   − 0.366

10. 9.936
    − 1.755

Find the sums or differences.

11. 79.03 + 52.9 + 81.325

12. 32.08 + 17.48 + 9.54

13. 8.26 + 12.7 + 9.06

14. 21.73 + 9.406 + 15.225

15. 32.15 − 24.8

16. 9.05 − 6.723

Find the total amounts or differences.

17. $ 12.44
    + 15.98

18. $ 293.66
    + 174.83

19. $ 12.95
    − 8.46

20. $ 5.00
    − 1.79

The Matching Sides Puzzle

Make copies of these nine squares. Cut out the squares. Make a 3 by 3 square with nine small squares.

Follow this rule: Where any two squares touch, their sides must have matching colors.

Using Your Skills

Car Expenses

	Gasoline	Cost	Odometer Reading
March 3	31.2 L	$4.68	7948.3 km
March 8	54.0 L	$8.10	8499.1 km
March 14	41.6 L	$6.24	8910.9 km

	Oil Change	Tune Up	Odometer Reading
March 15	$6.16	$42.50	8976.4 km

Getting started

Carol Johnson made this record of her automobile expenses.

1. What was the total amount of gasoline bought?

2. How far did Carol drive her car from March 3 to March 8?

3. What other problems can you solve?

Each problem has a question. The kind of question it is will help you decide what to do to solve the problem.

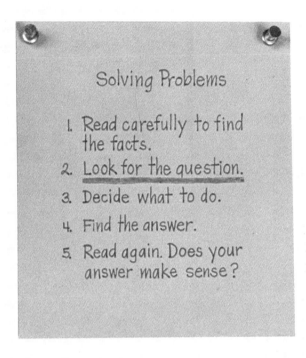

Solving Problems

1. Read carefully to find the facts.
2. Look for the question.
3. Decide what to do.
4. Find the answer.
5. Read again. Does your answer make sense?

Read each problem. Look at the question in the problem. Then tell what you would do to solve the problem.

1. Carol bought 31.2 L of gasoline on March 3. She bought 54.0 L on March 8. What was the total amount of gasoline bought for these two days?

2. Carol bought 31.2 L of gasoline on March 3. She bought 41.6 L on March 14. How much more did she buy on March 14?

3. The odometer reading on March 3 was 7948.3. On March 15 the odometer reading was 8976.4. What was the distance traveled during this time?

4. The tune-up cost $42.50. The oil change cost $6.16. How much more did the tune-up cost than the oil change?

5. The tune-up cost $42.50. The oil change cost $6.16. What was the total cost of the tune-up and oil change?

6. Carol spent $4.68, $8.10, and $6.24 for gasoline. The tune-up cost $42.50. Which cost more, the tune-up or the total amount for gasoline? How much more?

Finding balances

A bookkeeper keeps records of all the money a business takes in or pays out. Bookkeepers must do correct number work. Special books and machines help bookkeepers pay attention to details.

Many businesses sell goods on an **installment plan.** A customer buys an item by paying a certain amount, or installment, each month or each week until the cost of the item has been completely paid.

Stereo Music Co. 1129 State Street Sold to: Jerry Williams 2774 East 18th St.		
		$239 95
Stereo Hi-fi Set		14 40
Sales Tax		254 35
Total		- 50 00
- Down payment		$204 35
Balance		

A bookkeeper must keep a record of the amount paid and the **balance** owed.

Find the new balance.

1. $ 189.95   Old balance
   −   32.75   Payment
                 New balance

2. $ 347.52   Old balance
   −   43.44   Payment
                 New balance

3. $ 280.80   Old balance
   −   31.20   Payment
                 New balance

4. $228.42   Old balance
   −   25.38   Payment
                 New balance

Copy and complete each of the tables below.

1.

Month	Balance	Payment	New Balance
1	$204.35	$40.87	$163.48
2	$163.48	$40.87	
3		$40.87	
4		$40.87	
5		$40.87	

←— $204.35 − $40.87
←— $163.48 − $40.87

2.

Month	Balance	Payment	New Balance
1	$170.56	$42.64	
2		$42.64	
3		$42.64	
4		$42.64	

3.

Month	Balance	Payment	New Balance
1	$326.60	$65.32	
2		$65.32	
3		$65.32	
4		$65.32	
5		$65.32	

4.

Month	Balance	Payment	New Balance
1	$1887.00	$314.50	
2		$314.50	
3		$314.50	
4		$314.50	
5		$314.50	
6		$314.50	

Jetliner sizes

The tail of a 727 jet airplane is 10.36 m high. What are the heights of the tails of the other three planes?

Plane	Number of Passengers	Length	Wingspan	Tail Height
727	131	40.80 m	32.92 m	10.36 m
707	135	44.04 m	43.41 m	
DC-10	250	55.29 m	47.35 m	
747	370	70.51 m	59.64 m	

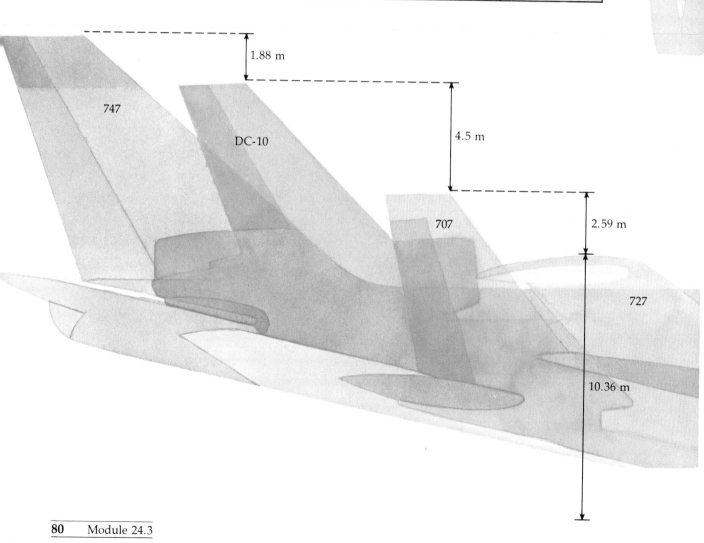

1.88 m

747

DC-10

4.5 m

707

2.59 m

727

10.36 m

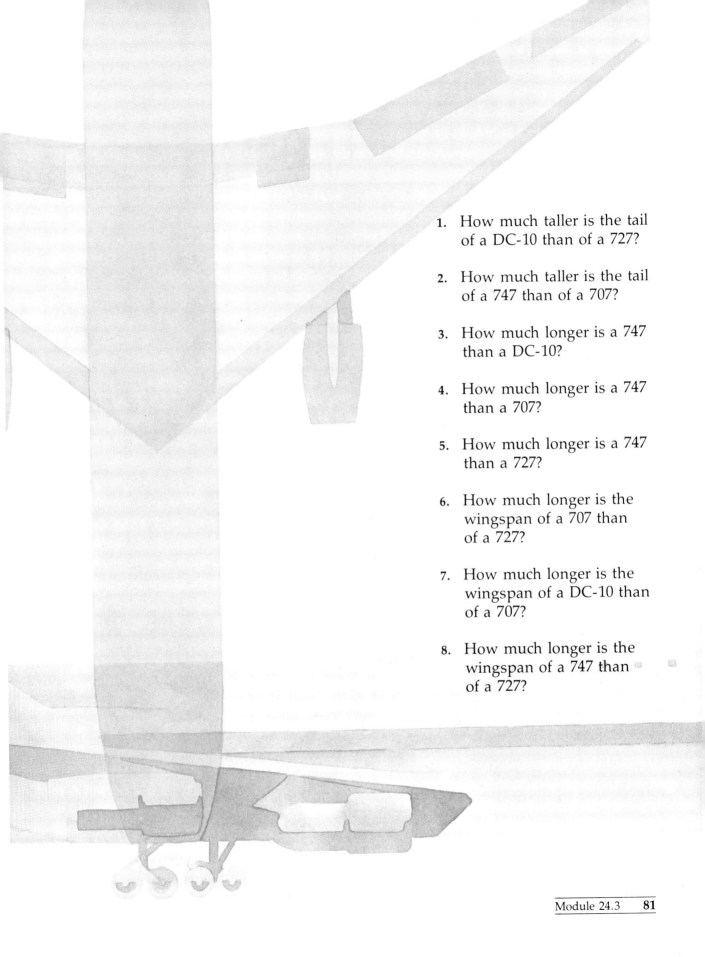

1. How much taller is the tail of a DC-10 than of a 727?

2. How much taller is the tail of a 747 than of a 707?

3. How much longer is a 747 than a DC-10?

4. How much longer is a 747 than a 707?

5. How much longer is a 747 than a 727?

6. How much longer is the wingspan of a 707 than of a 727?

7. How much longer is the wingspan of a DC-10 than of a 707?

8. How much longer is the wingspan of a 747 than of a 727?

⊗ The air we breathe

The air we breathe is made up of
several kinds of gases. The graph
below shows the part of a liter
of air for each gas.

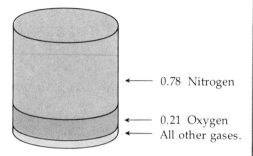

← 0.78 Nitrogen

← 0.21 Oxygen
← All other gases.

1. The graph shows that 0.78 of air
   is nitrogen. It shows that
   0.21 of air is oxygen. What
   part of air is nitrogen
   and oxygen together?

2. What part of air is all other
   gases? (Subtract the answer in
   exercise 1 from 1.00.)

3. About 9 parts out of every
   thousand parts of air is a gas
   called argon. Write a decimal to
   show what part of air is argon.

4. At rest a person breathes about
   0.5 L of air in one breath. When
   active, a person breathes
   about 3.8 L of air in one breath.
   How much more air is breathed
   when a person is active?

5. A person breathes about 2.3
   kiloliters (kL) of oxygen every
   day. About 0.6 kL of the oxygen
   is used by the body. How many
   kiloliters are not used?

6. At sea level, air pressure is
   about 1.034 kg on each square
   centimeter of surface. At a
   height of 10 000 m above the
   earth, the pressure is only
   0.265 kg on each square
   centimeter of surface. How
   much less is the pressure at
   10 000 m?

7. Clean air may have as few as
   915 dust particles in one cubic
   centimeter of air. Polluted air
   may have 315 000 dust particles
   in one cubic centimeter. How
   many more particles does the
   polluted air have?

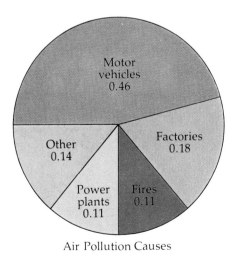

Air Pollution Causes

8. The circle graph shows that 0.46 of all air pollution is caused by motor vehicles. What part of air pollution is caused by factories?

9. What part of air pollution is caused by motor vehicles, factories, and power plants combined?

10. What part of air pollution is caused by other causes?

Answers for Self-check   1. 116.1 L   2. 229.5 km   3. 16.23 m   4. $14.95   5. $9.44   6. $93.85

Self-check

1. One week Nita used 62.4 L of gasoline. The next week she used 53.7 L. How many liters did she use in all?

2. Odometer reading on Monday: 4937.2 km
   Odometer reading on Saturday: 5166.7 km
   What was the distance traveled between Monday and Saturday?

3. The wingspan of a 707 jet is 43.41 m. A 747 jet has a wingspan of 59.64 m. How much longer is the wingspan of the 747?

4. A radio costs $24.95. Made a down payment of $10.00. What is the balance?

5. Spent $3.78 on Monday. Spent $5.66 on Wednesday. How much in all?

6. Owed $127.47. Paid $33.62. What is the balance?

Answers for Self-check—page 83

Test

1. On Tuesday Bob bought 36.7 L of gasoline. On Friday he bought 42.8 L more. How much did he buy in all?

2. Odometer reading before the trip: 2377.4 km
   Odometer reading after the trip: 3642.2 km
   How many kilometers were traveled during the trip?

3. Small plane: 6.86 m long
   Large plane: 70.51 m long
   How much longer is the large plane?

4. Had $127.69 in the bank. Put in $44.75 more. How much is in the bank now?

5. A bicycle costs $83.50. Paid $16.70. What is the balance?

6. A desk costs $48.55. Made a down payment of $20.00. What is the balance?

For fun

Name "Lengths"

0	0.1	0.2	0.3	0.4	0.5	0.6	0.7	0.8	0.9	1.0	1.1	1.2	1.3	1.4	1.5	1.6	1.7	1.8	1.9	2.0	2.1	2.2	2.3	2.4	2.5
E	T	O	A	N	I	R	S	H	D	L	C	U	M	F	P	Y	B	G	W	V	K	X	J	Q	Z
0	0.1	0.2	0.3	0.4	0.5	0.6	0.7	0.8	0.9	1.0	1.1	1.2	1.3	1.4	1.5	1.6	1.7	1.8	1.9	2.0	2.1	2.2	2.3	2.4	2.5

Use this special ruler to find the "length" of your name.

Match each letter in the name with the number for the letter on the ruler. Then add the numbers.

Examples:

J   A   N   E
$2.3 + 0.3 + 0.4 + 0 = 3.0$

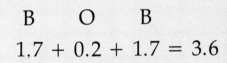

B   O   B
$1.7 + 0.2 + 1.7 = 3.6$

Bob is a "longer" name than Jane.

How "long" is your name?

Who has the "longest" name in your room?

Who has the "shortest" name in your room?

Length

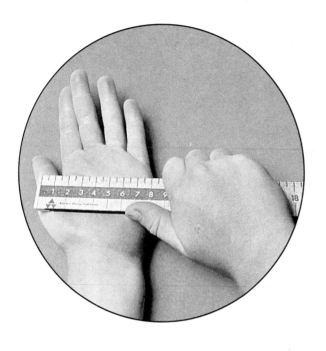

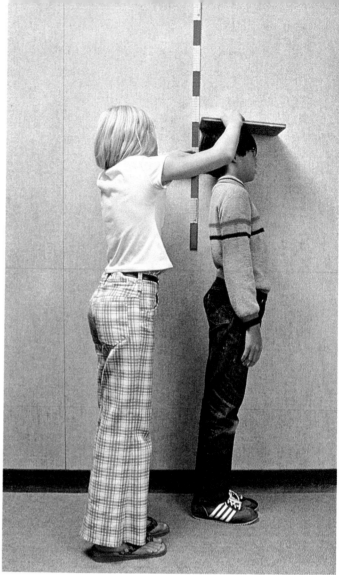

Getting started

Kevin is about 152 cm tall.

Becky's hand is about 8 cm wide.

Here is a centimeter ruler.

```
|0  1  2  3  4  5  6  7  8  9  10  11  12  13  14  15|
 cm
```

Estimate in centimeters

1. your height

2. the width of your hand

3. the length of your shoe

4. the length of your arm

Check your estimates by measuring.

The basic unit of length in the
metric system is the meter (m).

The table is a little less than 1 m wide.

A meter is divided into smaller units called
decimeters (dm), centimeters (cm), and millimeters (mm).

1 decimeter (dm) ⊢———————————————————┤

1 centimeter (cm) ⊢———┤

1 millimeter (mm) ⊢

10 mm = 1 cm   10 dm = 1 m

10 cm = 1 dm   100 cm = 1 m

Find some objects in your classroom that are about these lengths.

1. 1 m	2. 2 m	3. 1 dm
4. 1 cm	5. 1 mm	6. 50 cm
7. 150 cm	8. 5 mm	9. 180 cm

Cindy built a birdhouse.

1. How many millimeters long were the nails that Cindy used?

0   2 cm

2. How many millimeters thick was the wood?

Top
Make two pieces

3. How many centimeters long is this piece?
4. How many centimeters wide is this piece?

Cindy used this pattern for the front
and back of the birdhouse.

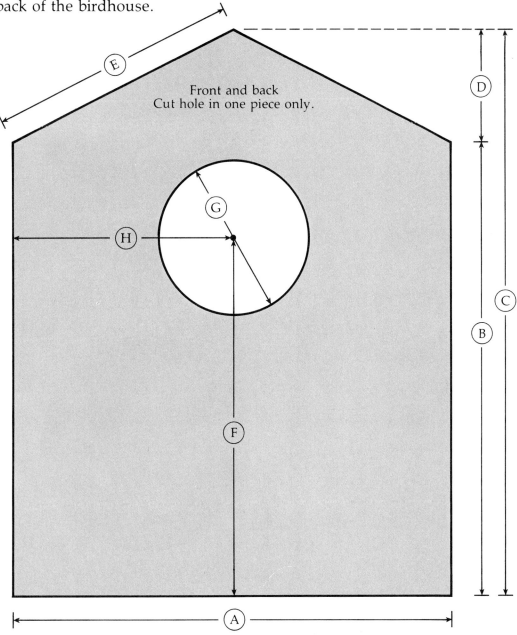

Front and back
Cut hole in one piece only.

Give each length in centimeters and in millimeters.

1. A
2. B
3. C
4. D
5. E
6. F
7. G
8. H

Measuring circles

The **diameter** of the spool
is 25 mm or 2.5 cm.

The **radius** of the button is
28 mm or 2.8 cm.

Give the diameter of each circle in millimeters and in centimeters.

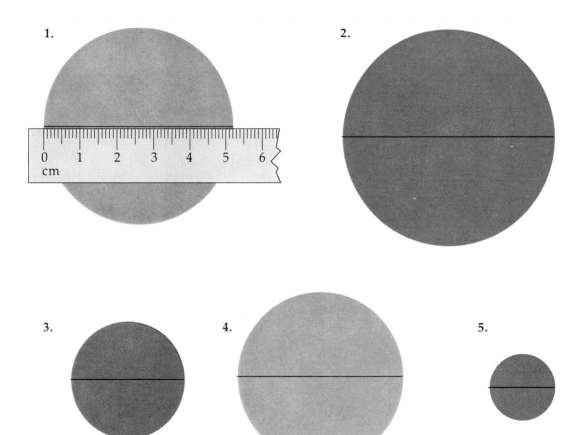

1.

2.

3.

4.

5.

Give the diameter in centimeters.

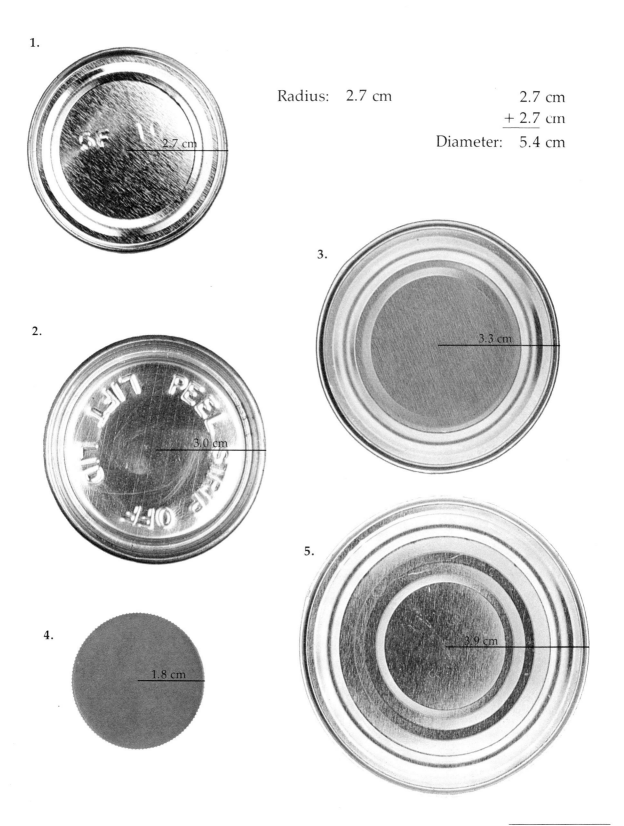

1.

Radius: 2.7 cm

2.7 cm
+ 2.7 cm
Diameter: 5.4 cm

2.7 cm

3.

3.3 cm

2.

3.0 cm

5.

3.9 cm

4.

1.8 cm

1 kilometer

Give the correct unit, **centimeters, meters,**
or **kilometers,** for each measurement.

1. A door is about 2 _?_ in height.
2. You can walk about 6 _?_ in one hour.
3. An adult may be 1.8 _?_ in height.
4. Marsha's waist is about 51 _?_ around.
5. John's height is 147 _?_.
6. You might travel 80 _?_ in one hour on a freeway.
7. Linda threw a softball 45 _?_.
8. A jet airplane traveled 900 _?_ in one hour.
9. Ingrid swam 200 _?_ in 2 minutes 22 seconds.
10. Jason ran 1500 _?_ in 5 minutes.

Men's World Running Records		
Distance	Name	Time
1000 m	Rick Wohlhuter	2 min 13.9 s
1500 m	Filbert Bayi	3 min 32.2 s
2000 m	Michel Jazy	4 min 56.2 s
3000 m	Brendon Foster	7 min 35.2 s
5000 m	Emiel Puttemans	13 min 13.0 s
10 000 m	Dave Bedford	27 min 30.8 s
20 000 m	Gaston Roelants	57 min 44.4 s
25 000 m	Seppo Nikkari	1 h 14 min 55.6 s
30 000 m	Jim Alder	1 h 31 min 30.4 s

1000 m = 1 km

This table gives men's world running records for a recent year.

Use the data in the table to answer each question.

1. Which person holds the 1 kilometer running record?
2. Brendon Foster holds the record for running how many kilometers?
3. How many kilometers did Seppo Nikkari run in setting his record?
4. Which distance did Filbert Bayi run: 1.5 km, 15 km, or 150 km?
5. Who holds the 2 km running record?
6. How many kilometers did Jim Alder run?
7. The record time of 13 min 13.0 s is for running how many kilometers?
8. Who holds the 20 km record, Michel Jazy or Gaston Roelants?

Practicing your skills

Find the sums.

1. $\begin{array}{r} 7.4 \\ + 8.9 \\ \hline \end{array}$
2. $\begin{array}{r} 3.7 \\ + 6.8 \\ \hline \end{array}$
3. $\begin{array}{r} 12.4 \\ + 28.3 \\ \hline \end{array}$
4. $\begin{array}{r} 1.77 \\ + 2.48 \\ \hline \end{array}$
5. $\begin{array}{r} 6.9 \\ + 15.4 \\ \hline \end{array}$

6. $\begin{array}{r} 3.8 \\ 7.9 \\ + 6.4 \\ \hline \end{array}$
7. $\begin{array}{r} 12.7 \\ 8.6 \\ + 15.4 \\ \hline \end{array}$
8. $\begin{array}{r} 23.47 \\ 16.95 \\ + 43.66 \\ \hline \end{array}$
9. $\begin{array}{r} 72.9 \\ 84.7 \\ + 66.5 \\ \hline \end{array}$
10. $\begin{array}{r} 8.99 \\ 6.03 \\ + 7.48 \\ \hline \end{array}$

Perimeter

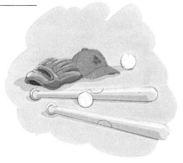

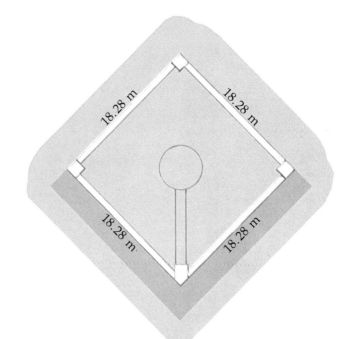

Softball diamond

The distance around a region is called the **perimeter** of the region. What is the perimeter of the softball diamond?

Add the lengths of the sides.	18.28
	18.28
	18.28
	+ 18.28
	73.12

The perimeter of the softball diamond is 73.12 m.

Find the perimeter of each.

1.

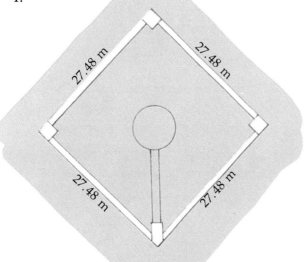

Baseball diamond

2.

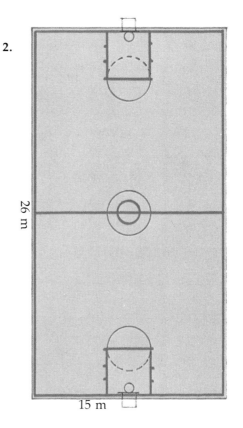

Basketball court

Find the perimeter.

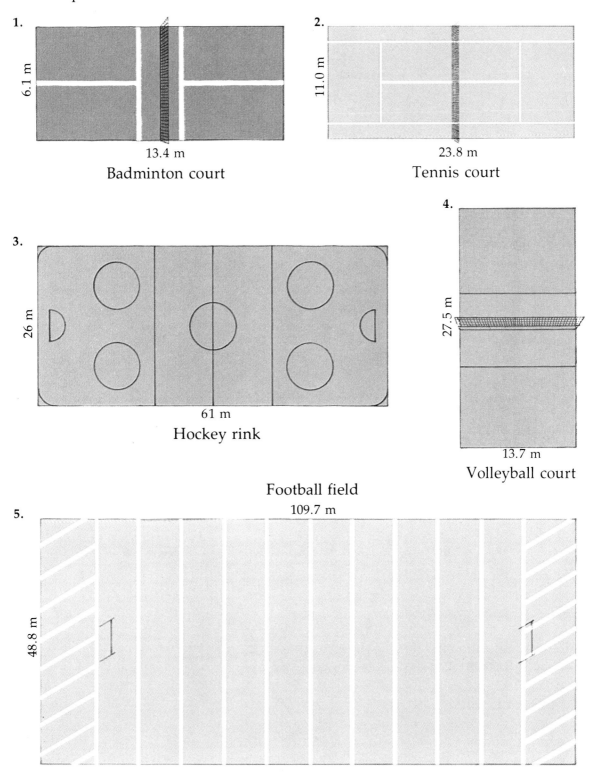

1.

6.1 m

13.4 m

Badminton court

2.

11.0 m

23.8 m

Tennis court

3.

26 m

61 m

Hockey rink

4.

27.5 m

13.7 m

Volleyball court

Football field

109.7 m

5.

48.8 m

Answers for Self-check   1. 25 mm; 2.5 cm   2. 18 mm; 1.8 cm   3. 41 mm; 4.1 cm   4. 10 mm
5. 100 cm   6. 1000 m   7. radius 1.7 cm; diameter: 3.4 cm   8. 33.2 m   9. 34.0 m

Self-check

Give the length of each nail in millimeters and in centimeters.

1.

2.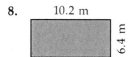

3.

Complete. **4.** 1 cm = ▨ mm **5.** 1 m = ▨ cm **6.** 1 km = ▨ m

7. Give the radius and the diameter of this circle in centimeters.

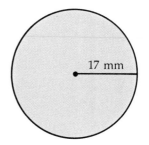

17 mm

Find the perimeters.

8.
10.2 m
6.4 m

9.
8.5 m 8.5 m
8.5 m 8.5 m

Answers for Self-check—page 95

Answers for Self-check—page 95

Test

Give the length of each segment in millimeters and in centimeters.

1.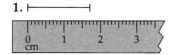

2.

3.

Complete. **4.** 1 cm = ▨ mm **5.** 100 cm = ▨ m **6.** 1000 m = ▨ km

7. Give the radius and the diameter of this circle in centimeters.

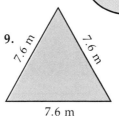

12 mm

Find the perimeters.

8.
46 cm
22 cm

9.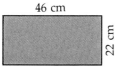
7.6 m 7.6 m
7.6 m

Stepping through a Sheet of Paper

Can you make a hole in a piece of tablet paper big enough to step through?

Try this:
Fold the paper in half.
Then cut along the solid lines through both halves.
Then cut on the fold line **between the arrows.**

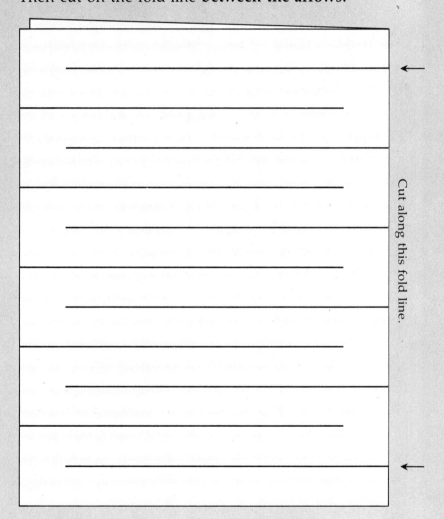

Now step through the hole you have made.

Polygons

Getting started

The geoboards in the picture show two squares
of different sizes.

How many squares of different sizes can
you find on a 5 by 5 geoboard?

Show your squares on graph paper or dot paper.

Polygons are simple closed figures formed by line segments. Each segment is a side of the polygon. This polygon has 5 sides.

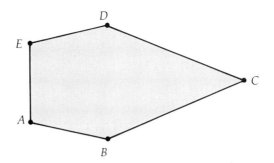

How many sides does each polygon have?

1.

triangle

2.

rectangle

3.

octagon

4.

pentagon

5.

hexagon

6.

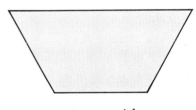

trapezoid

7.

parallelogram

8.

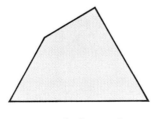

quadrilateral

9.

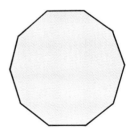

decagon

Congruent segments

This geoboard shows two segments that have the same length.

We say: Segment *AB* **is congruent to** segment *CD*.

We write: $\overline{AB} \cong \overline{CD}$

Complete each statement.

1.

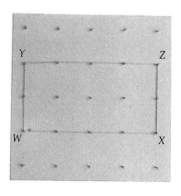

$\overline{WX} \cong$ ▥
$\overline{WY} \cong$ ▥

2.

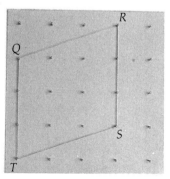

$\overline{QR} \cong$ ▥
$\overline{TQ} \cong$ ▥

3.

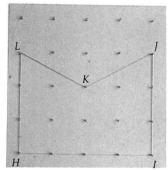

$\overline{HL} \cong$ ▥
$\overline{JK} \cong$ ▥

List two pairs of congruent segments for each geoboard.

1.

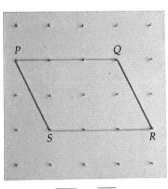

$$\overline{PQ} \cong \overline{SR}$$
$$\overline{PS} \cong \overline{QR}$$

2.

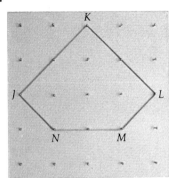

3.

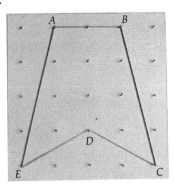

4.

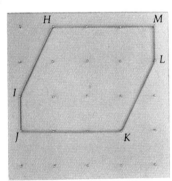

5.

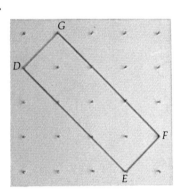

6.

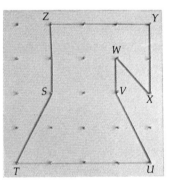

☆ 7. How many different segments can you show on a geoboard that are congruent to $\overline{AB}$?

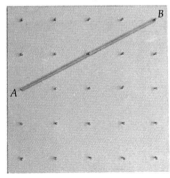

If you stacked 1 penny on one small square, 2 pennies on another small square, 4 pennies on another, 8 on another, and so on, how many pennies would you need for all 16 small squares?

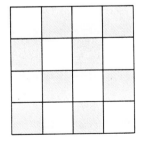

Congruent polygons

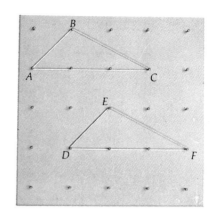

The pair of triangles on the
geoboard have the same size
and shape.

We say: Triangle *ABC* is congruent
to triangle *DEF*.

We write: $\triangle ABC \cong \triangle DEF$.

Congruent polygons can be matched so that matching pairs
of segments are congruent and matching pairs of angles
are congruent.

For example: $\overline{AC} \cong \overline{DF}$ and $\angle BAC \cong \angle EDF$

Each pair of polygons on the geoboards are congruent.
Complete each statement.

1.

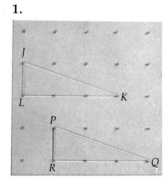

$\overline{PQ} \cong$ ▓

2.

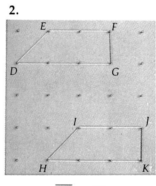

$\overline{EF} \cong$ ▓

3.

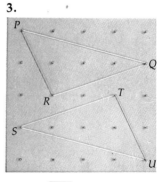

$\overline{RQ} \cong$ ▓

4.

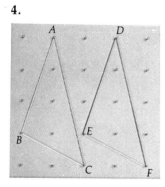

$\angle BAC \cong$ ▓

5.

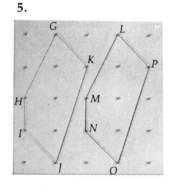

$\angle OPL \cong$ ▓

6.

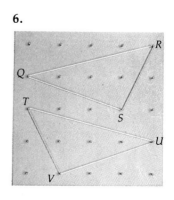

$\angle QSR \cong$ ▓

Match the pairs of congruent triangles.

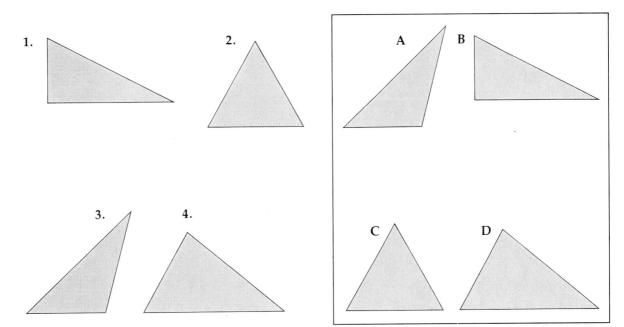

1. 2.

3. 4.

A B

C D

Match the pairs of congruent triangles.

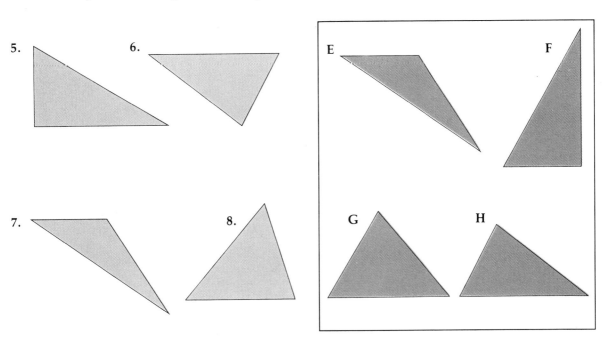

5. 6.

7. 8.

E F

G H

Lines of symmetry

A polygon has a **line of symmetry** if a fold on that line makes two halves of the polygon that match exactly.

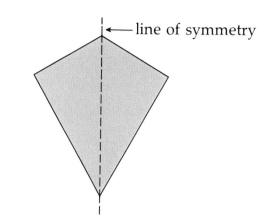

line of symmetry

This **rhombus** can be folded two ways to make the halves match.

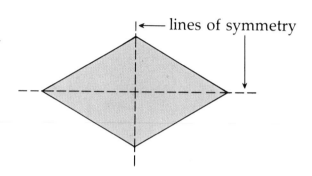

lines of symmetry

Give the number of lines of symmetry of each triangle.

	Geometric figure	Description	Picture	Number of lines of symmetry
1.	Equilateral triangle	All sides have the same length.		
2.	Isosceles triangle	Two sides have the same length.		
3.	Scalene triangle	No two sides have the same length.		

Give the number of lines of symmetry.

	Polygon	Description	Picture	Number of lines of symmetry
1.	Rectangle	Opposite sides have the same length. All angles are right angles.		
2.	Square	All sides have the same length. All angles are right angles.		
3.	Parallelogram	Opposite sides are congruent. Opposite angles are congruent.		
4.	Rhombus	All 4 sides have the same length.		
5.	Regular pentagon	All 5 sides have the same length. All angles are congruent.		
6.	Regular hexagon	All 6 sides have the same length. All angles are congruent.		

Practicing your skills

Subtract.

1. $\begin{array}{r} 31.49 \\ -\ 17.62 \\ \hline \end{array}$
2. $\begin{array}{r} 84.63 \\ -\ 52.75 \\ \hline \end{array}$
3. $\begin{array}{r} 0.712 \\ -\ 0.346 \\ \hline \end{array}$
4. $\begin{array}{r} 2.379 \\ -\ 0.949 \\ \hline \end{array}$
5. $\begin{array}{r} 16.32 \\ -\ 8.67 \\ \hline \end{array}$

6. $\begin{array}{r} 0.801 \\ -\ 0.578 \\ \hline \end{array}$
7. $\begin{array}{r} 65.17 \\ -\ 36.41 \\ \hline \end{array}$
8. $\begin{array}{r} 342.7 \\ -\ 161.9 \\ \hline \end{array}$
9. $\begin{array}{r} 0.730 \\ -\ 0.469 \\ \hline \end{array}$
10. $\begin{array}{r} 110.5 \\ -\ 92.8 \\ \hline \end{array}$

Similar polygons

The two polygons are **similar** polygons. Similar polygons have the same shape, but not necessarily the same size.

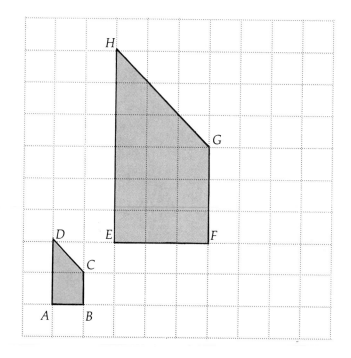

Which two polygons in each row are similar?

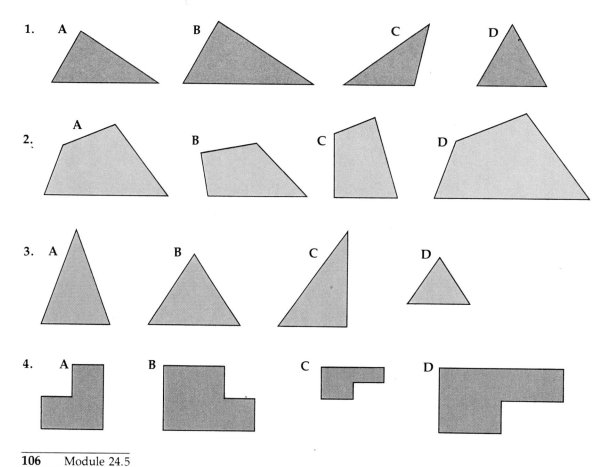

1.   A   B   C   D

2.   A   B   C   D

3.   A   B   C   D

4.   A   B   C   D

Copy each figure on graph paper. Then draw similar figures, with sides as many times as long as the number given.

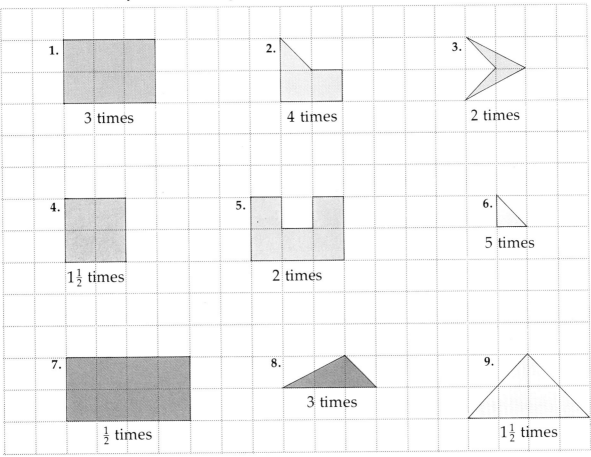

1. 3 times

2. 4 times

3. 2 times

4. $1\frac{1}{2}$ times

5. 2 times

6. 5 times

7. $\frac{1}{2}$ times

8. 3 times

9. $1\frac{1}{2}$ times

Practicing your skills

Add or subtract.

1. $\quad$ 349.1 $\quad$ $-$ 164.5	2. $\quad$ 12.77 $\quad$ $+$ 48.95	3. $\quad$ 0.358 $\quad$ $+$ 0.916	4. $\quad$ 32.76 $\quad$ $-$ 15.98	5. $\quad$ 7.115 $\quad$ $-$ 4.096
6. $\quad$ 50.18 $\quad$ $+$ 79.02	7. $\quad$ 0.913 $\quad$ $-$ 0.627	8. $\quad$ 18.41 $\quad$ $-$ $\quad$ 9.08	9. $\quad$ 413.7 $\quad$ $+$ 829.5	10. $\quad$ 5.172 $\quad$ $+$ 2.859

11. $34.5 + 2.76 + 118.1$

12. $203.7 - 19.28$

Answers for Self-check 1. $\overline{WU}$ 2. $\overline{WV}$ 3. $\overline{UV}$ 4. $\triangle WVU$ 5. no 6. similar 7. a

Self-check

Complete each sentence.

1. $\overline{RT} \cong$ ▓

2. $\overline{RS} \cong$ ▓

3. $\overline{TS} \cong$ ▓

4. $\triangle RST \cong$ ▓

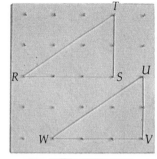

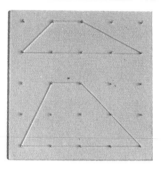

5. Are the two polygons congruent?

6. Are the two triangles congruent or similar?

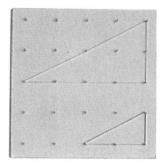

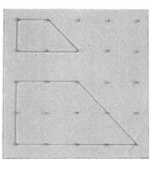

7. Which is a line of symmetry, *a* or *b*?

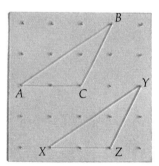

Answers for Self-check—page 107

Test

Complete each sentence.

1. $\overline{AC} \cong$ ▓

2. $\overline{AB} \cong$ ▓

3. $\overline{BC} \cong$ ▓

4. $\triangle ACB \cong$ ▓

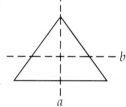

6. Are these two polygons congruent or similar?

5. Are the two triangles congruent?

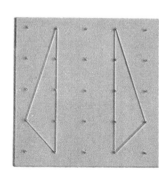

7. Which is a line of symmetry, *a* or *b*?

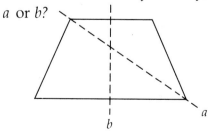

Enlargements

Cut out a picture from a newspaper or magazine.
Trace around it on a piece of graph paper. Mark
several points on the drawing, especially at corners.

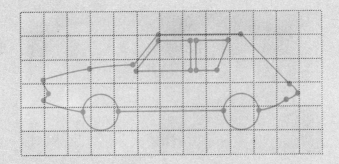

Use another sheet of graph paper with larger
squares. Mark points on the larger squares in the
same places they are marked on the small squares.
Now connect these points to form a larger copy of
the picture.

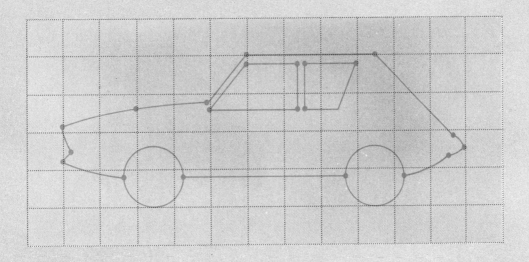

Level 24 review

Write the decimal.

1. seven tenths
2. four and five tenths
3. sixty-three hundredths
4. eight and thirty-one hundredths
5. nineteen and two hundredths

6. sixty-four and seventy-eight hundredths
7. four hundred fifteen thousandths
8. two and three hundred one thousandths
9. five and twelve hundredths
10. seven hundred fifty-three thousandths

Add.

11.	71.69	12.	82.16	13.	2.458	14.	41.637	15.	92.14
	+ 26.58		+ 47.35		+ 9.075		+ 27.398		+ 85.68

16.	5.859	17.	302.10	18.	0.447	19.	0.713	20.	8.307
	+ 2.736		+ 248.09		+ 0.386		+ 1.920		+ 2.699

Subtract.

21.	0.973	22.	9.102	23.	50.41	24.	8.551	25.	86.01
	− 0.586		− 6.543		− 23.78		− 3.297		− 75.10

26.	2.804	27.	34.57	28.	7.206	29.	0.631	30.	82.75
	− 1.637		− 21.49		− 3.524		− 0.372		− 36.89

Find the perimeters.

31.

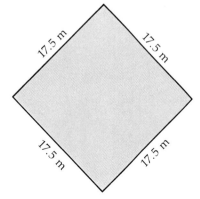

17.5 m · 17.5 m · 17.5 m · 17.5 m

32.

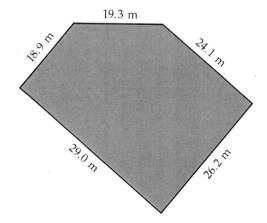

19.3 m · 18.9 m · 24.1 m · 29.0 m · 26.2 m

Multiplication and Division Facts
Special Products and Quotients
Multiplying
Using Your Skills
Area

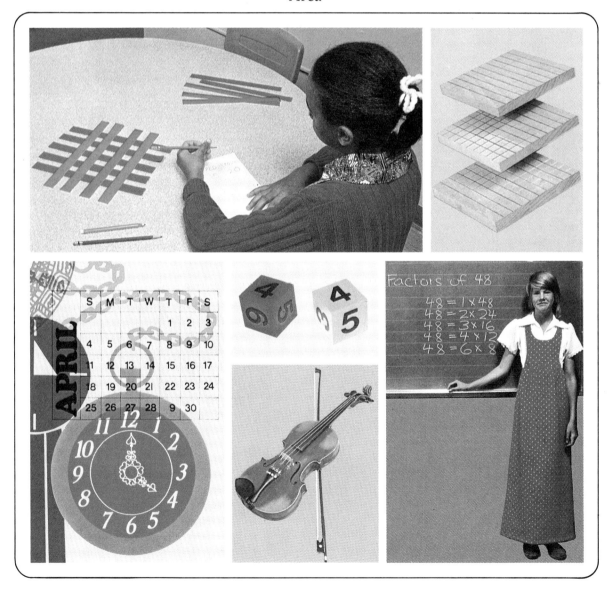

Multiplication and Division Facts

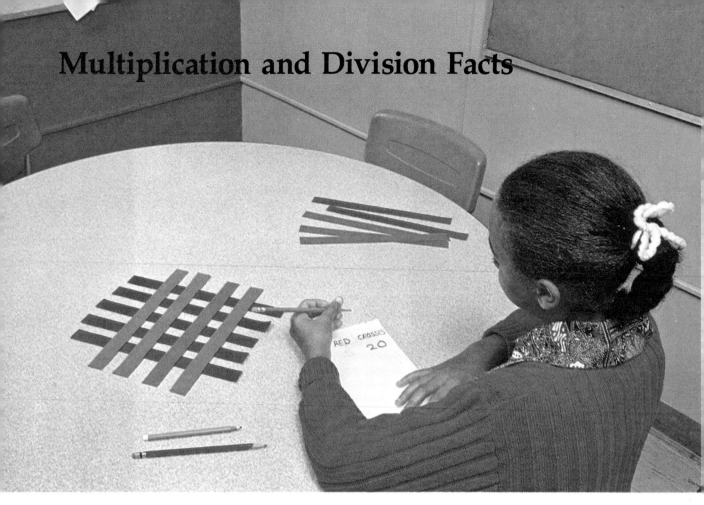

Getting started

Kathy used strips of paper to show this multiplication fact.

$$4 \quad \times \quad 5 \quad = \quad 20$$

blue strips   red strips   crosses

What multiplication facts do these strips show?

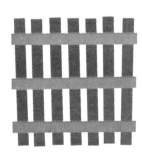 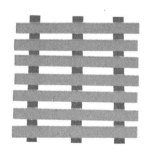

We see: 3 rows of crosses
         4 crosses in each row

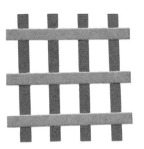

We say: 3 times 4 is 12.

We write: 3 × 4 = 12
        ↑ ↑   ↑
     factors   product

Give the missing numbers.

1.

2.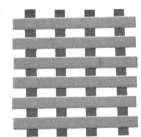

3. 6 + 6 + 6 = 18.

   3 sixes are 18.

   3 × 6 = n

4. 7 + 7 + 7 + 7 = 28

   4 sevens are 28.

   4 × 7 = n

5. 8 + 8 + 8 + 8 = 32

   n × 8 = 32

6. 5 + 5 + 5 = 15

   n × 5 = 15

7. 6 eights are 3 eights and 3 eights.

   6 × 8 = (3 × 8) + (3 × 8)

   6 × 8 = 24 + 24

   6 × 8 = n

8. 8 nines are 4 nines and 4 nines.

   8 × 9 = (4 × 9) + (4 × 9)

   8 × 9 = 36 + 36

   8 × 9 = n

9. 7 sixes are 5 sixes and 2 sixes.

   7 × 6 = (5 × 6) + (2 × 6)

   7 × 6 = 30 + 12

   7 × 6 = n

10. 9 eights are 5 eights and 4 eights.

   9 × 8 = (5 × 8) + (4 × 8)

   9 × 8 = 40 + 32

   9 × 8 = n

Reviewing multiplication facts

A guitar has 6 strings.
How many strings are
there on 4 guitars?

$$4 \times 6 = 24$$

There are 24 strings on 4 guitars.

Find the products.

1. 3×4	**2.** 2×8	**3.** 3×3	**4.** 1×7	**5.** 2×9
6. 5×0	**7.** 4×4	**8.** 2×6	**9.** 5×2	**10.** 3×5
11. 6×7	**12.** 6×3	**13.** 4×2	**14.** 3×6	**15.** 5×5
16. 1×9	**17.** 4×6	**18.** 5×3	**19.** 4×5	**20.** 4×0

21. $\begin{array}{r} 7 \\ \times 5 \\ \hline \end{array}$	**22.** $\begin{array}{r} 7 \\ \times 2 \\ \hline \end{array}$	**23.** $\begin{array}{r} 8 \\ \times 4 \\ \hline \end{array}$	**24.** $\begin{array}{r} 9 \\ \times 3 \\ \hline \end{array}$	**25.** $\begin{array}{r} 5 \\ \times 2 \\ \hline \end{array}$
26. $\begin{array}{r} 8 \\ \times 6 \\ \hline \end{array}$	**27.** $\begin{array}{r} 8 \\ \times 3 \\ \hline \end{array}$	**28.** $\begin{array}{r} 6 \\ \times 6 \\ \hline \end{array}$	**29.** $\begin{array}{r} 4 \\ \times 5 \\ \hline \end{array}$	**30.** $\begin{array}{r} 7 \\ \times 3 \\ \hline \end{array}$
31. $\begin{array}{r} 4 \\ \times 6 \\ \hline \end{array}$	**32.** $\begin{array}{r} 9 \\ \times 6 \\ \hline \end{array}$	**33.** $\begin{array}{r} 7 \\ \times 4 \\ \hline \end{array}$	**34.** $\begin{array}{r} 8 \\ \times 5 \\ \hline \end{array}$	**35.** $\begin{array}{r} 6 \\ \times 5 \\ \hline \end{array}$

Find the products.

1. 3×7 2. 5×4 3. 2×8 4. 5×6 5. 6×3

6. 4×2 7. 5×7 8. 3×9 9. 4×4 10. 0×4

11. 3×4 12. 4×7 13. 2×2 14. 3×5 15. 6×1

16. 5×5 17. 4×3 18. 4×9 19. 2×6 20. 6×5

21. $\begin{array}{r} 9 \\ \times 2 \\ \hline \end{array}$ 22. $\begin{array}{r} 8 \\ \times 3 \\ \hline \end{array}$ 23. $\begin{array}{r} 1 \\ \times 5 \\ \hline \end{array}$ 24. $\begin{array}{r} 0 \\ \times 6 \\ \hline \end{array}$ 25. $\begin{array}{r} 3 \\ \times 3 \\ \hline \end{array}$

26. $\begin{array}{r} 8 \\ \times 6 \\ \hline \end{array}$ 27. $\begin{array}{r} 6 \\ \times 6 \\ \hline \end{array}$ 28. $\begin{array}{r} 6 \\ \times 4 \\ \hline \end{array}$ 29. $\begin{array}{r} 5 \\ \times 2 \\ \hline \end{array}$ 30. $\begin{array}{r} 7 \\ \times 0 \\ \hline \end{array}$

31. $\begin{array}{r} 8 \\ \times 1 \\ \hline \end{array}$ 32. $\begin{array}{r} 1 \\ \times 1 \\ \hline \end{array}$ 33. $\begin{array}{r} 9 \\ \times 5 \\ \hline \end{array}$ 34. $\begin{array}{r} 5 \\ \times 6 \\ \hline \end{array}$ 35. $\begin{array}{r} 4 \\ \times 6 \\ \hline \end{array}$

36. $\begin{array}{r} 8 \\ \times 5 \\ \hline \end{array}$ 37. $\begin{array}{r} 6 \\ \times 3 \\ \hline \end{array}$ 38. $\begin{array}{r} 9 \\ \times 6 \\ \hline \end{array}$ 39. $\begin{array}{r} 8 \\ \times 4 \\ \hline \end{array}$ 40. $\begin{array}{r} 7 \\ \times 6 \\ \hline \end{array}$

41. A violin has 4 strings. How many strings do 8 violins have?

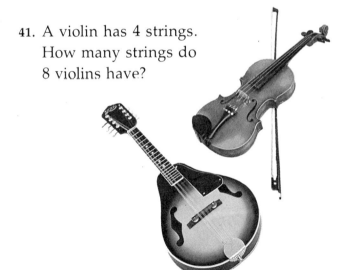

Find a pair of numbers for each sum and product.

☆ 42. A mandolin may use 4 pairs of strings. How many strings would be needed for 3 mandolins?

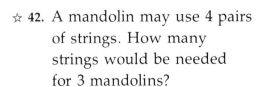

	Numbers	Sum	Product
	4,2	6	8
1.	▥▥ , ▥▥	8	15
2.	▥▥ , ▥▥	9	18
3.	▥▥ , ▥▥	11	30
4.	▥▥ , ▥▥	11	24
5.	▥▥ , ▥▥	12	35
6.	▥▥ , ▥▥	9	20

More multiplication facts

Linda and George are playing
Multiplication Concentration.

Linda turns up $\begin{array}{r} 8 \\ \times\, 7 \\ \hline \end{array}$. What product card
should she try to find?

$7 \times 8 = 56$

She should try to find this card: $\boxed{56}$

Find the products.

1. 6×7	2. 5×8	3. 8×7	4. 3×9	5. 7×9
6. 5×7	7. 6×6	8. 9×6	9. 7×4	10. 8×8
11. 4×8	12. 7×7	13. 9×9	14. 5×9	15. 9×3
16. 7×6	17. 9×5	18. 4×9	19. 8×6	20. 5×5
21. 7×3	22. 8×9	23. 9×7	24. 5×6	25. 7×2
26. 8×3	27. 9×2	28. 9×8	29. 6×8	30. 7×5

Find the products.

1. 8×3 2. 9×2 3. 7×4 4. 6×4 5. 5×5

6. 6×9 7. 0×8 8. 7×6 9. 7×9 10. 9×5

11. 8×6 12. 5×9 13. 7×7 14. 5×8 15. 8×4

16. 6×6 17. 5×6 18. 7×3 19. 8×6 20. 9×2

21. $\begin{array}{r} 5 \\ \times 7 \\ \hline \end{array}$ 22. $\begin{array}{r} 9 \\ \times 9 \\ \hline \end{array}$ 23. $\begin{array}{r} 4 \\ \times 9 \\ \hline \end{array}$ 24. $\begin{array}{r} 2 \\ \times 8 \\ \hline \end{array}$ 25. $\begin{array}{r} 8 \\ \times 6 \\ \hline \end{array}$

26. $\begin{array}{r} 7 \\ \times 5 \\ \hline \end{array}$ 27. $\begin{array}{r} 6 \\ \times 9 \\ \hline \end{array}$ 28. $\begin{array}{r} 8 \\ \times 8 \\ \hline \end{array}$ 29. $\begin{array}{r} 8 \\ \times 9 \\ \hline \end{array}$ 30. $\begin{array}{r} 8 \\ \times 7 \\ \hline \end{array}$

31. $\begin{array}{r} 5 \\ \times 6 \\ \hline \end{array}$ 32. $\begin{array}{r} 3 \\ \times 9 \\ \hline \end{array}$ 33. $\begin{array}{r} 9 \\ \times 4 \\ \hline \end{array}$ 34. $\begin{array}{r} 5 \\ \times 8 \\ \hline \end{array}$ 35. $\begin{array}{r} 8 \\ \times 4 \\ \hline \end{array}$

36. $\begin{array}{r} 7 \\ \times 6 \\ \hline \end{array}$ 37. $\begin{array}{r} 7 \\ \times 9 \\ \hline \end{array}$ 38. $\begin{array}{r} 3 \\ \times 7 \\ \hline \end{array}$ 39. $\begin{array}{r} 9 \\ \times 8 \\ \hline \end{array}$ 40. $\begin{array}{r} 7 \\ \times 8 \\ \hline \end{array}$

41. Multiplication concentration game: What fact card would match this product card?

☆ 42. Make some fact and product cards. Play a concentration game with a classmate. The player who finds the most matches wins.

This is a magic addition hexagon. Try to find out why it is magic.

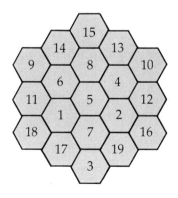

More practice, page 364, Set A; page 357A

Reviewing division facts

How many cartons of 6 are there in a case of 24 bottles?

$$24 \div 6 = 4 \qquad \text{or} \qquad 6\overline{)24}^{\,4}$$

There are 4 cartons of 6 in a case of 24 bottles.

Division and multiplication are related.
If you know the missing factor, $n \times 9 = 27$,
then you should know the missing quotient, $27 \div 9 = n$.
Since $3 \times 9 = 27$, then $27 \div 9 = 3$ and $27 \div 3 = 9$.

Copy and complete the table.

	Multiplication equations		Division equations	
1.	$3 \times 5 = 15$	$5 \times 3 = 15$	$15 \div 3 = 5$	$15 \div 5 = 3$
2.	$7 \times 2 = 14$		$14 \div 7 = 2$	
3.	$4 \times 5 = 20$			
4.		$2 \times 8 = 16$		
5.			$24 \div 8 = 3$	
6.				$18 \div 2 = 9$
7.		$3 \times 4 = 12$		
8.			$18 \div 6 = 3$	
9.	$6 \times 5 = 30$			
10.				$10 \div 2 = 5$

Divide.

1. $9 \div 3$ 2. $14 \div 2$ 3. $16 \div 4$ 4. $18 \div 9$ 5. $21 \div 3$

6. $20 \div 4$ 7. $12 \div 6$ 8. $10 \div 5$ 9. $16 \div 2$ 10. $25 \div 5$

11. $15 \div 5$ 12. $18 \div 3$ 13. $24 \div 4$ 14. $8 \div 2$ 15. $4 \div 4$

16. $12 \div 4$ 17. $8 \div 4$ 18. $30 \div 5$ 19. $36 \div 6$ 20. $28 \div 4$

21. $36 \div 4$ 22. $42 \div 6$ 23. $40 \div 5$ 24. $35 \div 5$ 25. $21 \div 7$

26. $18 \div 6$ 27. $14 \div 7$ 28. $4 \div 2$ 29. $0 \div 5$ 30. $28 \div 7$

31. $6\overline{)24}$ 32. $3\overline{)12}$ 33. $2\overline{)18}$ 34. $5\overline{)20}$ 35. $6\overline{)30}$

36. $8\overline{)16}$ 37. $6\overline{)6}$ 38. $5\overline{)45}$ 39. $4\overline{)32}$ 40. $3\overline{)27}$

41. 32 hot dogs
8 hot dogs in a package
How many packages?

42. Fried chicken wings:
12 in a package
How many servings
of 2 wings each?

Think !

Arrange the letters of
the sentence below to
form the name of a
school subject.

I MATCH TEAMS

More division facts

Each volleyball team has 6 players.
How many teams can be formed from 54 players?

$54 \div 6 = 9$

Nine teams can be formed.

Copy and complete the table.

	Multiplication equations		Division equations	
1.	$9 \times 6 = 54$	$6 \times 9 = 54$	$54 \div 9 = 6$	$54 \div 6 = 9$
2.	$8 \times 7 = 56$		$56 \div 8 = 7$	
3.		$6 \times 7 = 42$		
4.			$72 \div 9 = 8$	
5.	$9 \times 5 = 45$			
6.				$36 \div 9 = 4$
7.		$8 \times 5 = 40$		
8.			$63 \div 7 = 9$	
9.				$35 \div 7 = 5$
10.		$6 \times 8 = 48$		

Divide.

1. $42 \div 6$	**2.** $30 \div 5$	**3.** $18 \div 6$	**4.** $49 \div 7$	**5.** $24 \div 4$
6. $48 \div 6$	**7.** $32 \div 8$	**8.** $24 \div 6$	**9.** $24 \div 3$	**10.** $21 \div 7$
11. $56 \div 8$	**12.** $48 \div 8$	**13.** $35 \div 5$	**14.** $18 \div 3$	**15.** $63 \div 9$
16. $18 \div 2$	**17.** $24 \div 8$	**18.** $30 \div 6$	**19.** $36 \div 4$	**20.** $42 \div 7$
21. $27 \div 3$	**22.** $28 \div 4$	**23.** $9 \div 1$	**24.** $36 \div 6$	**25.** $45 \div 9$
26. $7\overline{)28}$	**27.** $9\overline{)72}$	**28.** $6\overline{)54}$	**29.** $9\overline{)27}$	**30.** $5\overline{)25}$
31. $4\overline{)32}$	**32.** $7\overline{)63}$	**33.** $8\overline{)72}$	**34.** $7\overline{)56}$	**35.** $5\overline{)45}$
36. $8\overline{)64}$	**37.** $7\overline{)35}$	**38.** $9\overline{)81}$	**39.** $8\overline{)40}$	**40.** $9\overline{)54}$

41. Baseball:
9 players per team
36 players
How many teams?

42. Basketball:
5 players per team
40 players
How many teams?

☆ **43.** How many children are in your class? How many volleyball teams could you form?

Choose a number and multiply it by itself.

Subtract the odd numbers, beginning with 1, from the product.

How many odd numbers did you subtract?

Choose some other numbers and try it again. Can you discover a pattern?

$5 \times 5 = 25$

$$
\begin{array}{r}
25 \\
-\ 1 \\
\hline
24 \\
-\ 3 \\
\hline
21 \\
-\ 5 \\
\hline
16 \\
-\ 7 \\
\hline
9 \\
-\ 9 \\
\hline
0 \\
\end{array}
$$

Answers for Self-check   1. 24   2. 42   3. 45   4. 24   5. 35   6. 64   7. 54   8. 81   9. 56   10. 18   11. 28   12. 8   13. 27   14. 49   15. 72   16. 5   17. 7   18. 5   19. 9   20. 9   21. 8   22. 8   23. 9   24. 1   25. 8   26. 8   27. 3   28. 9   29. 8   30. 9

More practice, page 357B and page 364, Set B

Self-check

Multiply.

1. 8×3 2. 7×6 3. 5×9 4. 4×6 5. 7×5

6. 8×8 7. 6×9 8. 9×9 9. 7×8 10. 2×9

11. $\begin{array}{r} 7 \\ \times\,4 \\ \hline \end{array}$
    12. $\begin{array}{r} 8 \\ \times\,1 \\ \hline \end{array}$
    13. $\begin{array}{r} 9 \\ \times\,3 \\ \hline \end{array}$
    14. $\begin{array}{r} 7 \\ \times\,7 \\ \hline \end{array}$
    15. $\begin{array}{r} 8 \\ \times\,9 \\ \hline \end{array}$

Divide.

16. $40 \div 8$ 17. $35 \div 5$ 18. $45 \div 9$ 19. $27 \div 3$ 20. $36 \div 4$

21. $72 \div 9$ 22. $64 \div 8$ 23. $63 \div 7$ 24. $8 \div 8$ 25. $16 \div 2$

26. $3\overline{)24}$ 27. $9\overline{)27}$ 28. $8\overline{)72}$ 29. $7\overline{)56}$ 30. $6\overline{)54}$

Answers for Self-check—page 121

Test

Multiply.

1. 5×7 2. 8×9 3. 6×0 4. 8×8 5. 9×3

6. 8×7 7. 4×9 8. 7×7 9. 6×8 10. 3×8

11. $\begin{array}{r} 9 \\ \times\,6 \\ \hline \end{array}$
    12. $\begin{array}{r} 5 \\ \times\,8 \\ \hline \end{array}$
    13. $\begin{array}{r} 4 \\ \times\,7 \\ \hline \end{array}$
    14. $\begin{array}{r} 3 \\ \times\,6 \\ \hline \end{array}$
    15. $\begin{array}{r} 5 \\ \times\,9 \\ \hline \end{array}$

Divide.

16. $20 \div 4$ 17. $24 \div 8$ 18. $15 \div 5$ 19. $18 \div 9$ 20. $42 \div 6$

21. $45 \div 5$ 22. $49 \div 7$ 23. $54 \div 9$ 24. $36 \div 4$ 25. $16 \div 8$

26. $8\overline{)72}$ 27. $6\overline{)54}$ 28. $8\overline{)32}$ 29. $7\overline{)56}$ 30. $4\overline{)24}$

For fun

Three in a Row

Play this game with two or more players.

Use 2 cubes numbered 4 through 9,
this playing board, and markers
of 2 different colors.

Playing Board

36	54	35	45	20	30
42	49	24	63	48	56
35	32	16	25	40	28
56	28	64	81	54	42
20	45	30	24	72	36
48	36	40	72	32	63

Rules:
1. Take turns rolling the cubes.
2. For each toss, multiply the numbers on top of the cubes and place a marker on that product on the board.
3. The first player to get 3 markers in a row, horizontally ⟷ vertically ↕, or diagonally ↗ wins the game.

Special Products and Quotients

Getting started

This multiplication game uses two cubes and two score sheets.

The faces on this cube show 4, 5, 6, 7, 8, 9.

The faces on this cube show 10, 100, 1000, 10, 100, 1000.

$$5 \qquad \times \qquad 100 \qquad = 500$$

The score is the product of the two top numbers.

Player: Tony		
Numbers rolled		Score
5	100						
8	10						
7	1000						
9	100						
4	1000						
Total		|||||

Player: Iris		
Numbers rolled		Score
6	10						
9	100						
6	1000						
4	10						
5	1000						
Total		|||||

Find the missing scores.
Then find the totals.

Which player has the highest total?

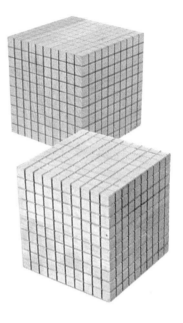

| 4 tens | 3 hundreds | 2 thousands |
| $4 \times 10 = 40$ | $3 \times 100 = 300$ | $2 \times 1000 = 2000$ |

Give the products.

1. 6×10 2. 2×100 3. 4×1000 4. 3×100 5. 7×1000

6. 2×10 7. 8×100 8. 9×1000 9. 6×100 10. 5×10

11. 7×100 12. 9×10 13. 1×1000 14. 8×1000 15. 4×100

16. 5×100 17. 3×1000 18. 7×10 19. 10×10 20. 12×10

21. 10×100 22. 10×1000 23. 17×10 24. 23×100 25. 11×100

Give the missing zeros in each product.

26. $9 \times 100 = 9\,\|\|\|\|\|$ 27. $6 \times 10 = 6\,\|\|\|\|\|$ 28. $3 \times 1000 = 3\,\|\|\|\|\|$

29. $30 \times 10 = 3\,\|\|\|\|\|$ 30. $40 \times 100 = 4\,\|\|\|\|\|$ 31. $90 \times 1000 = 9\,\|\|\|\|\|$

32. Give a rule for multiplying a number by 10.

33. Give a rule for multiplying a number by 100.

34. Give a rule for multiplying a number by 1000.

Multiplying by a multiple of 10, 100, or 1000

Three school buses each carried 40 children on a trip to the art museum. How many children were on the 3 buses?

Finding the answer

$$3 \times 40$$

$$3 \times 4 \times 10$$

$$12 \times 10$$

$$120$$

$$3 \times 40 = 120$$

There were 120 children on the buses.

Other examples

$$7 \times 50 = 350 \qquad 8 \times 600 = 4800 \qquad 5 \times 7000 = 35\ 000$$

Find the products.

1. 4×20 2. 5×60 3. 7×30 4. 6×40 5. 9×30

6. 8×60 7. 3×60 8. 4×40 9. 9×50 10. 6×90

11. 3×70 12. 7×80 13. 6×60 14. 2×70 15. 9×40

16. 8×80 17. 8×90 18. 7×40 19. 5×40 20. 7×70

Find the products.

1. 3×800 2. 2×600 3. 5×700

4. 4×200 5. 9×300 6. 5×300

7. 8×400 8. 7×300 9. 4×400

10. 7×600 11. 8×700 12. 9×400

13. 5×900 14. 6×300 15. 9×200

16. 4×6000 17. 3×5000 18. 7×4000

19. 9×6000 20. 7×3000 21. 3×9000

22. 8×6000 23. 2×7000 24. 3×3000

25. 6×6000 26. 7×8000 27. 4×8000

28. 9×2000 29. 5×6000 30. 5×3000

31. 5×100 32. 8×1000 33. 3×10

34. 5×1000 35. 7×10 36. 4×1000

37. 2×100 38. 9×100 39. 8×10

40. 6×1000 41. 8×100 42. 9×1000

43. Postcards of paintings at the museum cost 40 cents each. How much would 6 postcards cost?

44. The art museum plans to buy 7 paintings. Each painting costs $500. What will be the total cost?

45. The museum also plans to buy 3 very old paintings. Each costs $8000. What will be the total cost?

50 is our product
As you can clearly see
When you know my partner
Is twice as large as me.

Who are we?

Multiples of 10, 100, and 1000 as factors

One section of a stadium has 20 rows of seats. There are 30 seats in each row. How many seats are in the section?

Finding the answer

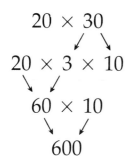

$$20 \times 30$$

$$20 \times 3 \times 10$$

$$60 \times 10$$

$$600$$

$$20 \times 30 = 600$$

There are 600 seats in the section.

Other examples

$$70 \times 40 = 2800 \qquad 90 \times 70 = 6300 \qquad 80 \times 50 = 4000$$

Find the products.

1. 20×40	2. 30×50	3. 70×30	4. 30×30	5. 50×60
6. 40×80	7. 90×20	8. 40×40	9. 70×60	10. 60×40
11. 80×80	12. 90×80	13. 50×90	14. 70×80	15. 20×70
16. 60×60	17. 60×30	18. 90×60	19. 50×70	20. 90×90

Find the products.

1. 30×50	**2.** 70×40	**3.** 40×30	**4.** 70×90
5. 20×20	**6.** 40×10	**7.** 80×60	**8.** 50×50
9. 50×80	**10.** 30×90	**11.** 40×90	**12.** 70×80
13. 20×90	**14.** 90×50	**15.** 60×70	**16.** 80×20
17. 40×50	**18.** 80×90	**19.** 80×40	**20.** 70×20
21. 30×60	**22.** 7×500	**23.** 4×3000	**24.** 20×60
25. 8×40	**26.** 9×400	**27.** 7×60	**28.** 2×8000
29. 90×60	**30.** 6×600	**31.** 50×90	**32.** 2×600
33. 60×60	**34.** 80×80	**35.** 5×500	**36.** 3×700
37. 80×30	**38.** 7×2000	**39.** 60×80	**40.** 20×30

41. 40 rows of seats
60 seats in each row
How many seats in all?

42. 30 rows of seats
50 seats in each row
How many seats in all?

Find these products.

1. $4 \times 8 \times 10 \times 10 \times 10$ **2.** $25 \times 10 \times 32 \times 4$
3. $64 \times 4 \times 5 \times 25$ **4.** $20 \times 20 \times 20 \times 4$
5. $16 \times 20 \times 10 \times 5 \times 2$ **6.** $5 \times 4 \times 4 \times 4 \times 4 \times 25$
7. $5 \times 128 \times 25 \times 2$ **8.** $50 \times 40 \times 16$
9. $2 \times 2 \times 2 \times 2 \times 2 \times 2 \times 2 \times 2 \times 5 \times 5 \times 5$ **10.** 256×125

What did you find out about the products?

More practice, page 365, Set A

Dividing multiples of 10, 100, and 1000

A dance teacher has 120 students. She wants to put them into 6 equal groups. How many will there be in each group?

Finding the answer

$$120 \div 6 = n$$

$$\text{Since } 6 \times 20 = 120,$$

$$\text{then } 120 \div 6 = 20.$$

There will be 20 in each group.

Other examples

$15 \div 3 = 5$ $150 \div 3 = 50$ $1500 \div 3 = 500$ $15\,000 \div 3 = 5000$

Divide.

1. $36 \div 4$ 2. $360 \div 4$ 3. $3600 \div 4$ 4. $36\,000 \div 4$

5. $9 \div 3$ 6. $90 \div 3$ 7. $900 \div 3$ 8. $9000 \div 3$

9. $24 \div 6$ 10. $240 \div 6$ 11. $2400 \div 6$ 12. $24\,000 \div 6$

13. $28 \div 4$ 14. $280 \div 4$ 15. $2800 \div 4$ 16. $28\,000 \div 4$

17. $54 \div 9$ 18. $540 \div 9$ 19. $5400 \div 9$ 20. $54\,000 \div 9$

21. $20 \div 5$ 22. $200 \div 5$ 23. $2000 \div 5$ 24. $20\,000 \div 5$

Divide.

1. $210 \div 7$

2. $180 \div 6$

3. $160 \div 8$

4. $350 \div 7$

5. $630 \div 9$

6. $6400 \div 8$

7. $4500 \div 9$

8. $1500 \div 5$

9. $7200 \div 8$

10. $3600 \div 9$

11. $8000 \div 4$

12. $6000 \div 3$

13. $14\,000 \div 2$

14. $25\,000 \div 5$

15. $42\,000 \div 7$

16. $1600 \div 4$

17. $450 \div 5$

18. $180 \div 9$

19. $9000 \div 3$

20. $2400 \div 8$

21. $490 \div 7$

22. $560 \div 8$

23. $72\,000 \div 9$

24. $5400 \div 6$

25. $16\,000 \div 8$

26. $200 \div 5$

27. $4200 \div 6$

28. $240 \div 8$

29. $270 \div 3$

30. $5400 \div 9$

31. Swimming school: 180 students
9 classes a week
(same number in each class)
How many students in each class?

32. Art school: 210 students
7 classes a week
(same number in each class)
How many students in each class?

Think!

Jean and Marie split a 44¢ milk shake. Marie did not have enough to pay for her half. If she owes Jean 6¢, how much money did Marie pay to Jean?

Dividing by a multiple of ten

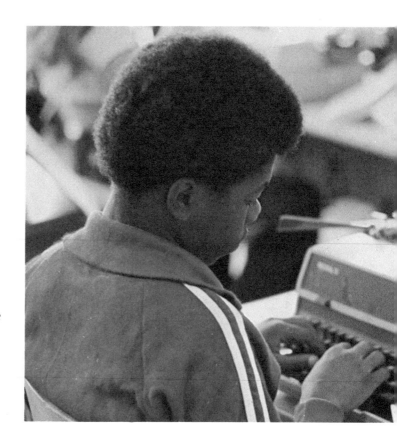

Brian set his typewriter so he could type 70 letters or spaces on a line. How many lines will he use to type 2800 letters or spaces?

Finding the answer

$2800 \div 70 = n$
Since $70 \times 40 = 2800$,
then $2800 \div 70 = 40$.

He will use 40 lines to type 2800 letters or spaces.

Other examples

$1200 \div 40 = 30$ $\qquad$ $2400 \div 30 = 80$ $\qquad$ $800 \div 10 = 80$

Divide.

1. $1600 \div 40$	2. $1800 \div 30$	3. $2500 \div 50$	4. $800 \div 20$	5. $3500 \div 70$
6. $3200 \div 80$	7. $1800 \div 90$	8. $1400 \div 20$	9. $4500 \div 50$	10. $8100 \div 90$
11. $300 \div 10$	12. $5400 \div 60$	13. $4200 \div 70$	14. $2700 \div 30$	15. $3600 \div 40$
16. $4900 \div 70$	17. $2000 \div 40$	18. $1600 \div 80$	19. $4800 \div 60$	20. $150 \div 10$
21. $6400 \div 80$	22. $5600 \div 70$	23. $2700 \div 90$	24. $1800 \div 60$	25. $6300 \div 90$

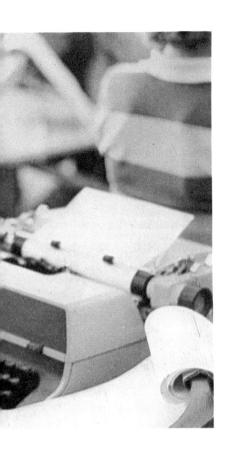

Divide.

1. 2400 ÷ 60	**2.** 1200 ÷ 30	**3.** 400 ÷ 20
4. 900 ÷ 30	**5.** 3500 ÷ 50	**6.** 4200 ÷ 60
7. 1500 ÷ 50	**8.** 160 ÷ 10	**9.** 2100 ÷ 70
10. 3600 ÷ 40	**11.** 1800 ÷ 20	**12.** 2400 ÷ 80
13. 5600 ÷ 80	**14.** 2000 ÷ 50	**15.** 6400 ÷ 80
16. 5400 ÷ 90	**17.** 600 ÷ 30	**18.** 800 ÷ 20
19. 6300 ÷ 70	**20.** 1200 ÷ 60	**21.** 4000 ÷ 50
22. 7200 ÷ 90	**23.** 200 ÷ 20	**24.** 2400 ÷ 40
25. 600 ÷ 20	**26.** 8100 ÷ 90	**27.** 1400 ÷ 70
28. 2700 ÷ 30	**29.** 7200 ÷ 80	**30.** 1000 ÷ 50

31. Rita can type 30 words in one minute. How long does it take her to type 2400 words?

32. Tom can type 40 words in one minute. How long does it take him to type 2400 words?

☆ **33.** Set a typewriter to type 50 letters to a line. Type 1000 letters. How many lines? How long did it take you?

Enter 10 000 000 on the calculator. Divide by 10. Divide by ten again. Continue dividing by ten until the answer is 1.

How many times did you divide by 10?

Can you find out how many times 100 000 000 000 000 000 would have to be divided by ten to give an answer of 1?

Answers for Self-check 1. 90 2. 700 3. 8000 4. 60 5. 300 6. 150 7. 240 8. 4000 9. 1800
10. 3500 11. 1800 12. 5600 13. 2700 14. 1600 15. 7200 16. 100 17. 10 18. 1000 19. 100 20. 10
21. 30 22. 80 23. 200 24. 5000 25. 300 26. 30 27. 50 28. 60 29. 80 30. 40

More practice, page 365, Set B

Self-check

Multiply.

1. 9×10	**2.** 7×100	**3.** 8×1000	**4.** 6×10	**5.** 3×100
6. 3×50	**7.** 4×60	**8.** 5×800	**9.** 6×300	**10.** 7×500
11. 30×60	**12.** 70×80	**13.** 90×30	**14.** 40×40	**15.** 90×80

Divide.

16. $300 \div 3$	**17.** $70 \div 7$	**18.** $4000 \div 4$	**19.** $500 \div 5$	**20.** $80 \div 8$
21. $150 \div 5$	**22.** $240 \div 3$	**23.** $1200 \div 6$	**24.** $35\,000 \div 7$	**25.** $2700 \div 9$
26. $1800 \div 60$	**27.** $2500 \div 50$	**28.** $4200 \div 70$	**29.** $7200 \div 90$	**30.** $3200 \div 80$

Answers for Self-check—page 133

Test

Multiply.

1. 8×10	**2.** 9×1000	**3.** 4×100	**4.** 7×100	**5.** 3×1000
6. 5×60	**7.** 7×80	**8.** 4×300	**9.** 2×7000	**10.** 9×70
11. 80×30	**12.** 90×50	**13.** 60×60	**14.** 50×70	**15.** 90×90

Divide.

16. $90 \div 9$	**17.** $700 \div 7$	**18.** $5000 \div 5$	**19.** $60 \div 10$	**20.** $400 \div 4$
21. $270 \div 9$	**22.** $1800 \div 6$	**23.** $6300 \div 7$	**24.** $2500 \div 5$	**25.** $600 \div 2$
26. $2400 \div 40$	**27.** $3500 \div 50$	**28.** $1800 \div 20$	**29.** $4800 \div 80$	**30.** $600 \div 20$

A Coded-Shapes Riddle

What did the tree say when it was asked why it was cut down?

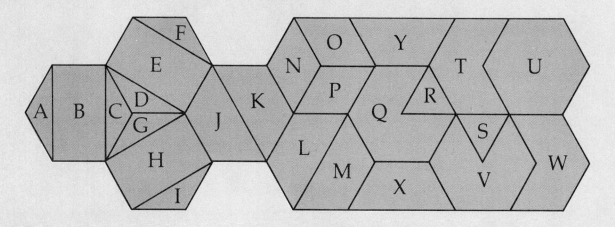

Find the answer to the riddle by finding the letters
for the coded shapes in these positions.

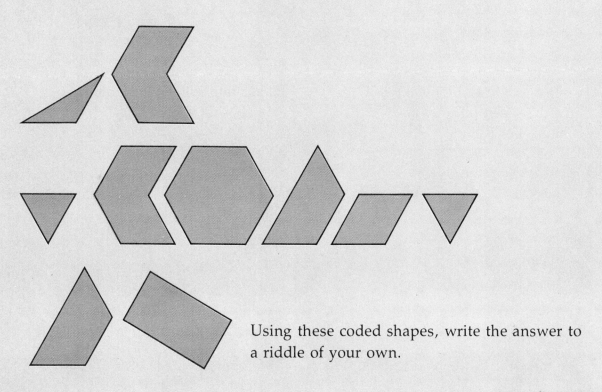

Using these coded shapes, write the answer to
a riddle of your own.

Multiplying

Getting started

This spinner is for a Spin-by-Six game.

Rules: Each player takes two spins.

First spin:

Player chooses either the red or the green number and multiplies it by 6.

Second spin:

Player multiplies the number on the other color by 6.

Both colors must be used.
Add the two products.
The player with the highest total wins.

Sample:

Josie				Terry		
Green:	6 × 2	=	12	Red:	6 × 70 = ‖‖
Red:	6 × 50	=	300	Green:	6 × 3 = ‖‖
		Total =	312		Total = ‖‖

Complete the scores and find out who won the game.

Find the products and the total score for each of these games.

1. Red: 6×40 = |||||
   Green: 6×3 = |||||
            Total = |||||

2. Green: 6×2 = |||||
   Red: 6×50 = |||||
            Total = |||||

3. Red: 6×70 = |||||
   Green: 6×7 = |||||
            Total = |||||

4. Green: 6×5 = |||||
   Red: 6×30 = |||||
            Total = |||||

For a new game, change the rule and multiply by 8.
Find the products and the total score.

5. Green: 8×4 = |||||
   Red: 8×60 = |||||
            Total = |||||

6. Green: 8×6 = |||||
   Red: 8×20 = |||||
            Total = |||||

7. Green: 8×2 = |||||
   Red: 8×70 = |||||
            Total = |||||

8. Green: 8×5 = |||||
   Red: 8×40 = |||||
            Total = |||||

Jack found his total like this:

$$
\begin{array}{r}
43 \\
\times\ 8 \\
\end{array}
$$

Green: $8 \times 3 \rightarrow$ 24
Red: $8 \times 40 \rightarrow$ 320
          Total   344

9. Find the product. Use Jack's method.

$$
\begin{array}{r}
76 \\
\times\ 8 \\
\hline
\end{array}
$$

Multiplying by a 1-digit factor

In an automobile factory, 45 cars are put together each hour. How many cars will be put together in 8 hours?

Finding the answer

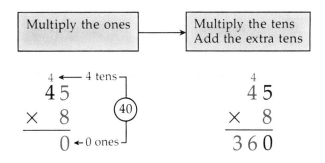

$$
\begin{array}{r}
4 \leftarrow \text{4 tens} \\
4\,5 \\
\times \quad 8 \\
\hline
0 \leftarrow \text{0 ones}
\end{array}
\qquad (40) \qquad
\begin{array}{r}
4 \\
4\,5 \\
\times \quad 8 \\
\hline
3\,6\,0
\end{array}
$$

In 8 hours, 360 cars will be put together.

Other examples

$$
\begin{array}{r}
71 \\
\times\ 6 \\
\hline
426
\end{array}
\qquad
\begin{array}{r}
{\scriptstyle 2} \\
129 \\
\times\ \ 3 \\
\hline
387
\end{array}
\qquad
\begin{array}{r}
{\scriptstyle 2\ 1} \\
254 \\
\times\ \ 4 \\
\hline
1016
\end{array}
\qquad
\begin{array}{r}
{\scriptstyle 1\ 4\ 5} \\
3\,258 \\
\times\quad 7 \\
\hline
22\,806
\end{array}
$$

Multiply.

1. $\begin{array}{r} 27 \\ \times\ 3 \\ \hline \end{array}$
2. $\begin{array}{r} 39 \\ \times\ 4 \\ \hline \end{array}$
3. $\begin{array}{r} 76 \\ \times\ 2 \\ \hline \end{array}$
4. $\begin{array}{r} 47 \\ \times\ 8 \\ \hline \end{array}$
5. $\begin{array}{r} 73 \\ \times\ 9 \\ \hline \end{array}$

6. $\begin{array}{r} 123 \\ \times\ 4 \\ \hline \end{array}$
7. $\begin{array}{r} 217 \\ \times\ 5 \\ \hline \end{array}$
8. $\begin{array}{r} 186 \\ \times\ 7 \\ \hline \end{array}$
9. $\begin{array}{r} 651 \\ \times\ 9 \\ \hline \end{array}$
10. $\begin{array}{r} 293 \\ \times\ 6 \\ \hline \end{array}$

Multiply.

1.	96 × 2	2.	63 × 4	3.	35 × 9	4.	29 × 6
5.	94 × 8	6.	78 × 5	7.	44 × 3	8.	59 × 7
9.	76 × 6	10.	55 × 5	11.	746 × 3	12.	839 × 9
13.	534 × 9	14.	576 × 8	15.	680 × 9	16.	367 × 4
17.	219 × 7	18.	177 × 8	19.	308 × 6	20.	425 × 9
21.	3276 × 2	22.	5843 × 7	23.	8439 × 6	24.	9206 × 8

25. Auto factory:
    720 cars a day
    5 days
    How many cars in all?

26. Truck factory:
    28 trucks an hour
    6 hours
    How many trucks?

Find the product:
(your age) × 37 × 91 × 3.

Multiplying by multiples of 10 and 100

There are 24 hours in one day.
How many hours in a month
of 30 days?

Finding the answer

Write zero in the ones' place	→	Multiply by the tens' number

$$\begin{array}{r} 24 \\ \times 30 \\ \hline 0 \end{array} \qquad \begin{array}{r} \overset{1}{2}4 \\ \times 30 \\ \hline 720 \end{array}$$

There are 720 hours in 30 days.

Other examples

$$\begin{array}{r} \overset{3}{3}8 \\ \times 40 \\ \hline 1520 \end{array} \qquad \begin{array}{r} \overset{1}{1}\overset{4}{2}8 \\ \times \ 60 \\ \hline 7680 \end{array} \qquad \begin{array}{r} 431 \\ \times 200 \\ \hline 86\,200 \end{array} \qquad \begin{array}{r} \overset{2}{2}\overset{3}{5}7 \\ \times 500 \\ \hline 128\,500 \end{array}$$

Multiply.

1.	56 × 30	**2.**	48 × 40	**3.**	23 × 50	**4.**	65 × 70	**5.**	37 × 80
6.	74 × 20	**7.**	98 × 60	**8.**	26 × 90	**9.**	19 × 40	**10.**	66 × 70
11.	253 × 50	**12.**	133 × 70	**13.**	621 × 80	**14.**	225 × 30	**15.**	171 × 90

Multiply.

1. 27 × 50	**2.** 93 × 30	**3.** 33 × 60	**4.** 78 × 80	**5.** 47 × 90
6. 231 × 40	**7.** 231 × 400	**8.** 714 × 80	**9.** 714 × 800	**10.** 526 × 90
11. 526 × 900	**12.** 743 × 30	**13.** 743 × 300	**14.** 276 × 90	**15.** 276 × 900

16. 819 × 30   **17.** 927 × 200   **18.** 556 × 700   **19.** 919 × 80

20. 810 × 70   **21.** 46 × 50   **22.** 374 × 900   **23.** 641 × 500

24. 923 × 80   **25.** 128 × 600

26. 60 minutes in one hour
60 seconds in each minute
How many seconds in one hour?

27. There are 30 days in April.
There are 24 hours in each day.
How many hours in April?

☆ **28.** How many seconds are
there in one week?

The number shown below
is called a **googol.** How
many zeros does it have?

How many times would ten
have to be multiplied by
itself to make a googol?

10 000 000 000 000 000 000 000 000 000
000 000 000 000 000 000 000 000 000
000 000 000 000 000 000 000 000 000
000 000 000 000 000 000

Multiplying by 2-digit factors

Honeybees can fly for only 15 minutes before refueling. Fruit flies can fly about 23 times as long as this before refueling. How many minutes can the fruit fly fly before refueling?

Finding the answer

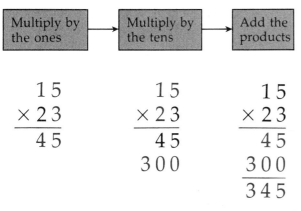

Multiply by the ones	→	Multiply by the tens	→	Add the products

```
    15            15            15
  × 23          × 23          × 23
  ————          ————          ————
    45            45            45
                 300           300
                             ————
                               345
```

The fruit fly can fly about 345 minutes before refueling.

Other examples

```
      35              59              365
    × 73            × 76            ×  37
    ————            ————            ————
     105             354           2 555
   2450            4130           10 950
   ————            ————           ——————
   2555            4484           13 505
```

Multiply.

1. 49   2. 91   3. 48   4. 57   5. 54
  × 38   × 37   × 68   × 83   × 66

6. 526   7. 324   8. 514   9. 621   10. 284
  × 34   × 36   × 23   × 57   × 62

Multiply.

1. 72 ×18	2. 97 ×36	3. 75 ×33	4. 26 ×62	5. 37 ×46
6. 24 ×35	7. 56 ×14	8. 41 ×52	9. 88 ×57	10. 75 ×75
11. 256 ×25	12. 137 ×45	13. 891 ×36	14. 227 ×58	15. 514 ×19
16. 705 ×46	17. 370 ×53	18. 665 ×27	19. 585 ×63	20. 192 ×88

21. 89 × 64

22. 677 × 58

23. 307· × 47

24. 75 × 35

25. 886 × 59

26. The honeybee is about 14 mm long. The longest insect, the tropical stick insect, is about 24 times as long. How long is the longest insect?

27. A housefly might have a wingspan of 22 mm. The Atlas moth has a wingspan about 12 times as long. About how long is the wingspan of the Atlas moth?

Find the number for a, b, and c in each equation.

a × a = 5329
b × b × b = 2197
c × c × c × c = 6561

More practice, page 366, Set A; page 366A

Multiplying by 3-digit factors

A jetliner might carry an average
of 178 passengers per flight.
How many passengers might
be carried per day if there
are 775 jetliner flights per day?

Finding the answer

Multiply by the ones	Multiply by the tens	Multiply by the hundreds	Add the products

```
   775          775          775           775
 ×178         ×178         ×178          ×178
 6 200        6 200        6 200         6 200
             54 250       54 250        54 250
                          77 500        77 500
                                       137 950
```

137 950 passengers are carried per day.

Other examples

```
    718           564            629
  ×364          ×690           ×807
  2 872         50 760         4 403
 43 080        338 400        503 200
215 400        389 160        507 603
261 352
```

Find the products.

1. 213   2. 126   3. 416   4. 507   5. 344
  × 345   × 237   × 248   × 128   × 257

6. 622   7. 737   8. 276   9. 982   10. 803
  × 417   × 451   × 340   × 256   × 354

Find the products.

1. 643 × 192	**2.** 336 × 633	**3.** 975 × 466	**4.** 868 × 230	**5.** 179 × 627	**6.** 429 × 259
7. 625 × 160	**8.** 286 × 777	**9.** 315 × 172	**10.** 163 × 709	**11.** 234 × 508	**12.** 516 × 704
13. 624 × 473	**14.** 949 × 138	**15.** 783 × 250	**16.** 722 × 919	**17.** 940 × 376	**18.** 828 × 107

19. One jetliner seats 145 passengers. How many passengers could it carry in 225 flights?

20. A 747 jetliner seats 363 passengers. How many passengers could it carry in 450 flights?

Add the numbers in the circle. Subtract the numbers in the square. Multiply by the numbers in the triangle that are not in the square or the circle. What do you get?

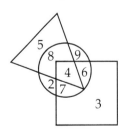

Answers for Self-check 1. 104 2. 340 3. 301 4. 472 5. 1284 6. 1215 7. 2124 8. 9348 9. 1480 10. 2910 11. 140 800 12. 313 500 13. 4234 14. 1610 15. 7735 16. 55 158 17. 9312 18. 257 985 19. 149 179 20. 143 202

Self-check

1. 26
    × 4

2. 68
    × 5

3. 43
    × 7

4. 59
    × 8

5. 214
    × 6

6. 135
    × 9

7. 708
    × 3

8. 2337
    × 4

9. 74
    × 20

10. 97
    × 30

11. 352
    × 400

12. 627
    × 500

13. 73
    × 58

14. 35
    × 46

15. 91
    × 85

16. 634
    × 87

17. 582
    × 16

18. 637
    × 405

19. 241
    × 619

20. 823
    × 174

Answers for Self-check—page 145

Test

1. 43
    × 5

2. 62
    × 7

3. 74
    × 8

4. 29
    × 6

5. 273
    × 3

6. 304
    × 9

7. 156
    × 7

8. 4167
    × 4

9. 61
    × 70

10. 252
    × 80

11. 643
    × 500

12. 287
    × 400

13. 57
    × 19

14. 84
    × 62

15. 87
    × 53

16. 786
    × 35

17. 472
    × 18

18. 915
    × 206

19. 873
    × 362

20. 490
    × 183

Paper Clip Designs

The figure shows how a paper clip and two pencils can be used to draw circles.

Each design below was made with a paper clip and two pencils. How many of them can you make?

Make others of your own.

Using Your Skills

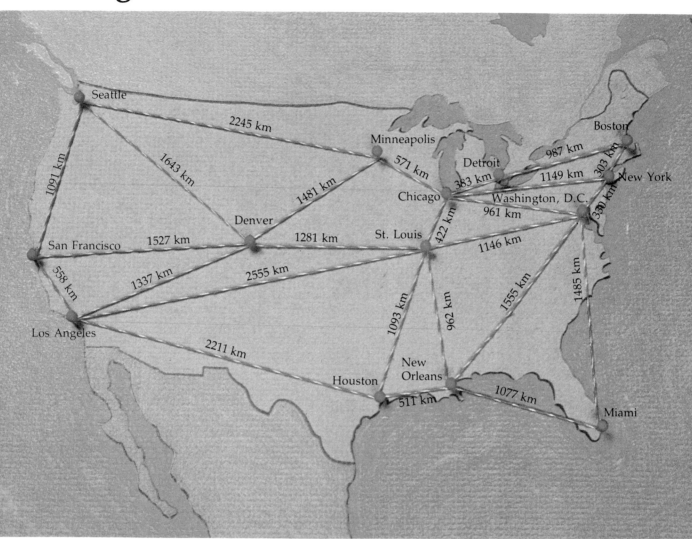

Getting started

1. Which two cities are 175 km closer together than
    Los Angeles and San Francisco?

2. Which two cities are 5 times as far apart as
    Houston and New Orleans?

3. What other problems can you solve?

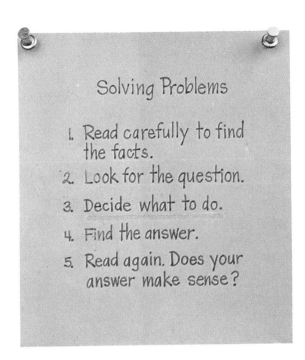

Solving Problems

1. Read carefully to find the facts.
2. Look for the question.
3. Decide what to do.
4. Find the answer.
5. Read again. Does your answer make sense?

For these problems you will need to add, subtract, or multiply. Use the map on the opposite page to find the facts.

1. How far is it from San Francisco to St. Louis by way of Denver?

2. What is the distance from Houston to St. Louis to Chicago?

3. How much farther is it from Miami to Washington than from Miami to New Orleans?

4. The map shows that Chicago is 383 km from Detroit. What city is 3 times as far from Chicago?

5. The distance from Denver to Seattle is how much greater than the distance from Denver to Los Angeles?

6. A person who made 3 round trips from San Francisco to Los Angeles would have traveled how many kilometers?

Estimating products

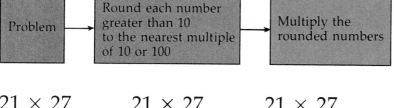

In Mark's classroom, there are 21 rows of floor tiles. Each row has 27 tiles. Estimate the number of floor tiles.

Finding the answer

Problem	→	Round each number greater than 10 to the nearest multiple of 10 or 100	→	Multiply the rounded numbers

21×27

21×27
$\downarrow \quad \downarrow$
20×30

21×27
$20 \times 30 = 600$

There are about 600 tiles.

Other examples

33×42
$\downarrow \quad \downarrow$
$30 \times 40 = 1200$

729×6
$\downarrow \quad \downarrow$
$700 \times 6 = 4200$

45×812
$\downarrow \quad \downarrow$
$50 \times 800 = 40\ 000$

Give an estimate for each product.

1. 29×53
$\downarrow \quad \downarrow$
$30 \times 50 = n$

2. 49×78
$\downarrow \quad \downarrow$
$50 \times 80 = n$

3. 6×823
$\downarrow \quad \downarrow$
$6 \times 800 = n$

4. 39×674
$\downarrow \quad \downarrow$
$40 \times 700 = n$

5. $88 \times 17 = n$

6. $65 \times 42 = n$

7. $3 \times 283 = n$

8. $9 \times 407 = n$

Estimate the products.
Then find the exact products.

1. 26×44 2. 78×49 3. 36×31 4. 25×52 5. 93×4

6. 38×29 7. 9×72 8. 88×51 9. 4×32 10. 63×59

11. $\begin{array}{r} 42 \\ \times\, 31 \\ \hline \end{array}$ 12. $\begin{array}{r} 19 \\ \times\, 53 \\ \hline \end{array}$ 13. $\begin{array}{r} 28 \\ \times\, 29 \\ \hline \end{array}$ 14. $\begin{array}{r} 76 \\ \times\, 11 \\ \hline \end{array}$ 15. $\begin{array}{r} 99 \\ \times\, 23 \\ \hline \end{array}$

16. 377×4 17. 427×7 18. 882×6 19. 239×8 20. 502×3

21. $\begin{array}{r} 319 \\ \times\quad 7 \\ \hline \end{array}$ 22. $\begin{array}{r} 476 \\ \times\quad 8 \\ \hline \end{array}$ 23. $\begin{array}{r} 117 \\ \times\quad 6 \\ \hline \end{array}$ 24. $\begin{array}{r} 889 \\ \times\quad 3 \\ \hline \end{array}$ 25. $\begin{array}{r} 211 \\ \times\quad 5 \\ \hline \end{array}$

26. $\begin{array}{r} 709 \\ \times\quad 9 \\ \hline \end{array}$ 27. $\begin{array}{r} 419 \\ \times\quad 5 \\ \hline \end{array}$ 28. $\begin{array}{r} 778 \\ \times\quad 6 \\ \hline \end{array}$ 29. $\begin{array}{r} 994 \\ \times\quad 7 \\ \hline \end{array}$ 30. $\begin{array}{r} 687 \\ \times\quad 8 \\ \hline \end{array}$

31. 17 ceiling tiles in one row
23 rows
Estimate how many ceiling
tiles in all.

32. Hallway: 12 tiles wide
74 tiles long
Estimate how many tiles.

☆ 33. Use estimation to find the
number of tiles in a floor,
ceiling, or hallway of your
school.

A penny has a mass of 3 g.
If you were given a bag of
pennies with a mass equal to
your mass, how much money
would you have?

Estimating products

Choose the best estimate for each problem.

1. There are about 26 children
   in each of 14 class rooms.
   About how many children in all?

   A 200   B 300   C 500

2. John drinks about 3 glasses of milk
   a day. About how many glasses of
   milk does he drink in a year?

   A 1200   B 12 000   C 120 000

3. Diane took 69 steps in one minute.
   About how many steps would she
   take in an hour?

   A 3600   B 4200   C 5000

4. Jo's heart was beating 78 times
   a minute. About how many times
   would it beat in a half hour?

   A 4800   B 2000   C 2400

5. In one minute, 32 cars passed a point
   on the freeway. About how many cars
   will pass in an hour?

   A 180   B 1800   C 18 000

6. A telephone book had 408 names on one
   page. There were 5 pages of names
   beginning with the letter V. About
   how many names began with V?

   A 200 000   B 20 000   C 2000

7. A car travels an average of 78 km in 1 hour. About how far will it travel in 6 hours?

   A 600 km   B 550 km
   C 480 km   D 420 km

8. A jet plane flies an average of 896 km in 1 hour. About how far will the plane fly in 4 hours?

   A 3200 km   B 3600 km
   C 4000 km   D 4400 km

9. Carla's heart was beating 68 times a minute. About how many times would it beat in 60 minutes?

   A 4200   B 420
   C 3600   D 360

10. A sound travels through the air a distance of about 332 m in one second. About how far would a sound travel in 5 seconds?

   A 15 m   B 150 m
   C 1500 m   D 15 000 m

11. Rita's car traveled 11 km on 1 L of gasoline. About how far would the car travel on 58 L of gasoline?

   A 500 km   B 5000 km
   C 600 km   D 6000 km

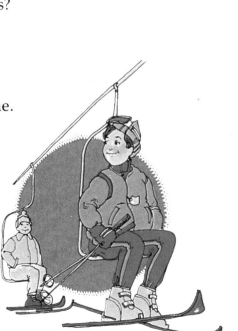

12. A ski lift can carry 196 people in 1 hour. About how many people could the lift carry in 8 hours?

   A 800   B 8000
   C 1600   D 16 000

African animals

Years ago, large numbers of animals lived in the rich lands of Africa. Today, many of these animals are found in national parks and game preserves. The animals differ greatly in size and shape.

1. A large elephant is about 3.5 m tall. An adult giraffe is about 1.5 m taller. How tall is an adult giraffe?

2. An ostrich can run about 65 km per hour. A cheetah can run about 45 km per hour faster. How fast can a cheetah run?

3. A lion ate 33 kg of meat at one meal. The mass of the lion was about 5 times the mass of the meal. What was the lion's mass?

4. A pygmy hippopotamus has a mass of about 250 kg. A large hippopotamus has a mass that is 10 times as much. What is the mass of the large hippopotamus?

5. At birth, a gorilla has a mass of about 2 kg. As an adult, its mass is about 90 times as much. What is the mass of an adult gorilla?

6. A lion usually eats once every three days. About how many times does a lion eat in 30 days?

7. An elephant had a mass of 89 kg at birth. The mass of an adult elephant was 57 times as much. What was the mass of the adult?

8. An impala can jump about 1.8 m high. A springbok can jump 3.0 m high. How much higher can a springbok jump?

9. A baboon troop was made up of 2 adult males, 21 adult females, and 33 young baboons. How many baboons were in the troop?

10. The smallest African antelope, the dik-dik, is about 38 cm tall. A large antelope, called an eland, is about 5 times as tall. How tall is an eland?

11. The mass of a white rhinoceros is about 3200 kg. The mass of a hippopotamus is 570 kg less. What is the mass of the hippopotamus?

12. In a 5 year period, about 20 000 leopards were killed in some parts of Africa. About how many leopards were killed each year?

Multiplication and money

Ronald and his family are planning
a camping trip. They bought 4 camp
stools. Each stool cost $1.89.
What was the total cost of
the four stools?

Finding the answer

Multiply as with whole numbers	→	Show the answer in dollars and cents

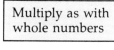

$$\begin{array}{r} \$\,1.89 \\ \times\ \ \ \ 4 \\ \hline 7\,5\,6 \end{array} \qquad \begin{array}{r} \$\,1.89 \\ \times\ \ \ \ 4 \\ \hline \$\,7.56 \end{array}$$

The total cost of the camp stools was $7.56.

Other examples

$$\begin{array}{r} \$\,2.63 \\ \times\ \ \ \ 5 \\ \hline \$13.15 \end{array} \qquad \begin{array}{r} \$0.79 \\ \times\ \ \ 13 \\ \hline 2\,37 \\ 7\,90 \\ \hline \$10.27 \end{array} \qquad \begin{array}{r} \$\,24.79 \\ \times\ \ \ \ \ 28 \\ \hline 198\,32 \\ 495\,80 \\ \hline \$694.12 \end{array}$$

Multiply.

1. $\begin{array}{r} \$\,1.76 \\ \times\ \ \ \ 3 \end{array}$
2. $\begin{array}{r} \$\,4.09 \\ \times\ \ \ \ 5 \end{array}$
3. $\begin{array}{r} \$\,2.53 \\ \times\ \ \ \ 7 \end{array}$
4. $\begin{array}{r} \$\,10.44 \\ \times\ \ \ \ 6 \end{array}$
5. $\begin{array}{r} \$\,22.50 \\ \times\ \ \ \ 8 \end{array}$

6. $\begin{array}{r} \$\,5.64 \\ \times\ \ \ 65 \end{array}$
7. $\begin{array}{r} \$\,8.00 \\ \times\ \ \ 98 \end{array}$
8. $\begin{array}{r} \$\,0.87 \\ \times\ \ \ 94 \end{array}$
9. $\begin{array}{r} \$\,36.98 \\ \times\ \ \ 32 \end{array}$
10. $\begin{array}{r} \$\,0.95 \\ \times\ \ \ 98 \end{array}$

11. $\begin{array}{r} \$\,1.47 \\ \times\ \ 120 \end{array}$
12. $\begin{array}{r} \$\,3.62 \\ \times\ \ 435 \end{array}$
13. $\begin{array}{r} \$\,6.09 \\ \times\ \ 227 \end{array}$
14. $\begin{array}{r} \$\,9.75 \\ \times\ \ 166 \end{array}$
15. $\begin{array}{r} \$\,4.11 \\ \times\ \ 376 \end{array}$

Solve.

1. A sleeping bag was priced at $54.95. It was put on sale at $39.88. How much less was the sale price?

2. Ronald's family bought these items for the camping trip: a tent for $59.99, an ice chest for $4.99, and a camp stove for $22.75. What was the total cost of these items?

3. A backpack with frame costs $18.88. How much would 4 backpacks with frames cost?

4. Ronald bought 6 fishing lures at 49¢ each. What was the total cost of the lures?

5. Hiking boots were regularly priced at $32.00 a pair. They were put on sale at $23.50 a pair. How much less was the sale price of the boots?

6. Ronald's family needed 6 water cans. The cans cost $3.99 each. What would be the total price of 6 cans?

7. Bottles of insect spray cost $1.29 each. How much would 12 bottles of insect spray cost?

8. Campsites in a camping area cost $6.25 a day. What would it cost to stay at the camping area for 5 days?

9. Ronald's family plans to rent a camping trailer. The rent is $18.75 a day. What will it cost to rent the camping trailer for 14 days?

☆ 10. A camping van rents for $125 a week plus 12¢ for each kilometer traveled. What would be the total cost for a week, if the distance traveled was 1263 km?

More practice, page 366, Set C

Factors

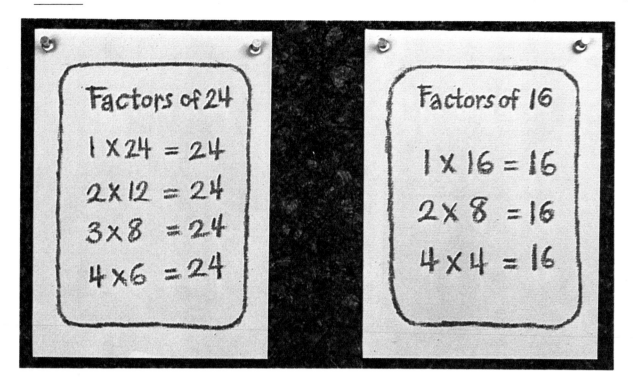

The factors of 24 are 1, 2, 3, 4, 6, 8, 12 and 24.
What are the factors of 16?

1. What are the factors of 30?

$1 \times 30 = 30$
$2 \times 15 = 30$
$3 \times 10 = 30$
$5 \times 6 = 30$

2. What are the factors of 20?

$1 \times 20 = 20$
$2 \times 10 = 20$
$4 \times 5 = 20$

3. What are the factors of 36?

$1 \times 36 = 36$
$2 \times 18 = 36$
$3 \times 12 = 36$
$4 \times 9 = 36$
$6 \times 6 = 36$

4. What are the factors of 12?

$1 \times 12 = 12$
$2 \times 6 = 12$
$3 \times 4 = 12$

5. What are the factors of 49?

$1 \times 49 = 49$
$7 \times 7 = 49$

6. What is the only factor of 1?

$1 \times 1 = 1$

List all the factors of each number.

1. 4	**2.** 14	**3.** 27	**4.** 7	**5.** 25	**6.** 32
7. 35	**8.** 12	**9.** 44	**10.** 21	**11.** 18	**12.** 16
13. 6	**14.** 15	**15.** 40	**16.** 9	**17.** 28	**18.** 100
19. 8	**20.** 11	**21.** 36	**22.** 50	**23.** 42	**24.** 26

Use division to tell whether the first number
is a factor of the second.

Examples

Is 3 a factor of 24?

$$\begin{array}{r} 8 \\ 3\overline{)24} \\ -24 \\ \hline 0 \end{array}$$

Yes, 3 is a factor of 24 because
there is zero remainder.

Is 4 a factor of 26?

$$\begin{array}{r} 6 \\ 4\overline{)26} \\ -24 \\ \hline 2 \end{array}$$

No, 4 is not a factor of 26 because
the remainder is not zero.

25. 3, 27	**26.** 4, 58	**27.** 9, 72	**28.** 7, 54	**29.** 2, 20
30. 8, 80	**31.** 6, 52	**32.** 5, 60	**33.** 3, 33	**34.** 9, 57

35. List all the whole numbers
less than 20. Which ones
have exactly 3 factors?

☆ **36.** What number less than 40
has the greatest number
of factors?

The number 28 is called a **perfect
number.** List all the factors of
28. Add all the factors and then
divide by 2. What do you get as
your answer?

1, 2, 3, and 6 are factors of both 30 and 48.

They are called **common factors** of 30 and 48.

6 is the **greatest common factor** of 30 and 48.

Give the missing numbers in the table.

	Numbers	Factors	Common factors	Greatest common factor
1.	8 12	1, 2, 4, 8 1, 2, 3, 4, 6, 12	1, 2, 4	▦
2.	12 20	1, 2, 3, 4, 6, 12 1, 2, 4, 5, 10, 20	1, ▦ , ▦	▦
3.	18 27	1, 2, 3, 6, 9, 18 1, 3, 9, 27	▦ , 3, ▦	▦
4.	14 15	1, 2, 7, 14 1, 3, 5, 15	▦	▦
5.	50 75	1, 2, 5, 10, 25, 50 1, 3, 5, 15, 25, 75	▦ , ▦ , ▦	▦

Find the greatest common factor for each pair of numbers.

1. 4, 10	**2.** 9, 12	**3.** 10, 14	**4.** 7, 13	**5.** 8, 20
6. 9, 27	**7.** 40, 50	**8.** 20, 25	**9.** 16, 24	**10.** 15, 28
11. 15, 25	**12.** 8, 14	**13.** 18, 24	**14.** 9, 10	**15.** 18, 30
16. 10, 30	**17.** 3, 21	**18.** 15, 18	**19.** 9, 12	**20.** 8, 18
21. 7,8	**22.** 20, 50	**23.** 16, 36	**24.** 10, 15	**25.** 27, 36
26. 8, 32	**27.** 16, 28	**28.** 15, 35	**29.** 15, 21	**30.** 16, 40

31. What is the greatest common factor of 3 and 5?

32. Factors of 12: 1, 2, 3, 4, 6, 12
Factors of 18: 1, 2, 3, 6, 9, 18
Factors of 27: 1, 3, 9, 27
What is the greatest common factor of 12, 18, 27?

33. What is the greatest common factor of 10, 15, 30?

34. What is the greatest common factor of 16, 32, 40?

Some numbers, when multiplied by themselves, have a product that ends in that same number.

$$1 \times 1 = 1$$
$$5 \times 5 = 25$$
$$6 \times 6 = 36$$
$$25 \times 25 = 625$$

Find another number like these.
Hint: There is one between 60 and 90.

⊛ Prime and composite numbers

Numbers that have exactly two
different factors are called
prime numbers.

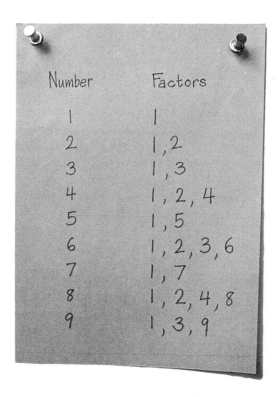

Number	Factors
1	1
2	1, 2
3	1, 3
4	1, 2, 4
5	1, 5
6	1, 2, 3, 6
7	1, 7
8	1, 2, 4, 8
9	1, 3, 9

1. Name the prime numbers less than ten.

2. Name the prime numbers between 10 and 20.

Composite numbers are larger than 1 and have more than 2 factors.
Example: 6 has four factors: 1, 2, 3, and 6.
        6 is a composite number.

Tell whether each number is a prime number or a composite number.

3. 4   4. 12   5. 13   6. 18   7. 19   8. 21

Factor trees show prime factors of a number. The top row must have
all prime numbers.

Copy and complete these factor trees.

9. $5 \times 3 \times$ ▥
   5 × 6
   30

10. $3 \times 2 \times$ ▥ $\times$ ▥
    6 × ▥
    36

11. $3 \times$ ▥ $\times$ ▥
    3 × 9
    27

Copy and complete each factor tree.

1. ▥ × ▥ × ▥ × 2
   ▥ × 4
   16

2. ▥ × ▥ × ▥
   7 × ▥
   42

3. ▥ × ▥ × ▥ × ▥
   10 × ▥
   40

4. ▥ × ▥ × ▥ × ▥
   ▥ × 6
   24

5. ▥ × ▥ × ▥ × ▥
   ▥ × 25
   100

6. ▥ × ▥ × ▥
   10 × ▥
   70

7. ▥ × ▥ × ▥ × ▥
   6 × ▥
   60

8. ▥ × ▥ × ▥ × ▥
   9 × ▥
   54

9. ▥ × ▥ × ▥ × ▥
   ▥ × 9
   81

Make a factor tree for each number.

10. 56   11. 72   12. 27   13. 32   14. 45

15. 35   16. 28   17. 48   18. 63   19. 64

20. What is the only prime number that is an even number?

☆ 21. List all the prime numbers between 1 and 100.

☆ 22. **Twin primes** have a difference of 2. 3 and 5 are twin primes. List all the pairs of twin primes less than 100.

Find 3 prime numbers, all less than 20, whose product is 1001.

▥ × ▥ × ▥ = 1001

Answers for Self-check   1. B   2. 960   3. $15.18   4. $359.86   5. $3.16   6. 1, 2, 4, 5, 8, 10, 20, 40
7. 6   8. 2×7×2×2   9. 23

Self-check

1. Truck: 88 km per hour
   About how far in 8 hours?

   A 72 km B 720 km C 7200 km

2. Mary takes 16 breaths in one minute. How many breaths does she take in 1 hour?

3. $ 2.53
   × 6

4. $ 9.47
   × 38

5. Find the cost of 4 felt-type pens at 79¢ each.

6. List all the factors of 40.

7. Give the greatest common factor of 12 and 30.

☆ 8. Copy and complete the factor tree.

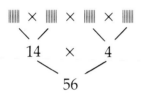

☆ 9. Which is a prime number, 23 or 32?

Answers for Self-check—page 163

Test

1. Jet plane: 885 km per hour
   About how far in 3 hours?

   A 2400 km B 2700 km C 3200 km

2. Carla took 164 steps to walk 100 meters. How many steps would she take in 1000 meters?

3. Find the cost of 6 loaves of bread at 39¢ a loaf.

4. $ 1.36
   × 7

5. $ 8.07
   × 45

6. List all the factors of 24.

7. Give the greatest common factor of 15 and 21.

☆ 8. Copy and complete the factor tree.

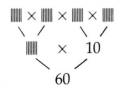

☆ 9. Which is a prime number, 21 or 31?

A Prime Number Game

You need: Two cubes with faces numbered 4 through 9.
One cube with faces numbered 1 through 6.

Rules: Take turns tossing the three cubes.

Multiply the numbers on two of the cubes, and then add or subtract the number on the third cube.

If you can get a prime number, score one point; otherwise you score zero.

The first player to get 5 points wins the game.

			Score
Examples:		$(4 \times 4) - 9 = 7$ prime	1
		$(4 \times 9) - 4 = 32$	0

No prime is possible   0

$(4 \times 1) + 9 = 13$ prime   1
$(9 \times 1) - 4 = 5$ prime   1
$(9 \times 1) + 4 = 13$ prime   1
$(9 \times 4) + 1 = 37$ prime   1
$(9 \times 4) - 1 = 35$ 0

A List of Prime Numbers

2	3	5	7	11	13	17	19	23	29
31	37	41	43	47	53	59	61	67	71
73	79	83	89	97	101	103	107	109	113

Area

Getting started

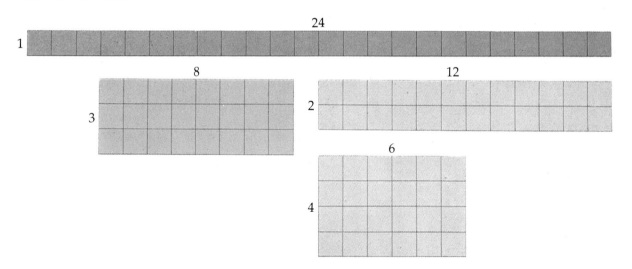

How many small squares are there in each rectangle?

How many different rectangles can you make that each have 60 small squares?

The number of unit squares covering
a region is the **area** of the region.

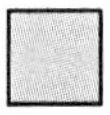

unit square

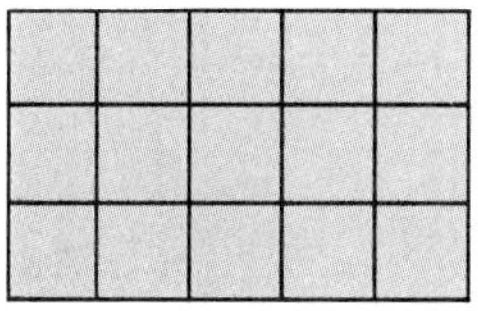

area: 15 square units

Give the area of each figure.
Each small square is a unit square.

1.

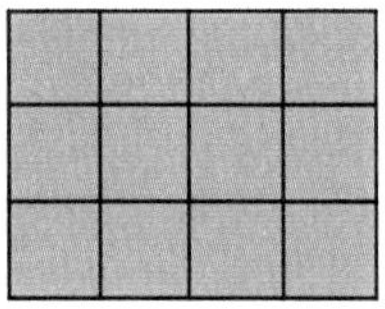

2.

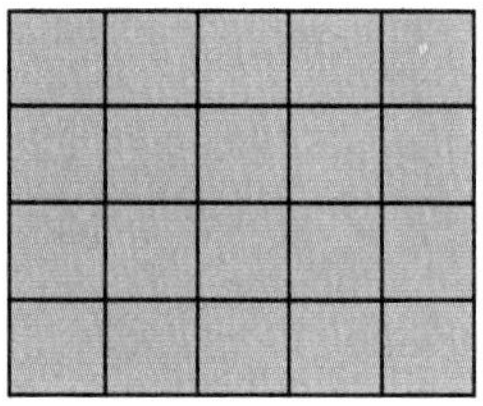

3.

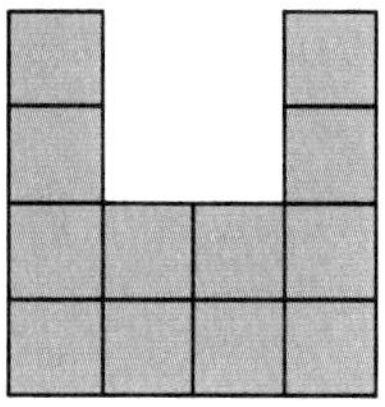

4.

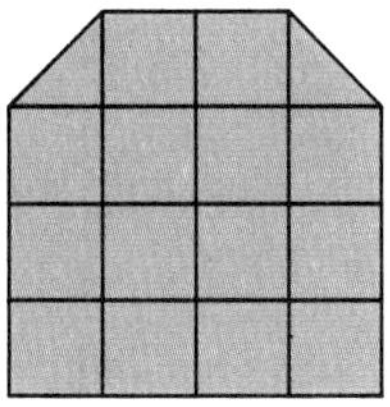

When this square
is the unit,

1 cm

1 cm

1 square centimeter

the area of this
rectangle is
6 **square centimeters.**

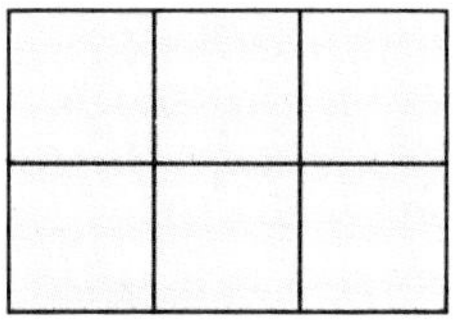

We write:
area = 6 cm²

Give the area in square centimeters.

5.

4 cm

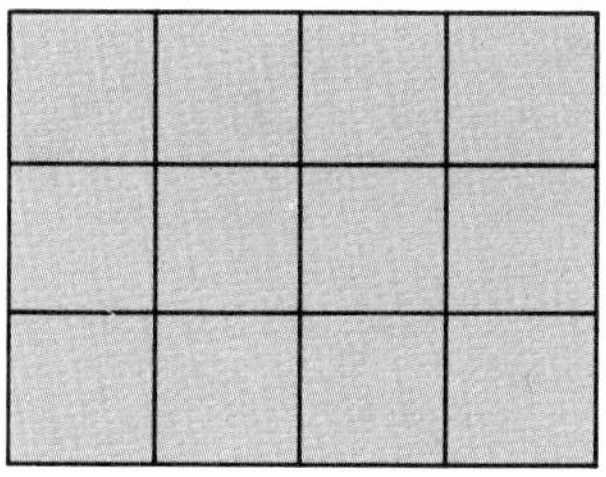

3 cm

6.

3 cm

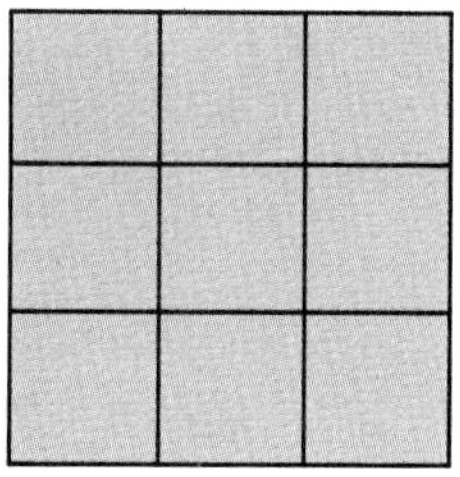

3 cm

7.

5 cm

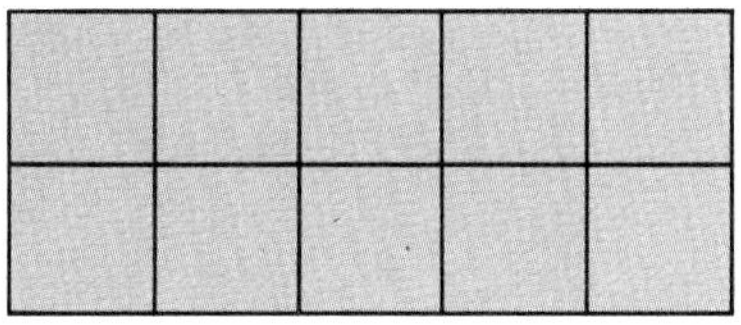

2 cm

8.

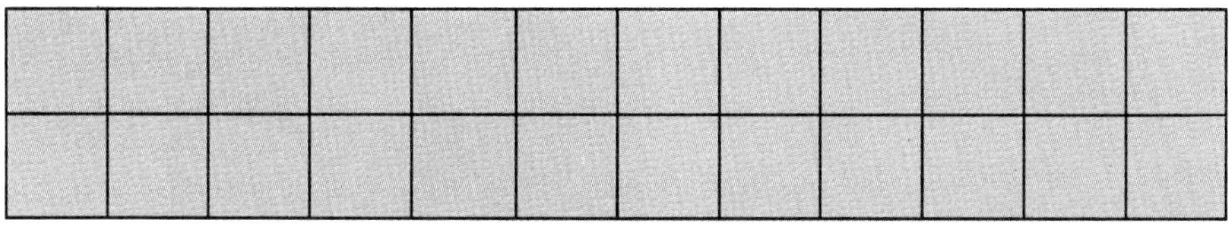

12 cm

2 cm

Area of rectangles

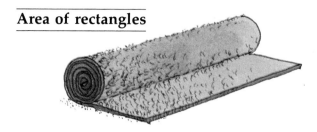

A rectangular room has a length of 12 m and a width of 8 m. How many square meters of carpet will be needed to cover the floor?

Finding the answer

Length of a rectangle	Multiply by the width	Area

12   12 × 8   96 m²

The area is 96 m².

Find the area of each of these rooms.

1.

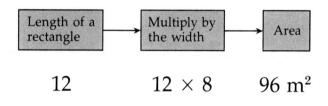

7 m

16 m

2.

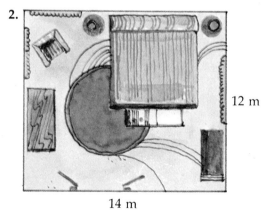

12 m

14 m

3.

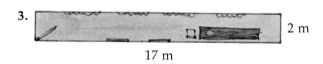

2 m

17 m

4.

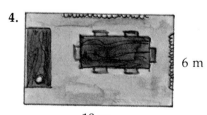

6 m

10 m

Find the area of each room.

1.

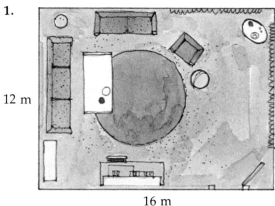

12 m

16 m

2.

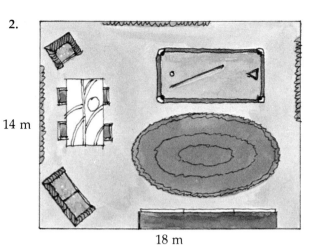

14 m

18 m

3.

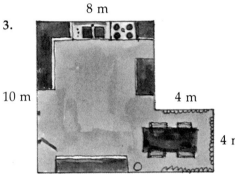

8 m

10 m

4 m

4 m

4.

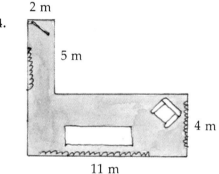

2 m

5 m

4 m

11 m

Find the area of each rectangle.

The length is *l* and the width is *w*.

5.   *l* = 15 cm
        w = 12 cm

6.   *l* = 32 cm
        w = 25 cm

7.   *l* = 60 cm
        w = 40 cm

8.   *l* = 18 mm
        w = 9 mm

9.   *l* = 25 m
        w = 19 m

10. *l* = 22 km
        w = 17 km

11. Find the area of the room.

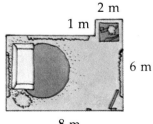

2 m

1 m

6 m

8 m

☆ **12.** Carpeting for the room in Exercise 11 costs $12.99 per square meter. What will it cost to carpet the room?

Area of a triangle

Draw and shade a triangle inside a rectangle, like this:

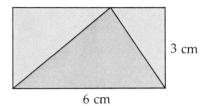

3 cm

6 cm

Cut off the two corner regions.

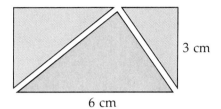

3 cm

6 cm

The two corner regions will exactly cover the triangle.

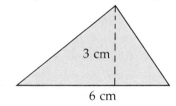

3 cm

6 cm

What is the area of the triangle?

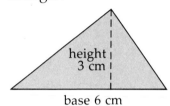

height 3 cm

base 6 cm

Finding the answer

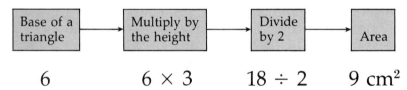

Base of a triangle	Multiply by the height	Divide by 2	Area

6   6 × 3   18 ÷ 2   9 cm²

The area of the triangle is 9 cm².

Find the area of each triangle.

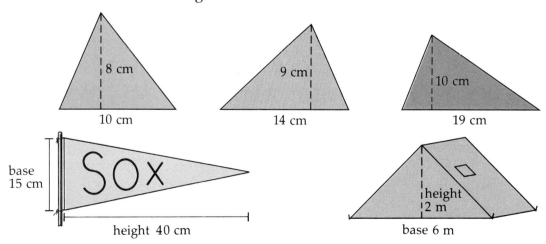

8 cm

10 cm

9 cm

14 cm

10 cm

19 cm

base 15 cm

SOX

height 40 cm

height 2 m

base 6 m

Find the base (*b*) and height (*h*) of each triangle.
Then give the area in square centimeters.

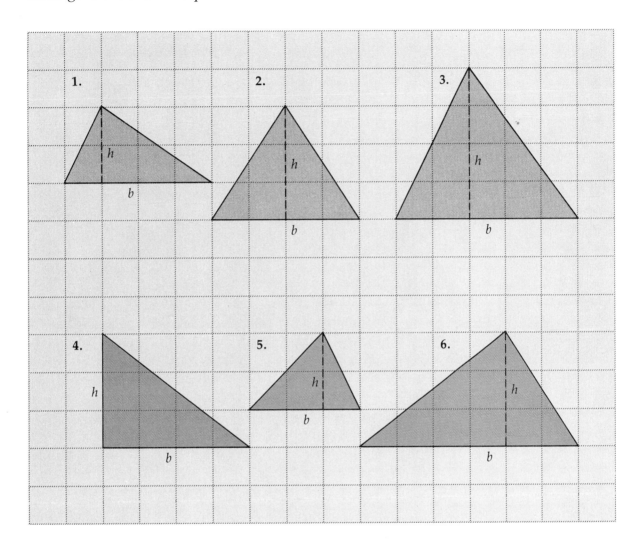

Find the area in square centimeters for triangles
with these bases and heights.

7. *b* = 10 cm   8. *b* = 18 cm   9. *b* = 12 cm   10. *b* = 24 cm   11. *b* = 48 cm
   h = 4 cm   *h* = 4 cm   *h* = 10 cm   *h* = 36 cm   *h* = 35 cm

12. *b* = 15 cm   13. *b* = 24 cm   14. *b* = 40 cm   15. *b* = 16 cm   16. *b* = 30 cm
    h = 8 cm   *h* = 12 cm   *h* = 10 cm   *h* = 9 cm   *h* = 30 cm

Answers for Self-check   1. 162 cm²   2. 25 cm²   3. 120 cm²   4. 24 cm²   5. 63 cm²   6. 143 cm²

Self-check

Find the area of each rectangle.

1.

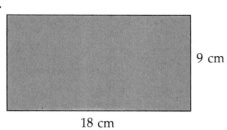

9 cm

18 cm

2.

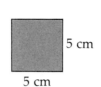

5 cm

5 cm

3.

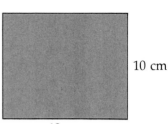

10 cm

12 cm

Find the area of each triangle.

4.

8 cm

6 cm

5.

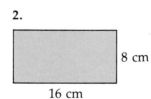

9 cm

14 cm

6.

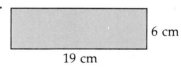

13 cm

22 cm

Answers for Self-check—page 171

Test

Find the area of each rectangle.

1.

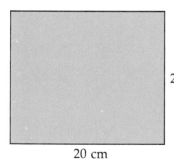

24 cm

20 cm

2.

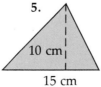

8 cm

16 cm

3.

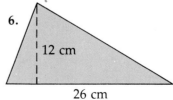

6 cm

19 cm

Find the area of each triangle.

4.

8 cm

10 cm

5.

10 cm

15 cm

6.

12 cm

26 cm

How Large Is Your Hand?

Put your hand on a sheet of centimeter graph paper
and trace around it. Count the squares and parts
of squares that it covers. Estimate the area.

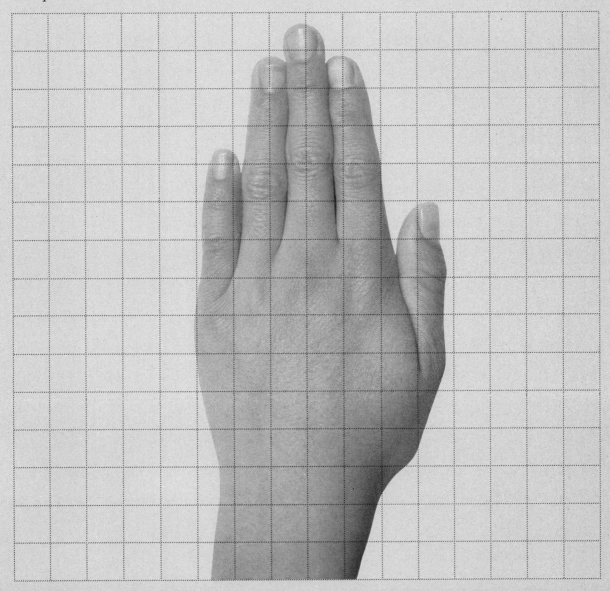

Find the area of the sole of your shoe.

Level 25 review

Multiply.

1. 6×7 2. 3×5 3. 7×9 4. 2×8 5. 9×8

6. 5×4 7. 8×8 8. 5×7 9. 8×6 10. 6×3

11. 8×10 12. 6×100 13. 4×30 14. 5×700 15. 9×800

16. 30×60 17. 70×50 18. 40×20 19. 90×80 20. 50×80

21. $\begin{array}{r} 34 \\ \times\ 5 \\ \hline \end{array}$
22. $\begin{array}{r} 82 \\ \times\ 7 \\ \hline \end{array}$
23. $\begin{array}{r} 38 \\ \times 29 \\ \hline \end{array}$
24. $\begin{array}{r} 59 \\ \times 78 \\ \hline \end{array}$
25. $\begin{array}{r} 27 \\ \times 66 \\ \hline \end{array}$

26. $\begin{array}{r} 345 \\ \times\ 71 \\ \hline \end{array}$
27. $\begin{array}{r} 619 \\ \times\ 82 \\ \hline \end{array}$
28. $\begin{array}{r} 825 \\ \times\ 64 \\ \hline \end{array}$
29. $\begin{array}{r} 965 \\ \times\ 73 \\ \hline \end{array}$
30. $\begin{array}{r} 709 \\ \times\ 91 \\ \hline \end{array}$

31. $\begin{array}{r} 715 \\ \times 402 \\ \hline \end{array}$
32. $\begin{array}{r} 473 \\ \times 326 \\ \hline \end{array}$
33. $\begin{array}{r} 684 \\ \times 532 \\ \hline \end{array}$
34. $\begin{array}{r} 927 \\ \times 802 \\ \hline \end{array}$
35. $\begin{array}{r} 835 \\ \times 614 \\ \hline \end{array}$

Divide.

36. $35 \div 7$ 37. $63 \div 9$ 38. $72 \div 8$ 39. $25 \div 5$ 40. $64 \div 8$

41. $42 \div 7$ 42. $28 \div 7$ 43. $36 \div 4$ 44. $45 \div 9$ 45. $16 \div 4$

46. $400 \div 4$ 47. $20 \div 2$ 48. $600 \div 6$ 49. $8000 \div 8$ 50. $5000 \div 5$

51. $320 \div 8$ 52. $2100 \div 3$ 53. $3600 \div 6$ 54. $640 \div 8$ 55. $1200 \div 6$

56. $240 \div 60$ 57. $4800 \div 80$ 58. $2700 \div 30$ 59. $45\,000 \div 50$ 60. $18\,000 \div 30$

Find the area of each figure.

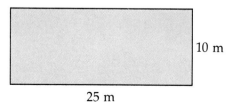

61.   10 m   25 m

62.   12 m   16 m

Dividing
2-Digit Divisors
Using Your Skills
Space Figures
Coordinate Geometry

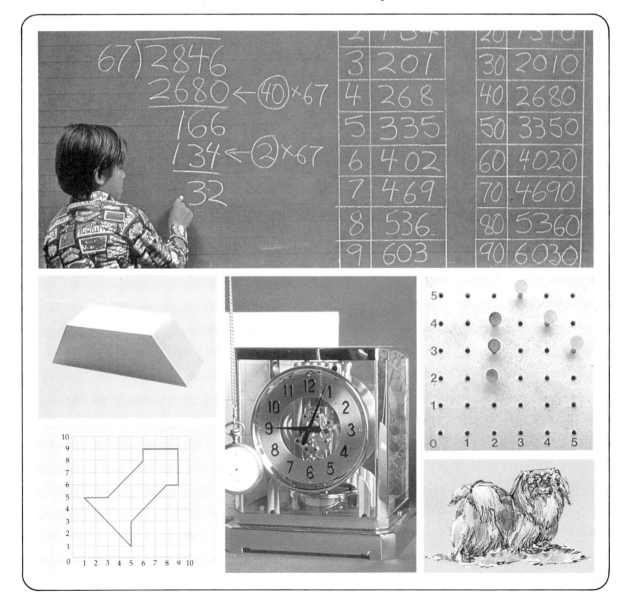

Dividing

Getting started

Some children planted seeds for a science project.
They used 6 seeds for each pot. They planted
78 seeds in all.

How many pots did they use?

$$
\begin{array}{r} 78 \\ -\ 6 \\ \hline 72 \end{array}
\qquad
\begin{array}{r} 72 \\ -\ 6 \\ \hline 66 \end{array}
\qquad
\begin{array}{r} 66 \\ -\ 6 \\ \hline 60 \end{array}
\qquad
\begin{array}{r} 60 \\ -\ 6 \\ \hline 54 \end{array}
\qquad ?
$$

1. Edward used this method to find how many sixes there are in 78.

   How many sixes did he subtract first?

   How many sixes did he subtract next?

   How many sixes did he subtract in all?

$$
\begin{array}{r}
78 \\
- 30 \quad \longleftarrow \quad 5 \text{ sixes} \\
\hline
48 \\
- 30 \quad \longleftarrow \quad 5 \text{ sixes} \\
\hline
18 \\
- 18 \quad \longleftarrow \quad 3 \text{ sixes} \\
\hline
0
\end{array}
$$

2. Marie used a shorter method.

   How many sixes did she subtract first?

   How many sixes did she subtract in all?

$$
\begin{array}{r}
78 \\
- 60 \quad \longleftarrow \quad 10 \text{ sixes} \\
\hline
18 \\
- 18 \quad \longleftarrow \quad 3 \text{ sixes} \\
\hline
0
\end{array}
$$

Study the example.

$$
\text{divisor} \longrightarrow 8\overline{)52} \qquad
\begin{array}{l}
6 \longleftarrow \text{ quotient} \\
\longleftarrow \text{ dividend}
\end{array}
$$
$$
\begin{array}{r}
- 48 \\
\hline
4 \longleftarrow \text{ remainder}
\end{array}
$$

Give the divisor, quotient, dividend, and remainder for each problem.

3.
$$
\begin{array}{r}
9 \\
3\overline{)28} \\
- 27 \\
\hline
1
\end{array}
$$

4.
$$
\begin{array}{r}
8 \\
7\overline{)59} \\
- 56 \\
\hline
3
\end{array}
$$

5.
$$
\begin{array}{r}
6 \\
9\overline{)54} \\
- 54 \\
\hline
0
\end{array}
$$

6.
$$
\begin{array}{r}
4 \\
8\overline{)35} \\
- 32 \\
\hline
3
\end{array}
$$

7.
$$
\begin{array}{r}
8 \\
5\overline{)42} \\
- 40 \\
\hline
2
\end{array}
$$

Find the quotients and remainders.

8. $3\overline{)22}$

9. $5\overline{)18}$

10. $6\overline{)45}$

11. $9\overline{)44}$

12. $4\overline{)38}$

13. $7\overline{)45}$

14. $6\overline{)27}$

15. $8\overline{)78}$

16. $5\overline{)28}$

17. $9\overline{)64}$

1-digit divisors

How many books, each 3 cm
thick, will fit on one 85 cm shelf?

Finding the answer

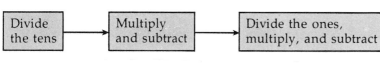

| Divide the tens | → | Multiply and subtract | → | Divide the ones, multiply, and subtract |

$$\begin{array}{r} 2 \\ 3\overline{)85} \end{array}$$

$$\begin{array}{r} 2 \\ 3\overline{)85} \\ -6 \\ \hline 2 \end{array}$$

$$\begin{array}{r} 28\,\text{R}1 \\ 3\overline{)85} \\ -6\downarrow \\ \hline 25 \\ -24 \\ \hline 1 \end{array}$$

One shelf will hold 28 books.
There will be 1 cm of space remaining.

Other examples

$$\begin{array}{r} 23\,\text{R}3 \\ 6\overline{)141} \\ 12 \\ \hline 21 \\ 18 \\ \hline 3 \end{array}$$

$$\begin{array}{r} 628\,\text{R}1 \\ 4\overline{)2513} \\ 24 \\ \hline 11 \\ 8 \\ \hline 33 \\ 32 \\ \hline 1 \end{array}$$

$$\begin{array}{r} 206\,\text{R}3 \\ 7\overline{)1445} \\ 14 \\ \hline 4 \\ 0 \\ \hline 45 \\ 42 \\ \hline 3 \end{array}$$

Find the quotients and remainders.

1. $4\overline{)95}$ 2. $3\overline{)79}$ 3. $4\overline{)613}$ 4. $4\overline{)143}$ 5. $6\overline{)773}$

6. $5\overline{)2800}$ 7. $5\overline{)1747}$ 8. $3\overline{)1151}$ 9. $8\overline{)2445}$ 10. $7\overline{)3807}$

11. $9\overline{)2758}$ 12. $7\overline{)2245}$ 13. $8\overline{)5208}$ 14. $2\overline{)1378}$ 15. $5\overline{)3107}$

Divide.

1. $6\overline{)95}$
2. $7\overline{)121}$
3. $4\overline{)206}$
4. $6\overline{)262}$
5. $7\overline{)341}$

6. $8\overline{)247}$
7. $2\overline{)137}$
8. $9\overline{)611}$
9. $8\overline{)555}$
10. $8\overline{)2495}$

11. $3\overline{)1069}$
12. $5\overline{)4293}$
13. $9\overline{)2984}$
14. $4\overline{)3555}$
15. $6\overline{)3627}$

16. $8\overline{)1651}$
17. $9\overline{)7134}$
18. $5\overline{)1826}$
19. $7\overline{)4218}$
20. $8\overline{)324}$

21. $2\overline{)96}$
22. $7\overline{)2268}$
23. $5\overline{)156}$
24. $7\overline{)734}$
25. $8\overline{)485}$

26. $9\overline{)3716}$
27. $4\overline{)1172}$
28. $3\overline{)1428}$
29. $5\overline{)1006}$
30. $7\overline{)4580}$

31. Full library shelf: 126 cm long
    Books: each 3 cm thick
    How many books on the shelf?

32. Full book shelf: 79 cm long
    Books: 4 cm thick
    How many books on the shelf?
    How much space remaining?

☆ 33. Find out how many books
    as thick as your math book
    would fit on a shelf in
    your classroom.

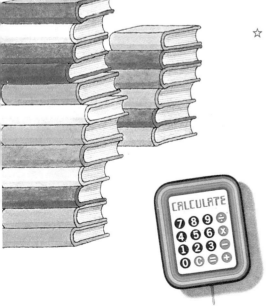

Choose a 4 by 4 square of dates on a calendar. Find the sum of all 16 numbers. Then try this shortcut: Add 12 to the smallest date in the square and multiply that answer by 16. Do you get the same answer? Try a different 4 by 4 square.

AUGUST						
S	M	T	W	T	F	S
					1	2
3	4	5	6	7	8	9
10	11	12	13	14	15	16
17	18	19	20	21	22	23
24/31	25	26	27	28	29	30

More practice, page 367, Set A

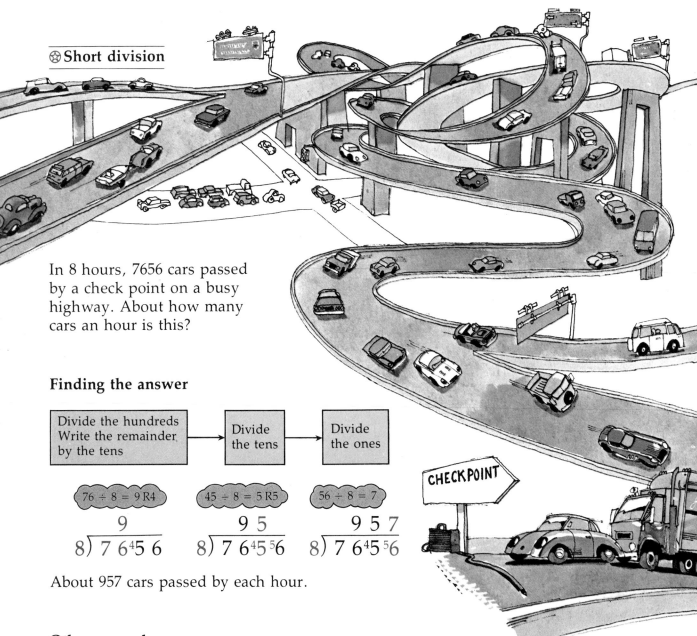

⊗ Short division

In 8 hours, 7656 cars passed by a check point on a busy highway. About how many cars an hour is this?

Finding the answer

Divide the hundreds Write the remainder by the tens	→	Divide the tens	→	Divide the ones

$$76 \div 8 = 9 \text{ R4}$$

$$\begin{array}{r} 9 \\ 8\overline{)7\ 6^4 5\ 6} \end{array}$$

$$45 \div 8 = 5 \text{ R5}$$

$$\begin{array}{r} 9\ 5 \\ 8\overline{)7\ 6^4 5^5 6} \end{array}$$

$$56 \div 8 = 7$$

$$\begin{array}{r} 9\ 5\ 7 \\ 8\overline{)7\ 6^4 5^5 6} \end{array}$$

About 957 cars passed by each hour.

CHECKPOINT

Other examples

$$\begin{array}{r} 7\ 5\ \text{R2} \\ 7\overline{)5\ 2^3 7} \end{array} \qquad \begin{array}{r} 4\ 0\ 8 \\ 3\overline{)1\ 2\ 2^2 4} \end{array} \qquad \begin{array}{r} 5\ 7\ 9\ 1\ \text{R3} \\ 6\overline{)3\ 4^4 7^5 4\ 9} \end{array}$$

Find the quotients and remainders.

1. $7\overline{)581}$ 2. $4\overline{)257}$ 3. $4\overline{)329}$ 4. $8\overline{)340}$ 5. $6\overline{)384}$

6. $6\overline{)4356}$ 7. $8\overline{)4296}$ 8. $9\overline{)2943}$ 9. $6\overline{)2738}$ 10. $4\overline{)1619}$

11. $5\overline{)6250}$ 12. $7\overline{)3678}$ 13. $3\overline{)2514}$ 14. $6\overline{)4130}$ 15. $8\overline{)5882}$

Divide. Use short division.

1. $3\overline{)251}$ 2. $7\overline{)388}$ 3. $9\overline{)281}$

4. $6\overline{)408}$ 5. $8\overline{)577}$ 6. $7\overline{)44}$

7. $6\overline{)3636}$ 8. $9\overline{)6498}$ 9. $5\overline{)2469}$

10. $3\overline{)1519}$ 11. $4\overline{)1776}$ 12. $8\overline{)3679}$

13. $2\overline{)1981}$ 14. $7\overline{)2505}$ 15. $6\overline{)5000}$

16. $3\overline{)1924}$ 17. $5\overline{)2550}$ 18. $9\overline{)7543}$

19. $4\overline{)3812}$ 20. $8\overline{)6666}$ 21. $8\overline{)47\,562}$

22. $5\overline{)23\,647}$ 23. $6\overline{)56\,213}$ 24. $8\overline{)31\,354}$

25. $9\overline{)12\,345}$ 26. $7\overline{)200}$ 27. $4\overline{)2775}$

28. $9\overline{)1836}$ 29. $5\overline{)42\,747}$ 30. $8\overline{)35\,456}$

31. In 7 hours, 2912 cars were counted passing a busy corner. About how many went by in one hour?

☆ 32. Find the number of cars that go by some busy corner in 6 hours. Find out how many cars go by in 1 hour.

Think !

Think of a number line that is stacked up in pieces. Imagine as many rows as you need.

Where will the 6th jump for each color end?

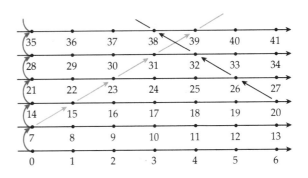

More practice, page 367, Set B

Dividing by a multiple of 10

A class of 30 collected 1927 kg of
newspapers for recycling. About how
many kilograms did each person collect?

Finding the answer

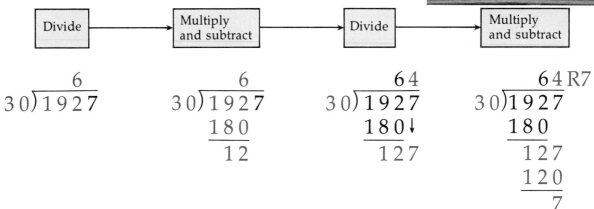

Divide	Multiply and subtract	Divide	Multiply and subtract

```
      6              6             64            64 R7
30)1927        30)1927        30)1927       30)1927
                180            180↓          180
                 12            127           127
                                            120
                                              7
```

Each person collected about 64 kg of newspapers.

Other examples

```
     82 R35           30 R13             856 R14
40)3315          70)2113          60)51 374
 320              210              48 0
 115               13              3 37
  80                0              3 00
  35               13              374
                                   360
                                    14
```

Find the quotients and remainders.

1. 20)1307   2. 40)2764   3. 30)1877   4. 40)3168   5. 70)5135

6. 60)2691   7. 50)4209   8. 60)1378   9. 20)1646   10. 40)2418

Divide.

1. $30\overline{)1623}$ 2. $50\overline{)2454}$ 3. $40\overline{)3307}$ 4. $70\overline{)5872}$ 5. $20\overline{)1774}$

6. $90\overline{)4738}$ 7. $60\overline{)5036}$ 8. $80\overline{)2594}$ 9. $30\overline{)1368}$ 10. $40\overline{)2751}$

11. $80\overline{)25\ 616}$ 12. $50\overline{)32\ 742}$ 13. $90\overline{)47\ 451}$ 14. $20\overline{)15\ 965}$ 15. $60\overline{)18\ 949}$

16. $70\overline{)221}$ 17. $30\overline{)2558}$ 18. $40\overline{)2107}$ 19. $80\overline{)17\ 743}$ 20. $40\overline{)348}$

21. $60\overline{)4336}$ 22. $90\overline{)73\ 524}$ 23. $50\overline{)415}$ 24. $20\overline{)1910}$ 25. $70\overline{)38\ 662}$

26. $80\overline{)61\ 298}$ 27. $30\overline{)1600}$ 28. $90\overline{)2845}$ 29. $40\overline{)2199}$ 30. $60\overline{)16\ 587}$

31. 40 students collected 2170 kg of newspapers. About how many kilograms did each person collect?

32. 20 students collected 940 kg of newspapers. About how many kilograms did each person collect?

Find both sums.

```
8 7 6 5 4 3 2 1            1 2 3 4 5 6 7 8
  7 6 5 4 3 2 1            1 2 3 4 5 6 7 0
    6 5 4 3 2 1            1 2 3 4 5 6 0 0
      5 4 3 2 1            1 2 3 4 5 0 0 0
        4 3 2 1            1 2 3 4 0 0 0 0
          3 2 1            1 2 3 0 0 0 0 0
            2 1            1 2 0 0 0 0 0 0
+             1          + 1 0 0 0 0 0 0 0
```

Answers for Self-Check   1. 39 R4   2. 38 R3   3. 75 R2   4. 676   5. 897 R2   6. 783   7. 540
8. 2697 R2   9. 3369   10. 3323 R3   11. 42 R5   12. 74 R6   13. 53 R34   14. 64 R20   15. 52 R15
16. 447 R11   17. 457 R2   18. 630 R28   19. 360 R23   20. 834 R26

Self-check

Divide.

1. $6\overline{)238}$
2. $5\overline{)193}$
3. $3\overline{)227}$
4. $8\overline{)5408}$

5. $7\overline{)6281}$
6. $9\overline{)7047}$
7. $4\overline{)2160}$
8. $5\overline{)13\ 487}$

9. $4\overline{)13\ 476}$
10. $8\overline{)26\ 587}$
11. $70\overline{)2945}$
12. $90\overline{)6666}$

13. $50\overline{)2684}$
14. $80\overline{)5140}$
15. $40\overline{)2095}$
16. $60\overline{)26\ 831}$

17. $30\overline{)13\ 712}$
18. $70\overline{)44\ 128}$
19. $90\overline{)32\ 423}$
20. $50\overline{)41\ 726}$

Answers for Self-check—page 183

Test

Divide.

1. $7\overline{)437}$
2. $3\overline{)138}$
3. $8\overline{)257}$
4. $5\overline{)2709}$

5. $7\overline{)23\ 714}$
6. $5\overline{)3645}$
7. $8\overline{)5132}$
8. $3\overline{)11\ 632}$

9. $9\overline{)41\ 552}$
10. $7\overline{)31\ 806}$
11. $60\overline{)327}$
12. $30\overline{)2517}$

13. $80\overline{)3849}$
14. $90\overline{)5504}$
15. $70\overline{)3697}$
16. $50\overline{)1867}$

17. $30\overline{)26\ 684}$
18. $80\overline{)57\ 713}$
19. $60\overline{)32\ 517}$
20. $70\overline{)61\ 427}$

A Road Maze

There are 4 roads in this maze. Each
road starts at one letter and ends at
another letter. Find the pair of letters
for each road of the maze.

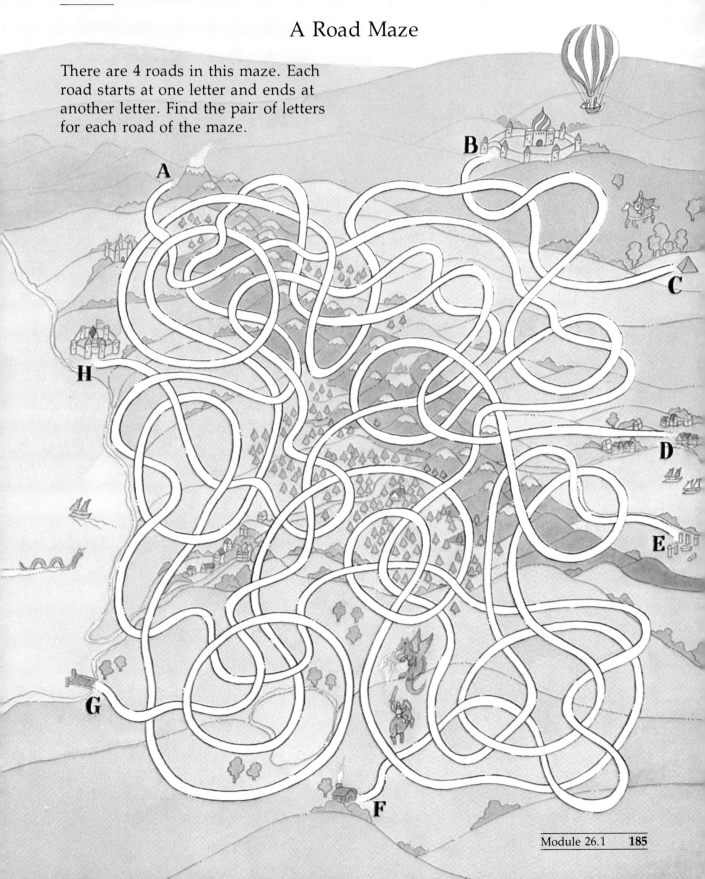

2-Digit Divisors

$$67\overline{)2846}$$

×	67		×	67
1	67		10	670
2	134		20	1340
3	201		30	2010
4	268		40	2680
5	335		50	3350
6	402		60	4020
7	469		70	4690
8	536		80	5360
9	603		90	6030

Getting started

Ron used the multiplication tables to do his division problem.
Try these problems. Use the multiplication tables above.

1.

$$67\overline{)\,\rule{2cm}{0pt}}$$

number of pages in your math book

2.

$$67\overline{)\,\rule{2.5cm}{0pt}}$$

last 4 digits of a telephone number you know

3.

$$67\overline{)\,\rule{2.5cm}{0pt}}$$

year of your birth

You can estimate 1-digit quotients by using the first digit of the divisor.

$$\begin{array}{r} 8 \\ 4\overline{)35} \\ -32 \leftarrow 8 \times 4 \\ \hline 3 \end{array}$$

$$\begin{array}{r} 8 \\ 43\overline{)351} \\ -344 \leftarrow 8 \times 43 \\ \hline 7 \end{array}$$

Estimate these 1-digit quotients.

1. $6\overline{)37}$ $62\overline{)378}$

2. $2\overline{)17}$ $21\overline{)174}$

3. $5\overline{)24}$ $51\overline{)243}$

4. $8\overline{)61}$ $83\overline{)619}$

Sometimes an estimate is too large.   →

$$\begin{array}{r} 6 \\ 54\overline{)312} \\ -324 \\ \hline \end{array}$$

Try again.   →

$$\begin{array}{r} 5 \\ 54\overline{)312} \\ 270 \\ \hline 42 \end{array}$$

Now estimate these 1-digit quotients.

5. $63\overline{)458}$ 6. $22\overline{)178}$ 7. $44\overline{)229}$ 8. $33\overline{)288}$

Sometimes an estimate is too small.
The remainder is greater than the divisor.

$$\begin{array}{r} 6 \\ 73\overline{)528} \\ 438 \\ \hline 90 \end{array}$$

Try again.

$$\begin{array}{r} 7 \\ 73\overline{)528} \\ 511 \\ \hline 17 \end{array}$$

Which of these estimated quotients may be used?

9. $\overset{7}{52\overline{)396}}$ 10. $\overset{6}{49\overline{)253}}$ 11. $\overset{5}{82\overline{)493}}$ 12. $\overset{9}{32\overline{)294}}$

Finding 1-digit quotients

An earth satellite makes 1 trip around the earth every 92 minutes. How many trips does it make in 600 minutes?

Finding the answer

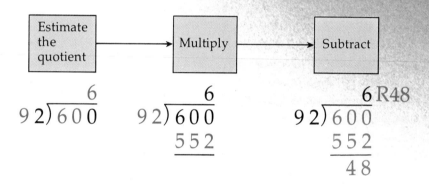

| Estimate the quotient | Multiply | Subtract |

$$
\begin{array}{r} 6 \\ 92\overline{)600} \end{array}
\qquad
\begin{array}{r} 6 \\ 92\overline{)600} \\ 552 \end{array}
\qquad
\begin{array}{r} 6\,\text{R}48 \\ 92\overline{)600} \\ 552 \\ \hline 48 \end{array}
$$

In 600 minutes, the satellite makes 6 trips around the earth, with 48 minutes remaining.

Other examples

$$
\begin{array}{r} 5\,\text{R}32 \\ 63\overline{)347} \\ 315 \\ \hline 32 \end{array}
\qquad
\begin{array}{r} 3\,\text{R}28 \\ 77\overline{)259} \\ 231 \\ \hline 28 \end{array}
\qquad
\begin{array}{r} 6\,\text{R}37 \\ 54\overline{)361} \\ 324 \\ \hline 37 \end{array}
$$

Find the quotients and remainders.

1. $52\overline{)376}$ 2. $41\overline{)375}$ 3. $73\overline{)594}$ 4. $94\overline{)487}$ 5. $21\overline{)156}$

6. $33\overline{)200}$ 7. $84\overline{)356}$ 8. $75\overline{)229}$ 9. $95\overline{)284}$ 10. $76\overline{)572}$

Divide.

Check your work by multiplying.

1. $31\overline{)142}$ 2. $43\overline{)354}$ 3. $73\overline{)624}$ 4. $51\overline{)427}$ 5. $64\overline{)476}$

6. $85\overline{)203}$ 7. $48\overline{)304}$ 8. $41\overline{)205}$ 9. $60\overline{)500}$ 10. $22\overline{)156}$

11. $69\overline{)208}$ 12. $94\overline{)648}$ 13. $30\overline{)237}$ 14. $75\overline{)298}$ 15. $86\overline{)731}$

16. $32\overline{)265}$ 17. $52\overline{)438}$ 18. $91\overline{)835}$ 19. $25\overline{)169}$ 20. $78\overline{)500}$

21. A satellite traveled 425 km in 1 minute (60 seconds). About how far did it travel in 1 second?

22. Astronauts from the Apollo X trip to the moon traveled 665 km in one minute at re-entry. About how far did they travel in one second?

Check the equations to be sure they are true. Then estimate the sum of the whole numbers 1 through 30. Check your estimate with a calculator.

$1 + 2 = (2 \times 3) \div 2$
$1 + 2 + 3 = (3 \times 4) \div 2$
$1 + 2 + 3 + 4 = (4 \times 5) \div 2$
$1 + 2 + 3 + 4 + 5 = (5 \times 6) \div 2$
$1 + 2 + 3 + 4 + 5 + 6 = (6 \times 7) \div 2$

More practice, page 368, Set A

Finding 2-digit quotients

There are 52 weeks in a year.
How many years old will you be
when you have lived 3796 weeks?

Finding the answer

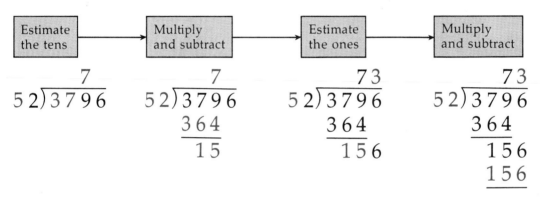

| Estimate the tens | Multiply and subtract | Estimate the ones | Multiply and subtract |

```
        7              7             73             73
52)3796       52)3796       52)3796       52)3796
                 364            364            364
                  15            156            156
                                              156
```

You will be 73 years old.

Other examples

```
     58 R3            33 R8           40 R16
41)2381          23)767          82)3296
   205              69              328
   331              77               16
   328              69                0
     3               8               16
```

Find the quotients and remainders.

1. 53)3828　　2. 81)3529　　3. 42)3371　　4. 74)5347　　5. 32)757

6. 31)458　　7. 94)2166　　8. 35)1166　　9. 68)775　　10. 55)3901

Divide.

1. $71\overline{)3704}$ 2. $32\overline{)2375}$ 3. $64\overline{)5388}$

4. $53\overline{)1863}$ 5. $85\overline{)1957}$ 6. $44\overline{)977}$

7. $92\overline{)3155}$ 8. $73\overline{)6068}$ 9. $65\overline{)3258}$

10. $24\overline{)576}$ 11. $80\overline{)6053}$ 12. $24\overline{)534}$

13. $36\overline{)1476}$ 14. $97\overline{)2922}$ 15. $41\overline{)2385}$

16. $55\overline{)3472}$ 17. $61\overline{)3845}$ 18. $82\overline{)6150}$

19. $43\overline{)1810}$ 20. $50\overline{)2872}$ 21. $74\overline{)2520}$

22. $21\overline{)319}$ 23. $91\overline{)7746}$ 24. $64\overline{)5896}$

25. $82\overline{)5911}$ 26. $63\overline{)5300}$ 27. $95\overline{)5700}$

28. $45\overline{)560}$ 29. $42\overline{)1054}$ 30. $55\overline{)3470}$

31. An **octogenarian** has lived at least 4160 weeks. How many years is this?

32. A **nonagenarian** has lived at least 4680 weeks. How many years is this?

33. In some places you must be at least 884 weeks old to drive a car. How many years old must you be?

Think!

The name of a certain number also tells how many letters are in its word name. What is the number?

More practice, page 368, Set B

Rounding divisors

In 1960 a 57 year old woman walked from New York City to San Francisco in 86 days. She walked 4867 km.

About how many kilometers a day did she walk?

Finding the answer

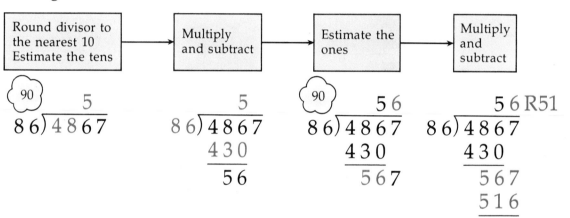

Round divisor to the nearest 10 Estimate the tens	Multiply and subtract	Estimate the ones	Multiply and subtract

```
  90    5              5           90    56           56 R51
86)4867       86)4867       86)4867       86)4867
                430               430            430
                 56               567            567
                                                 516
                                                  51
```

She walked more than 56 km a day.

Other examples

```
Round              Round              Round
to                 to                 to
50      58 R8      30      49 R2      20      78 R9
   47)2734            29)1423            18)1413
      235                116                126
      384                263                153
      376                261                144
        8                  2                  9
```

Find the quotients and remainders.

1. 48)3057   2. 27)1551   3. 59)4407   4. 35)1000   5. 66)5000

6. 37)2335   7. 85)6549   8. 96)1835   9. 54)3123   10. 75)5755

Divide.

1. $38\overline{)1420}$ 2. $59\overline{)3163}$ 3. $98\overline{)7685}$ 4. $86\overline{)7316}$ 5. $17\overline{)442}$

6. $65\overline{)3781}$ 7. $42\overline{)1849}$ 8. $27\overline{)1568}$ 9. $74\overline{)5047}$ 10. $56\overline{)1156}$

11. $47\overline{)3874}$ 12. $82\overline{)1776}$ 13. $94\overline{)5579}$ 14. $67\overline{)1920}$ 15. $39\overline{)1601}$

16. $51\overline{)1672}$ 17. $76\overline{)5891}$ 18. $19\overline{)1220}$ 19. $45\overline{)2000}$ 20. $97\overline{)4760}$

21. $83\overline{)3296}$ 22. $49\overline{)2745}$ 23. $33\overline{)1210}$ 24. $66\overline{)4457}$ 25. $35\overline{)1296}$

26. The walking record from New York City to Los Angeles is 54 days. The distance is 4628 km. About how many kilometers per day is this?

27. The record walking distance in 24 hours is 214 km. About how many kilometers in one hour is this?

28. A "walking record" for a snail might be 1152 meters in 24 hours. How many meters in one hour is this?

Try this problem.

Start with any 3 digit number. Subtract the sum of the digits. Divide the answer by 9. What is the remainder?

Try the problem again with a different number. What do you find?

More practice, page 368, Set C

✵ Larger quotients

The planet Mercury travels around the sun in 88 Earth days. Uranus takes 30 686 Earth days to travel around the sun. About how many times as long as Mercury does Uranus take?

Finding the answer

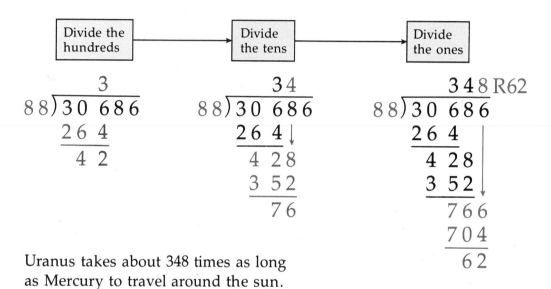

Uranus takes about 348 times as long as Mercury to travel around the sun.

Other examples

```
     435 R10            306 R7           130 R22
53)23 065          57)17 449         64)8342
  21 2               17 1              64
  ─────              ────             ────
   1 86                34             194
   1 59                 0             192
   ────              ────             ───
    275               349              22
    265               342               0
    ───               ───             ───
     10                 7              22
```

Divide.

1. 51)11 934   2. 32)16 482   3. 64)14 784   4. 65)33 025

Find the quotients and remainders.

1. $62\overline{)72\ 630}$ 2. $75\overline{)41\ 625}$ 3. $23\overline{)14\ 763}$ 4. $78\overline{)30\ 342}$

5. $89\overline{)61\ 143}$ 6. $76\overline{)67\ 376}$ 7. $67\overline{)32\ 378}$ 8. $93\overline{)66\ 274}$

9. $42\overline{)10\ 813}$ 10. $61\overline{)26\ 119}$ 11. $39\overline{)6438}$ 12. $72\overline{)9375}$

13. $50\overline{)20\ 900}$ 14. $36\overline{)33\ 199}$ 15. $43\overline{)25\ 353}$ 16. $96\overline{)41\ 966}$

17. $43\overline{)7435}$ 18. $81\overline{)65\ 271}$ 19. $72\overline{)50\ 832}$ 20. $27\overline{)21\ 854}$

21. $54\overline{)8626}$ 22. $90\overline{)82\ 746}$ 23. $65\overline{)24\ 055}$ 24. $86\overline{)79\ 137}$

25. A year on Mercury: 88 Earth days
A year on Saturn: 10 759 Earth days
About how many times as long
on Saturn?

26. A year on Mercury: 88 Earth days
A year on Earth: 365 Earth days
About how many times as long
on Earth?

☆ 27. Find out how many days you
have lived. Divide by 88 to find
your age on Mercury.

What is the divisor
in each problem?

1. $\dfrac{75\ \text{R1}}{\text{▓▓}\overline{)3901}}$

2. $\dfrac{21\ \text{R7}}{\text{▓▓}\overline{)2002}}$

3. $\dfrac{34\ \text{R11}}{\text{▓▓}\overline{)1065}}$

Answers for Self-check 1. 6 R13 2. 6 R20 3. 2 R83 4. 9 R28 5. 67 R5 6. 52 R16 7. 73 R2
8. 83 R25 9. 240 R10 10. 140 R31 11. 144 R13 12. 153 R52 13. 719 R40 14. 310 R63 15. 722 R27
16. 707 R6

More practice, page 369, Set A

Self-check

Find the quotients and remainders.

1. $42\overline{)265}$
2. $59\overline{)374}$
3. $87\overline{)257}$
4. $38\overline{)370}$

5. $72\overline{)4829}$
6. $48\overline{)2512}$
7. $63\overline{)4601}$
8. $91\overline{)7578}$

☆ 9. $35\overline{)8410}$
☆ 10. $48\overline{)6751}$
☆ 11. $63\overline{)9085}$
☆ 12. $54\overline{)8314}$

☆ 13. $52\overline{)37\,428}$
☆ 14. $73\overline{)22\,693}$
☆ 15. $44\overline{)31\,795}$
☆ 16. $85\overline{)60\,101}$

Answers for Self-check—page 195

Test

Find the quotients and remainders.

1. $32\overline{)208}$
2. $88\overline{)481}$
3. $43\overline{)356}$
4. $19\overline{)148}$

5. $61\overline{)2161}$
6. $75\overline{)6476}$
7. $52\overline{)4315}$
8. $94\overline{)6633}$

☆ 9. $21\overline{)8505}$
☆ 10. $72\overline{)8164}$
☆ 11. $39\overline{)7624}$
☆ 12. $47\overline{)6185}$

☆ 13. $92\overline{)49\,514}$
☆ 14. $45\overline{)15\,726}$
☆ 15. $86\overline{)35\,088}$
☆ 16. $66\overline{)37\,629}$

Russian Peasant Multiplication

An old method of multiplying two numbers is shown below.
It is called Russian Peasant multiplication.

Study the example which shows how to multiply 37 × 53.

Rules:

1. Divide the number in column A by 2. Omit the remainder.

2. Double the number in column B.

3. Repeat steps 1 and 2 until you get 1 in column A.

4. Draw lines through the even numbers in column A and the matching numbers in column B.

5. Add the remaining numbers in column B to find the product.

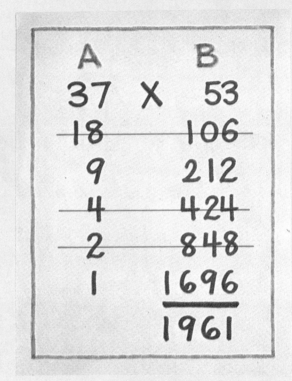

37 × 53 = 1961

Use the Russian Peasant multiplication method to find these products.
Check by multiplying the usual way.

1. 12 × 52
2. 25 × 35
3. 43 × 71
4. 23 × 23

5. 44 × 63
6. 16 × 59
7. 27 × 48
8. 101 × 101

Using Your Skills

Mastiff 64 kg

Chihuahua 1 kg

Great Dane 60 kg

Greyhound 30 kg

Dalmatian 21 kg

Pekingese 4 kg

Getting started

1. About how many Pekingese dogs would it take to equal the mass of one mastiff?
2. How much heavier is the greyhound than the Dalmatian?
3. What other problems can you solve?

It helps to make an estimate of the answer to a problem to see if your answer makes sense. Use rounded numbers to help make an estimate.

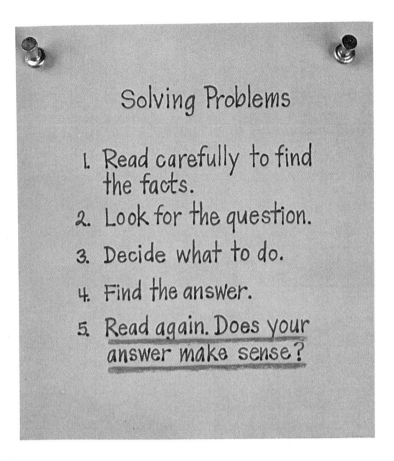

Solving Problems

1. Read carefully to find the facts.
2. Look for the question.
3. Decide what to do.
4. Find the answer.
5. Read again. Does your answer make sense?

Which answer makes the best sense?

1. A Chihuahua is 12 cm tall. An Irish wolfhound is 84 cm tall. How many times as tall is the wolfhound?

   A 4   B 7   C 10

2. Dogs can hear sounds that are about 10 times as far away as sounds humans can hear. A dog can hear a certain sound at a distance of 270 m. At what distance would a human be able to hear this sound?

   A 2700 m   B 270 m   C 27 m

3. A fast greyhound can run a kilometer in 72 seconds. About how many kilometers could the greyhound run in an hour at this speed?

   A 40 km   B 50 km   C 60 km

4. A Pekingese had a mass of 4 kg. An English mastiff was 29 times as heavy. What was the mass of the mastiff?

   A 96 kg   B 156 kg   C 116 kg

Finding averages

What is the **average** height of the children? (measurements in centimeters)

Finding the answer

Find the sum of all the numbers	→	Divide by the number of addends	→	The quotient is the average of the numbers

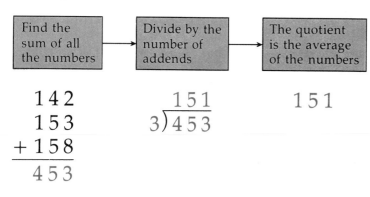

```
  142        151        151
  153      3)453
+ 158
─────
  453
```

The average height of the children is 151 cm.

Other examples

Find the average of 32, 30, and 43.

```
  32      35
  30    3)105
+ 43      9
─────    ──
 105      15
          15
          ──
```

Find the average of 19, 27, 18, and 23.

```
  19       21      →  The average to the
  27     4)87         nearest whole
  18       8          number is 22.
+ 23      ──
─────      7
  87       4
          ──
           3
```

Find the average of each list of numbers to the nearest whole number.

1. 3, 2, 7

2. 5, 2, 2, 4

3. 5, 9, 10, 4

4. 3, 8, 4

5. 55, 29

6. 6, 9, 12, 5, 7

7. 20, 32, 35

8. 63, 75, 47, 27

9. 4, 12, 7, 9, 13, 8

10. 58, 37, 69, 93

11. 156, 266, 187

12. 478, 644, 823

1. Jerry's scores on three math tests were 82, 86, and 93. What was his average score?

2. The chart shows daily high temperatures for a week. What was the average daily high temperature?

Day	S	M	T	W	Th	F	S
Temperature (°C)	21	24	28	29	26	30	31

3. This graph shows how far some children threw a baseball. Find the average distance.

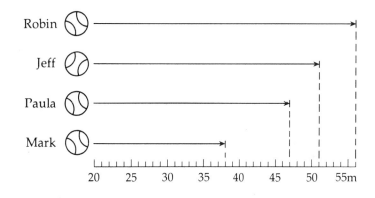

4. The bar graph shows the heights of 6 children. Find the average height of these children.

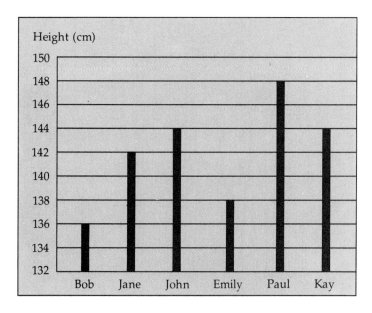

☆ 5. Find the height of six of your classmates. Find their average height. Which classmate has a height nearest the average?

Dividing money

Ken bought three long-playing records. They cost a total of $10.41. What was the average cost of a record?

Finding the answer

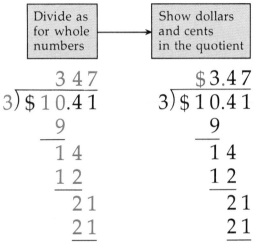

Divide as for whole numbers	Show dollars and cents in the quotient

```
      3 4 7              $ 3.4 7
3)$ 1 0.4 1        3)$ 1 0.4 1
    9                    9
   ──                   ──
    1 4                  1 4
    1 2                  1 2
      2 1                  2 1
      2 1                  2 1
      ──                   ──
```

The average cost of each record was $3.47.

Other examples

```
        $ 2.1 5              $ 0.4 3                 $ 5.2 5
   6)$ 1 2.9 0         32)$ 1 3.7 6          78)$ 4 0 9.5 0
      1 2                   1 2 8                  3 9 0
      ──                    ────                   ────
        9                     9 6                  1 9 5
        6                     9 6                  1 5 6
        ─                     ──                   ────
        3 0                                          3 9 0
        3 0                                          3 9 0
        ──                                           ────
```

Divide.

1. 2)$6.18

2. 9)$25.11

3. 5)$12.45

4. 3)$8.13

5. 60)$22.80

6. 45)$41.85

7. 36)$332.64

8. 25)$77.75

Give the missing amount. Multiply or divide.

1.

4 books: $23.60
1 book: ▦

2.

5 cassettes: $8.45
1 cassette: ▦

3.

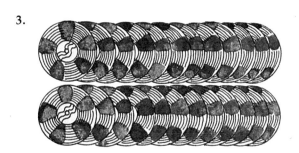

24 records: $25.20
1 record: ▦

4.

1 record: $4.59
5 records: ▦

5.

64 records: $316.80
1 record: ▦

6.

1 recorder: $3.25
4 recorders: ▦

7.

1 piece of sheet music: $2.85
6 pieces: ▦

8.

2 guitars: $125.50
1 guitar: ▦

Automobiles through the years

The first road car was built in 1769 in France. It ran on steam. The first gasoline-powered car was built in 1885. After 1900, the number of cars being used grew every year. Now over 25 million cars a year are manufactured throughout the world.

1915 Buick

1918 Model T Ford

1920 Chevrolet

1947 Kaiser

1. In 1903, a car made a trip across the United States in 63 days. If the distance traveled was 4977 km, how many kilometers were traveled each day?

2. A new car may cost $5100. This is 6 times as much as a Model T Ford cost in 1908. What was the cost of the Ford in 1908?

3. Balloon tires were first used on cars in 1922. Twenty-six years later, cars with tubeless tires were introduced. What year were tubeless tires introduced?

4. In 1909, there were only about 300 000 km of surfaced roads. There are about 12 times that many kilometers today. How many kilometers of surfaced roads are there today?

1930 Cord

1932 Essex

1934 Chrysler Airflow

5. One out of every 6 American workers has a job related to the automobile. If there are 78 million workers, how many have jobs related to the automobile?

6. New automobiles are often shipped by train on special flatcars. Each flatcar holds 12 cars. How many flatcars are needed to ship 492 new cars?

7. For safe driving, cars should stay at least 1 m apart for every 3 km per hour of speed. At least how far apart should two cars be when traveling 84 km per hour?

8. About 57 million American families own cars. One out of every 3 families owns more than 1 car. About how many families own more than one car?

Finding speed

A large sailing ship once sailed 492 km in 12 hours. What was the average speed of the ship?

Finding the answer

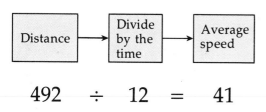

$$492 \div 12 = 41$$

The average speed was 41 kilometers per hour (km/h).

Other examples

Distance: 268 km
Time: 4 h
Speed: 67 km/h

```
     67
 4)268
     24
     28
     28
```

Distance: 2128 km
Time: 38 h
Speed: 56 km/h

```
        56
 38)2128
      190
      228
      228
```

Find the speed for each trip.

1. Distance: 413 km
   Time: 7 h
   Speed: ▦ km/h

2. Distance: 3648 km
   Time: 4 h
   Speed: ▦ km/h

3. Distance: 198 km
   Time: 18 h
   Speed: ▦ km/h

4. Distance: 1824 km
   Time: 24 h
   Speed: ▦ km/h

5. Distance: 1280 km
   Time: 20 h
   Speed: ▦ km/h

6. Distance: 1056 km
   Time: 11 h
   Speed: ▦ km/h

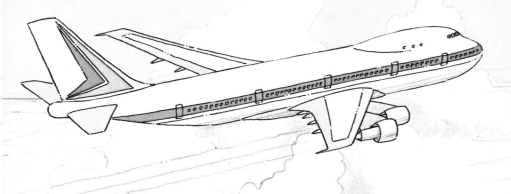

1. A sailing ship once traveled 851 km in 23 hours. What was the ship's speed?

2. It takes 2 hours to travel by jet airplane from Vancouver, B.C., to San Francisco. The distance is 1636 km. What is the speed for the trip?

3. The ocean liner *United States* made a record crossing of the Atlantic Ocean. She traveled 5478 km in about 83 hours. What was the speed?

4. The longest straight railroad track is in Australia. It is 480 km long. If a train travels this distance in 6 hours, what is its speed?

5. The winner of a bicycle race went 272 km in 8 hours. What was the winner's speed?

☆ 6. In 1927, Charles A. Lindbergh flew his plane alone across the Atlantic Ocean. He traveled 5808 km in about 33 hours. What was his speed?

☆ 7. An astronaut once traveled about 1 970 000 km in 71 hours. What was the astronaut's average speed?

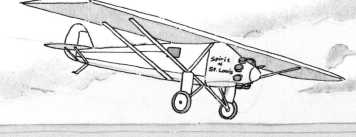

1. 60 minutes in 1 hour
   How many hours in 420 minutes?

2. 52 weeks in 1 year
   How many years in 1300 weeks?

3. 7 days in 1 week
   How many weeks in 266 days?

4. 60 seconds in 1 minute
   How many seconds in 5 minutes?

5. 60 seconds in 1 minute
   60 minutes in 1 hour
   How many seconds in an hour?

6. 12 months in a year
   276 months
   How many years?

7. 365 days in 1 year
   Paul is 12 years old.
   How many days old?

8. Metronome: 96 beats in 1 minute
   How many beats in 15 minutes?

9. Seven months have 31 days each.
   How many days in these 7 months?

10. One **decade:** 10 years
    52 weeks in one year
    How many weeks in a decade?

11. One **century:** 100 years
    How many weeks in a century?

12. Light from the sun:
    About 480 seconds to reach Earth
    How many minutes to reach Earth?

Answers for Self-check   1. $2.63   2. $4.63   3. $3.94   4. $3.49   5. 17   6. 141 cm   7. 36 h
8. 73 km/h

Self-check

Divide.

1. 6)$15.78   2. 8)$37.04   3. 23)$90.62

4. Two potted plants were selling for $6.98.
   How much did each plant cost?

5. Find the average of 10, 15, 18 and 25.

6. Find the average height of these three children:
   Rickey: 140 cm; Diane: 135 cm; Paula: 148 cm

7. How many hours are there in 2160 minutes?

8. Ralph drove 657 km in 9 hours. What was his average speed?

Answers for Self-check—page 209

Test

Divide.

1. 5)$8.15   2. 9)$20.52   3. 39)$21.06

4. The price of 6 rolls of wallpaper is $37.50.
   How much does each roll cost?

5. Find the average of 32, 18, 46, and 28.

6. Find the average mass of these four children:
   Betty: 34 kg; Wayne: 41 kg; Lon: 31 kg; Peggy: 34 kg.

7. There are 7 days in one week. How many weeks are
   there in 294 days?

8. A 747 jet plane flew 2724 km in 3 hours. What was the
   speed of the plane?

Eyes Right?

Which piece is larger?

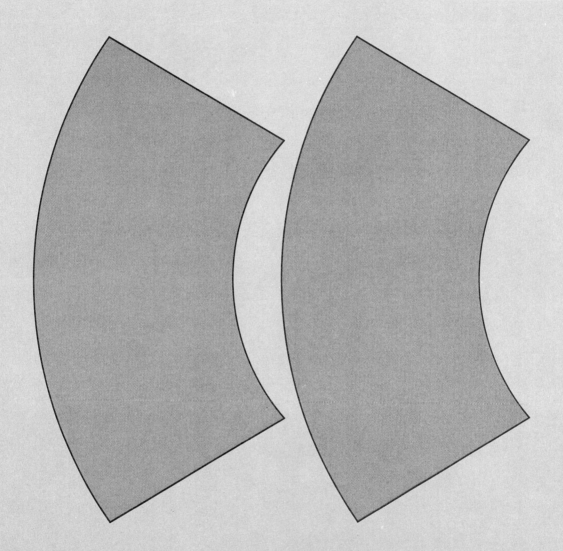

Check your answer.

Trace the pieces and cut them out. Reverse the
positions of the two pieces and compare their sizes.

Space Figures

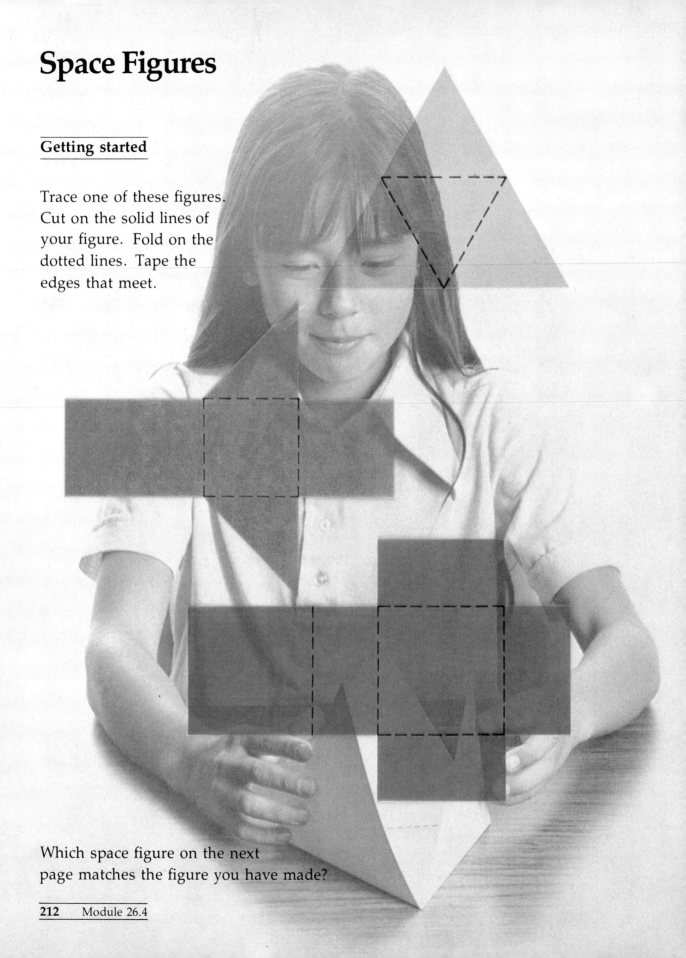

Getting started

Trace one of these figures. Cut on the solid lines of your figure. Fold on the dotted lines. Tape the edges that meet.

Which space figure on the next page matches the figure you have made?

Match the space figure with the picture of a real object.

Space figure   Real Object

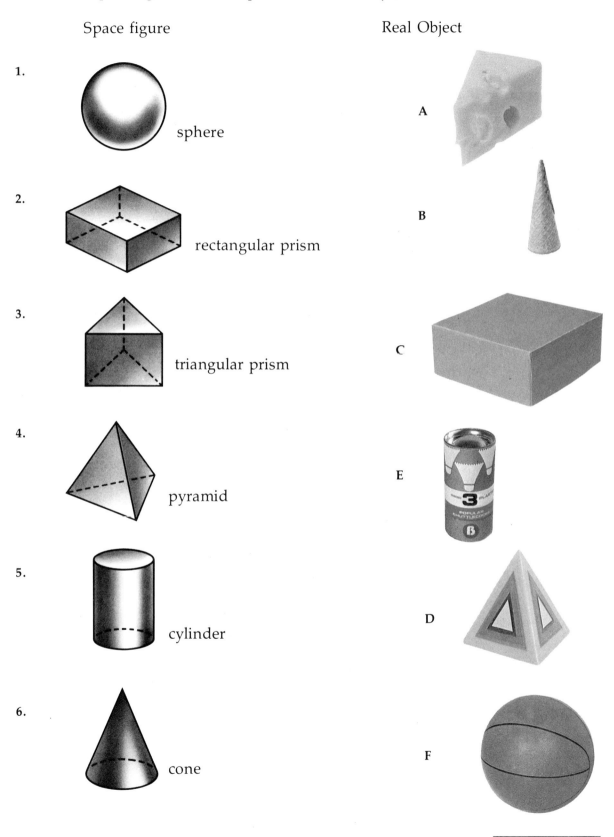

1.   sphere

2.   rectangular prism

3.   triangular prism

4.   pyramid

5.   cylinder

6.   cone

A

B

C

E

D

F

Faces, edges, and vertices

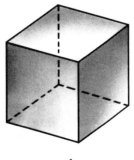

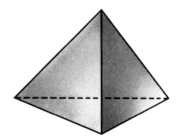

Give the number of faces, edges, and vertices of each figure.

1.

cube

2.

triangular pyramid

Copy and complete the table.

	Space figure	Number of faces	Number of vertices	Number of edges
1.		5	5	▦
2.		▦	▦	9
3.		▦	7	▦
4.		▦	▦	18
5.		8	▦	▦
6.		▦	10	▦

☆ 7. There is a pattern in the number of faces, vertices, and edges of space figures. Can you discover the pattern?

⊛ Views of space figures

What do you see if you view this space figure from the front, side, and top?

Front view	Side view	Top view

Give the correct word, **front, side,** or **top,** for each view.

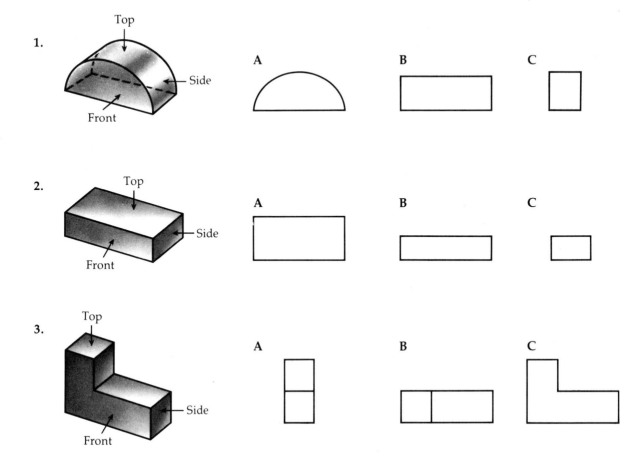

1.

2.

3.

Tell which view, **front, side,** or **top,** is shown.

1.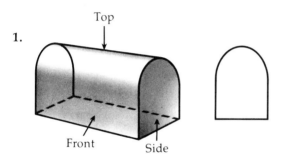

2.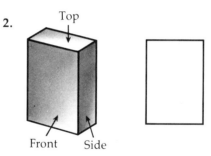

3.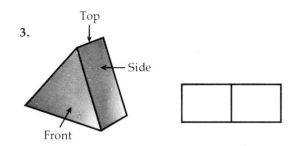

4.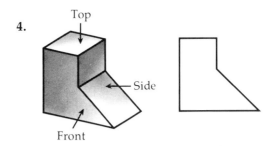

5.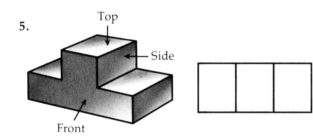

6.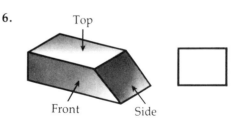

Practicing your skills

Divide.

1. $7\overline{)84}$ 2. $9\overline{)321}$ 3. $8\overline{)622}$ 4. $6\overline{)1355}$ 5. $7\overline{)6214}$

6. $5\overline{)2144}$ 7. $3\overline{)7047}$ 8. $8\overline{)2957}$ 9. $2\overline{)5496}$ 10. $9\overline{)3096}$

11. $22\overline{)337}$ 12. $51\overline{)495}$ 13. $73\overline{)1825}$ 14. $69\overline{)5184}$ 15. $95\overline{)5000}$

16. $43\overline{)3284}$ 17. $87\overline{)1953}$ 18. $56\overline{)2991}$ 19. $70\overline{)6273}$ 20. $39\overline{)2145}$

Answers for Self-check   1. 6   2. 5   3. 9   4. 8   5. 6   6. 12   7. 12   8. 8   9. 18   10. **B**

Self-check

Give the number of vertices, faces, and edges
for each space figure.

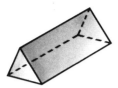 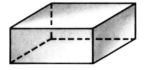 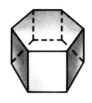

1. <u>?</u> vertices
2. <u>?</u> faces
3. <u>?</u> edges

4. <u>?</u> vertices
5. <u>?</u> faces
6. <u>?</u> edges

7. <u>?</u> vertices
8. <u>?</u> faces
9. <u>?</u> edges

☆ 10. Choose the figure that shows the front view.

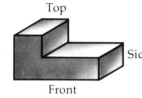

A

B

Answers for Self-check—page 217

Test

Give the number of vertices, faces, and edges
for each space figure.

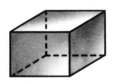 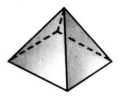

1. <u>?</u> vertices
2. <u>?</u> faces
3. <u>?</u> edges

4. <u>?</u> vertices
5. <u>?</u> faces
6. <u>?</u> edges

7. <u>?</u> vertices
8. <u>?</u> faces
9. <u>?</u> edges

☆ 10. Choose the figure that shows the side view.

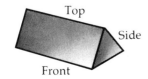

A

B

The Plus and Minus Game

Use 2 cubes of different colors.
Put the numbers 1, 2, 3, 4, 5, 6
on each cube.

Rules:
1. Players take turns tossing the cubes.
2. Each player keeps his or her own score.
3. Start with the top number on the green cube.
4. Take away the top number on the red cube.
   The score may be a plus score (+) or a minus score (−).

Examples:

Start with 4.   Start with 2.
Take away 1.   Take away 4.
Score: +3   Score: −2

The total score for these 2 tosses is +1.

Play the game with two or more players.
Each player should take at least 3 tosses.
The player with the highest total score wins the game.

Coordinate Geometry

Getting started

The 3 green golf tees mark the location of a sunken treasure ship.

The 3 yellow tees mark another sunken ship.

To try to land on a sunken ship, roll a red and a blue cube, each numbered 0 through 5.

Example: over 5 up 3

This roll locates part of the yellow ship at the point (5,3).

What are some other rolls that will locate parts of the ships?

Give the missing location numbers.
Then write the coordinates.

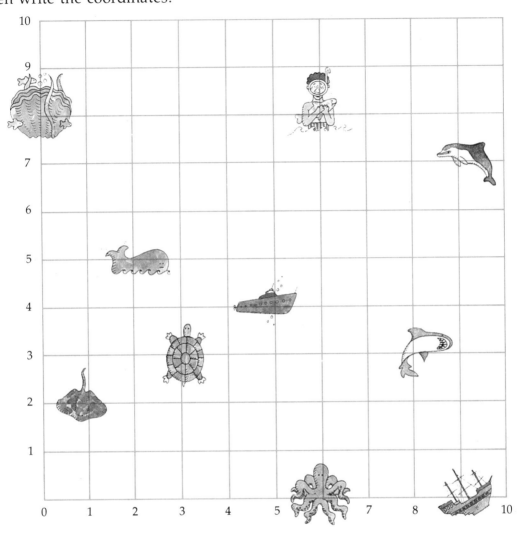

Object	Location	Coordinates
1. Turtle	over 3, up 3	(3,3)
2. Shark	over ▦, up 3	(▦,3)
3. Whale	over 2, up ▦	(2, ▦)
4. Octopus	over ▦, up 0	(▦,0)
5. Diver	over ▦, up ▦	(▦, ▦)
6. Giant clam	over ▦, up ▦	(▦, ▦)
7. Porpoise	over ▦, up ▦	(▦, ▦)
8. Submarine	over ▦, up ▦	(▦, ▦)
9. Sting-ray	over ▦, up ▦	(▦, ▦)
10. Sunken ship	over ▦, up ▦	(▦, ▦)

Graphing points and pictures

The picture shows how to **graph the point** whose coordinates are $(3, 2)$.

Use graph paper. Start at $(0, 0)$.
Go **over** 3 and **up** 2. Mark the point.

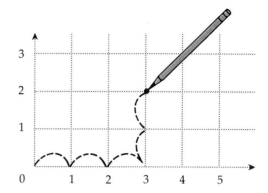

Three points are graphed below.
Give the coordinates of each point.

1.

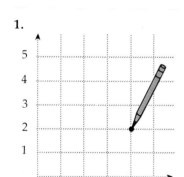

2.

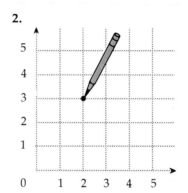

3.

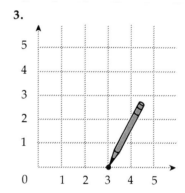

4. Use graph paper. Graph each of these points and write the letter beside it.

A $(7, 3)$ E $(8, 1)$

B $(3, 7)$ F $(0, 3)$

C $(5, 5)$ G $(2, 1)$

D $(1, 6)$ H $(6, 0)$

Example

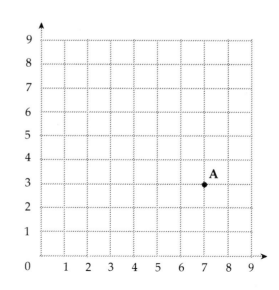

To "graph a picture," graph the points in order.
Then draw lines from point to point.

START $(1,5) \rightarrow (1,8) \rightarrow (2,9) \rightarrow (4,9) \rightarrow (5,8) \rightarrow (6,9) \rightarrow$
$(8,9) \rightarrow (9,8) \rightarrow (9,5) \rightarrow (5,2) \rightarrow (1,5)$

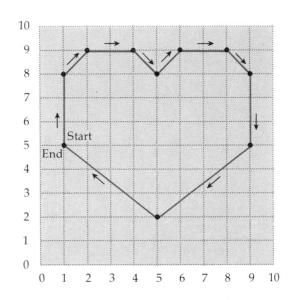

Graph the points. Connect them in the order given, to form a picture.

1. $(2,1)$, $(5,9)$, $(8,1)$,
    $(1,6)$, $(9,6)$, $(2,1)$

2. $(1,6)$, $(3,9)$, $(7,9)$, $(9,6)$,
    $(7,3)$, $(3,3)$, $(1,6)$

3. $(5,10)$, $(3,8)$, $(4,8)$, $(2,6)$,
    $(3,6)$, $(1,4)$, $(4,4)$, $(4,2)$,
    $(6,2)$, $(6,4)$, $(9,4)$, $(7,6)$,
    $(8,6)$, $(6,8)$, $(7,8)$, $(5,10)$

4. $(6,9)$, $(7,8)$, $(7,6)$, $(6,3)$,
    $(4,3)$, $(3,4)$, $(4,5)$, $(3,5)$,
    $(3,6)$, $(2,6)$, $(3,7)$, $(3,8)$,
    $(4,9)$, $(6,9)$

5. $(4,0)$, $(5,3)$, $(7,1)$, $(8,1)$,
    $(8,2)$, $(9,1)$, $(10,2)$, $(9,4)$,
    $(5,8)$, $(5,10)$, $(4,8)$, $(3,10)$,
    $(0,4)$, $(4,0)$

6. $(0,1)$, $(0,3)$, $(1,2)$, $(4,6)$,
    $(0,9)$, $(1,10)$, $(6,8)$, $(9,10)$,
    $(10,10)$, $(10,9)$, $(8,6)$, $(10,1)$,
    $(9,0)$, $(6,4)$, $(2,1)$, $(3,0)$,
    $(1,0)$, $(0,1)$

These points were graphed, and connected to form the figure at the right.

$(3, 2)$, $(7, 2)$, $(10, 7)$, $(7, 7)$,
$(5, 9)$, $(3, 7)$, $(0, 7)$, $(3, 2)$

Next, the line of symmetry of the figure was drawn. This line intersects the figure at the points whose coordinates are $(5, 2)$ and $(5, 9)$.

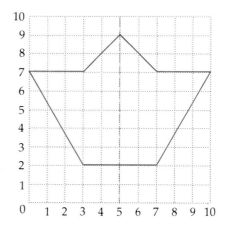

Give the coordinates that show where a line of symmetry intersects each figure.

1.

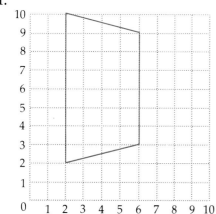

2.

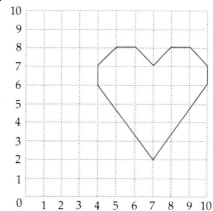

3.

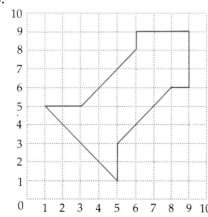

4.

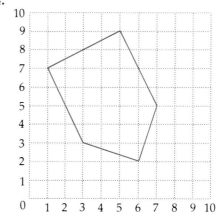

Graph the points and connect them in the order given.
Then find and draw the line of symmetry of the figure formed.

1. $(1, 2)$, $(3, 9)$, $(5, 2)$, $(1, 2)$

2. $(4, 8)$, $(10, 8)$, $(9, 4)$,
   $(5, 4)$, $(4, 8)$

3. $(3, 9)$, $(8, 9)$, $(9, 7)$, $(8, 5)$,
   $(3, 5)$, $(4, 7)$, $(3, 9)$

4. $(7, 1)$, $(9, 3)$, $(9, 6)$, $(3, 6)$,
   $(3, 3)$, $(5, 1)$, $(7, 1)$

5. $(2, 1)$, $(1, 6)$, $(2, 9)$, $(4, 9)$,
   $(5, 6)$, $(4, 1)$, $(2, 1)$

6. $(5, 4)$, $(4, 5)$, $(4, 3)$, $(2, 3)$,
   $(2, 9)$, $(5, 7)$, $(8, 9)$, $(8, 3)$,
   $(6, 3)$, $(6, 5)$, $(5, 4)$

One half of a figure and a line of symmetry are shown.
Show the whole figure on graph paper.

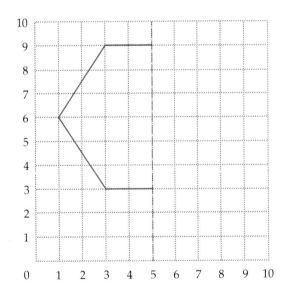
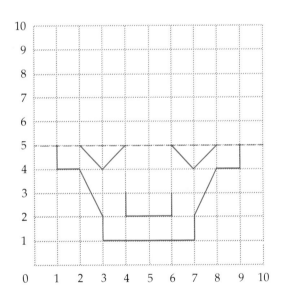

☆ 9. Draw one half of a figure that has a line of symmetry.
Have a classmate draw the other half.

⊛ Graphing congruent figures

Each point of the starting figure was moved **over 3 and up 5.** Then a "moved figure" was drawn.
The two figures are congruent to each other.

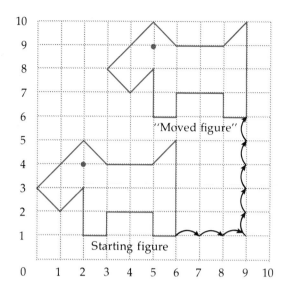

Use graph paper. Graph the figure shown. Then show the "moved figure."

1. Move: over 2 and up 5

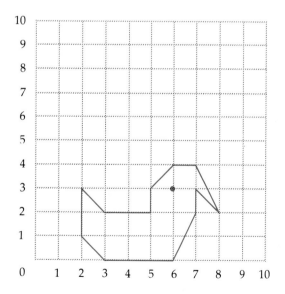

2. Move: over 4 and down 4

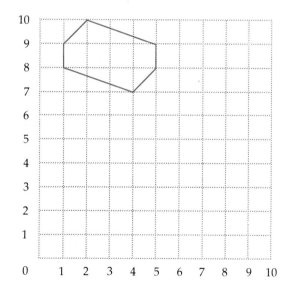

3. Move: over 4, up 2

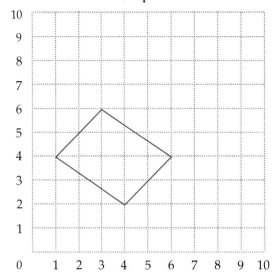

4. Move: over 5, down 4

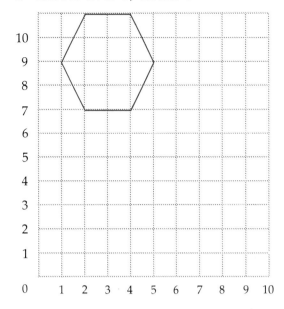

5. Move: over 1, up 5

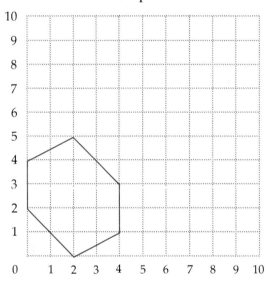

6. Move: over 2, down 4

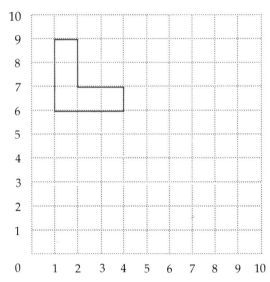

Practicing your skills

Find the quotients and remainders.

1. $3\overline{)284}$ **2.** $7\overline{)341}$ **3.** $6\overline{)3514}$ **4.** $9\overline{)6225}$ **5.** $8\overline{)1746}$

6. $40\overline{)3152}$ **7.** $60\overline{)2774}$ **8.** $21\overline{)629}$ **9.** $43\overline{)929}$ **10.** $52\overline{)789}$

11. $27\overline{)1457}$ **12.** $63\overline{)2001}$ **13.** $59\overline{)2842}$ **14.** $93\overline{)12\,845}$ **15.** $88\overline{)16\,358}$

You can graph similar figures by using graph paper with different size squares.

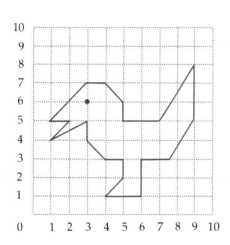

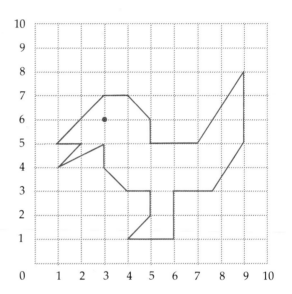

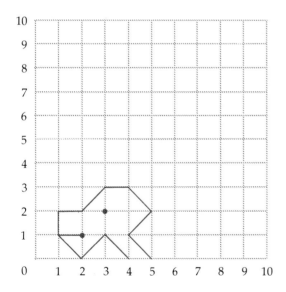

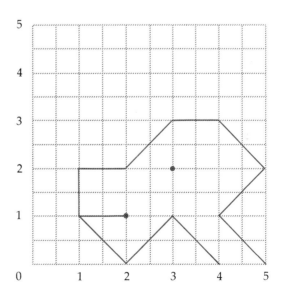

These two figures are similar.
The spaces between the numbers on the grid at the right are twice as large as those on the grid at the left.

Copy each figure on graph paper. Then graph a figure similar to it.

1.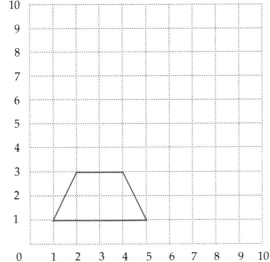

2.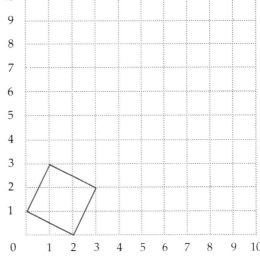

3.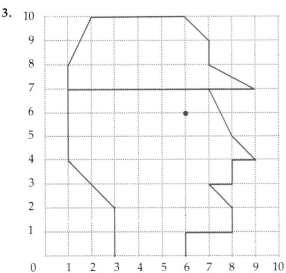

4.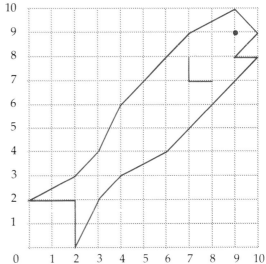

5. Make up your own figure. Then graph a figure similar to it.

 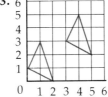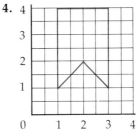

Self-check

1. Give the coordinates of points A, B, C, and D.

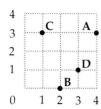

☆ 3. Show the figure after a move of **over 3, up 2.**

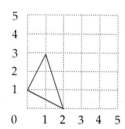

Answers for Self-check—page 229

2. Graph these points and connect them in order.
$(2,1)$, $(3,1)$, $(4,2)$, $(4,3)$,
$(3,4)$, $(2,4)$, $(1,3)$, $(1,2)$, $(2,1)$

☆ 4. Copy this figure. Then graph a figure similar to it.

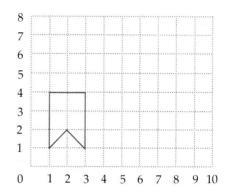

Test

1. Give the coordinates of points W, X, Y, and Z.

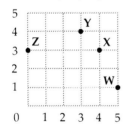

☆ 3. Show the figure after a move of **over 2, down 3.**

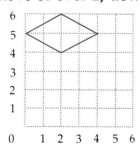

2. Graph these points and connect them in order.
$(2,6)$, $(4,6)$, $(7,2)$, $(5,2)$,
$(5,0)$, $(2,3)$, $(2,6)$

☆ 4. Copy this figure. Then graph a figure similar to it.

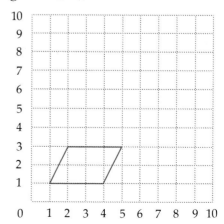

Secret Messages

Here is a **code graph** some students made.

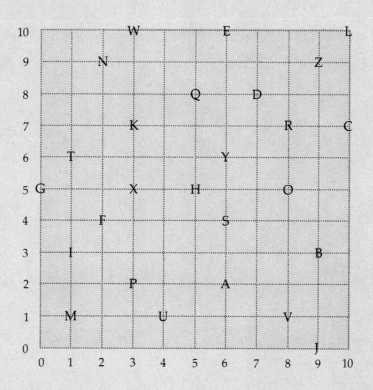

Use the code graph to find this message.

| $(10,10)\ (6,10)\ (1,6)\ (6,4)$ | $(1,1)\ (6,10)\ (6,10)\ (1,6)$ |

| $(9,3)\ (6,6)$ | $(1,6)\ (5,5)\ (6,10)$ | $(9,3)\ (1,3)\ (0,5)$ |

| $(1,6)\ (8,7)\ (6,10)\ (6,10)$ | $(6,2)\ (2,4)\ (1,6)\ (6,10)\ (8,7)$ |

| $(6,4)\ (10,7)\ (5,5)\ (8,5)\ (8,5)\ (10,10)$ |

Make a code graph of your own.

Level 26 review

Divide.

1. $7\overline{)322}$

2. $5\overline{)715}$

3. $8\overline{)236}$

4. $4\overline{)336}$

5. $9\overline{)528}$

6. $8\overline{)1452}$

7. $3\overline{)2641}$

8. $6\overline{)3095}$

9. $7\overline{)1132}$

10. $8\overline{)7501}$

11. $40\overline{)5315}$

12. $90\overline{)4179}$

13. $60\overline{)2757}$

14. $50\overline{)14\,892}$

15. $80\overline{)62\,485}$

16. $85\overline{)700}$

17. $32\overline{)186}$

18. $74\overline{)4201}$

19. $42\overline{)3986}$

20. $67\overline{)8251}$

21. $56\overline{)64\,123}$

22. $81\overline{)85\,406}$

23. $26\overline{)54\,018}$

24. $47\overline{)31\,206}$

25. $65\overline{)82\,371}$

26. A car traveled 352 km in 4 hours. What was its speed?

27. Jean drove 680 km on Tuesday, 704 km on Wednesday, and 635 km on Thursday. Find the average number of kilometers she drove a day.

28. Fremont basketball team:

First game: 32 points
Second game: 25 points
Third game: 28 points
Fourth game: 23 points

Find the average number of points per game.

29. Four pairs of ski boots cost $119.40. How much does 1 pair cost?

30. Twenty-five children will attend a music performance. Each ticket costs $0.80. What will all 25 tickets cost?

31. Sue kept a record of daily temperature highs. What is the average high temperature?

Monday: 27° C   Thursday: 23° C
Tuesday: 29° C   Friday: 22° C
Wednesday: 25° C

Fractional Numbers
Larger Fractional Numbers
Adding and Subtracting Fractional Numbers
Ratio
Graphs

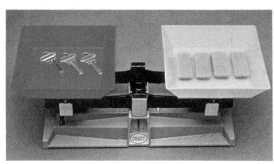

Favorite Sport

Soccer
Baseball
other
Basketball
Football
Hockey

Fractional Numbers

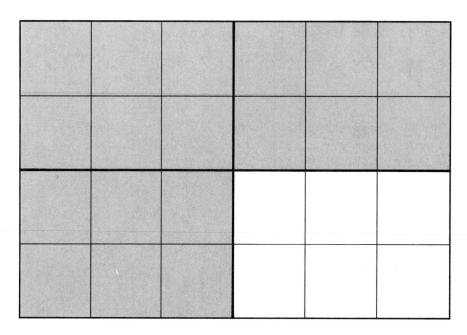

Three fourths of this rectangle is shaded.

parts shaded → $\dfrac{3}{4}$
parts in all →

Give a fractional number that tells what part of each rectangle is shaded.

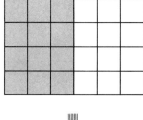   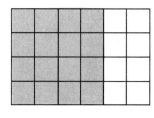   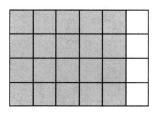

Choose some fractional number.
Shade part of a rectangle to show it.

numerator $\dfrac{3}{10}$ parts torn off
denominator parts in all

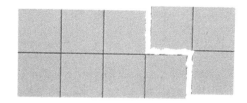

1. Which pizza has $\frac{1}{8}$ missing?

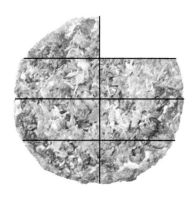  

Give a fractional number for each.

2.

3.

4.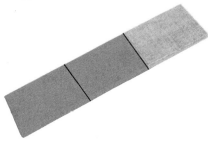

Complete the fraction that tells how much of each region is shaded.

5.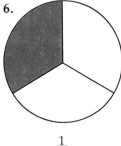

$\dfrac{||||}{3}$

6.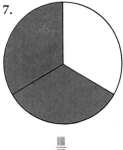

$\dfrac{1}{||||}$

7.

$\dfrac{||||}{||||}$

8.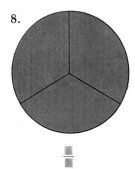

$\dfrac{||||}{||||}$

Fractional numbers—sets

What fractional part of the bottles
have been knocked down?
What fractional part of the bottles
are still standing?

$\dfrac{1}{6}$ → bottle knocked down
→ bottles in all

One sixth of the bottles have
been knocked down.

$\dfrac{5}{6}$ → bottles standing
→ bottles in all

Five sixths of the bottles
are still standing.

Give the fractional number for each ▥ .

1.

▥ are goldfish.

2.

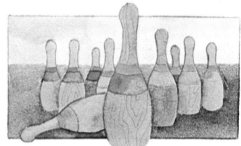

▥ are standing.

3.

▥ have 2 scoops.

4.

▥ are red.

Give the missing fractional number.

1.

||||| of the pennies are heads.

2.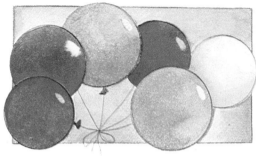

||||| of the balloons are blue.

3.

||||| of the tickets are for adults.

4

||||| of the banners are yellow.

5.

||||| of the balls are green.

6.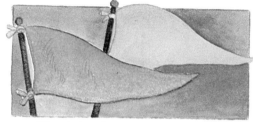

||||| of the prizes are plants.

7.

||||| of the drinks are orange.

8.

||||| of the letters are **a**'s.

The missing digits are all different. Find them.

||||| ||||| ||||| ||||| ||||| ||||| ||||| |||||
———————————————— × 9
1 1 1 1 1 1 1 1 1

Equivalent fractions

Vicki and James tossed 4 coins.
Two coins came up heads.
Two coins came up tails.

2 out of 4 coins
are heads.

Vicki said:
$\frac{2}{4}$ of the coins
came up heads.

1 out of every 2
coins are heads.

James said:
$\frac{1}{2}$ of the coins
came up heads.

$\frac{2}{4}$ and $\frac{1}{2}$ are equivalent fractions. They name the same fractional number.

We write: $\frac{2}{4} = \frac{1}{2}$

What part of these coins are heads?
Use two equivalent fractions.

What part of the coins are heads? Write two equivalent fractions.

1.

2.

Give two equivalent fractions that tell what part of each region or set is shaded.

3.

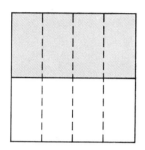

4.

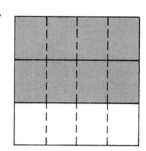

5.

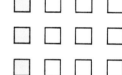

6.

7.

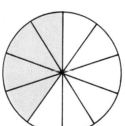

8.

Which fraction does not belong in this set?

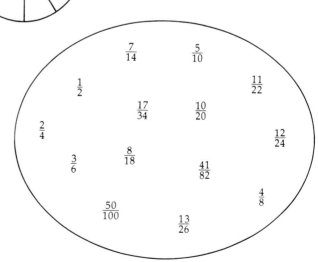

$$\frac{7}{14} \qquad \frac{5}{10}$$

$$\frac{1}{2} \qquad\qquad\qquad \frac{11}{22}$$

$$\frac{17}{34} \qquad \frac{10}{20}$$

$$\frac{2}{4} \qquad\qquad\qquad\qquad \frac{12}{24}$$

$$\frac{3}{6} \qquad \frac{8}{18} \qquad \frac{41}{82}$$

$$\frac{4}{8}$$

$$\frac{50}{100} \qquad \frac{13}{26}$$

Finding equivalent fractions

Two thirds of the blocks are blue. What is another fraction that is equivalent to $\frac{2}{3}$?

Finding the answer

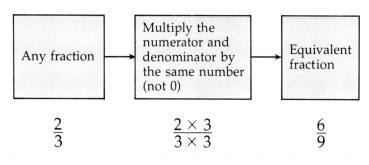

$$\frac{2}{3} \qquad \frac{2 \times 3}{3 \times 3} \qquad \frac{6}{9}$$

We write: $\frac{2}{3} = \frac{6}{9}$ $\frac{6}{9}$ is equivalent to $\frac{2}{3}$.

Other examples $\frac{2}{3} = \frac{2 \times 4}{3 \times 4} = \frac{8}{12}$ $\frac{1}{2} = \frac{1 \times 5}{2 \times 5} = \frac{5}{10}$ $\frac{3}{4} = \frac{3 \times 10}{4 \times 10} = \frac{30}{40}$

Give the missing fractions in each exercise.

1. $\frac{1 \times 1}{5 \times 1}$ $\frac{1 \times 2}{5 \times 2}$ $\frac{1 \times 3}{5 \times 3}$ $\frac{1 \times 4}{5 \times 4}$ $\frac{1 \times 5}{5 \times 5}$ $\frac{1 \times 6}{5 \times 6}$

   ↓   ↓   ↓   ↓   ↓   ↓

   $\frac{1}{5}$ $\frac{2}{10}$ ▥   ▥   ▥   ▥

2. $\frac{3 \times 1}{10 \times 1}$ $\frac{3 \times 2}{10 \times 2}$ $\frac{3 \times 3}{10 \times 3}$ $\frac{3 \times 10}{10 \times 10}$ $\frac{3 \times 100}{10 \times 100}$ $\frac{3 \times 1000}{10 \times 1000}$

   ↓   ↓   ↓   ↓   ↓   ↓

   $\frac{3}{10}$ ▥   ▥   ▥   ▥   ▥

3. $\frac{3 \times 1}{8 \times 1}$ $\frac{3 \times 2}{8 \times 2}$ $\frac{3 \times 3}{8 \times 3}$ $\frac{3 \times 10}{8 \times 10}$ $\frac{3 \times 12}{8 \times 12}$ $\frac{3 \times 50}{8 \times 50}$

   ↓   ↓   ↓   ↓   ↓   ↓

   $\frac{3}{8}$ ▥   ▥   ▥   ▥   ▥

4. $\frac{3 \times 1}{4 \times 1}$ $\frac{3 \times 2}{4 \times 2}$ $\frac{3 \times 3}{4 \times 3}$ $\frac{3 \times 10}{4 \times 10}$ $\frac{3 \times 100}{4 \times 100}$ $\frac{3 \times 1000}{4 \times 1000}$

   ↓   ↓   ↓   ↓   ↓   ↓

   $\frac{3}{4}$ ▥   ▥   ▥   ▥   ▥

Give the missing numerator.

1. $\frac{1}{2} = \frac{}{12}$ 2. $\frac{2}{3} = \frac{}{12}$ 3. $\frac{3}{4} = \frac{}{12}$ 4. $\frac{5}{6} = \frac{}{12}$ 5. $\frac{3}{10} = \frac{}{100}$

6. $\frac{7}{20} = \frac{}{100}$ 7. $\frac{4}{5} = \frac{}{100}$ 8. $\frac{3}{4} = \frac{}{100}$ 9. $\frac{1}{4} = \frac{}{36}$ 10. $\frac{5}{6} = \frac{}{36}$

11. $\frac{7}{12} = \frac{}{36}$ 12. $\frac{2}{3} = \frac{}{36}$ 13. $\frac{1}{3} = \frac{}{30}$ 14. $\frac{2}{3} = \frac{}{30}$ 15. $\frac{3}{3} = \frac{}{30}$

16. $\frac{4}{3} = \frac{}{30}$ 17. $\frac{3}{4} = \frac{}{24}$ 18. $\frac{1}{6} = \frac{}{24}$ 19. $\frac{5}{8} = \frac{}{24}$ 20. $\frac{2}{3} = \frac{}{24}$

Give equivalent fractions. Use the same denominator for each pair.

21. $\frac{1}{2} = $ 22. $\frac{3}{4} = $ 23. $\frac{2}{5} = $ 24. $\frac{1}{6} = $

  $\frac{2}{3} = $ $\frac{1}{3} = $ $\frac{1}{2} = $ $\frac{3}{5} = $

25. $\frac{1}{3} = $ 26. $\frac{1}{4} = $ 27. $\frac{2}{3} = $ 28. $\frac{3}{10} = $

  $\frac{5}{8} = $ $\frac{4}{5} = $ $\frac{2}{5} = $ $\frac{5}{6} = $

Find the missing fractions.

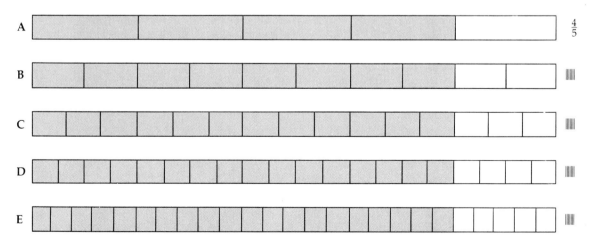

A $\frac{4}{5}$

B

C

D

E

$$\frac{15}{24} \quad \frac{2}{3} \quad \frac{5}{2} \quad \frac{5}{8} \quad \frac{10}{40}$$

$$\frac{1}{4} \quad \frac{12}{18} \quad \frac{20}{8} \quad \frac{4}{6} \quad \frac{8}{12}$$

Cross products can help you find out whether or not two fractions are equivalent.

$$\frac{3}{5} \begin{array}{c} \\ \times \\ \end{array} \frac{12}{20}$$
→ 5 × 12 = 60   The cross products $\frac{3}{5} = \frac{12}{20}$
→ 3 × 20 = 60   are equal.

Two fractions are equivalent if their cross products are equal.

$$\frac{3}{4} \begin{array}{c} \\ \times \\ \end{array} \frac{8}{12}$$
→ 4 × 8 = 32   The cross products $\frac{3}{4} \neq \frac{8}{12}$
→ 3 × 12 = 36   are not equal.

The fractions are not equivalent if their cross products are not equal.

Give the missing cross products.
Then tell whether the fractions are equivalent or not equivalent.

1. $\frac{3}{4} \times \frac{9}{12}$ → 4 × 9 = ▥
→ 3 × 12 = ▥

2. $\frac{3}{8} \times \frac{2}{5}$ → 8 × 2 = ▥
→ 3 × 5 = ▥

3. $\frac{5}{10} \times \frac{3}{6}$ → 10 × 3 = ▥
→ 5 × 6 = ▥

4. $\frac{10}{15} \times \frac{3}{4}$ → 15 × 3 = ▥
→ 10 × 4 = ▥

5. $\frac{6}{10} \times \frac{2}{3}$ → 10 × 2 = ▥
→ 6 × 3 = ▥

6. $\frac{5}{8} \times \frac{15}{24}$ → 8 × 15 = ▥
→ 5 × 24 = ▥

7. $\frac{4}{6} \times \frac{5}{8}$ → 6 × 5 = ▥
→ 4 × 8 = ▥

8. $\frac{4}{12} \times \frac{6}{18}$ → 12 × 6 = ▥
→ 4 × 18 = ▥

Write = or ≠ for each ◍.

1. $\frac{3}{4}$ ◍ $\frac{9}{12}$
2. $\frac{10}{15}$ ◍ $\frac{2}{3}$
3. $\frac{4}{5}$ ◍ $\frac{8}{10}$
4. $\frac{3}{8}$ ◍ $\frac{4}{10}$

5. $\frac{7}{21}$ ◍ $\frac{3}{9}$
6. $\frac{6}{8}$ ◍ $\frac{10}{12}$
7. $\frac{5}{10}$ ◍ $\frac{3}{6}$
8. $\frac{6}{15}$ ◍ $\frac{10}{25}$

9. $\frac{6}{9}$ ◍ $\frac{9}{12}$
10. $\frac{1}{10}$ ◍ $\frac{10}{100}$
11. $\frac{4}{15}$ ◍ $\frac{1}{3}$
12. $\frac{30}{40}$ ◍ $\frac{3}{4}$

13. $\frac{50}{100}$ ◍ $\frac{1}{2}$
14. $\frac{5}{8}$ ◍ $\frac{20}{24}$
15. $\frac{8}{10}$ ◍ $\frac{12}{25}$
16. $\frac{4}{4}$ ◍ $\frac{18}{64}$

17. $\frac{2}{3}$ ◍ $\frac{4}{9}$
18. $\frac{15}{24}$ ◍ $\frac{3}{8}$
19. $\frac{6}{5}$ ◍ $\frac{24}{30}$
20. $\frac{1}{3}$ ◍ $\frac{33}{100}$

Give the missing numerator or denominator.

Example: $\frac{2}{3} = \frac{8}{n}$ $2 \times n = 24$, $n = 12$

21. $\frac{5}{10} = \frac{4}{n}$
22. $\frac{3}{4} = \frac{9}{n}$
23. $\frac{4}{4} = \frac{n}{3}$
24. $\frac{2}{3} = \frac{10}{n}$

25. $\frac{1}{2} = \frac{6}{n}$
26. $\frac{2}{6} = \frac{n}{9}$
27. $\frac{5}{6} = \frac{10}{n}$
28. $\frac{3}{10} = \frac{n}{100}$

29. $\frac{4}{5} = \frac{12}{n}$
30. $\frac{3}{9} = \frac{n}{6}$
31. $\frac{2}{5} = \frac{10}{n}$
32. $\frac{6}{8} = \frac{3}{n}$

33. $\frac{7}{10} = \frac{70}{n}$
34. $\frac{5}{10} = \frac{7}{n}$
35. $\frac{4}{12} = \frac{2}{n}$
36. $\frac{2}{7} = \frac{6}{n}$

37. $\frac{3}{5} = \frac{n}{10}$
38. $\frac{2}{3} = \frac{n}{12}$
39. $\frac{1}{4} = \frac{6}{n}$
40. $\frac{4}{10} = \frac{n}{100}$

☆ 41. Use the fact that
$9 \times 4 = 3 \times 12$
to write different pairs
of equivalent fractions
using the numbers 9, 4,
3, and 12.

There are two different pairs of
equivalent fractions shown here.
Find them by checking cross products.

$\frac{91}{169}$ $\frac{99}{187}$ $\frac{117}{221}$ $\frac{161}{299}$

Lowest-terms fractions

The box holds 24 cans.
There are only 16 cans
in the box.
The box is $\frac{16}{24}$ full.
What is the lowest-terms
fraction for $\frac{16}{24}$?

Finding the answer

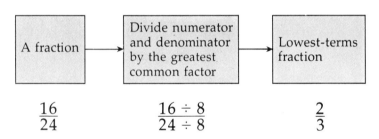

| A fraction | → | Divide numerator and denominator by the greatest common factor | → | Lowest-terms fraction |

$$\frac{16}{24} \qquad \frac{16 \div 8}{24 \div 8} \qquad \frac{2}{3}$$

The **lowest-terms** fraction for $\frac{16}{24}$ is $\frac{2}{3}$.

Other examples

$$\frac{9}{15} = \frac{9 \div 3}{15 \div 3} = \frac{3}{5} \qquad\qquad \frac{14}{20} = \frac{14 \div 2}{20 \div 2} = \frac{7}{10}$$

$$\frac{80}{100} = \frac{80 \div 20}{100 \div 20} = \frac{4}{5} \qquad\qquad \frac{15}{25} = \frac{15 \div 5}{25 \div 5} = \frac{3}{5}$$

Give the lowest-terms fraction.

1. $\frac{12}{30}$ 2. $\frac{35}{50}$ 3. $\frac{6}{16}$ 4. $\frac{15}{40}$ 5. $\frac{10}{15}$ 6. $\frac{28}{40}$

7. $\frac{4}{6}$ 8. $\frac{49}{70}$ 9. $\frac{9}{24}$ 10. $\frac{8}{12}$ 11. $\frac{50}{60}$ 12. $\frac{10}{100}$

13. $\frac{14}{21}$ 14. $\frac{10}{25}$ 15. $\frac{5}{15}$ 16. $\frac{6}{18}$ 17. $\frac{5}{20}$ 18. $\frac{90}{100}$

Find the lowest-terms fraction.

1. $\frac{5}{10}$ 2. $\frac{9}{30}$ 3. $\frac{12}{16}$ 4. $\frac{12}{20}$ 5. $\frac{25}{100}$ 6. $\frac{8}{10}$

7. $\frac{6}{18}$ 8. $\frac{25}{35}$ 9. $\frac{6}{10}$ 10. $\frac{4}{8}$ 11. $\frac{10}{16}$ 12. $\frac{5}{15}$

13. $\frac{20}{30}$ 14. $\frac{4}{6}$ 15. $\frac{40}{70}$ 16. $\frac{8}{80}$ 17. $\frac{3}{24}$ 18. $\frac{8}{20}$

19. $\frac{40}{60}$ 20. $\frac{7}{14}$ 21. $\frac{6}{8}$ 22. $\frac{10}{20}$ 23. $\frac{7}{35}$ 24. $\frac{75}{100}$

Write the lowest-terms fraction.

25. It rained $\frac{10}{30}$ of the days in April.

26. The race took $\frac{10}{60}$ of a minute.

27. Larry did $\frac{18}{20}$ of the problems.

28. $\frac{6}{30}$ of the class is in the library.

29. Laurel scored $\frac{3}{6}$ of the points.

30. John drank $\frac{250}{1000}$ liters of milk.

31. Maureen spelled $\frac{90}{100}$ of the words correctly.

32. Bonnie spent $\frac{5}{25}$ of her money.

33. Ingrid walked to school $\frac{6}{8}$ of the time.

34. Warren slept $\frac{9}{24}$ of a day.

Find a fraction that is equivalent to $\frac{3}{5}$ **and** has a denominator that is 8 more than its numerator.

More practice, page 368A, Set B

Self-check

Give a fraction that tells what part of each region
or set is shaded.

1.

2. □ △ ● △
   △ □ ●

3.

4.

5.

6. ◇ ○ ◇ ○
   ◇ ○ ◇ ○

Give the missing numerator or denominator.

7. $\frac{2}{3} = \frac{n}{12}$

8. $\frac{3}{4} = \frac{n}{8}$

9. $\frac{4}{5} = \frac{16}{n}$

Write = or ≠ for each .   10. $\frac{2}{3}$ ▥ $\frac{10}{12}$ 11. $\frac{5}{6}$ ▥ $\frac{15}{18}$

Give the lowest-terms fraction.

12. $\frac{9}{12}$ 13. $\frac{18}{27}$ 14. $\frac{50}{60}$ 15. $\frac{14}{28}$ 16. $\frac{12}{40}$

Answers for Self-check—page 245

Test

Give a fraction that tells what part of each region or set is shaded.

1.

2. △ △ △ △ △
   △ △ △ △

3.

4.

5.

6. □ □ ◇ ◇
   ◇ ◇ □ □

Give the missing numerator or denominator.

7. $\frac{5}{6} = \frac{n}{12}$

8. $\frac{7}{10} = \frac{14}{n}$

9. $\frac{2}{5} = \frac{n}{20}$

Write = or ≠ for each ▥.   10. $\frac{3}{4}$ ▥ $\frac{4}{5}$ 11. $\frac{7}{10}$ ▥ $\frac{7}{8}$

Give the lowest-terms fraction.

12. $\frac{14}{16}$ 13. $\frac{75}{100}$ 14. $\frac{81}{90}$ 15. $\frac{33}{55}$ 16. $\frac{12}{18}$

A Two Shape Puzzle

Trace and cut out 4 of these shapes.
Put them together to form
each of the figures below.

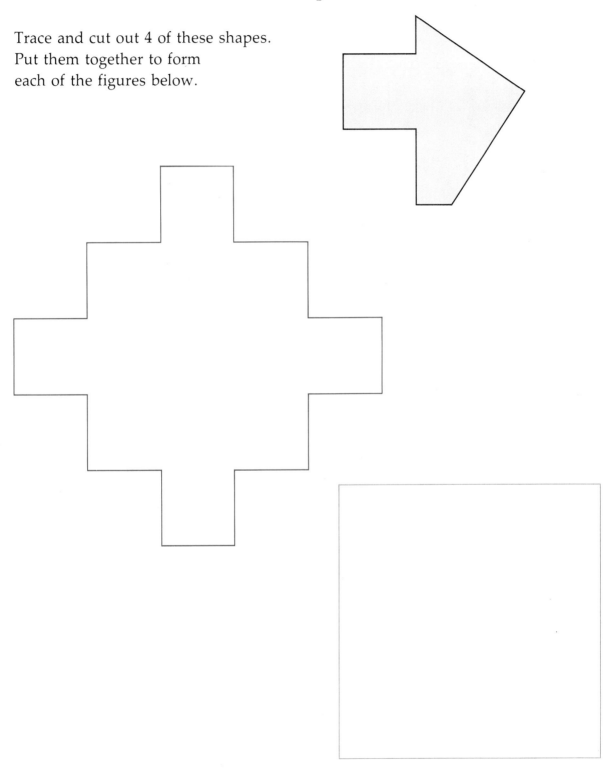

Larger Fractional Numbers

Getting started

Which pieces from the poster would you use to
show each of the numbers below?

1. $2\frac{1}{2}$ 2. $\frac{3}{2}$ 3. $2\frac{3}{4}$ 4. $\frac{6}{4}$

$2\frac{1}{2}$ ← mixed numeral
two and one half

$\frac{5}{2}$ ← improper fraction
five halves

Give the mixed numeral or improper fraction that each picture suggests.

1.

$\frac{1}{2}$ $\frac{1}{2}$ $\frac{1}{2}$

2.

$\frac{1}{2}$ $\frac{1}{2}$ $\frac{1}{2}$ $\frac{1}{2}$ $\frac{1}{2}$ $\frac{1}{2}$

3.

1       $\frac{1}{4}$

4.

1   1 $\frac{3}{4}$

5.

1            $\frac{1}{2}$

Mixed numerals to improper fractions

Marian jogged $2\frac{3}{4}$ times around the track without stopping. Express this mixed numeral as an improper fraction.

Finding the answer

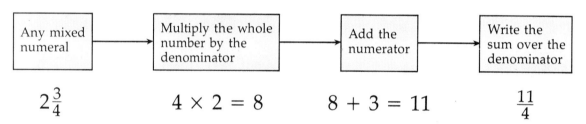

Any mixed numeral	→	Multiply the whole number by the denominator	→	Add the numerator	→	Write the sum over the denominator

$2\frac{3}{4}$ $4 \times 2 = 8$ $8 + 3 = 11$ $\frac{11}{4}$

Marian jogged $\frac{11}{4}$ times around the track.

Other examples

$2\frac{1}{5} = \frac{11}{5}$ $3\frac{7}{8} = \frac{31}{8}$ $5\frac{3}{10} = \frac{53}{10}$ $3\frac{1}{7} = \frac{22}{7}$

Express as improper fractions.

1. $1\frac{2}{3}$ 2. $3\frac{4}{5}$ 3. $2\frac{1}{2}$ 4. $1\frac{7}{8}$ 5. $3\frac{4}{5}$

6. $2\frac{9}{10}$ 7. $6\frac{7}{10}$ 8. $1\frac{75}{100}$ 9. $4\frac{1}{10}$ 10. $7\frac{5}{6}$

11. $4\frac{5}{6}$ 12. $5\frac{1}{8}$ 13. $3\frac{1}{5}$ 14. $3\frac{2}{3}$ 15. $8\frac{7}{10}$

16. $6\frac{7}{8}$ 17. $9\frac{7}{10}$ 18. $7\frac{3}{8}$ 19. $4\frac{5}{8}$ 20. $9\frac{3}{4}$

Express as improper fractions.

1. $1\frac{1}{4}$ 2. $2\frac{3}{4}$ 3. $2\frac{1}{8}$ 4. $3\frac{1}{5}$ 5. $2\frac{2}{5}$

6. $3\frac{1}{7}$ 7. $4\frac{1}{8}$ 8. $6\frac{2}{3}$ 9. $10\frac{1}{3}$ 10. $3\frac{2}{3}$

11. $1\frac{5}{6}$ 12. $5\frac{5}{8}$ 13. $7\frac{1}{2}$ 14. $6\frac{1}{10}$ 15. $7\frac{3}{4}$

16. $8\frac{3}{8}$ 17. $1\frac{9}{10}$ 18. $4\frac{4}{5}$ 19. $2\frac{7}{10}$ 20. $3\frac{3}{10}$

21. $2\frac{13}{100}$ 22. $7\frac{3}{5}$ 23. $16\frac{2}{3}$ 24. $33\frac{1}{3}$ 25. $62\frac{1}{2}$

26. John ran $4\frac{1}{5}$ times around the track. Express this number as an improper fraction.

27. Jenny swam $8\frac{1}{2}$ laps of the swimming pool. Express this number as an improper fraction.

Find the missing numbers. Is there a pattern in the answers?

$(9 - 1) \div 8 = |||||$
$(98 - 2) \div 8 = |||||$
$(987 - 3) \div 8 = |||||$
$(9876 - 4) \div 8 = |||||$
$(98\,765 - 5) \div 8 = |||||$
$(987\,654 - 6) \div 8 = |||||$
$(9\,876\,543 - 7) \div 8 = |||||$
$(98\,765\,432 - 8) \div 8 = |||||$

Renaming improper fractions as mixed numerals

Karen uses each triangle as $\frac{1}{4}$ of a square for her quilt. She has 23 triangles or $\frac{23}{4}$ squares. Express $\frac{23}{4}$ as a mixed numeral.

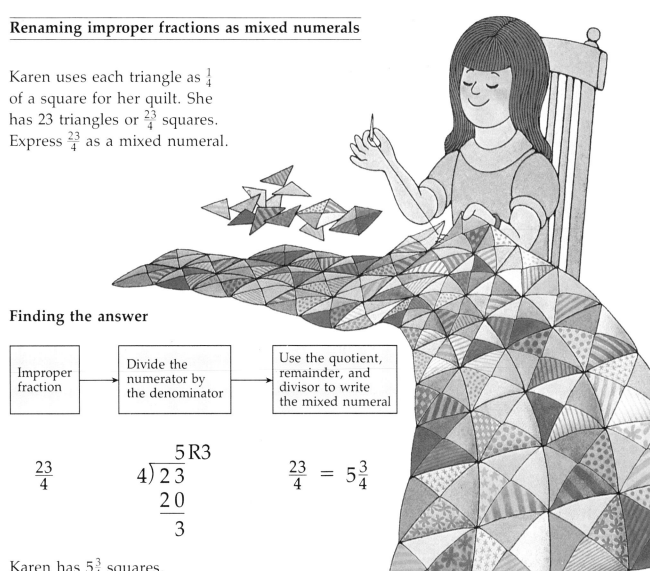

Finding the answer

Improper fraction	→	Divide the numerator by the denominator	→	Use the quotient, remainder, and divisor to write the mixed numeral

$$\frac{23}{4}$$

$$4)\overline{\begin{array}{l} 5\,R3 \\ 2\,3 \\ \underline{2\,0} \\ 3 \end{array}}$$

$$\frac{23}{4} = 5\frac{3}{4}$$

Karen has $5\frac{3}{4}$ squares.

Other examples

$$\frac{8}{3} = 2\frac{2}{3} \qquad \frac{23}{10} = 2\frac{3}{10} \qquad \frac{353}{100} = 3\frac{53}{100} \qquad \frac{20}{5} = 4$$

Express as mixed numerals.

1. $\frac{7}{5}$ 2. $\frac{13}{3}$ 3. $\frac{27}{10}$ 4. $\frac{9}{2}$ 5. $\frac{19}{8}$

6. $\frac{33}{10}$ 7. $\frac{37}{6}$ 8. $\frac{41}{20}$ 9. $\frac{11}{10}$ 10. $\frac{15}{4}$

11. $\frac{15}{8}$ 12. $\frac{12}{5}$ 13. $\frac{19}{6}$ 14. $\frac{59}{8}$ 15. $\frac{501}{100}$

16. $\frac{31}{6}$ 17. $\frac{27}{2}$ 18. $\frac{11}{8}$ 19. $\frac{25}{3}$ 20. $\frac{31}{2}$

Express each improper fraction as a mixed numeral.

1. $\frac{7}{2}$
2. $\frac{26}{3}$
3. $\frac{41}{10}$
4. $\frac{27}{5}$
5. $\frac{19}{10}$

6. $\frac{123}{100}$
7. $\frac{42}{5}$
8. $\frac{35}{8}$
9. $\frac{37}{2}$
10. $\frac{15}{4}$

11. $\frac{751}{100}$
12. $\frac{13}{2}$
13. $\frac{7}{4}$
14. $\frac{19}{8}$
15. $\frac{73}{10}$

Give a whole number for each improper fraction.

16. $\frac{2}{1}$
17. $\frac{8}{2}$
18. $\frac{14}{2}$
19. $\frac{20}{10}$
20. $\frac{18}{3}$

21. $\frac{24}{2}$
22. $\frac{12}{3}$
23. $\frac{50}{10}$
24. $\frac{700}{100}$
25. $\frac{54}{6}$

26. $\frac{1}{1}$
27. $\frac{100}{25}$
28. $\frac{27}{3}$
29. $\frac{0}{4}$
30. $\frac{40}{5}$

Express as mixed numerals, with lowest-terms fractions.
Example: $\frac{14}{4} = 3\frac{2}{4} = 3\frac{1}{2}$

31. $\frac{12}{8}$
32. $\frac{22}{4}$
33. $\frac{16}{6}$
34. $\frac{24}{10}$
35. $\frac{12}{9}$

36. $\frac{27}{12}$
37. $\frac{32}{6}$
38. $\frac{26}{8}$
39. $\frac{33}{15}$
40. $\frac{38}{10}$

41. Josie uses a triangle of cloth as $\frac{1}{6}$ of a hexagon for her quilt. She has 17 triangles or $\frac{17}{6}$ hexagons. Express $\frac{17}{6}$ as a mixed numeral.

Think!

Write a symbol for 100 using four 9's.

9   9   9   9

Comparing fractional numbers

Shaded parts of regions can help you compare fractional numbers that have the same denominator.

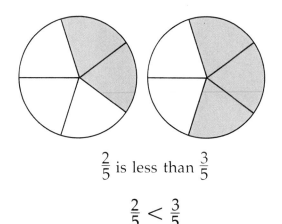

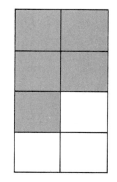 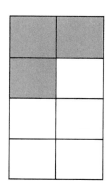

$\frac{2}{5}$ is less than $\frac{3}{5}$

$$\frac{2}{5} < \frac{3}{5}$$

$\frac{5}{8}$ is greater than $\frac{3}{8}$

$$\frac{5}{8} > \frac{3}{8}$$

Study these examples, comparing fractions with different denominators.

Compare $\frac{2}{3}$ and $\frac{4}{5}$

$$\begin{array}{cc} \frac{2}{3} & \frac{4}{5} \\ \downarrow & \downarrow \\ \frac{10}{15} & \frac{12}{15} \end{array} \quad \frac{10}{15} < \frac{12}{15} \text{ so } \frac{2}{3} < \frac{4}{5}$$

Compare $\frac{1}{3}$ and $\frac{3}{10}$

$$\begin{array}{cc} \frac{1}{3} & \frac{3}{10} \\ \downarrow & \downarrow \\ \frac{10}{30} & \frac{9}{30} \end{array} \quad \frac{10}{30} > \frac{9}{30} \text{ so } \frac{1}{3} > \frac{3}{10}$$

Give the correct sign, $>$ or $<$, for each ▥ .

1. $\frac{1}{2}$ ▥ $\frac{2}{5}$
$$\begin{array}{cc} \downarrow & \downarrow \\ \frac{5}{10} & \frac{4}{10} \end{array}$$

2. $\frac{2}{3}$ ▥ $\frac{3}{4}$
$$\begin{array}{cc} \downarrow & \downarrow \\ \frac{8}{12} & \frac{9}{12} \end{array}$$

3. $\frac{3}{8}$ ▥ $\frac{1}{6}$
$$\begin{array}{cc} \downarrow & \downarrow \\ \frac{9}{24} & \frac{4}{24} \end{array}$$

4. $\frac{1}{2}$ ▥ $\frac{3}{7}$
$$\begin{array}{cc} \downarrow & \downarrow \\ \frac{7}{14} & \frac{6}{14} \end{array}$$

5. $\frac{5}{6}$ ▥ $\frac{7}{12}$
$$\begin{array}{cc} \downarrow & \downarrow \\ \frac{10}{12} & \frac{7}{12} \end{array}$$

6. $\frac{7}{8}$ ▥ $\frac{9}{10}$
$$\begin{array}{cc} \downarrow & \downarrow \\ \frac{35}{40} & \frac{36}{40} \end{array}$$

7. $\frac{2}{3}$ ▥ $\frac{5}{6}$
$$\begin{array}{cc} \downarrow & \downarrow \\ \frac{4}{6} & \frac{5}{6} \end{array}$$

8. $\frac{1}{2}$ ▥ $\frac{5}{8}$
$$\begin{array}{cc} \downarrow & \downarrow \\ \frac{4}{8} & \frac{5}{8} \end{array}$$

9. $\frac{2}{3}$ ▥ $\frac{5}{8}$
$$\begin{array}{cc} \downarrow & \downarrow \\ \frac{16}{24} & \frac{15}{24} \end{array}$$

Give the correct sign, > or <, for each  .

1. $\frac{1}{2}$ ⬤ $\frac{2}{3}$ 2. $\frac{4}{5}$ ⬤ $\frac{3}{4}$ 3. $\frac{3}{10}$ ⬤ $\frac{2}{5}$

4. $\frac{5}{8}$ ⬤ $\frac{3}{4}$ 5. $\frac{1}{5}$ ⬤ $\frac{1}{4}$ 6. $\frac{1}{3}$ ⬤ $\frac{2}{3}$

7. $\frac{5}{6}$ ⬤ $\frac{11}{12}$ 8. $\frac{7}{8}$ ⬤ $\frac{7}{10}$ 9. $\frac{1}{3}$ ⬤ $\frac{1}{2}$

10. $\frac{5}{8}$ ⬤ $\frac{7}{8}$ 11. $\frac{1}{2}$ ⬤ $\frac{7}{16}$ 12. $\frac{7}{10}$ ⬤ $\frac{3}{4}$

13. $\frac{1}{5}$ ⬤ $\frac{21}{100}$ 14. $\frac{1}{4}$ ⬤ $\frac{1}{3}$ 15. $\frac{1}{6}$ ⬤ $\frac{1}{8}$

16. $\frac{5}{12}$ ⬤ $\frac{1}{3}$ 17. $\frac{5}{8}$ ⬤ $\frac{1}{2}$ 18. $\frac{3}{10}$ ⬤ $\frac{9}{10}$

19. $\frac{9}{16}$ ⬤ $\frac{3}{4}$ 20. $\frac{1}{4}$ ⬤ $\frac{1}{6}$ 21. $\frac{7}{10}$ ⬤ $\frac{69}{100}$

22. Vicki erased $\frac{3}{8}$ of the blackboard. Jason erased $\frac{1}{2}$ of the blackboard. Who erased the smaller part?

23. Gary mowed $\frac{1}{3}$ of the lawn. Arlene mowed $\frac{1}{4}$ of the lawn. Who mowed the larger part?

Each of these fractions has a simple lowest-terms fraction. What is it?

1. $\frac{6381}{57429}$ 2. $\frac{3942}{15768}$ 3. $\frac{5823}{17469}$

4. $\frac{6729}{13458}$ 5. $\frac{2943}{17658}$ 6. $\frac{2394}{16758}$

7. $\frac{5963}{23852}$ 8. $\frac{2769}{13845}$

Answers for Self-check 1. $\frac{3}{2}$ 2. $\frac{11}{4}$ 3. $\frac{73}{10}$ 4. $\frac{33}{8}$ 5. $\frac{17}{3}$ 6. $3\frac{2}{5}$ 7. $2\frac{7}{10}$ 8. $1\frac{9}{100}$ 9. $4\frac{2}{3}$ 10. $5\frac{1}{4}$
11. < 12. > 13. > 14. > 15. < 16. > 17. < 18. <

Self-check

Express as improper fractions.

1. $1\frac{1}{2}$

2. $2\frac{3}{4}$

3. $7\frac{3}{10}$

4. $4\frac{1}{8}$

5. $5\frac{2}{3}$

Express as mixed numerals.

6. $\frac{17}{5}$

7. $\frac{27}{10}$

8. $\frac{109}{100}$

9. $\frac{14}{3}$

10. $\frac{21}{4}$

Give the correct symbol, > or <, for each ▒.

11. $\frac{7}{10}$ ▒ $\frac{9}{10}$

12. $\frac{7}{8}$ ▒ $\frac{5}{8}$

13. $\frac{2}{5}$ ▒ $\frac{3}{10}$

14. $\frac{3}{4}$ ▒ $\frac{1}{2}$

15. $\frac{7}{9}$ ▒ $\frac{5}{6}$

16. $\frac{1}{3}$ ▒ $\frac{1}{4}$

17. $\frac{2}{3}$ ▒ $\frac{3}{4}$

18. $\frac{1}{8}$ ▒ $\frac{1}{4}$

Answers for Self-check—page 255

Test

Express as improper fractions.

1. $4\frac{2}{3}$

2. $2\frac{7}{10}$

3. $3\frac{1}{2}$

4. $6\frac{1}{4}$

5. $9\frac{2}{5}$

Express as mixed numerals.

6. $\frac{23}{10}$

7. $\frac{15}{4}$

8. $\frac{131}{100}$

9. $\frac{22}{5}$

10. $\frac{23}{4}$

Give the correct symbol, > or <, for each ▒.

11. $\frac{5}{12}$ ▒ $\frac{7}{12}$

12. $\frac{3}{4}$ ▒ $\frac{1}{4}$

13. $\frac{1}{3}$ ▒ $\frac{1}{2}$

14. $\frac{4}{5}$ ▒ $\frac{9}{10}$

15. $\frac{1}{5}$ ▒ $\frac{1}{4}$

16. $\frac{4}{5}$ ▒ $\frac{5}{8}$

17. $\frac{2}{9}$ ▒ $\frac{3}{8}$

18. $\frac{1}{6}$ ▒ $\frac{1}{5}$

Star Nim

This game is for two players.
Place a counter on each star.
The players take turns picking up 1 or 2 counters.
A player may take 2 counters only if the stars
under the counters are connected by a line.
The player who picks up the last counter is the winner.

Adding and Subtracting Fractional Numbers

Think of this rectangle as the unit.
Trace and cut out each colored piece.

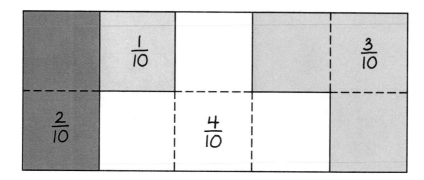

Which pieces of the unit rectangle would cover each
of these regions?

A

B

C

D

$$\frac{2}{10} + \frac{1}{10} = \frac{3}{10}$$

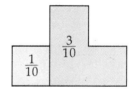

$$\frac{1}{10} + \frac{3}{10} = \frac{4}{10}$$

Write an addition equation for each figure.

1.

2.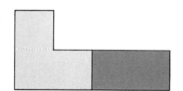

3.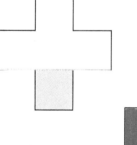

5.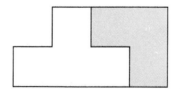

6.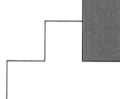

4.

Add.

7. $\frac{1}{10} + \frac{1}{10} = n$

8. $\frac{2}{10} + \frac{3}{10} = n$

9. $\frac{2}{10} + \frac{7}{10} = n$

10. $\frac{5}{10} + \frac{2}{10} = n$

11. $\frac{7}{10} + \frac{3}{10} = n$

12. $\frac{6}{10} + \frac{4}{10} = n$

Adding fractional numbers

Carol has painted $\frac{4}{10}$ of the fence.
Bonnie has painted $\frac{3}{10}$ of the fence.
How much of the fence
have they painted?

Finding the answer

Two fractions with the same denominator	→	Add the numerators	→	Write the sum over the denominator

$$\frac{4}{10} + \frac{3}{10} \qquad 4 + 3 = 7 \qquad \frac{7}{10}$$

They have painted $\frac{7}{10}$ of the fence.

Other examples

$$\frac{5}{12} + \frac{9}{12} = \frac{14}{12} = 1\frac{1}{6}$$

$$\begin{array}{r} \frac{3}{8} \\ + \frac{2}{8} \\ \hline \frac{5}{8} \end{array} \qquad \begin{array}{r} \frac{9}{10} \\ + \frac{7}{10} \\ \hline \frac{16}{10} = 1\frac{6}{10} = 1\frac{3}{5} \end{array}$$

Find the sums.

1. $\frac{3}{8} + \frac{4}{8}$ 2. $\frac{1}{6} + \frac{1}{6}$ 3. $\frac{2}{10} + \frac{1}{10}$ 4. $\frac{3}{16} + \frac{9}{16}$

5. $\frac{1}{8} + \frac{5}{8}$ 6. $\frac{1}{3} + \frac{1}{3}$ 7. $\frac{3}{5} + \frac{4}{5}$ 8. $\frac{7}{10} + \frac{8}{10}$

9. $\frac{1}{4} + \frac{1}{4}$ 10. $\frac{5}{12} + \frac{2}{12}$ 11. $\frac{5}{8} + \frac{1}{8}$ 12. $\frac{4}{9} + \frac{3}{9}$

13. $\begin{array}{r} \frac{1}{8} \\ + \frac{2}{8} \\ \hline \end{array}$ 14. $\begin{array}{r} \frac{5}{6} \\ + \frac{3}{6} \\ \hline \end{array}$ 15. $\begin{array}{r} \frac{2}{5} \\ + \frac{4}{5} \\ \hline \end{array}$ 16. $\begin{array}{r} \frac{3}{10} \\ + \frac{7}{10} \\ \hline \end{array}$

17. $\begin{array}{r} \frac{4}{10} \\ + \frac{5}{10} \\ \hline \end{array}$ 18. $\begin{array}{r} \frac{2}{4} \\ + \frac{1}{4} \\ \hline \end{array}$ 19. $\begin{array}{r} \frac{14}{15} \\ + \frac{7}{15} \\ \hline \end{array}$ 20. $\begin{array}{r} \frac{5}{12} \\ + \frac{11}{12} \\ \hline \end{array}$

Add.

1. $\frac{1}{5} + \frac{3}{5}$ 2. $\frac{3}{8} + \frac{3}{8}$ 3. $\frac{1}{10} + \frac{7}{10}$ 4. $\frac{5}{12} + \frac{8}{12}$

5. $\begin{array}{r} \frac{3}{4} \\ + \frac{3}{4} \\ \hline \end{array}$ 6. $\begin{array}{r} \frac{8}{5} \\ + \frac{2}{5} \\ \hline \end{array}$ 7. $\begin{array}{r} \frac{15}{24} \\ + \frac{7}{24} \\ \hline \end{array}$ 8. $\begin{array}{r} \frac{7}{16} \\ + \frac{3}{16} \\ \hline \end{array}$

9. $\begin{array}{r} \frac{9}{10} \\ + \frac{3}{10} \\ \hline \end{array}$ 10. $\begin{array}{r} \frac{4}{6} \\ + \frac{2}{6} \\ \hline \end{array}$ 11. $\begin{array}{r} \frac{7}{8} \\ + \frac{5}{8} \\ \hline \end{array}$ 12. $\begin{array}{r} \frac{5}{6} \\ + \frac{5}{6} \\ \hline \end{array}$

13. $\begin{array}{r} 6\frac{1}{5} \\ + 7\frac{2}{5} \\ \hline \end{array}$ 14. $\begin{array}{r} 1\frac{1}{4} \\ + 6\frac{1}{4} \\ \hline \end{array}$ 15. $\begin{array}{r} 3\frac{5}{8} \\ + 2\frac{1}{8} \\ \hline \end{array}$ 16. $\begin{array}{r} 7\frac{1}{10} \\ + 4\frac{2}{10} \\ \hline \end{array}$

17. $\begin{array}{r} 10\frac{1}{3} \\ + 12\frac{1}{3} \\ \hline \end{array}$ 18. $\begin{array}{r} 16\frac{2}{8} \\ + 17\frac{3}{8} \\ \hline \end{array}$ 19. $\begin{array}{r} 23\frac{3}{10} \\ + 47\frac{3}{10} \\ \hline \end{array}$ 20. $\begin{array}{r} 58\frac{13}{100} \\ + 47\frac{57}{100} \\ \hline \end{array}$

21. $\begin{array}{r} 158\frac{1}{4} \\ + 236\frac{1}{4} \\ \hline \end{array}$ 22. $\begin{array}{r} 309\frac{5}{8} \\ + 644\frac{2}{8} \\ \hline \end{array}$ 23. $\begin{array}{r} 18\frac{5}{10} \\ + 39\frac{4}{10} \\ \hline \end{array}$ 24. $\begin{array}{r} 66\frac{1}{3} \\ + 79\frac{1}{3} \\ \hline \end{array}$

25. Chris ran $2\frac{3}{10}$ km.
She walked $1\frac{1}{10}$ km.
How far in all?

26. Paul painted for $1\frac{1}{3}$ hours on Wednesday.
He painted for $2\frac{1}{3}$ hours on Thursday.
How many hours in all?

There are 16 girls and 14 boys in one class. 20 of the children ride the bus.

1. Is it possible that all the girls ride the bus?

2. What is the least number of girls that might ride the bus?

3. What is the least number of boys that might ride the bus?

Subtracting fractional numbers

A water tank was $\frac{7}{8}$ full of water. After a day of use, it was $\frac{3}{8}$ full. What part of the tank of water was used during the day?

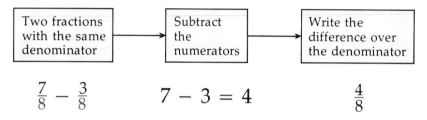

Finding the answer

Two fractions with the same denominator	→	Subtract the numerators	→	Write the difference over the denominator

$$\frac{7}{8} - \frac{3}{8} \qquad\qquad 7 - 3 = 4 \qquad\qquad \frac{4}{8}$$

During the day, $\frac{4}{8}$ or $\frac{1}{2}$ of the tank of water was used.

Other examples

$$\frac{11}{12} - \frac{3}{12} = \frac{8}{12} = \frac{2}{3}$$

$$\begin{array}{r} \frac{9}{16} \\ -\frac{5}{16} \\ \hline \frac{4}{16} = \frac{1}{4} \end{array} \qquad \begin{array}{r} 5\frac{3}{4} \\ -3\frac{2}{4} \\ \hline 2\frac{1}{4} \end{array} \qquad \begin{array}{r} 4\frac{9}{10} \\ -2\frac{3}{10} \\ \hline 2\frac{6}{10} = 2\frac{3}{5} \end{array}$$

Find the differences.

1. $\frac{4}{5} - \frac{1}{5}$
2. $\frac{3}{6} - \frac{2}{6}$
3. $\frac{2}{3} - \frac{1}{3}$
4. $\frac{3}{4} - \frac{1}{4}$

5. $\frac{7}{10} - \frac{5}{10}$
6. $\frac{7}{10} - \frac{4}{10}$
7. $\frac{5}{8} - \frac{1}{8}$
8. $\frac{6}{7} - \frac{3}{7}$

9. $\frac{10}{15} - \frac{4}{15}$
10. $\frac{13}{16} - \frac{9}{16}$
11. $\frac{11}{12} - \frac{4}{12}$
12. $\frac{5}{6} - \frac{3}{6}$

13. $\begin{array}{r} \frac{3}{8} \\ -\frac{1}{8} \\ \hline \end{array}$
14. $\begin{array}{r} \frac{8}{10} \\ -\frac{3}{10} \\ \hline \end{array}$
15. $\begin{array}{r} \frac{7}{8} \\ -\frac{4}{8} \\ \hline \end{array}$
16. $\begin{array}{r} \frac{14}{16} \\ -\frac{9}{16} \\ \hline \end{array}$

17. $\begin{array}{r} \frac{5}{7} \\ -\frac{2}{7} \\ \hline \end{array}$
18. $\begin{array}{r} \frac{17}{20} \\ -\frac{9}{20} \\ \hline \end{array}$
19. $\begin{array}{r} \frac{13}{15} \\ -\frac{4}{15} \\ \hline \end{array}$
20. $\begin{array}{r} \frac{8}{9} \\ -\frac{2}{9} \\ \hline \end{array}$

Subtract.

1. $\dfrac{5}{8} - \dfrac{1}{8}$ 2. $\dfrac{7}{10} - \dfrac{5}{10}$ 3. $\dfrac{5}{6} - \dfrac{4}{6}$ 4. $\dfrac{9}{16} - \dfrac{1}{16}$

5. $\dfrac{7}{12} - \dfrac{4}{12}$ 6. $\dfrac{7}{5} - \dfrac{4}{5}$ 7. $\dfrac{13}{8} - \dfrac{7}{8}$ 8. $\dfrac{5}{3} - \dfrac{2}{3}$

9. $\begin{array}{r} \frac{8}{10} \\ -\frac{3}{10} \\ \hline \end{array}$ 10. $\begin{array}{r} \frac{15}{16} \\ -\frac{3}{16} \\ \hline \end{array}$ 11. $\begin{array}{r} \frac{8}{3} \\ -\frac{5}{3} \\ \hline \end{array}$ 12. $\begin{array}{r} \frac{5}{2} \\ -\frac{1}{2} \\ \hline \end{array}$

13. $\begin{array}{r} 7\frac{3}{4} \\ -2\frac{1}{4} \\ \hline \end{array}$ 14. $\begin{array}{r} 6\frac{4}{5} \\ -3\frac{2}{5} \\ \hline \end{array}$ 15. $\begin{array}{r} 12\frac{9}{10} \\ -9\frac{3}{10} \\ \hline \end{array}$ 16. $\begin{array}{r} 16\frac{7}{8} \\ -8\frac{1}{8} \\ \hline \end{array}$

17. $\begin{array}{r} 13\frac{2}{3} \\ -9\frac{1}{3} \\ \hline \end{array}$ 18. $\begin{array}{r} 21\frac{7}{10} \\ -16\frac{5}{10} \\ \hline \end{array}$ 19. $\begin{array}{r} 126\frac{5}{8} \\ -97\frac{3}{8} \\ \hline \end{array}$ 20. $\begin{array}{r} 215\frac{3}{8} \\ -176\frac{1}{8} \\ \hline \end{array}$

21. $\begin{array}{r} 72\frac{1}{2} \\ -66\frac{1}{2} \\ \hline \end{array}$ 22. $\begin{array}{r} 83\frac{9}{10} \\ -44\frac{8}{10} \\ \hline \end{array}$ 23. $\begin{array}{r} 100\frac{3}{10} \\ -65\frac{1}{10} \\ \hline \end{array}$ 24. $\begin{array}{r} 67\frac{4}{5} \\ -38\frac{1}{5} \\ \hline \end{array}$

25. Had $\frac{7}{10}$ of a pitcher of water. Drank $\frac{3}{10}$. How much was left?

26. Watered the front lawn in $\frac{1}{4}$ hour. Watered the back lawn in $\frac{3}{4}$ hour. How much longer did it take to water the back lawn?

Pick a 3-digit number.   351
Repeat it to make a 6-digit number.   351 351

Divide by 7. $\begin{array}{r} 50\,193 \\ 7\overline{)351\,351} \end{array}$

Divide by your starting number. $\begin{array}{r} 143 \\ 351\overline{)50\,193} \end{array}$

Divide by 11. $\begin{array}{r} 13 \\ 11\overline{)143} \end{array}$

Try again with a different number.
Will your answer always be the same?

More practice, page 369, Set B

Adding with unlike denominators

Jim tossed two fraction cubes.
He added the two numbers
on the top faces.
What was the sum?

Finding the answer

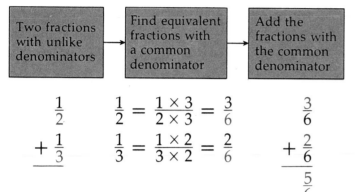

Two fractions with unlike denominators	→	Find equivalent fractions with a common denominator	→	Add the fractions with the common denominator

$$\frac{1}{2}$$
$$+\frac{1}{3}$$

$$\frac{1}{2} = \frac{1 \times 3}{2 \times 3} = \frac{3}{6}$$
$$\frac{1}{3} = \frac{1 \times 2}{3 \times 2} = \frac{2}{6}$$

$$\frac{3}{6}$$
$$+\frac{2}{6}$$
$$\frac{5}{6}$$

Jim's sum was $\frac{5}{6}$.

Common denominators of 12, 18, 24, or larger numbers
could have been used to find the sum $\frac{1}{2} + \frac{1}{3}$.

$$\frac{1}{2} = \frac{6}{12}$$
$$+\frac{1}{3} = \frac{4}{12}$$
$$\frac{10}{12} = \frac{5}{6}$$

$$\frac{1}{2} = \frac{9}{18}$$
$$+\frac{1}{3} = \frac{6}{18}$$
$$\frac{15}{18} = \frac{5}{6}$$

$$\frac{1}{2} = \frac{12}{24}$$
$$+\frac{1}{3} = \frac{8}{24}$$
$$\frac{20}{24} = \frac{5}{6}$$

All the sums are equivalent to $\frac{5}{6}$.
The **least common denominator** for $\frac{1}{2}$ and $\frac{1}{3}$ is 6.

Other examples

$$\frac{1}{4} = \frac{3}{12}$$
$$+\frac{2}{3} = \frac{8}{12}$$
$$\frac{11}{12}$$

$$\frac{1}{2} = \frac{5}{10}$$
$$+\frac{3}{5} = \frac{6}{10}$$
$$\frac{11}{10} = 1\frac{1}{10}$$

$$\frac{1}{3} = \frac{4}{12}$$
$$+\frac{3}{4} = \frac{9}{12}$$
$$\frac{13}{12} = 1\frac{1}{12}$$

Find the sums.

1. $\dfrac{2}{5}$
    $+\dfrac{7}{10}$

2. $\dfrac{5}{8}$
    $+\dfrac{3}{16}$

3. $\dfrac{3}{10}$
    $+\dfrac{4}{5}$

4. $\dfrac{3}{8}$
    $+\dfrac{1}{2}$

5. $\dfrac{1}{2}$
    $+\dfrac{4}{5}$

6. $\dfrac{9}{10}$
    $+\dfrac{3}{100}$

7. $\dfrac{3}{4}$
    $+\dfrac{1}{2}$

8. $\dfrac{1}{4}$
    $+\dfrac{37}{100}$

9. $\dfrac{5}{12}$
    $+\dfrac{1}{3}$

10. $\dfrac{9}{100}$
    $+\dfrac{9}{10}$

11. $\dfrac{8}{15}$
    $+\dfrac{4}{15}$

12. $\dfrac{1}{3}$
    $+\dfrac{5}{6}$

13. $\dfrac{3}{4}$
    $+\dfrac{7}{16}$

14. $\dfrac{1}{4}$
    $+\dfrac{1}{5}$

15. $\dfrac{3}{4}$
    $+\dfrac{5}{8}$

16. $\dfrac{27}{100}$
    $+\dfrac{251}{1000}$

17. $\dfrac{3}{10}$
    $+\dfrac{7}{20}$

18. $\dfrac{1}{4}$
    $+\dfrac{2}{3}$

19. $\dfrac{7}{8}$
    $+\dfrac{7}{16}$

20. $\dfrac{3}{10}$
    $+\dfrac{49}{100}$

21. $\dfrac{1}{8} + \dfrac{3}{4}$

22. $\dfrac{1}{2} + \dfrac{7}{10}$

23. $\dfrac{9}{10} + \dfrac{4}{5}$

24. $\dfrac{17}{100} + \dfrac{7}{10}$

25. $\dfrac{3}{4} + \dfrac{7}{8}$

26. Brian tossed these cubes.

What is Brian's total?

27. Tracy tossed the cubes.

What is Tracy's total?

☆ 28. Mark the faces of two cubes with these fractions, $\dfrac{1}{2}, \dfrac{1}{4}, \dfrac{3}{4}, \dfrac{1}{3}, \dfrac{2}{3}, \dfrac{3}{10}, \dfrac{2}{5}, \dfrac{9}{10}, \dfrac{1}{5}, \dfrac{4}{5}, \dfrac{3}{5}, \dfrac{7}{10}$. Play a fraction game with a classmate.

Think!

Arrange 24 toothpicks as in the figure below.

1. Pick up 8 toothpicks and have 5 small squares left.
2. Pick up 4 toothpicks and have 5 small squares left.

Subtracting with unlike denominators

Kay tossed the fraction cubes.
Then she subtracted the
two numbers for her score.
What was her score?

Finding the answer

Fractions with unlike denominators	→	Find equivalent fractions with a common denominator	→	Subtract the fractions with a common denominator

$$\frac{3}{4}$$
$$-\frac{1}{3}$$

$$\frac{3}{4} = \frac{3 \times 3}{4 \times 3} = \frac{9}{12}$$
$$\frac{1}{3} = \frac{1 \times 4}{3 \times 4} = \frac{4}{12}$$

$$\frac{9}{12}$$
$$-\frac{4}{12}$$
$$\frac{5}{12}$$

Kay's score was $\frac{5}{12}$.

Other examples

$$\frac{7}{10} = \frac{7}{10}$$
$$-\frac{1}{2} = \frac{5}{10}$$
$$\frac{2}{10} = \frac{1}{5}$$

$$\frac{9}{10} = \frac{18}{20}$$
$$-\frac{3}{4} = \frac{15}{20}$$
$$\frac{3}{20}$$

$$\frac{7}{10} = \frac{70}{100}$$
$$-\frac{37}{100} = \frac{37}{100}$$
$$\frac{33}{100}$$

Find the differences.

1. $\frac{1}{2}$
    $-\frac{1}{8}$

2. $\frac{3}{8}$
    $-\frac{1}{4}$

3. $\frac{9}{10}$
    $-\frac{1}{2}$

4. $\frac{3}{4}$
    $-\frac{1}{2}$

5. $\frac{7}{10}$
    $-\frac{2}{5}$

6. $\frac{1}{3}$
    $-\frac{1}{6}$

7. $\frac{7}{8}$
    $-\frac{3}{4}$

8. $\frac{4}{5}$
    $-\frac{1}{10}$

9. $\frac{5}{6}$
    $-\frac{1}{3}$

10. $\frac{1}{2}$
    $-\frac{3}{8}$

Subtract.

1. $\dfrac{1}{2}$
   $-\dfrac{1}{5}$

2. $\dfrac{3}{8}$
   $-\dfrac{1}{4}$

3. $\dfrac{7}{8}$
   $-\dfrac{1}{2}$

4. $\dfrac{2}{3}$
   $-\dfrac{1}{2}$

5. $\dfrac{7}{10}$
   $-\dfrac{1}{5}$

6. $\dfrac{13}{10}$
   $-\dfrac{1}{4}$

7. $\dfrac{1}{3}$
   $-\dfrac{1}{12}$

8. $\dfrac{2}{3}$
   $-\dfrac{1}{4}$

9. $\dfrac{9}{10}$
   $-\dfrac{3}{5}$

10. $\dfrac{5}{2}$
    $-\dfrac{5}{8}$

11. $\dfrac{17}{100}$
    $-\dfrac{1}{10}$

12. $\dfrac{9}{10}$
    $-\dfrac{87}{100}$

13. $\dfrac{1}{2}$
    $-\dfrac{347}{1000}$

14. $\dfrac{87}{100}$
    $-\dfrac{3}{4}$

15. $\dfrac{15}{16}$
    $-\dfrac{7}{8}$

16. $\dfrac{2}{3}$
    $-\dfrac{1}{6}$

17. $\dfrac{3}{5}$
    $-\dfrac{3}{10}$

18. $\dfrac{11}{8}$
    $-\dfrac{1}{2}$

19. $\dfrac{19}{20}$
    $-\dfrac{3}{4}$

20. $\dfrac{9}{16}$
    $-\dfrac{1}{4}$

21. $\dfrac{7}{10} - \dfrac{3}{100}$

22. $\dfrac{5}{12} - \dfrac{1}{3}$

23. $\dfrac{21}{100} - \dfrac{177}{1000}$

24. $\dfrac{5}{3} - \dfrac{1}{2}$

25. $\dfrac{83}{100} - \dfrac{7}{10}$

26. Pat tossed these cubes.

What is the difference?

27. Michelle tossed these cubes.

What is the difference?

☆ 28. Make a pair of fraction cubes.
Play a "Difference of Fractions"
game with a classmate.

Think!

Complete this Fraction
Magic Square.

$\dfrac{2}{5}$	$\dfrac{1}{20}$	
$\dfrac{3}{20}$		
$\dfrac{1}{5}$		$\dfrac{1}{10}$

Each row, column, and
diagonal have the same sum.

Answers for Self-check 1. $\dfrac{5}{8}$ 2. $\dfrac{8}{10}$ or $\dfrac{4}{5}$ 3. $\dfrac{3}{4}$ 4. $\dfrac{7}{8}$ 5. $9\dfrac{4}{10}$ or $9\dfrac{2}{5}$ 6. $21\dfrac{4}{8}$ or $21\dfrac{1}{2}$ 7. $\dfrac{3}{6}$ or $\dfrac{1}{2}$ 8. $\dfrac{11}{14}$
9. $\dfrac{3}{10}$ 10. $\dfrac{5}{16}$ 11. $\dfrac{3}{10}$ 12. $\dfrac{1}{4}$ 13. $7\dfrac{2}{8}$ or $7\dfrac{1}{4}$ 14. $7\dfrac{2}{10}$ or $7\dfrac{1}{5}$ 15. $\dfrac{2}{6}$ or $\dfrac{1}{3}$ 16. $\dfrac{5}{16}$

Self-check

Add.

1. $\frac{2}{8} + \frac{3}{8}$

2. $\frac{3}{10} + \frac{5}{10}$

3. $\frac{1}{2} + \frac{1}{4}$

4. $\frac{3}{4} + \frac{1}{8}$

5. $\begin{array}{r} 5\frac{3}{10} \\ + 4\frac{1}{10} \\ \hline \end{array}$

6. $\begin{array}{r} 12\frac{3}{8} \\ + 9\frac{1}{8} \\ \hline \end{array}$

7. $\begin{array}{r} \frac{1}{3} \\ + \frac{1}{6} \\ \hline \end{array}$

8. $\begin{array}{r} \frac{1}{2} \\ + \frac{2}{7} \\ \hline \end{array}$

Subtract.

9. $\begin{array}{r} \frac{9}{10} \\ - \frac{6}{10} \\ \hline \end{array}$

10. $\begin{array}{r} \frac{11}{16} \\ - \frac{6}{16} \\ \hline \end{array}$

11. $\begin{array}{r} \frac{7}{10} \\ - \frac{2}{5} \\ \hline \end{array}$

12. $\begin{array}{r} \frac{1}{2} \\ - \frac{1}{4} \\ \hline \end{array}$

13. $\begin{array}{r} 10\frac{7}{8} \\ - 3\frac{5}{8} \\ \hline \end{array}$

14. $\begin{array}{r} 16\frac{7}{10} \\ - 9\frac{5}{10} \\ \hline \end{array}$

15. $\begin{array}{r} \frac{1}{2} \\ - \frac{1}{6} \\ \hline \end{array}$

16. $\begin{array}{r} \frac{13}{16} \\ - \frac{1}{2} \\ \hline \end{array}$

Answers for Self-check—page 267

Test

Add.

1. $\frac{1}{6} + \frac{4}{6}$

2. $\frac{3}{10} + \frac{4}{10}$

3. $\frac{1}{3} + \frac{1}{6}$

4. $\frac{3}{8} + \frac{1}{4}$

5. $\begin{array}{r} 4\frac{3}{10} \\ + 8\frac{1}{10} \\ \hline \end{array}$

6. $\begin{array}{r} 12\frac{3}{8} \\ + 15\frac{11}{8} \\ \hline \end{array}$

7. $\begin{array}{r} \frac{43}{100} \\ + \frac{1}{10} \\ \hline \end{array}$

8. $\begin{array}{r} \frac{3}{4} \\ + \frac{9}{10} \\ \hline \end{array}$

Subtract.

9. $\frac{7}{10} - \frac{6}{10}$

10. $\frac{5}{8} - \frac{1}{4}$

11. $\frac{8}{9} - \frac{2}{3}$

12. $\frac{15}{16} - \frac{1}{4}$

13. $\begin{array}{r} 16\frac{3}{10} \\ - 8\frac{1}{10} \\ \hline \end{array}$

14. $\begin{array}{r} 26\frac{7}{8} \\ - 19\frac{3}{8} \\ \hline \end{array}$

15. $\begin{array}{r} \frac{3}{4} \\ - \frac{3}{16} \\ \hline \end{array}$

16. $\begin{array}{r} \frac{2}{3} \\ - \frac{1}{6} \\ \hline \end{array}$

Straight Line Designs

You can make curved designs using only straight lines.

In the figure at the right, 10 equally spaced points were marked on two lines. Then the pairs of points having the same number were connected to complete the design.

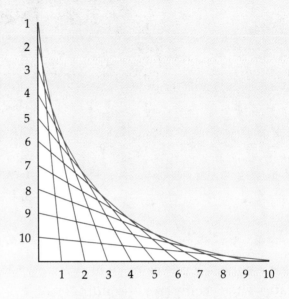

Can you make copies of these designs?
Make a design of your own.

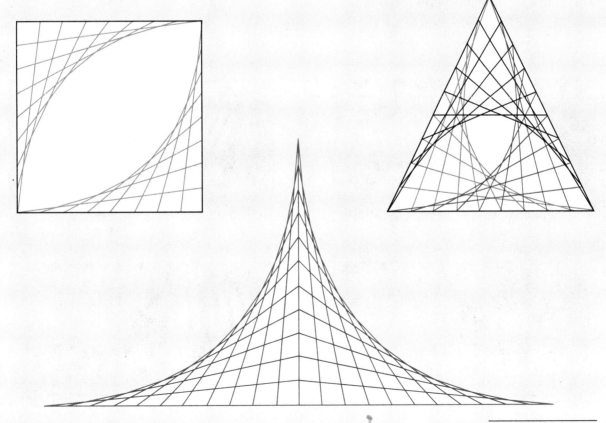

Ratio

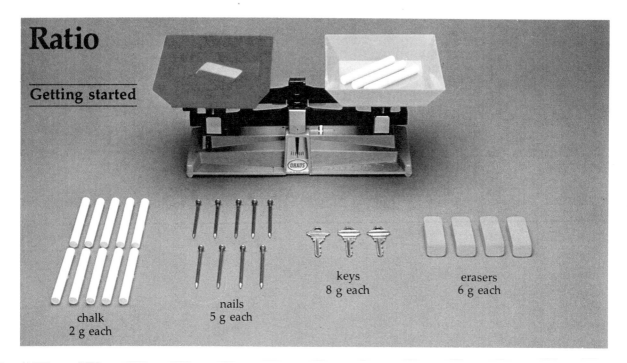

chalk
2 g each

nails
5 g each

keys
8 g each

erasers
6 g each

1 eraser balances 3 pieces of chalk.
The **ratio** 1 to 3 compares the number of
erasers to the number of pieces of chalk.

The pairs of objects below also balance.
For each pair, give a ratio that compares the number of objects.

1.

2.

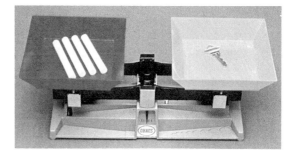

3.

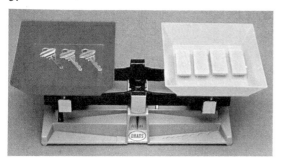

4.

It takes 3 keys to balance 4 erasers.
The **ratio** of keys to erasers is 3 to 4.

The ratio 3 to 4 can also be written as the fraction $\frac{3}{4}$.

The ratio of erasers to keys is 4 to 3 or $\frac{4}{3}$.

1. 2 nails will balance 5 pieces of chalk.
   What is the ratio of nails to chalk?
   What is the ratio of chalk to nails?

2. 1 key will balance 4 pieces of chalk.
   What is the ratio of keys to chalk?
   What is the ratio of chalk to keys?

3. 8 nails will balance 5 keys.
   What is the ratio of nails to keys?
   Keys to nails?

4. 5 erasers will balance 6 nails.
   What is the ratio of erasers to nails?
   Nails to erasers?

Write each ratio as a fraction.

5. 1 to 4   6. 7 to 5   7. 2 to 3   8. 5 to 6
9. 2 to 1   10. 3 to 10   11. 4 to 3   12. 2 to 5

Write each fraction as a ratio.

13. $\frac{1}{3}$ 14. $\frac{4}{5}$ 15. $\frac{7}{6}$ 16. $\frac{8}{3}$
17. $\frac{1}{10}$ 18. $\frac{5}{8}$ 19. $\frac{4}{3}$ 20. $\frac{5}{2}$

Writing ratios

There are 3
tennis balls
in 1 can.

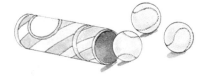

ratio of balls to cans: $\dfrac{3}{1}$ balls
cans

Give each ratio.

1. 1 carton holds 6 bottles.

ratio: bottles to cartons

2. 1 flashlight holds 2 batteries.

ratio: batteries to flashlights

3. 4 tomatoes cost 39¢.

ratio: tomatoes to cents

4. There are 8 crayons in 1 box.

ratio: crayons to boxes

5. 1 paintbox has 10 colors.

ratio: colors to paintboxes

6. 5 oranges make 2 glasses of juice.

ratio: oranges to glasses of juice

7. 3 apples cost 25¢.

ratio: apples to cents

8. There are 4 chairs around 1 table.

ratio: chairs to tables

Write the ratio.

1. Ran 100 m in 13 s. 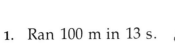  ratio: meters to seconds

2. Rode a bicycle 6 km in 15 min.  ratio: kilometers to minutes

3. Walked 2 km in 19 min. ratio: kilometers to minutes

4. Flew 2847 km in 3 h.  ratio: kilometers to hours

5. Drove a car 210 km in 3 h.  ratio: kilometers to hours

6. Walked 3 blocks in 5 min.  ratio: blocks to minutes

7. Jogged 4 km in 23 min.  ratio: kilometers to minutes

8. Ran 1500 m in 6 min.  ratio: meters to minutes

Making and using ratio tables

Orange juice:
1 can of frozen orange juice
3 cans of cold water

This **ratio table**
shows other amounts
of frozen juice and
water that could be used.

cans of frozen juice	1	2	3	4	5
cans of cold water	3	6	9	12	15

The ratios $\frac{1}{3}$, $\frac{2}{6}$, $\frac{3}{9}$, $\frac{4}{12}$, and $\frac{5}{15}$ are **equal ratios.**
You can use cross products to see if two ratios are equal.

$$\frac{2}{6} \quad \frac{3}{9} \rightarrow 6 \times 3 = 18 \qquad \frac{2}{6} = \frac{3}{9}$$
$$\rightarrow 2 \times 9 = 18$$

$$\frac{3}{5} \quad \frac{2}{3} \rightarrow 5 \times 2 = 10 \qquad \frac{3}{5} \neq \frac{2}{3}$$
$$\rightarrow 3 \times 3 = 9$$

Copy and complete each ratio table.

1.   Lemonade:
1 can of frozen juice
4 cans of cold water

cans of frozen juice	1	2	3	4	5
cans of cold water	4	▥	▥	▥	▥

2.  A record turns
3 times every
4 seconds.

turns	3	6	9	12	15
seconds	4	▥	▥	▥	▥

Find the cross products. Tell whether the ratios are **equal** or **not equal.**

3. $\frac{3}{5}, \frac{9}{15}$ 4. $\frac{2}{3}, \frac{6}{10}$ 5. $\frac{8}{12}, \frac{2}{3}$ 6. $\frac{4}{3}, \frac{24}{21}$

7. $\frac{3}{10}, \frac{2}{5}$ 8. $\frac{4}{12}, \frac{5}{15}$ 9. $\frac{4}{3}, \frac{12}{9}$ 10. $\frac{6}{9}, \frac{16}{24}$

Solve the problems.
Complete the ratio tables as needed.

1. Jody can walk 1 km in 11 minutes. How long will it take her to walk 5 km?

kilometers	1	2	3	4	5
minutes	11	22			

2. A candle burns down 2 cm every 5 minutes. How far will it burn down in 25 minutes?

centimeters	2				
minutes	5				

3. On a map, 1 cm represents a distance of 50 km. How many centimeters represent a distance of 200 km?

centimeters	1				
kilometers	50				

4. 1 box of fruit gelatin needs 2 cups of water. How many cups of water are needed for 3 boxes of gelatin?

boxes of gelatin	1				
cups of water	2				

5. A leaky faucet dripped 7 ml of water every 10 seconds. How many milliliters would it drip in 60 seconds?

seconds	10	20	30	60	70
milliliters	7				

6. In a box of sugar cubes, 1 layer has 18 cubes. The box holds 126 cubes. How many layers are there?

layers	1				
cubes	18	36	54	72	126

Using equal ratios

3 out of every 5 children are playing soccer. There are 30 children in all. How many are playing soccer?

Finding the answer

Write an equation with equal ratios	→	Find the cross products	→	Divide to find n

children playing soccer → $\dfrac{3}{5} = \dfrac{n}{30}$
children in all →

$5 \times n = 3 \times 30$
$5 \times n = 90$

$n = 90 \div 5$
$n = 18$

There are 18 children playing soccer.

Other examples

$\dfrac{3}{5} = \dfrac{n}{20}$

$5 \times n = 3 \times 20$
$5 \times n = 60$
$\quad n = 60 \div 5$
$\quad n = 12$

$\dfrac{4}{3} = \dfrac{n}{36}$

$3 \times n = 4 \times 36$
$3 \times n = 144$
$\quad n = 144 \div 3$
$\quad n = 48$

Solve the equations.

1. $\dfrac{2}{7} = \dfrac{n}{70}$

2. $\dfrac{1}{5} = \dfrac{n}{45}$

3. $\dfrac{3}{8} = \dfrac{n}{40}$

4. $\dfrac{9}{12} = \dfrac{n}{16}$

Solve each problem.
Use the equation to help you.

1. 3 out of every 8 children
   in a room wear glasses.
   There are 24 children
   in the room. How many
   wear glasses?

   $$\text{children with glasses} \rightarrow \frac{3}{8} = \frac{n}{24} \leftarrow \text{children in all}$$

2. There were 2 tables for every
   7 people. There were 28 people.
   How many tables were there?

   $$\text{tables} \rightarrow \frac{2}{7} = \frac{n}{28} \leftarrow \text{people}$$

3. In a group of 35 people,
   1 person out of 7 is left-handed.
   How many in the group are
   left-handed?

   $$\text{left-handed} \rightarrow \frac{1}{7} = \frac{n}{35} \leftarrow \text{people}$$

4. In a group of 40 people,
   2 out of 5 have blue eyes.
   How many in the group have
   blue eyes?

   $$\text{blue-eyed} \rightarrow \frac{2}{5} = \frac{n}{40} \leftarrow \text{people}$$

Write and solve an equation for each problem.

5. 2 out of every 9 children
   play in the orchestra.
   There are 27 children. How
   many play in the orchestra?

6. Lisa spelled 7 out of every
   8 words correctly. There
   were 40 words in all. How
   many did she spell correctly?

7. In one room, 3 out of every
   4 children have dark hair.
   There are 24 children in the
   room. How many children
   are there with dark hair?

☆ 8. Make up and solve a ratio problem
   about the children in your room.

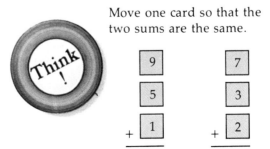

Move one card so that the
two sums are the same.

9   7
5   3
+ 1 + 2

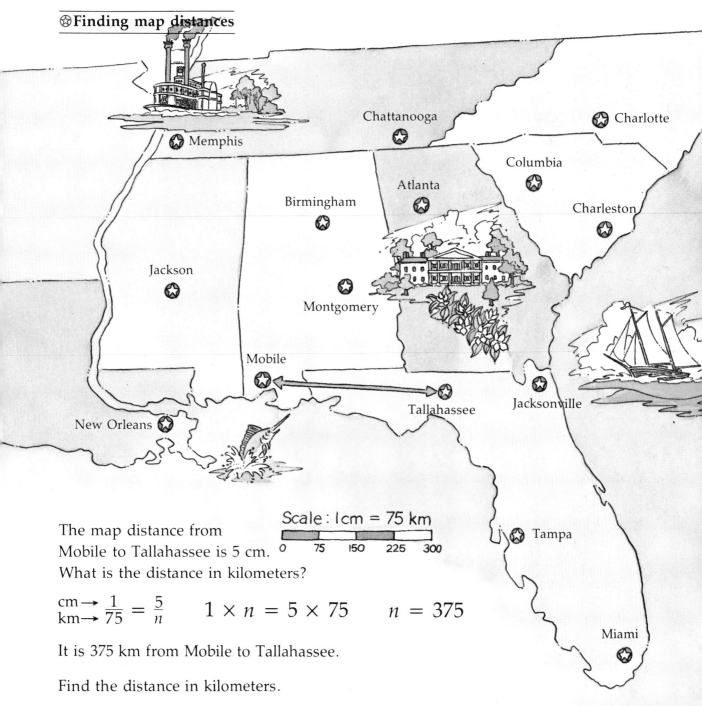

The map distance from
Mobile to Tallahassee is 5 cm.
What is the distance in kilometers?

Scale: 1cm = 75 km

0 75 150 225 300

$\begin{array}{c}\text{cm}\rightarrow\\\text{km}\rightarrow\end{array}\dfrac{1}{75}=\dfrac{5}{n}$ $1 \times n = 5 \times 75$ $n = 375$

It is 375 km from Mobile to Tallahassee.

Find the distance in kilometers.

1. Atlanta to Jacksonville
   map distance: 6 cm

2. New Orleans to Tampa
   map distance: 10 cm

3. Miami to Atlanta
   map distance: 13 cm

4. Memphis to Atlanta
   map distance: 7 cm

5. Chattanooga to Atlanta
   map distance: 2 cm

6. Tampa to Mobile
   map distance: 8 cm

Famous Western Trails

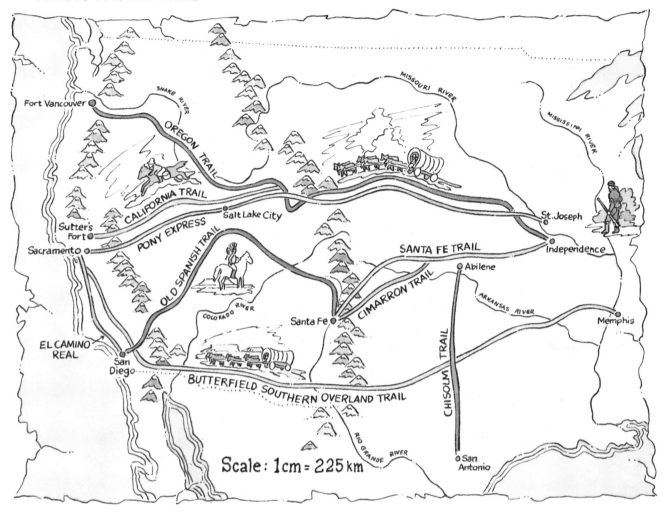

Scale: 1cm = 225 km

Find the length of each trail in kilometers.

1. Chisholm Trail
   map distance: 5 cm

2. Cimarron Trail
   map distance: 3 cm

3. Old Spanish Trail
   map distance: 9 cm

4. Santa Fe Trail
   map distance: 7 cm

5. Pony Express Route
   map distance: 14 cm

6. El Camino Real
   map distance: 4 cm

7. Oregon Trail
   map distance: 15 cm

8. Butterfield Southern Overland Trail
   map distance: 20 cm

Answers for Self-check 1. $\frac{2}{1}$ 2. $\frac{3}{5}$ 3. $\frac{5}{3}$ 4. $\frac{6}{5}$ 5. $\frac{7}{3}$ 6. $\frac{28}{3}$ 7. no 8. 12 9. 9 10. 6 11. 500 km
12. 2250 km

Self-check

Write each ratio as a fraction.

1. 2 to 1

2. 3 to 5

3. 5 to 3

4. 6 to 5

5. 7 oranges make 3 glasses of juice. What is the ratio of oranges to glasses?

6. Jane walked 3 km in 28 minutes. What is the ratio of minutes to kilometers?

7. Is the ratio $\frac{3}{4}$ equal to $\frac{4}{6}$?

8. Give the missing number in the ratio table.

4	8							16
3	6	9	12

9. Solve: $\frac{3}{8} = \frac{n}{24}$

10. Solve: $\frac{2}{7} = \frac{n}{21}$

☆ 11. A distance of 1 cm on a map represents 100 km. How many kilometers does 5 cm represent?

☆ 12. A distance of 1 cm on a map represents 375 km. How many kilometers does 6 cm represent?

Answers for Self-check—page 279

Test

Write each ratio as a fraction.

1. 4 to 5

2. 3 to 2

3. 2 to 3

4. 1 to 5

5. 4 chairs for every 3 students. What is the ratio of students to chairs?

6. Mike ran 100 meters in 14 seconds. What is the ratio of meters to seconds?

7. Is the ratio $\frac{10}{3}$ equal to the ratio $\frac{40}{12}$?

8. Give the missing number in the ratio table.

2	4	6	8
5	10	15						

9. Solve: $\frac{5}{3} = \frac{n}{12}$

10. Solve: $\frac{2}{3} = \frac{n}{15}$

☆ 11. A distance of 1 cm on a map represents 125 km. How many kilometers does 4 cm represent?

☆ 12. A distance of 1 cm on a map represents a distance of 65 km. How many kilometers does 8 cm represent?

A Linkage Puzzle

Here is a puzzle for you to make.
You will need to make 6 cardboard strips like the ones
shown below. You will also need 7 paper fasteners.

Punch small holes in the strips at the distances shown.
Put the strips together with the paper fasteners to make
a linkage like the one below. Be certain that the strips
overlap as shown.

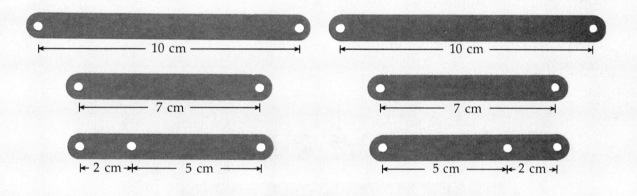

The object of the puzzle
is to get the small triangle
outside the large triangle.
The dotted lines show how the
linkage puzzle should look
after you have solved it.

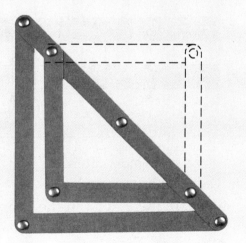

Graphs

Getting started

Two and a half hours later, the astronauts unlatched their spacecraft from the spent booster. They spun the craft around and docked with an airlock housed in the rocket hull.

Don counted the number of times each of the vowels, **a, e, i, o,** and **u,** was used in the newspaper clipping. The bar graph below shows his findings.

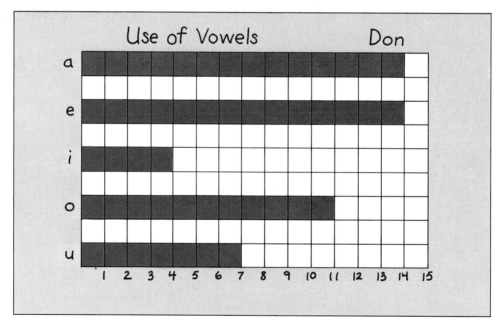

Which vowels were used most often?
Which vowel was used least often?
How many vowels are there in all in the clipping?
Choose a few sentences from a book, newspaper, or magazine. Count the number of times each vowel is used. Make a bar graph to show your findings.

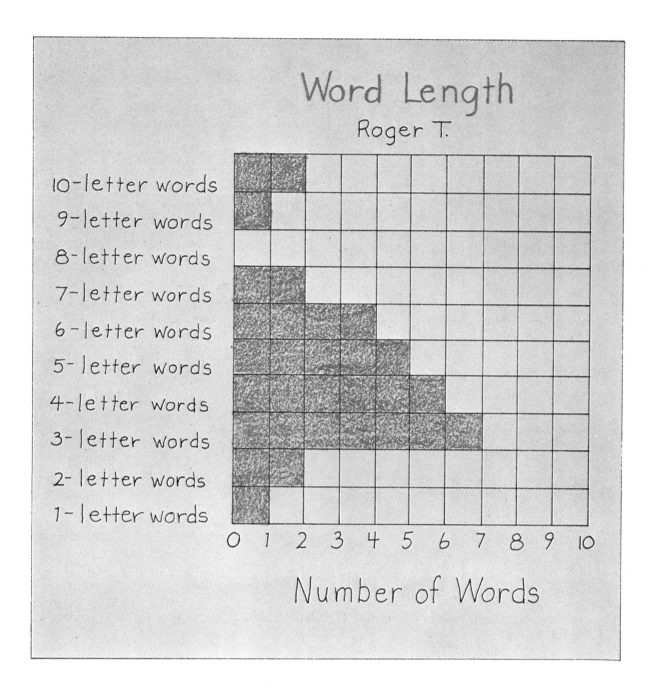

This bar graph shows the number of times words
of different lengths are used in the clipping.

1. How many letters are there in the longest words?
2. How many 5-letter words are used?
3. Which words are used most often?
4. Are there any 8-letter words used?
5. How many words are there in all in the clipping?

Pictographs

Number of Clear Days in One Year

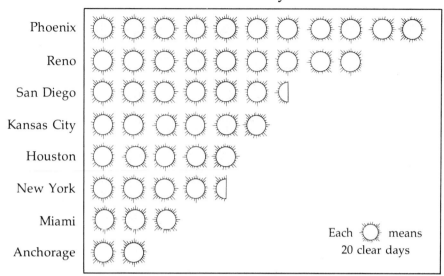

Study the pictograph above.

Since ☼ means 20 clear days, ◖ means 10 days.

Give the number of clear days per year for each city.

1. Phoenix   2. Reno   3. San Diego   4. Kansas City
5. Houston   6. New York   7. Miami   8. Anchorage

Rainy and Snowy Days per Year

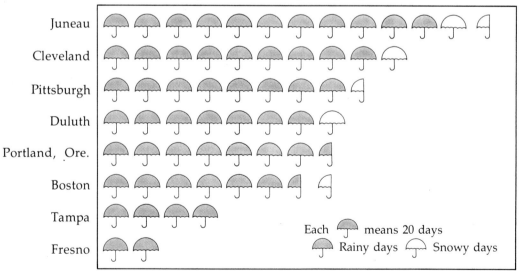

Give the number of rainy days and snowy days per year for each city.

9. Juneau   10. Cleveland   11. Pittsburgh   12. Duluth
13. Portland   14. Boston   15. Tampa   16. Fresno

Circle graphs

The children in Room 23 asked two questions of the children
in the classroom next door.

> What is your favorite TV channel?
> What is your favorite sport?

The circle graphs below show their findings.

This **circle graph** shows
that more children chose
channel 5 as their favorite
TV channel than any other.

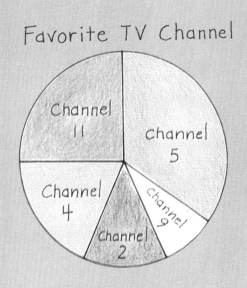

Favorite TV Channel

Tell which channel was chosen
by more children.

1. Channel 4 or channel 11
2. Channel 9 or channel 2
3. Channel 2 or channel 4
4. Channel 5 or channels 11
   and 4 together
5. Which channel was chosen by the
   fewest number of children?
6. About what part of the
   children chose Channel 11?

Tell which sport was chosen by
more children.

Favorite Sport

7. Soccer or baseball
8. Baseball or hockey
9. Basketball or football
10. Which sport was the favorite
    of more children than any
    other?

✪Graphs in science: pendulums

In science class, the students made pendulums by tying weights on strings of different lengths. They counted the number of swings (back and forth) made by each pendulum in one minute. Then they used the pendulums to make a graph showing their results.

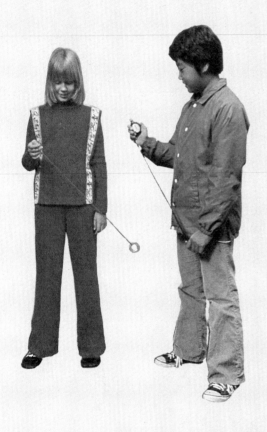

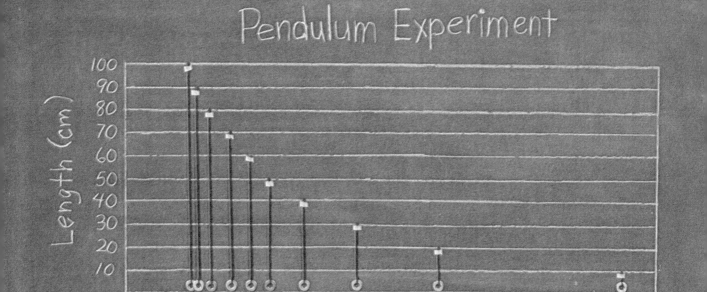

1. How long is the pendulum that swings 55 times a minute?

2. How long is the pendulum that makes about 30 swings per minute?

Estimate the number of swings for each length of pendulum.

3. 100 cm	4. 80 cm	5. 70 cm	6. 60 cm	7. 50 cm
8. 40 cm	9. 30 cm	10. 20 cm	11. 10 cm	12. 90 cm

13. About how long should you make a pendulum so that it would swing 60 times per minute?

☆ 14. Make a pendulum that you think will swing 60 times a minute. Check your guess by counting the swings.

Some students measured the length of the shadow
of a 10 cm rod every 15 minutes. They made the
line graph on page 289 to show how the length of
the shadow changed.

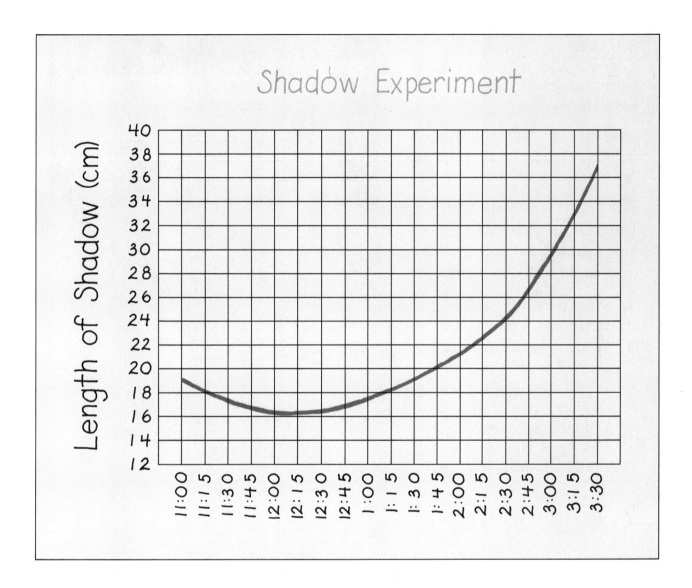

Give the length to the nearest centimeter of the shadow at each of these times.

1. 11:00   2. 11:30   3. 1:00   4. 1:45   5. 2:30   6. 3:15

7. At what time was the shadow the shortest?

8. Give two times at which the shadow was 18 cm long.

☆ 9. Work with several classmates and measure the length of the shadow of some object during the day. Make a graph of your findings.

Answers for Self-check   1. 84   2. 88   3. 80   4. 95   5. 100   6. $\frac{1}{2}$ 7. $\frac{1}{4}$ 8. green   9. red   10. blue

Self-check

Give the spelling score
for each day.

1. Monday
2. Tuesday
3. Wednesday
4. Thursday
5. Friday

The circle graph shows
how a group of children voted
on their favorite of 4 colors.

6. What part of the children voted for red?
7. What part of the children voted for blue?
8. Which color was chosen by the fewest number of children?
9. Which color was chosen by the greatest number of children?
10. Did more vote for blue or for yellow?

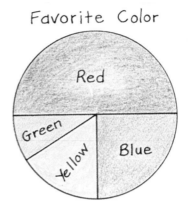

Answers for Self-check—page 289

Test

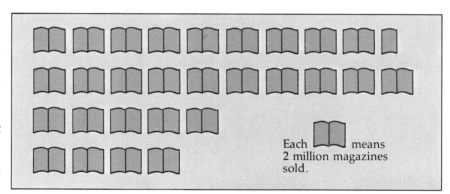

Give the number of magazines sold.

1. TV Guide
2. Reader's Digest
3. National Geographic
4. Family Circle

Give the temperature for each time.

5. 8 a.m.
6. 9 a.m.
7. 11 a.m.
8. 1 p.m.
9. 2 p.m.
10. 4 p.m.

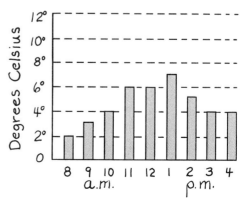

The Unsquare Game

This is a game for 2 players.
You need a 5 by 5 dot grid
like the one shown.

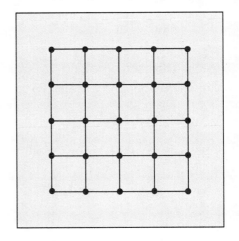

Rules:

1. The players take turns
   marking one of the dots on
   the grid. One player marks
   O and the other X.

2. The object is to force one player
   to make 4 marks on the corners
   of some square.

3. If one player has 4 marks on the
   corners of a square, the other player
   wins the game.

Sample games

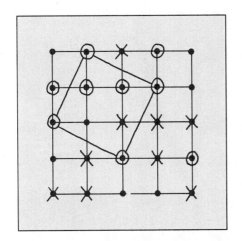

O loses this game.
X wins.

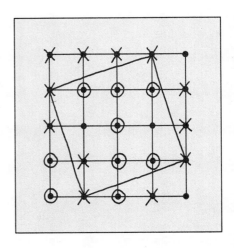

X loses this game.
O wins.

Level 27 review

Give the missing numerator or denominator.

1. $\frac{1}{2} = \frac{n}{12}$ 2. $\frac{3}{5} = \frac{12}{n}$ 3. $\frac{3}{4} = \frac{n}{24}$ 4. $\frac{1}{3} = \frac{n}{9}$

5. $\frac{5}{8} = \frac{15}{n}$ 6. $\frac{2}{3} = \frac{10}{n}$ 7. $\frac{1}{4} = \frac{n}{16}$ 8. $\frac{4}{5} = \frac{n}{15}$

Write = or ≠ for each ⬤ .

9. $\frac{1}{2}$ ⬤ $\frac{2}{5}$ 10. $\frac{5}{8}$ ⬤ $\frac{16}{24}$ 11. $\frac{1}{3}$ ⬤ $\frac{4}{12}$ 12. $\frac{3}{5}$ ⬤ $\frac{6}{12}$

Give the lowest-terms fractions.

13. $\frac{4}{8}$ 14. $\frac{3}{12}$ 15. $\frac{6}{9}$ 16. $\frac{8}{10}$ 17. $\frac{5}{20}$

Express as mixed numerals.

18. $\frac{25}{4}$ 19. $\frac{7}{2}$ 20. $\frac{20}{3}$ 21. $\frac{49}{5}$ 22. $\frac{35}{10}$

Add.

23. $\frac{3}{4}$
    $+ \frac{1}{2}$

24. $\frac{1}{2}$
    $+ \frac{2}{3}$

25. $2\frac{6}{8}$
    $+ 4\frac{1}{8}$

26. $6\frac{2}{24}$
    $+ 4\frac{3}{24}$

27. $5\frac{4}{10}$
    $+ 8\frac{3}{10}$

Subtract.

28. $\frac{7}{8}$
    $- \frac{1}{4}$

29. $\frac{4}{5}$
    $- \frac{1}{2}$

30. $9\frac{5}{6}$
    $- 3$

31. $4\frac{9}{12}$
    $- 1\frac{4}{12}$

32. $12\frac{5}{6}$
    $- 9\frac{2}{6}$

Express each ratio as a fraction.

33. 4 to 7   34. 2 to 3   35. 1 to 5   36. 6 to 3

37. 3 out of 4 students ride to school. There are 32 students. How many ride?

38. 2 out of 5 students will be in a class play. There are 30 students. How many will be in the play?

Multiplication of Fractional Numbers
Multiplying with Decimals
Using your Skills
Adding and Subtracting with Mixed Numerals
Volume, Capacity, Mass, and Temperature
Measurement: Other Units

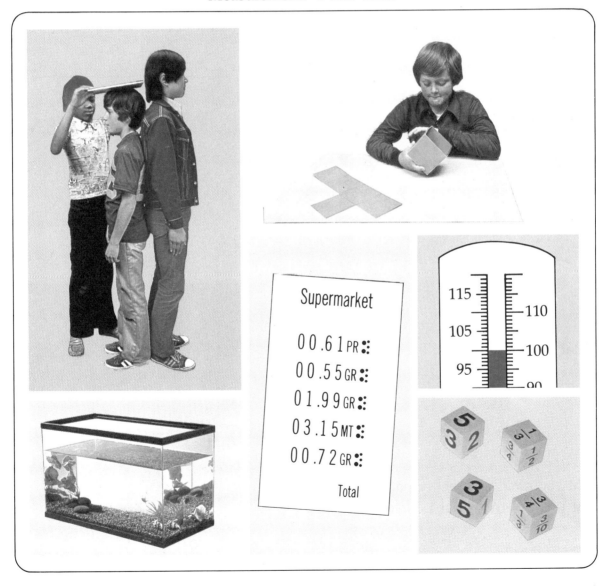

Multiplication of Fractional Numbers

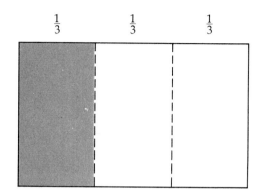

$\frac{1}{3}$ of the region is shaded pink.

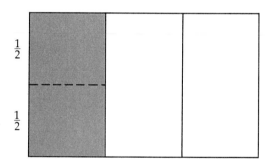

This region is divided in half.

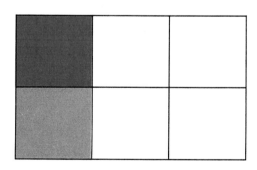

$\frac{1}{2}$ of $\frac{1}{3}$ of the region is shaded red.
What part of the region is shaded red?

Fold and shade a sheet of paper so
that $\frac{1}{3}$ of $\frac{1}{4}$ of the paper is shaded dark red.

Study the figures. Then give the fractional number for each ▥.

Example:

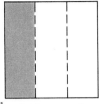

$\frac{1}{3}$ of the region
is shaded pink.

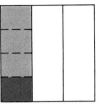

$\frac{1}{4}$ of $\frac{1}{3}$ is
shaded red.

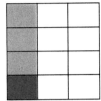

$\frac{1}{12}$ of the region
is shaded red.

We write:
$\frac{1}{4} \times \frac{1}{3} = \frac{1}{12}$

1.

$\frac{1}{4}$ of the region
is shaded pink.

$\frac{1}{2}$ of $\frac{1}{4}$ is
shaded red.

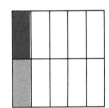

$\frac{1}{8}$ of the region
is shaded red.

We write:
$\frac{1}{2} \times \frac{1}{4} = $ ▥

2.

$\frac{1}{5}$ of the region
is shaded pink.

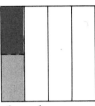

$\frac{1}{2}$ of $\frac{1}{5}$ is
shaded red.

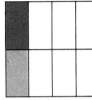

▥ of the region
is shaded red.

We write:
$\frac{1}{2} \times \frac{1}{5} = $ ▥

Example:

$\frac{1}{2}$ of the region
is shaded pink.

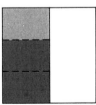

$\frac{2}{3}$ of $\frac{1}{2}$ is
shaded red.

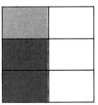

$\frac{2}{6}$ of the region
is shaded red.

We write:
$\frac{2}{3} \times \frac{1}{2} = \frac{2}{6}$

3.

$\frac{2}{3}$ of the region
is shaded pink.

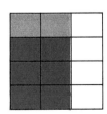

$\frac{3}{4}$ of $\frac{2}{3}$ is
shaded red.

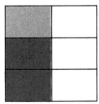

▥ of the region
is shaded red.

We write:
$\frac{3}{4} \times \frac{2}{3} = $ ▥

Multiplying with fractions

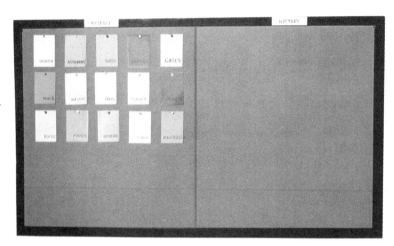

The class decided to use $\frac{1}{2}$ of the bulletin board for science papers. Only $\frac{3}{5}$ of the $\frac{1}{2}$ was used. How much of the whole board was used for science papers?

Finding the answer

Two fractional numbers	Multiply the numerators	Multiply the denominators

$$\frac{3}{5} \times \frac{1}{2} \qquad \frac{3}{5} \times \frac{1}{2} = \frac{3}{\text{||||||}} \qquad \frac{3}{5} \times \frac{1}{2} = \frac{3}{10}$$

The class used $\frac{3}{10}$ of the board for science papers.

Other examples

$$\frac{2}{5} \times \frac{1}{3} = \frac{2}{15} \qquad \frac{3}{4} \times \frac{1}{2} = \frac{3}{8} \qquad \frac{3}{10} \times \frac{5}{4} = \frac{15}{40} \text{ or } \frac{3}{8}$$

Find the products.

1. $\frac{1}{2} \times \frac{1}{2}$
2. $\frac{1}{2} \times \frac{1}{5}$
3. $\frac{1}{3} \times \frac{2}{3}$
4. $\frac{1}{4} \times \frac{1}{3}$

5. $\frac{1}{10} \times \frac{1}{10}$
6. $\frac{2}{3} \times \frac{2}{5}$
7. $\frac{3}{4} \times \frac{2}{5}$
8. $\frac{5}{8} \times \frac{2}{3}$

9. $\frac{3}{4} \times \frac{2}{3}$
10. $\frac{5}{6} \times \frac{1}{2}$
11. $\frac{1}{4} \times \frac{1}{2}$
12. $\frac{1}{2} \times \frac{4}{5}$

13. $\frac{3}{8} \times \frac{3}{4}$
14. $\frac{3}{10} \times \frac{7}{10}$
15. $\frac{1}{10} \times \frac{1}{100}$
16. $\frac{5}{8} \times \frac{3}{5}$

Multiply.

1. $\frac{1}{2} \times \frac{3}{10}$ 2. $\frac{3}{4} \times \frac{5}{8}$ 3. $\frac{3}{5} \times \frac{2}{3}$ 4. $\frac{5}{6} \times \frac{3}{5}$

5. $\frac{2}{5} \times \frac{3}{3}$ 6. $\frac{1}{2} \times \frac{3}{4}$ 7. $\frac{5}{8} \times \frac{10}{10}$ 8. $\frac{7}{10} \times \frac{9}{10}$

9. $\frac{1}{4} \times \frac{3}{2}$ 10. $\frac{1}{2} \times \frac{3}{5}$ 11. $\frac{7}{2} \times \frac{1}{10}$ 12. $\frac{3}{10} \times \frac{7}{100}$

13. $\frac{7}{3} \times \frac{1}{2}$ 14. $\frac{3}{4} \times \frac{5}{3}$ 15. $\frac{2}{3} \times \frac{9}{10}$ 16. $\frac{2}{5} \times \frac{3}{5}$

17. $\frac{1}{3} \times \frac{5}{8}$ 18. $\frac{3}{10} \times \frac{3}{2}$ 19. $\frac{5}{4} \times \frac{3}{2}$ 20. $\frac{3}{4} \times \frac{4}{3}$

21. $\frac{5}{6} \times \frac{1}{2}$ 22. $\frac{3}{8} \times \frac{2}{3}$ 23. $\frac{7}{10} \times \frac{2}{5}$ 24. $\frac{3}{4} \times \frac{3}{4}$

Find the products. Multiply the numbers in parentheses first.

Example: $\left(\frac{1}{2} \times \frac{1}{3}\right) \times \frac{2}{5} = \frac{1}{6} \times \frac{2}{5} = \frac{2}{30}$ or $\frac{1}{15}$

25. $\left(\frac{1}{4} \times \frac{1}{2}\right) \times \frac{1}{3}$ 26. $\frac{1}{4} \times \left(\frac{1}{2} \times \frac{1}{3}\right)$ 27. $\left(\frac{2}{3} \times \frac{1}{5}\right) \times \frac{1}{2}$

28. $\frac{2}{3} \times \left(\frac{1}{5} \times \frac{1}{2}\right)$ 29. $\left(\frac{1}{10} \times \frac{1}{2}\right) \times \frac{1}{5}$ 30. $\frac{1}{10} \times \left(\frac{1}{2} \times \frac{1}{5}\right)$

31. $\frac{1}{2}$ of the bulletin board was to be used for history papers. Only $\frac{3}{4}$ of this $\frac{1}{2}$ was used. What part of the board was used for history papers?

32. $\frac{3}{4}$ of a bulletin board was to be used for student maps. $\frac{2}{3}$ of the $\frac{3}{4}$ was used. What part of the bulletin board was used for maps?

Draw and cut out a figure like the one shown here. Cut along the dotted lines. Fit the four pieces together to make a square.

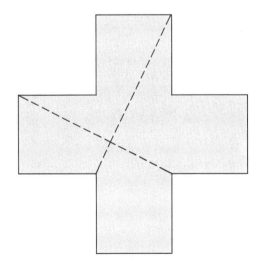

✪ Multiplying with mixed numerals

Chocolate Chip Cookies

$1\frac{1}{2}$ c flour	$\frac{1}{2}$ c granulated sugar
$\frac{1}{2}$ tsp soda	$\frac{1}{2}$ c brown sugar
$\frac{1}{4}$ tsp salt	1 tbs cream
$\frac{2}{3}$ c shortening	1 tsp vanilla
1 egg	1 package chocolate bits

Sift flour, soda, and salt together and set aside. Cream shortening and sugar. Stir in vanilla. Beat in egg. Add flour mixture. Stir in cream and chocolate bits. Drop by spoonfuls on greased baking sheets. Makes 4 dozen cookies. Temperature: 190° C   Time: about 10 minutes

How much flour should be used to make $2\frac{1}{2}$ times the recipe?

Finding the answer

Mixed numeral multiplication problem	→	Write the mixed numerals as improper fractions	→	Multiply the fractions

$$2\frac{1}{2} \times 1\frac{1}{2} \qquad\qquad \frac{5}{2} \times \frac{3}{2} \qquad\qquad \frac{5}{2} \times \frac{3}{2} = \frac{15}{4} \text{ or } 3\frac{3}{4}$$

Use $3\frac{3}{4}$ cups of flour to make $2\frac{1}{2}$ times the recipe.

Other examples

$$2\frac{1}{3} \times \frac{3}{4} = \frac{7}{3} \times \frac{3}{4} = \frac{21}{12} \text{ or } 1\frac{3}{4} \qquad\qquad 5 \times \frac{2}{3} = \frac{5}{1} \times \frac{2}{3} = \frac{10}{3} \text{ or } 3\frac{1}{3}$$

$$1\frac{1}{4} \times 8 = \frac{5}{4} \times \frac{8}{1} = \frac{40}{4} \text{ or } 10 \qquad\qquad 1\frac{1}{3} \times \frac{3}{4} = \frac{4}{3} \times \frac{3}{4} = \frac{12}{12} \text{ or } 1$$

Multiply.

1. $1\frac{1}{4} \times \frac{1}{2}$ 2. $3\frac{1}{3} \times \frac{1}{3}$ 3. $2\frac{1}{2} \times \frac{2}{3}$ 4. $2\frac{1}{5} \times 1\frac{1}{2}$

5. $\frac{1}{8} \times 1\frac{1}{2}$ 6. $3 \times 4\frac{1}{2}$ 7. $\frac{5}{6} \times 1\frac{1}{3}$ 8. $1\frac{3}{10} \times 5$

Multiply.

1. $2\frac{1}{2} \times \frac{1}{4}$
2. $\frac{2}{3} \times 3\frac{1}{2}$
3. $\frac{3}{4} \times 1\frac{1}{2}$
4. $\frac{3}{10} \times 2\frac{1}{4}$

5. $1\frac{1}{2} \times 1\frac{1}{4}$
6. $2\frac{3}{4} \times \frac{3}{4}$
7. $2\frac{1}{3} \times 1\frac{1}{4}$
8. $\frac{1}{2} \times 7\frac{1}{2}$

9. $\frac{9}{10} \times 2\frac{1}{2}$
10. $1\frac{1}{3} \times \frac{2}{3}$
11. $4\frac{1}{2} \times \frac{1}{4}$
12. $5\frac{2}{3} \times \frac{1}{2}$

13. $\frac{1}{8} \times 5$
14. $\frac{2}{3} \times 4$
15. $\frac{3}{4} \times 7$
16. $\frac{2}{5} \times 8$

17. $\frac{1}{5} \times 10$
18. $\frac{7}{8} \times 16$
19. $\frac{1}{2} \times 9$
20. $\frac{1}{3} \times 21$

21. $2\frac{1}{3} \times 3$
22. $1\frac{1}{4} \times 6$
23. $8 \times 2\frac{1}{2}$
24. $5 \times 1\frac{2}{3}$

25. $10 \times 2\frac{1}{2}$
26. $5\frac{1}{4} \times 4$
27. $\frac{2}{3} \times 12$
28. $3\frac{3}{4} \times 5$

29. $1\frac{1}{3} \times 1\frac{1}{2}$
30. $2\frac{1}{5} \times 1\frac{1}{4}$
31. $8\frac{1}{2} \times 4$
32. $3\frac{2}{3} \times 12$

33. Recipe: $\frac{2}{3}$ cup shortening
How much for $2\frac{1}{2}$ times the recipe?

34. Recipe: $\frac{1}{4}$ tsp salt
How much for $1\frac{1}{2}$ times the recipe?

☆ 35. Find a recipe for your favorite dessert. For each item on it, find the amount you would need to use to make $2\frac{1}{2}$ times the recipe.

Find 3 different whole numbers, each less than 10, that have a product equal to their sum.
$a \times b \times c = a + b + c$

Answers for Self-check 1. $\frac{2}{9}$ 2. $\frac{3}{8}$ 3. $\frac{3}{8}$ 4. $\frac{1}{15}$ 5. $\frac{7}{30}$ 6. $\frac{5}{16}$ 7. $\frac{3}{16}$ 8. $\frac{3}{100}$ 9. $\frac{1}{1000}$ 10. $\frac{1}{12}$ 11. $\frac{7}{3}$ or $2\frac{1}{3}$ 12. $\frac{8}{4}$ or 2 13. $\frac{42}{2}$ or 21 14. $\frac{126}{3}$ or 42 15. $\frac{80}{10}$ or 8 16. $\frac{210}{20}$ or $10\frac{1}{2}$ 17. $\frac{90}{15}$ or 6 18. $\frac{33}{8}$ or $4\frac{1}{8}$

More practice, page 370, Set B

Module 28.1   **299**

Self-check

Find the products.

1.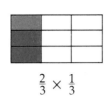

$\frac{2}{3} \times \frac{1}{3}$

2.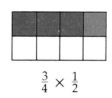

$\frac{3}{4} \times \frac{1}{2}$

3. $\frac{1}{2} \times \frac{3}{4}$

4. $\frac{1}{3} \times \frac{1}{5}$

5. $\frac{7}{10} \times \frac{1}{3}$

6. $\frac{5}{8} \times \frac{1}{2}$

7. $\frac{3}{4} \times \frac{1}{4}$

8. $\frac{1}{10} \times \frac{3}{10}$

9. $\frac{1}{100} \times \frac{1}{10}$

10. $\frac{1}{4} \times \frac{1}{3}$

☆ 11. $7 \times \frac{1}{3}$

☆ 12. $\frac{1}{4} \times 8$

☆ 13. $14 \times 1\frac{1}{2}$

☆ 14. $2\frac{1}{3} \times 18$

☆ 15. $2\frac{1}{2} \times 3\frac{1}{5}$

☆ 16. $8\frac{3}{4} \times 1\frac{1}{5}$

☆ 17. $3\frac{3}{5} \times 1\frac{2}{3}$

☆ 18. $1\frac{1}{2} \times 2\frac{3}{4}$

Answers for Self-check—page 299

Test

Find the products.

1.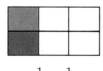

$\frac{1}{2} \times \frac{1}{3}$

2.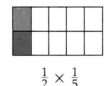

$\frac{1}{2} \times \frac{1}{5}$

3. $\frac{2}{3} \times \frac{1}{2}$

4. $\frac{3}{4} \times \frac{2}{3}$

5. $\frac{1}{8} \times \frac{4}{5}$

6. $\frac{1}{3} \times \frac{1}{8}$

7. $\frac{7}{10} \times \frac{1}{10}$

8. $\frac{1}{2} \times \frac{3}{4}$

9. $\frac{3}{8} \times \frac{2}{3}$

10. $\frac{4}{7} \times \frac{1}{4}$

☆ 11. $9 \times \frac{3}{5}$

☆ 12. $4 \times \frac{1}{3}$

☆ 13. $2 \times 1\frac{1}{4}$

☆ 14. $1\frac{1}{3} \times 3$

☆ 15. $2\frac{5}{8} \times 2\frac{1}{3}$

☆ 16. $8\frac{1}{3} \times 1\frac{3}{4}$

☆ 17. $1\frac{1}{2} \times 4\frac{1}{3}$

☆ 18. $1\frac{1}{5} \times 2\frac{5}{6}$

Heads or Tails?

Try this **probability** experiment.
You will need three pennies, or checkers,
or counters labeled **Heads** and **Tails.**

Toss the three pennies 50 times.
Keep a tally of the results of each toss.
Use a table like the one below.

Result	Tally
3 heads	
2 heads, 1 tail	
1 head, 2 tails	
3 tails	

Compare your results with those of your classmates.

Multiplying with Decimals

Getting started

The shaded parts of these regions can
be named by fractions or decimals.

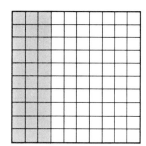 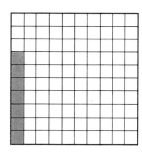 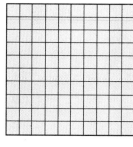 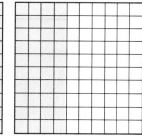

fraction: $\frac{3}{10}$ $\frac{7}{100}$ $1\frac{4}{10}$
decimal: 0.3   0.07   1.4

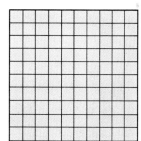 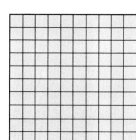 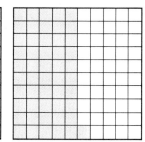

fraction: $2\frac{51}{100}$
decimal: 2.51

Match each fraction with a decimal from the list on the right.

1. $\frac{53}{100}$ **2.** $8\frac{3}{100}$

3. $\frac{7}{10}$ **4.** $\frac{1}{100}$

5. $2\frac{4}{10}$ **6.** $5\frac{3}{10}$

7. $\frac{83}{100}$ **8.** $13\frac{5}{10}$

9. $\frac{53}{1000}$ **10.** $2\frac{4}{1000}$

A 0.24	B 0.7	C 0.053
D 8.3	E 0.001	F 0.83
G 0.01	H 0.53	I 13.5
J 5.3	K 1.35	L 2.4
M 2.004	N 8.03	O 2.04

Multiplication of fractional numbers can help you understand multiplication with decimals.

$$\frac{3}{10} \times \frac{2}{10} = \frac{6}{100}$$

$$\downarrow \qquad \downarrow \qquad \downarrow$$

$$0.3 \times 0.2 = 0.06$$

$$\uparrow \qquad \uparrow \qquad \uparrow$$

1-place decimal   1-place decimal   2-place decimal

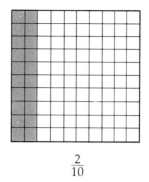

$\frac{2}{10}$

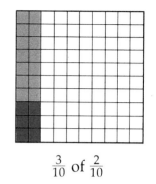

$\frac{3}{10}$ of $\frac{2}{10}$

Give the product as a decimal.

1. $\dfrac{3}{10} \times \dfrac{7}{100} = \dfrac{21}{1000}$

$$\downarrow \qquad \downarrow \qquad \downarrow$$

$$0.3 \times 0.07 = n$$

$$\uparrow \qquad \uparrow \qquad \uparrow$$

1-place decimal   2-place decimal   3-place decimal

2. $4 \times \dfrac{1}{10} = \dfrac{4}{10}$

$$\downarrow \qquad \downarrow \qquad \downarrow$$

$$4 \times 0.1 = n$$

$$\uparrow \qquad \uparrow \qquad \uparrow$$

0-place decimal   1-place decimal   1-place decimal

3. $\dfrac{9}{100} \times 7 = \dfrac{63}{100}$

$$\downarrow \qquad \downarrow \qquad \downarrow$$

$$0.09 \times 7 = n$$

$$\uparrow \qquad \uparrow \qquad \uparrow$$

2-place decimal   0-place decimal   2-place decimal

4. $\dfrac{12}{10} \times \dfrac{3}{10} = \dfrac{36}{100}$

$$\downarrow \qquad \downarrow \qquad \downarrow$$

$$1.2 \times 0.3 = n$$

$$\uparrow \qquad \uparrow \qquad \uparrow$$

1-place decimal   1-place decimal   2-place decimal

5. $0.2 \times 0.4 = n$

6. $0.03 \times 0.5 = n$

For each equation, give the name of the decimal place in the product.

7. $0.3 \times 0.2 = 0.06$
tenths $\times$ tenths = __?__

8. $3 \times 0.4 = 1.2$
units $\times$ tenths = __?__

9. $0.05 \times 0.3 = 0.015$
hundredths $\times$ tenths = __?__

10. $6 \times 0.04 = 0.24$
units $\times$ hundredths = __?__

Multiplying with decimals

John's height is 1.4 m.
Bill's height is 0.9 of John's height.
What is Bill's height?

Finding the answer

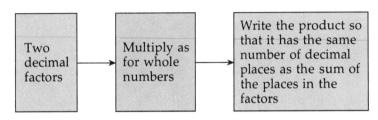

| Two decimal factors | → | Multiply as for whole numbers | → | Write the product so that it has the same number of decimal places as the sum of the places in the factors |

$$
\begin{array}{r} 1.4 \\ \times\, 0.9 \\ \hline \end{array}
\qquad
\begin{array}{r} 1.4 \\ \times\, 0.9 \\ \hline 1\,2\,6 \end{array}
\qquad
\begin{array}{r} 1.4 \\ \times\, 0.9 \\ \hline 1.2\,6 \end{array}
$$

1.4 ←1-place decimal
× 0.9 ←1-place decimal
1.2 6 ←2-place decimal

Bill's height is 1.26 m.

Other examples

$$
\begin{array}{r} 8.23 \\ \times\ 0.4 \\ \hline 3.292 \end{array}
\qquad
\begin{array}{r} 0.025 \\ \times\quad 7 \\ \hline 0.175 \end{array}
\qquad
\begin{array}{r} 21.7 \\ \times\quad 6 \\ \hline 130.2 \end{array}
\qquad
\begin{array}{r} 5.4 \\ \times\,1.6 \\ \hline 3\,2\,4 \\ 5\,4\,0 \\ \hline 8.6\,4 \end{array}
$$

Find the products.

1. $\begin{array}{r} 2.3 \\ \times\ \ 5 \\ \hline \end{array}$
2. $\begin{array}{r} 7.1 \\ \times\,0.2 \\ \hline \end{array}$
3. $\begin{array}{r} 0.14 \\ \times\quad 8 \\ \hline \end{array}$
4. $\begin{array}{r} 0.046 \\ \times\qquad 3 \\ \hline \end{array}$

5. $\begin{array}{r} 12.5 \\ \times\ 0.8 \\ \hline \end{array}$
6. $\begin{array}{r} 24 \\ \times\,0.5 \\ \hline \end{array}$
7. $\begin{array}{r} 0.17 \\ \times\ \ 0.7 \\ \hline \end{array}$
8. $\begin{array}{r} 35 \\ \times\,0.9 \\ \hline \end{array}$

9. $\begin{array}{r} 6.3 \\ \times\ \ 7 \\ \hline \end{array}$
10. $\begin{array}{r} 8.9 \\ \times\,0.3 \\ \hline \end{array}$
11. $\begin{array}{r} 62.4 \\ \times\ \ 0.8 \\ \hline \end{array}$
12. $\begin{array}{r} 20.9 \\ \times\quad 8 \\ \hline \end{array}$

Multiply.

| 1. | 8.1 × 0.7 | 2. | 6.22 × 5 | 3. | 1.1 × 3.4 | 4. | 0.99 × 2.8 |

1. 8.1
 × 0.7

2. 6.22
 × 5

3. 1.1
 × 3.4

4. 0.99
 × 2.8

5. 250
 × 0.6

6. 13.5
 × 3

7. 58
 × 0.06

8. 32.4
 × 9

9. 3.2
 × 1.3

10. 6.7
 × 2.1

11. 38
 × 5.4

12. 3.7
 × 10

13. 0.55
 × 2.6

14. 1.03
 × 36

15. 1.21
 × 1.2

16. 9.6
 × 0.75

17. 1.6×0.7

18. 3.09×5

19. 0.72×1.3

20. 6.6×9.2

21. 40×0.06

22. 25×2.5

23. 64×0.08

24. 87.1×4.7

25. 0.37×85

26. 6.6×10

27. 25×0.4

28. 72.8×3.8

29. Carla's height is 138 cm. Mary's height is 1.05 times Carla's height. How tall is Mary?

☆ 30. Measure the length of your arm from your shoulder to your fingertips. Multiply by 2.3 to find your approximate height.

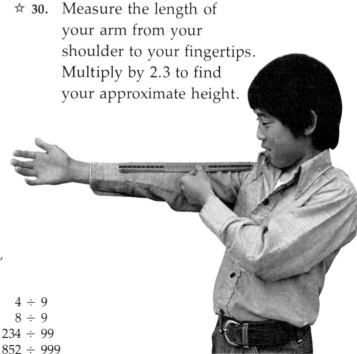

You can make your calculator "stutter." Try these division problems.

$1 \div 9$	$2 \div 9$	$3 \div 9$	$4 \div 9$
$5 \div 9$	$6 \div 9$	$7 \div 9$	$8 \div 9$
$1 \div 99$	$2 \div 99$	$37 \div 99$	$234 \div 99$
$306 \div 999$	$542 \div 999$	$715 \div 999$	$852 \div 999$

More decimal multiplication

Norma lives 0.4 km from school.
Her friend Jan lives 0.2 of the way
from Norma's house to school.
How far does Jan live from Norma?

Finding the answer

0.4 ← 1-place decimal
$\times\ 0.2$ ← 1-place decimal
$\overline{0.08}$ ← 2-place decimal ←

Notice that a zero is placed to the right of the decimal point to form a 2-place decimal

Jan lives 0.08 km from Norma.

Other examples

$$\begin{array}{r} 0.08 \\ \times\ \ 0.7 \\ \hline 0.056 \end{array} \qquad \begin{array}{r} 0.2 \\ \times\ 0.03 \\ \hline 0.006 \end{array} \qquad \begin{array}{r} 0.014 \\ \times\ \ \ \ \ 6 \\ \hline 0.084 \end{array}$$

Find the products.

1. $\begin{array}{r} 0.1 \\ \times\ 0.5 \\ \hline \end{array}$
2. $\begin{array}{r} 0.06 \\ \times\ \ 0.2 \\ \hline \end{array}$
3. $\begin{array}{r} 0.31 \\ \times\ \ 0.3 \\ \hline \end{array}$
4. $\begin{array}{r} 1.5 \\ \times\ 0.4 \\ \hline \end{array}$
5. $\begin{array}{r} 0.27 \\ \times\ \ 0.3 \\ \hline \end{array}$

6. $\begin{array}{r} 6.2 \\ \times\ 0.01 \\ \hline \end{array}$
7. $\begin{array}{r} 0.9 \\ \times\ 0.4 \\ \hline \end{array}$
8. $\begin{array}{r} 0.45 \\ \times\ \ 0.3 \\ \hline \end{array}$
9. $\begin{array}{r} 0.009 \\ \times\ \ \ \ \ \ 8 \\ \hline \end{array}$
10. $\begin{array}{r} 57 \\ \times\ .004 \\ \hline \end{array}$

11. $\begin{array}{r} 0.018 \\ \times\ \ \ \ \ 4 \\ \hline \end{array}$
12. $\begin{array}{r} 6.02 \\ \times\ 0.7 \\ \hline \end{array}$
13. $\begin{array}{r} 0.01 \\ \times\ 0.1 \\ \hline \end{array}$
14. $\begin{array}{r} 100 \\ \times\ 0.01 \\ \hline \end{array}$
15. $\begin{array}{r} 0.07 \\ \times\ 0.9 \\ \hline \end{array}$

Multiply.

1. 6.3
   × 0.05

2. 1.03
   × 0.9

3. 0.06
   × 0.8

4. 0.11
   × 0.7

5. 50
   × 0.06

6. 3.8
   × 0.7

7. 0.19
   × 0.5

8. 2.6
   × 0.04

9. 0.93
   × 0.2

10. 7.4
    × 0.06

11. 0.53
    × 1.2

12. 66
    × 3.5

13. 4.5
    × 2.7

14. 89
    × 0.16

15. 0.58
    × 10

16. 1.38
    × 0.8

17. 0.715
    × 6

18. 208
    × 0.07

19. 439
    × .009

20. 3.64
    × 0.7

21. 7.43
    × 3.5

22. 39.6
    × 4.3

23. 0.798
    × 56

24. 5.77
    × 7.8

25. 63.4
    × 8.2

26. 607
    × 2.39

27. 0.776
    × 439

28. 93.5
    × 27.8

29. 500
    × 2.46

30. 0.738
    × 400

31. Mike lives 2.1 km from school and Jason lives about 0.4 times that distance. How far from school does Jason live?

32. It took Karl 13.5 seconds to run 100 m. Alan took only 0.8 as long as Karl. How long did it take Alan to run 100 meters?

Find the products.

0.143 × 7
0.143 × 14
0.143 × 21
0.143 × 28
0.143 × 35

Is there a pattern in the answers? Make up some other problems in this pattern.

More practice, page 371

Finding money products

Ramon bought 4 felt-tip pens of different colors. Each pen cost $1.19. How much did the pens cost?

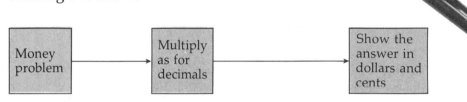

Finding the answer

Money problem	→	Multiply as for decimals	→	Show the answer in dollars and cents

$$\begin{array}{r} \$\ 1.19 \\ \times\quad 4 \\ \hline \end{array}$$

$$\begin{array}{r} \$\ 1.19 \leftarrow \text{2-place decimal} \\ \times\quad 4 \leftarrow \text{0-place decimal} \\ \hline 4.76 \leftarrow \text{2-place decimal} \end{array}$$

$$\begin{array}{r} \$\ 1.19 \leftarrow \text{2-place decimal} \\ \times\quad 4 \leftarrow \text{0-place decimal} \\ \hline \$\ 4.76 \leftarrow \text{2-place decimal} \end{array}$$

The pens cost $4.76.

Other examples

$$\begin{array}{r} \$\ 2.15 \\ \times\quad 6 \\ \hline \$12.90 \end{array}$$

$$\begin{array}{r} \$\ 12.48 \\ \times\quad 8 \\ \hline \$\ 99.84 \end{array}$$

$$\begin{array}{r} \$\ 0.25 \\ \times\quad 15 \\ \hline 1\ 25 \\ 2\ 50 \\ \hline \$\ 3.75 \end{array}$$

$$\begin{array}{r} \$\ 3.95 \\ \times\quad 36 \\ \hline 23\ 70 \\ 118\ 50 \\ \hline \$142.20 \end{array}$$

Find the products.

1. $\begin{array}{r} \$\ 1.75 \\ \times\quad 3 \\ \hline \end{array}$

2. $\begin{array}{r} \$\ 6.09 \\ \times\quad 4 \\ \hline \end{array}$

3. $\begin{array}{r} \$\ 0.69 \\ \times\quad 6 \\ \hline \end{array}$

4. $\begin{array}{r} \$\ 3.44 \\ \times\quad 2 \\ \hline \end{array}$

5. $\begin{array}{r} \$\ 7.25 \\ \times\quad 8 \\ \hline \end{array}$

6. $\begin{array}{r} \$\ 5.55 \\ \times\quad 5 \\ \hline \end{array}$

7. $\begin{array}{r} \$\ 11.22 \\ \times\quad 7 \\ \hline \end{array}$

8. $\begin{array}{r} \$\ 0.35 \\ \times\quad 9 \\ \hline \end{array}$

9. $\begin{array}{r} \$\ 1.05 \\ \times\quad 26 \\ \hline \end{array}$

10. $\begin{array}{r} \$\ 3.76 \\ \times\quad 12 \\ \hline \end{array}$

11. $\begin{array}{r} \$\ 26.98 \\ \times\quad 3 \\ \hline \end{array}$

12. $\begin{array}{r} \$\ 16.28 \\ \times\quad 4 \\ \hline \end{array}$

Find the products.

1. $ 1.50
   × 6

2. $ 0.66
   × 9

3. $ 2.13
   × 8

4. $ 20.15
   × 4

5. $ 2.98
   × 2

6. $ 3.44
   × 3

7. $ 89.95
   × 5

8. $ 17.50
   × 7

9. $ 0.77
   × 12

10. $ 1.23
    × 25

11. $ 5.77
    × 18

12. $ 0.29
    × 32

13. $ 16.50
    × 49

14. $ 2.98
    × 24

15. $ 43.75
    × 15

16. $ 20.00
    × 54

17. $ 0.85
    × 24

18. $ 0.49
    × 83

19. $ 42.90
    × 13

20. $ 8.00
    × 74

21. Desk set: $14.88
    How much for 4 desk sets?

22. Wall poster: $3.49
    How much for 3 posters?

☆ 23. Choose some article from a
    newspaper advertisement
    you would like to buy.
    How much would it cost
    if everyone in your class
    bought one?

Suppose you put 2¢ in a bank
on February 1, 4¢ on February 2,
8¢ on February 3, and so on,
doubling the amount each day.
After you made your last deposit
on Valentine's Day, would you have
enough money to buy a $5 box of
candy? How much would you have?

Answers for Self-check 1. 0.6 2. 2.4 3. 0.15 4. 0.28 5. 8.5 6. 5.67 7. 4.24 8. 1.095 9. 8.40
10. 2.916 11. 250.38 12. 239.02 13. 0.06 14. 0.075 15. 0.105 16. 0.024 17. $6.48 18. $2.34
19. $47.92 20. $82.08

Self-check

Find the products.

1. 0.3×2
2. 4×0.6
3. 0.5×0.3
4. 7×0.04

5.
$$\begin{array}{r} 1.7 \\ \times\ \ 5 \\ \hline \end{array}$$

6.
$$\begin{array}{r} 63 \\ \times\ 0.09 \\ \hline \end{array}$$

7.
$$\begin{array}{r} 0.53 \\ \times\ \ \ 8 \\ \hline \end{array}$$

8.
$$\begin{array}{r} 0.73 \\ \times\ 1.5 \\ \hline \end{array}$$

9.
$$\begin{array}{r} 3.5 \\ \times\ 2.4 \\ \hline \end{array}$$

10.
$$\begin{array}{r} 8.1 \\ \times\ 0.36 \\ \hline \end{array}$$

11.
$$\begin{array}{r} 32.1 \\ \times\ 7.8 \\ \hline \end{array}$$

12.
$$\begin{array}{r} 6.29 \\ \times\ \ 38 \\ \hline \end{array}$$

13.
$$\begin{array}{r} 0.2 \\ \times\ 0.3 \\ \hline \end{array}$$

14.
$$\begin{array}{r} 0.025 \\ \times\ \ \ \ \ 3 \\ \hline \end{array}$$

15.
$$\begin{array}{r} 0.15 \\ \times\ \ 0.7 \\ \hline \end{array}$$

16.
$$\begin{array}{r} 0.004 \\ \times\ \ \ \ \ 6 \\ \hline \end{array}$$

17.
$$\begin{array}{r} \$\ 1.62 \\ \times\ \ \ \ 4 \\ \hline \end{array}$$

18.
$$\begin{array}{r} \$\ 0.39 \\ \times\ \ \ \ 6 \\ \hline \end{array}$$

19.
$$\begin{array}{r} \$\ 5.99 \\ \times\ \ \ \ 8 \\ \hline \end{array}$$

20.
$$\begin{array}{r} \$\ 2.16 \\ \times\ \ \ 38 \\ \hline \end{array}$$

Answers for Self-check—page 309

Test

Find the products.

1. 0.1×0.3
2. 4×0.6
3. 0.9×0.3
4. 0.01×0.4

5.
$$\begin{array}{r} 3.5 \\ \times\ \ 5 \\ \hline \end{array}$$

6.
$$\begin{array}{r} 2.7 \\ \times\ \ 9 \\ \hline \end{array}$$

7.
$$\begin{array}{r} 6.18 \\ \times\ \ \ 4 \\ \hline \end{array}$$

8.
$$\begin{array}{r} 0.77 \\ \times\ \ 0.8 \\ \hline \end{array}$$

9.
$$\begin{array}{r} 7.4 \\ \times\ 1.2 \\ \hline \end{array}$$

10.
$$\begin{array}{r} 8.5 \\ \times\ 35 \\ \hline \end{array}$$

11.
$$\begin{array}{r} 2.09 \\ \times\ \ 0.8 \\ \hline \end{array}$$

12.
$$\begin{array}{r} 0.83 \\ \times\ 0.14 \\ \hline \end{array}$$

13.
$$\begin{array}{r} 0.3 \\ \times\ 0.3 \\ \hline \end{array}$$

14.
$$\begin{array}{r} 0.032 \\ \times\ \ \ \ \ 2 \\ \hline \end{array}$$

15.
$$\begin{array}{r} 0.16 \\ \times\ \ 0.8 \\ \hline \end{array}$$

16.
$$\begin{array}{r} 0.021 \\ \times\ \ \ \ \ 4 \\ \hline \end{array}$$

17.
$$\begin{array}{r} \$\ 2.53 \\ \times\ \ \ \ 7 \\ \hline \end{array}$$

18.
$$\begin{array}{r} \$\ 0.69 \\ \times\ \ \ \ 9 \\ \hline \end{array}$$

19.
$$\begin{array}{r} \$\ 12.75 \\ \times\ \ \ \ \ 4 \\ \hline \end{array}$$

20.
$$\begin{array}{r} \$\ 1.56 \\ \times\ \ \ 72 \\ \hline \end{array}$$

Toothpick Equations

These toothpick equations use Roman Numerals. **None** of the equations are correct as they now stand. You can make each equation correct by moving one, and only one, toothpick.

Example: $| - | = |||$

Solution: $| + | = ||$

Move one stick to make each of these equations correct.

$$IV - I = V$$

$$IX - V = VI$$

$$X + IV = V$$

$$VI - IV = XI$$

$$XL + X = ||$$

$$LV - X = XIV$$

$$C + L = I$$

$$| - ||| = ||$$

Make up some toothpick equations like these.

Using Your Skills

HOBBY SHOP

SPECIAL SALE

Stained-glass kit	$4.75
Mosaic tile kit	3.69
Paint-by-Numbers	2.75
Glass beads, packet	0.39
Wooden beads, packet	0.69
Decoupage kit	5.98
Wood plaques	1.19
Macrame cord	3.25
Candlemaking kit	7.49
Candle molds	3.75
Paint, jar	1.79

Getting started

1. How much would 4 candle molds cost?

2. How much change would you get back if you paid for a stained-glass kit with a 10-dollar bill?

3. What other problems can you solve?

Sometimes you must use more than one operation to solve a problem.

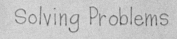

Solving Problems

1. Read carefully to find the facts.
2. Look for the question.
3. Decide what to do.
4. Find the answer
5. Read again. Does your answer make sense?

What would be the total cost of 4 wood plaques and 3 jars of paint?

$$\begin{array}{r} \$\,1.19 \\ \times\quad 4 \\ \hline \$\,4.76 \end{array} \qquad \begin{array}{r} \$\,1.79 \\ \times\quad 3 \\ \hline \$\,5.37 \end{array} \qquad \begin{array}{r} \$\,4.76 \\ +\,5.37 \\ \hline \$10.13 \end{array}$$

The total cost would be $10.13.

Solve these problems. Use the prices in the chart on page 312.

1. Margaret had $5.00. She bought some macrame cord for $3.25. The sales tax was 16 cents. How much money did she have left?

2. Kevin bought a candle-making kit and 3 candle molds. How much did he have to pay in all?

3. A jar of paint usually sells for $1.98. How much is saved by buying 6 jars of paint at the sale price?

4. Janet bought 3 packets of glass beads and 2 packets of wooden beads. How much change should she get from a 10-dollar bill?

Find the cost of the items in each problem.

1. 3 loaves of bread
   39¢ a loaf

2. 5 boxes of frozen peas
   33¢ a box

3. 2 boxes of cream cheese
   $1.39 a box

4. 3 cartons of milk
   74¢ a carton

5. 3 cans of coffee
   $1.19 a can

6. 2 cartons of butter
   95¢ a carton

7. 12 cans of baby food
   17¢ a can

8. 2 6-packs of cola
   16¢ for each bottle

9. 3 dozen eggs
   6¢ per egg

10. 5 kg of sugar
    57¢ per kilogram

11. 4 packages of ground beef
    $1.14 per package

12. 12 oranges
    3 for 29¢

Find the total for each sales slip. Then find the amount
of change due if each bill is paid with $20.00.

1.

Supermarket

01.22 MT ::
01.15 MT ::
00.45 GR ::
00.89 GR ::
01.09 GR ::
00.89 PR ::
00.39 MT ::
00.74 MT ::

Total

2.

Supermarket

00.61 PR ::
00.55 GR ::
01.99 GR ::
03.15 MT ::
00.72 GR ::

Total

3.

Supermarket

00.77 GR ::
00.69 PR ::
00.25 GR ::
00.49 GR ::
02.17 MT ::
01.27 MT ::
01.35 MT ::
00.39 PR ::
00.89 PR ::

Total

4.

Supermarket

03.66 MT ::
01.29 GR ::
01.75 GR ::
02.29 MT ::
00.68 PR ::
00.86 GR ::
02.43 MT ::
00.97 GR ::
00.35 PR ::

Total

5.

Supermarket

00.76 GR ::
01.08 GR ::
01.29 GR ::
00.53 GR ::
00.53 GR ::
00.53 GR ::
02.37 MT ::
01.16 GR ::
02.77 MT ::

Total

6.

Supermarket

00.39 GR ::
00.89 GR ::
00.89 GR ::
00.57 GR ::
00.15 PR ::
02.47 MT ::
02.07 MT ::
00.69 GR ::
01.79 MT ::
03.19 MT ::
00.98 GR ::

Total

Using decimals—scale models

A model of a ship is 28.6 cm long. The **scale** of the model is $\frac{1}{250}$. This means that the actual ship is 250 times as large as the model.
What is the length of the actual ship?

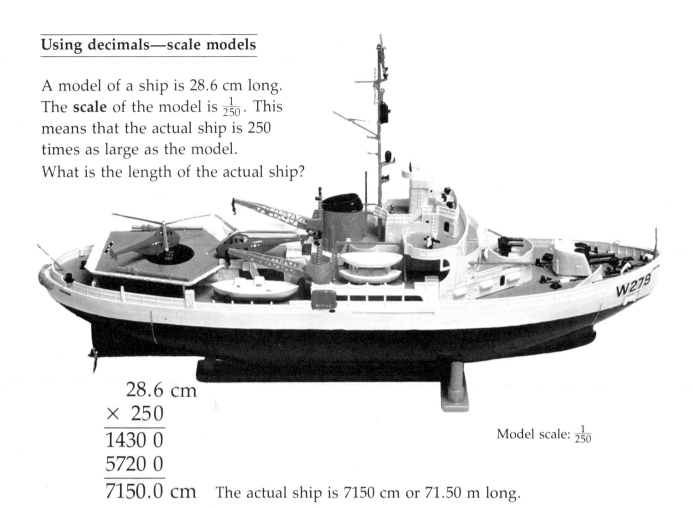

Model scale: $\frac{1}{250}$

$$
\begin{array}{r}
28.6 \text{ cm} \\
\times\ 250 \\
\hline
1430\ 0 \\
5720\ 0 \\
\hline
7150.0 \text{ cm}
\end{array}
$$

The actual ship is 7150 cm or 71.50 m long.

---

1. The scale for a model of a 1937 Packard car is $\frac{1}{16}$. The model is 34.3 cm long. How long is the car?

2. The scale of a model plane is $\frac{1}{72}$. The wingspan of the model is 26 cm. What is the wingspan of the actual plane?

3. The length of the fuselage (distance from nose to tail) of a model plane is 19.7 cm. The scale is $\frac{1}{72}$. What is the length of the full-sized plane?

4. The length of a model sports car is 25 cm. The scale is $\frac{1}{16}$. What is the length of the actual car?

5. The wingspan of a model DC-9 is 36.5 cm. The scale is $\frac{1}{72}$. What is the wingspan of a DC-9?

6. The length of a model ship is 32.6 cm. The scale is $\frac{1}{72}$. What is the length of the actual ship?

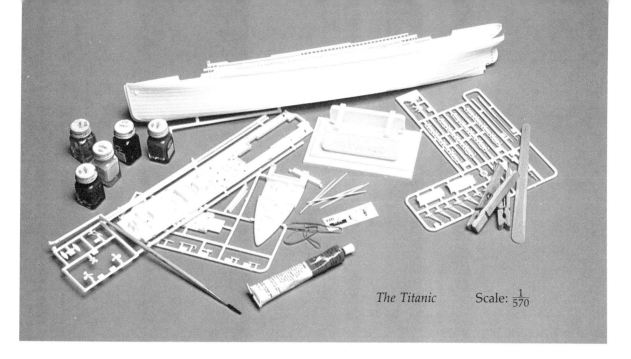

The Titanic   Scale: $\frac{1}{570}$

7. A model of the ship *Titanic* is 47 cm long. How long was the *Titanic*?

8. A model of the ocean liner *Queen Elizabeth 2* has a scale of $\frac{1}{570}$. The model is 51.5 cm long. About how long is the ship?

9. A model of a Spanish galleon has a scale of $\frac{1}{160}$. The model is 26.9 cm long. About how long was the Spanish galleon?

10.

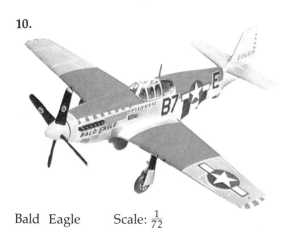

Bald Eagle   Scale: $\frac{1}{72}$

Model wingspan: 15.8 cm
Model body: 13.7 cm
Find the actual wingspan and length of body.

11.

Spitfire   Scale: $\frac{1}{32}$

Model wingspan: 47.0 cm
Model body: 39.3 cm
Find the actual wingspan and length of body.

Perimeter of regular polygons

Each figure is a **regular polygon.**

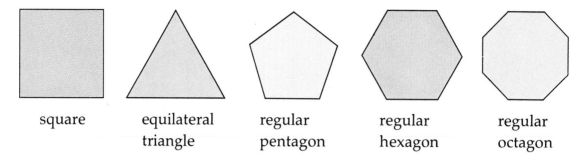

| square | equilateral triangle | regular pentagon | regular hexagon | regular octagon |

Each figure has sides of equal length
and angles of equal size.

The **perimeter** of a polygon is the total distance around the polygon.
What is the perimeter of a regular hexagon if each side is 1.3 cm?

Finding the answer

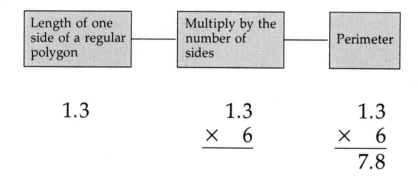

| Length of one side of a regular polygon | Multiply by the number of sides | Perimeter |

$$1.3 \qquad \begin{array}{r} 1.3 \\ \times\ \ 6 \\ \hline \end{array} \qquad \begin{array}{r} 1.3 \\ \times\ \ 6 \\ \hline 7.8 \end{array}$$

The perimeter of the hexagon is 7.8 cm.

Find the perimeter of each of these regular polygons.

1.

2.5 cm

2.

32.4 cm

3.

21.5 cm

Give the missing numbers.

Regular polygon		Length of each side	Perimeter
triangle		3.5 cm	1.
square		6.2 cm	2.
hexagon		5.0 cm	3.
octagon		2.7 cm	4.
pentagon		5.4 cm	5.
square		7.8 cm	6.
octagon		6.3 cm	7.
triangle		12 mm	8.
pentagon		83 mm	9.
hexagon		24 mm	10.

✷ Finding area—decimals

Mike's school picture is 5.2 cm long and 3.7 cm wide. What is the area of the picture?

$$\begin{array}{r} 5.2 \\ \times\ 3.7 \\ \hline 3\ 6\ 4 \\ 15\ 6\ 0 \\ \hline 19.2\ 4 \end{array}$$

5.2 cm

3.7 cm

The area is 19.24 cm².

Find the area of each rectangle.

1.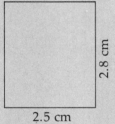

3.2 cm

2.0 cm

2.

4 cm

1.8 cm

3.

3.1 cm

3.1 cm

4.

2.5 cm

2.8 cm

5.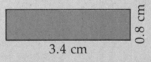

3.4 cm

0.8 cm

6.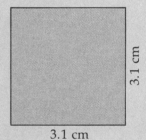

3.9 cm

2.1 cm

7.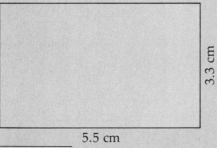

5.5 cm

3.3 cm

8.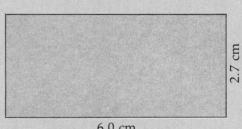

6.0 cm

2.7 cm

Find the area of each rectangular object.

1. window glass:
    length: 1.07 m
    width: 0.8 m

2. sheet of paper:
    length: 27.8 cm
    width: 21.5 cm

3. front cover of a book:
    length: 23.5 cm
    width: 20 cm

4. room:
    length: 4.4 m
    width: 3.6 m

5. ceiling:
    length: 7.3 m
    width: 6.1 m

6. bulletin board:
    length: 1.1 m
    width: 1.1 m

7. chalkboard:
    length: 1.7 m
    width: 0.9 m

8. table top:
    length: 1.8 m
    width: 0.7 m

9. door:
    length: 2.1 m
    width: 0.9 m

10. wall:
    length: 4.4 m
    height: 2.9 m

11. rug:
    length: 3.6 m
    width: 2.7 m

12. desk top:
    length: 1.7 m
    width: 0.9 m

☆ 13. Measure the length and width of your classroom. Find the area of the floor of the room.

Think !

The numeral for the year 1881 reads the same backward, forward, or upside down. What is the next year in which this will happen again?

Answers for Self-check: 1. $4.63   2. $2.55   3. 7050 cm or 70.50 m   4. 4197.6 cm or 41.976 m
5. 19.0 cm   6. 30.0 m   7. 39.42 cm²   8. 48.72 m²

Self-check

1. Lisa bought a roll of macrame cord for $3.25. She bought 2 packets of wooden beads at $0.69 a packet. How much did she spend?

2. Melons: 59¢ each
   Lettuce: 39¢ a head
   How much for 3 melons and 2 heads of lettuce?

3. The body of a model plane is 28.2 cm long. The scale is $\frac{1}{250}$. What is the length of the body of the plane?

4. The scale of a model ship is $\frac{1}{72}$. The model is 58.3 cm long. How long was the ship?

5. A regular pentagon has 5 sides. Each side is 3.8 cm long. What is the perimeter?

6. The length of each side of a square is 7.5 m. What is the perimeter of the square?

☆ 7. Find the area of a rectangle 7.3 cm long and 5.4 cm wide.

☆ 8. The floor of a room is 8.7 m long and 5.6 m wide. What is the area of the floor?

Answers for Self-check—page 321

Test

1. Adult tickets: $2.25
   Children's tickets: $1.50
   How much for 2 adults and 3 children?

2. Bread: $0.55 a loaf
   Milk: $0.68 a carton
   How much for 2 loaves of bread and 4 cartons of milk?

3. The scale of a model race car is $\frac{1}{16}$. The model is 28 cm long. What is the length of the actual race car?

4. The scale for a model of a 707 jet plane is $\frac{1}{100}$. The model is 43.4 cm long. How long is the plane?

5. Each side of an equilateral triangle is 12.7 cm long. What is the perimeter?

6. Each side of a regular nine-sided polygon is 13.6 cm long. What is the perimeter?

☆ 7. A throw rug is 1.5 m long and 0.9 m wide. What is the area of the rug?

☆ 8. A house lot is 45.7 m wide and 62 m long. What is the area of the lot?

A Slide Or Jump Puzzle

Place 3 red markers and 3 black markers on a board like the one below.

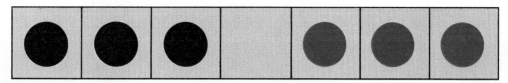

The object of the puzzle is to exchange the positions of the red and black markers.

Rules:

1. The red markers can be moved only to the left.

2. The black markers can be moved only to the right.

3. A marker can slide one place to an empty square.

4. A marker can jump one marker of a different color only if it can land on an empty square.

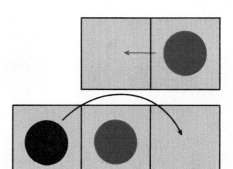

5. A marker cannot jump another marker of the same color.

Now use red and black markers and try to solve the puzzle at the top of the page.

Adding and Subtracting with Mixed Numerals

Getting started

Two people can play this mixed numeral game. The players take turns tossing a number cube to fill in three squares that form a mixed numeral. The player with the largest number wins.

Here is a sample game:

Player A	Player B
First toss	
Second toss	
Third toss	

$5\frac{3}{2} = 5 + \frac{3}{2} = 5 + 1\frac{1}{2} = 6\frac{1}{2}$ $3\frac{6}{5} = 3 + \frac{6}{5} = 3 + 1\frac{1}{5} = 4\frac{1}{5}$

Player A won this game.
Which player would win each of these games?

Player A	Player B	Player A	Player B	Player A	Player B
$4\frac{1}{2}$	$3\frac{4}{3}$	$6\frac{2}{3}$	$4\frac{5}{3}$	$5\frac{4}{2}$	$3\frac{3}{1}$

1. Give this player's number as an improper fraction.

2. Did these players get the same number?

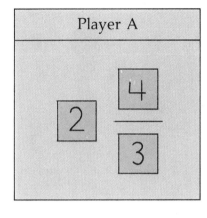 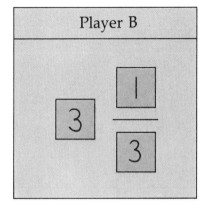

3. What is this player's number?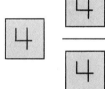

4. Can player B win with one more toss? Can player B tie?

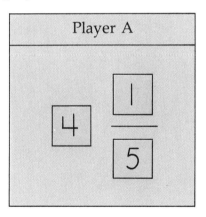 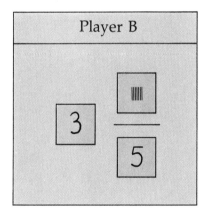

5. What is the smallest number you can get for this game?

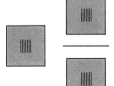

6. What is the largest number you can get?

Renaming mixed numerals

Joyce formed this mixed numeral by tossing a number cube three times. She renamed the numeral because $\frac{5}{4}$ is greater than 1.

$$3\frac{5}{4} = 3 + \frac{5}{4} = 3 + 1\frac{1}{4} = 4\frac{1}{4}$$

Other examples

$$10\frac{5}{3} = 10 + \frac{5}{3} = 10 + 1\frac{2}{3} = 11\frac{2}{3}$$

$$18\frac{4}{2} = 18 + \frac{4}{2} = 18 + 2 = 20$$

$$6\frac{8}{8} = 6 + \frac{8}{8} = 6 + 1 = 7$$

Rename each mixed numeral.

1. $3\frac{7}{6} = 4\frac{\square}{\square}$

2. $4\frac{13}{10} = 5\frac{\square}{\square}$

3. $26\frac{5}{3} = 27\frac{\square}{\square}$

4. $5\frac{8}{5} = 6\frac{\square}{\square}$

5. $16\frac{3}{2} = 17\frac{\square}{\square}$

6. $11\frac{19}{10} = 12\frac{\square}{\square}$

7. $7\frac{13}{10} = 8\frac{\square}{\square}$

8. $7\frac{11}{10} = 8\frac{\square}{\square}$

9. $6\frac{5}{4} = 7\frac{\square}{\square}$

10. $9\frac{7}{4} = 10\frac{\square}{\square}$

11. $3\frac{6}{5} = 4\frac{\square}{\square}$

12. $1\frac{5}{2} = 3\frac{\square}{\square}$

13. $15\frac{5}{3} = 16\frac{\square}{\square}$

14. $1\frac{11}{8} = 2\frac{\square}{\square}$

15. $29\frac{13}{10} = 30\frac{\square}{\square}$

Rename each of these mixed numerals.

16. $7\frac{3}{3}$

17. $16\frac{6}{2}$

18. $9\frac{4}{4}$

19. $3\frac{7}{4}$

20. $18\frac{20}{10}$

21. $39\frac{5}{5}$

22. $57\frac{24}{12}$

23. $46\frac{19}{10}$

Rename each mixed numeral by adding 1 to the fraction part.

Examples: $7\frac{1}{5} = (6 + 1) + \frac{1}{5} = 6 + \left(\frac{5}{5} + \frac{1}{5}\right) = 6\frac{6}{5}$

$\quad\quad\quad 4\frac{3}{4} = (3 + 1) + \frac{3}{4} = 3 + \left(\frac{4}{4} + \frac{3}{4}\right) = 3\frac{7}{4}$

1. $8\frac{1}{4} = 7\frac{\text{▥}}{4}$

2. $6\frac{2}{3} = 5\frac{\text{▥}}{3}$

3. $10\frac{1}{2} = 9\frac{\text{▥}}{2}$

4. $16\frac{2}{3} = 15\frac{\text{▥}}{3}$

5. $4\frac{3}{8} = 3\frac{\text{▥}}{8}$

6. $7\frac{2}{5} = 6\frac{\text{▥}}{5}$

7. $18\frac{3}{4} = 17\frac{\text{▥}}{4}$

8. $16\frac{7}{10} = 15\frac{\text{▥}}{10}$

9. $11\frac{5}{8} = 10\frac{\text{▥}}{8}$

10. $3\frac{1}{10} = 2\frac{\text{▥}}{10}$

11. $9\frac{3}{5} = 8\frac{\text{▥}}{5}$

12. $37\frac{1}{2} = 36\frac{\text{▥}}{2}$

13. $12\frac{2}{3} = 11\frac{\text{▥}}{3}$

14. $42\frac{1}{8} = 41\frac{\text{▥}}{8}$

15. $66\frac{2}{3} = 65\frac{\text{▥}}{3}$

16. $8\frac{4}{8} = 7\frac{\text{▥}}{8}$

17. $2\frac{4}{10} = 1\frac{\text{▥}}{10}$

18. $6\frac{3}{4} = 5\frac{\text{▥}}{4}$

19. $1\frac{5}{6} - \frac{\text{▥}}{6}$

20. $13\frac{9}{12} = 12\frac{\text{▥}}{12}$

21. $10\frac{1}{3} = 9\frac{\text{▥}}{3}$

22. $100\frac{1}{4} = 99\frac{\text{▥}}{4}$

23. $16\frac{6}{8} = 15\frac{\text{▥}}{8}$

24. $50\frac{4}{6} = 49\frac{\text{▥}}{6}$

Give the missing numerator.

25. $8 = 7\frac{\text{▥}}{2}$

26. $12 = 11\frac{\text{▥}}{5}$

27. $23 = 22\frac{\text{▥}}{10}$

28. $30 = 29\frac{\text{▥}}{4}$

29. $19 = 18\frac{\text{▥}}{6}$

30. $47 = 46\frac{\text{▥}}{8}$

31. $2 = 1\frac{\text{▥}}{3}$

32. $100 = 99\frac{\text{▥}}{100}$

33. $38 = 37\frac{\text{▥}}{12}$

Choose any number from 1 to 9.
Use the number 5 times as a factor.
Look at the ones' digit of your
answer. What do you discover?

$3 \times 3 \times 3 \times 3 \times 3 = n$
$8 \times 8 \times 8 \times 8 \times 8 = n$
$7 \times 7 \times 7 \times 7 \times 7 = n$

⊛ Adding with mixed numerals

Richard worked as a babysitter $3\frac{3}{4}$ hours on Friday and $3\frac{1}{2}$ hours on Saturday. How many hours did he work in all?

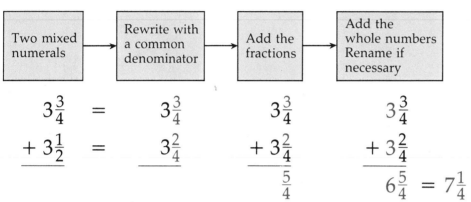

Finding the answer

Two mixed numerals	Rewrite with a common denominator	Add the fractions	Add the whole numbers Rename if necessary

$$3\frac{3}{4} = \qquad 3\frac{3}{4} \qquad 3\frac{3}{4} \qquad 3\frac{3}{4}$$

$$+\,3\frac{1}{2} = \qquad 3\frac{2}{4} \qquad +\,3\frac{2}{4} \qquad +\,3\frac{2}{4}$$

$$\frac{5}{4} \qquad\qquad 6\frac{5}{4} = 7\frac{1}{4}$$

Richard worked $7\frac{1}{4}$ hours.

Other examples

$$6\frac{5}{8} = 6\frac{5}{8}$$
$$+\,3\frac{3}{4} = 3\frac{6}{8}$$
$$9\frac{11}{8} = 10\frac{3}{8}$$

$$24\frac{4}{5} = 24\frac{8}{10}$$
$$37\frac{1}{2} = 37\frac{5}{10}$$
$$61\frac{13}{10} = 62\frac{3}{10}$$

Add.

1. $7\frac{2}{3}$
   $+\,8\frac{2}{3}$

2. $6\frac{5}{6}$
   $+\,9\frac{2}{3}$

3. $4\frac{7}{12}$
   $+\,8\frac{5}{6}$

4. $6\frac{7}{12}$
   $+\,7\frac{2}{3}$

5. $19\frac{1}{2}$
   $+\,2\frac{3}{4}$

6. $17\frac{7}{8}$
   $+\,26\frac{1}{4}$

7. $54\frac{3}{10}$
   $+\,37\frac{4}{5}$

8. $85\frac{1}{3}$
   $+\,61\frac{5}{6}$

9. $37\frac{7}{8}$
   $+\,84\frac{5}{6}$

10. $86\frac{7}{10}$
    $+\,25\frac{1}{5}$

11. $5\frac{5}{8}$
    $+\,6\frac{3}{4}$

12. $8\frac{1}{4}$
    $+\,7\frac{9}{10}$

13. $9\frac{4}{5}$
    $+\,2\frac{3}{5}$

14. $13\frac{9}{16}$
    $+\,6\frac{1}{2}$

15. $27\frac{3}{4}$
    $+\,8\frac{1}{2}$

Add.

1. $6\frac{4}{5}$
$+ 7\frac{1}{2}$

2. $3\frac{7}{10}$
$+ 5\frac{1}{2}$

3. $9\frac{2}{3}$
$+ 2\frac{5}{6}$

4. $8\frac{3}{5}$
$+ 7\frac{2}{5}$

5. $12\frac{9}{10}$
$+ 6\frac{1}{2}$

6. $18\frac{3}{4}$
$+ 13\frac{1}{2}$

7. $23\frac{1}{2}$
$+ 29\frac{1}{2}$

8. $16\frac{7}{8}$
$+ 20\frac{3}{4}$

9. $11\frac{1}{3}$
$+ 16\frac{3}{4}$

10. $34\frac{7}{10}$
$+ 46\frac{2}{5}$

11. $51\frac{2}{3}$
$+ 73\frac{1}{2}$

12. $9\frac{4}{5}$
$+ 8\frac{7}{10}$

13. $8\frac{7}{10}$
$+ 3\frac{1}{2}$

14. $12\frac{1}{4}$
$+ 17\frac{9}{10}$

15. $42\frac{7}{10}$
$+ 31\frac{41}{100}$

16. $66\frac{1}{2}$
$+ 48\frac{3}{8}$

17. $67\frac{3}{5}$
$+ 27\frac{7}{20}$

18. $35\frac{3}{10}$
$+ 72\frac{3}{5}$

19. $27\frac{1}{2}$
$18\frac{5}{8}$
$+ 12\frac{1}{4}$

20. $92\frac{3}{5}$
$88\frac{3}{5}$
$+ 63\frac{2}{5}$

21. $127\frac{1}{4}$
$328\frac{3}{4}$
$+ 256\frac{1}{2}$

22. $37\frac{1}{3}$
$29\frac{1}{2}$
$+ 43\frac{2}{3}$

23. $48\frac{1}{10}$
$65\frac{3}{5}$
$+ 82\frac{1}{2}$

24. Jan worked $1\frac{3}{4}$ hours on Tuesday and $2\frac{1}{3}$ hours on Wednesday. How many hours did she work in all?

25. Carl worked $5\frac{2}{3}$ hours Friday and $2\frac{3}{4}$ hours Saturday. How many hours did he work in all?

If you went to bed at 8:00 at night and set your alarm clock for 9:00, how many hours sleep would you get?

⊛ Subtracting with mixed numerals

Dave and Neil tossed two number cubes.

Dave's first toss:

The difference is Dave's score. What is Dave's score?

Dave's second toss:

Finding the answer

Two mixed numerals	→	Rewrite with a common denominator	→	Rename if necessary and subtract the fractions	→	Subtract the whole numbers

$$5\frac{1}{3} = 5\frac{4}{12} \qquad 4\frac{16}{12} \qquad 4\frac{16}{12}$$
$$-3\frac{3}{4} = 3\frac{9}{12} \qquad -3\frac{9}{12} \qquad -3\frac{9}{12}$$
$$\qquad \qquad \qquad \qquad \frac{7}{12} \qquad 1\frac{7}{12}$$

Dave's score is $1\frac{7}{12}$.

Other examples

$$8\frac{1}{4} = 8\frac{3}{12} = 7\frac{15}{12} \qquad 12\frac{1}{3} = 12\frac{2}{6} = 11\frac{8}{6} \qquad 16 \quad = 15\frac{10}{10}$$
$$-5\frac{1}{3} = 5\frac{4}{12} = 5\frac{4}{12} \qquad -9\frac{5}{6} = 9\frac{5}{6} = 9\frac{5}{6} \qquad -8\frac{3}{10} = 8\frac{3}{10}$$
$$\qquad \qquad 2\frac{11}{12} \qquad \qquad \qquad 2\frac{3}{6} \text{ or } 2\frac{1}{2} \qquad \qquad 7\frac{7}{10}$$

Subtract.

1. $8\frac{1}{4}$
   $-3\frac{5}{8}$

2. $9\frac{2}{3}$
   $-6\frac{5}{6}$

3. $8\frac{7}{8}$
   $-4\frac{5}{8}$

4. $7\frac{7}{10}$
   $-6\frac{2}{5}$

5. $19\frac{7}{12}$
   $-2\frac{3}{4}$

6. $54\frac{3}{10}$
   $-37\frac{4}{5}$

7. $6\frac{7}{9}$
   -5

8. $8\frac{5}{6}$
   $-7\frac{7}{8}$

9. $13\frac{3}{5}$
   $-6\frac{13}{15}$

10. $91\frac{1}{2}$
    $-88\frac{9}{16}$

11. $19\frac{2}{3}$
    $-5\frac{11}{12}$

12. $36\frac{1}{10}$
    $-29\frac{7}{10}$

13. 83
    $-42\frac{7}{8}$

14. $61\frac{4}{5}$
    $-39\frac{9}{10}$

15. 93
    $-39\frac{9}{10}$

Find the differences.

1. $24\frac{1}{4}$
   $-18\frac{1}{2}$

2. $37\frac{7}{10}$
   $-23\frac{1}{5}$

3. $13\frac{1}{3}$
   $-10\frac{5}{6}$

4. $54\frac{3}{10}$
   $-29\frac{7}{10}$

5. 18
   $-13\frac{9}{10}$

6. $60\frac{7}{8}$
   $-43\frac{1}{4}$

7. $16\frac{2}{3}$
   $-\ 9$

8. $31\frac{5}{8}$
   $-17\frac{1}{2}$

9. $83\frac{3}{10}$
   $-66\frac{1}{2}$

10. $53\frac{1}{4}$
    $-37\frac{3}{4}$

11. 50
    $-30\frac{1}{4}$

12. $41\frac{1}{2}$
    $-27\frac{1}{10}$

13. 12
    $-\ 1\frac{9}{10}$

14. $16\frac{4}{5}$
    $-11\frac{3}{10}$

15. $72\frac{9}{10}$
    $-30\frac{3}{5}$

16. $126\frac{3}{8}$
    $-\ 75\frac{5}{8}$

17. $247\frac{3}{10}$
    $-193\frac{9}{100}$

18. $506\frac{2}{3}$
    $-422\frac{1}{3}$

19. 100
    $-\ 72\frac{2}{5}$

20. $313\frac{5}{8}$
    $-274\frac{3}{4}$

21. $414\frac{1}{10}$
    $-342\frac{3}{10}$

22. $719\frac{23}{100}$
    $-426\frac{47}{100}$

23. 358
    $-329\frac{83}{100}$

24. $144\frac{93}{100}$
    $-\ 95\frac{1}{2}$

25. $344\frac{1}{2}$
    $-182\frac{9}{10}$

26. Find the difference of these tosses.

 $\longrightarrow 6\frac{1}{10}$

$\longrightarrow 2\frac{1}{2}$

☆ 27. Make a whole number cube and a fraction cube. Use the cubes to play a subtraction game.

Choose one number from each row, with no two numbers from the same column. Find the sum of the four numbers. Choose another set of four numbers. Do you get the same sum for both sets?

	3.3	4.0	5.5	3.7
Rows	2.7	3.4	4.9	3.1
	3.6	4.3	5.8	4.0
	2.8	3.5	5.0	3.2

Columns

Answers for Self-check 1. 3 2. 5 3. 3 4. 3 5. 9 6. $15\frac{1}{2}$ 7. 30 8. $8\frac{3}{5}$ 9. $11\frac{3}{8}$ 10. $17\frac{1}{3}$ 11. $5\frac{1}{2}$
12. $1\frac{1}{2}$ 13. $4\frac{3}{10}$ 14. $4\frac{3}{4}$ 15. $2\frac{7}{8}$ 16. $28\frac{1}{5}$ 17. $61\frac{7}{8}$ 18. $4\frac{3}{4}$ 19. $1\frac{87}{100}$ 20. $9\frac{1}{6}$

Give the missing numerators.

1. $3\frac{13}{10} = 4\frac{||||}{10}$ 2. $6\frac{1}{4} = 5\frac{||||}{4}$ 3. $10\frac{1}{2} = 9\frac{||||}{2}$ 4. $12\frac{7}{4} = 13\frac{||||}{4}$ 5. $6\frac{19}{10} = 7\frac{||||}{10}$

Add or subtract.

6. $\begin{array}{r} 6\frac{1}{4} \\ +\ 9\frac{1}{4} \\ \hline \end{array}$

7. $\begin{array}{r} 12\frac{1}{2} \\ +\ 17\frac{1}{2} \\ \hline \end{array}$

8. $\begin{array}{r} 3\frac{7}{10} \\ +\ 4\frac{9}{10} \\ \hline \end{array}$

9. $\begin{array}{r} 6\frac{7}{8} \\ +\ 4\frac{1}{2} \\ \hline \end{array}$

10. $\begin{array}{r} 9\frac{2}{3} \\ +\ 7\frac{2}{3} \\ \hline \end{array}$

11. $\begin{array}{r} 8\frac{3}{4} \\ -\ 3\frac{1}{4} \\ \hline \end{array}$

12. $\begin{array}{r} 6\frac{2}{10} \\ -\ 4\frac{7}{10} \\ \hline \end{array}$

13. $\begin{array}{r} 9\frac{3}{5} \\ -\ 5\frac{3}{10} \\ \hline \end{array}$

14. $\begin{array}{r} 7\frac{1}{2} \\ -\ 2\frac{3}{4} \\ \hline \end{array}$

15. $\begin{array}{r} 4\frac{1}{8} \\ -\ 1\frac{1}{4} \\ \hline \end{array}$

16. $\begin{array}{r} 12\frac{3}{10} \\ +\ 15\frac{9}{10} \\ \hline \end{array}$

17. $\begin{array}{r} 24\frac{3}{8} \\ +\ 37\frac{1}{2} \\ \hline \end{array}$

18. $\begin{array}{r} 9\frac{5}{8} \\ -\ 4\frac{7}{8} \\ \hline \end{array}$

19. $\begin{array}{r} 21\frac{7}{10} \\ -\ 19\frac{83}{100} \\ \hline \end{array}$

20. $\begin{array}{r} 66\frac{2}{3} \\ -\ 57\frac{1}{2} \\ \hline \end{array}$

Answers for Self-check—page 331

⊛ Test

Give the missing numerators.

1. $3\frac{1}{8} = 2\frac{||||}{8}$ 2. $9\frac{7}{10} = 8\frac{||||}{10}$ 3. $5\frac{7}{6} = 6\frac{||||}{6}$ 4. $10\frac{3}{4} = 9\frac{||||}{4}$ 5. $4\frac{3}{2} = 5\frac{||||}{2}$

Add or subtract.

6. $\begin{array}{r} 3\frac{1}{2} \\ +\ 7\frac{1}{2} \\ \hline \end{array}$

7. $\begin{array}{r} 8\frac{3}{4} \\ +\ 9\frac{3}{4} \\ \hline \end{array}$

8. $\begin{array}{r} 16\frac{1}{2} \\ +\ 12\frac{7}{10} \\ \hline \end{array}$

9. $\begin{array}{r} 27\frac{2}{3} \\ +\ 26\frac{1}{3} \\ \hline \end{array}$

10. $\begin{array}{r} 18\frac{4}{5} \\ +\ 26\frac{3}{5} \\ \hline \end{array}$

11. $\begin{array}{r} 7\frac{5}{8} \\ -\ 4\frac{1}{8} \\ \hline \end{array}$

12. $\begin{array}{r} 12\frac{3}{10} \\ -\ 3\frac{7}{10} \\ \hline \end{array}$

13. $\begin{array}{r} 5\frac{8}{15} \\ -\ 3\frac{7}{10} \\ \hline \end{array}$

14. $\begin{array}{r} 6\frac{3}{4} \\ -\ 2\frac{1}{5} \\ \hline \end{array}$

15. $\begin{array}{r} 10\frac{2}{5} \\ -\ 7\frac{1}{10} \\ \hline \end{array}$

16. $\begin{array}{r} 12\frac{5}{8} \\ +\ 8\frac{1}{2} \\ \hline \end{array}$

17. $\begin{array}{r} 31\frac{9}{10} \\ +\ 27\frac{7}{10} \\ \hline \end{array}$

18. $\begin{array}{r} 15\frac{1}{10} \\ -\ 8\frac{3}{10} \\ \hline \end{array}$

19. $\begin{array}{r} 12\frac{1}{4} \\ -\ 6\frac{7}{8} \\ \hline \end{array}$

20. $\begin{array}{r} 76\frac{3}{5} \\ -\ 38\frac{9}{10} \\ \hline \end{array}$

Geometric Rosettes

This geometric rosette was made by tracing and retracing the shape at the right as it was rotated about a point.

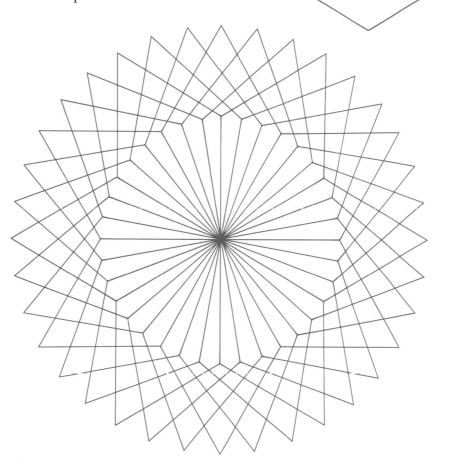

Make some rosettes of your own using other shapes such as the ones below.

  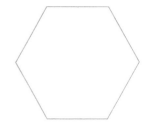

Volume, Capacity, Mass, and Temperature

Mickey had 18 wooden cubes.
She stacked them to make
some models of boxes.
Which models below could
she make from the 18 cubes?

1.

2.

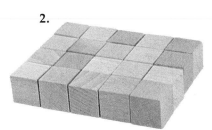

3.

4.

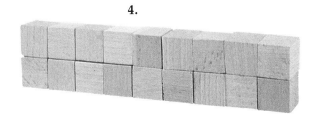

5.

6.

The **volume** of a box is
the number of **cubic units**
it will hold.

1 cubic centimeter
symbol: cm³

How many cubic centimeters will each box hold?

1.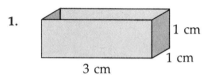

2.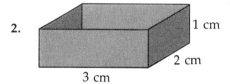

3.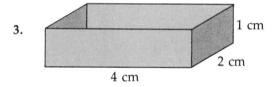

4.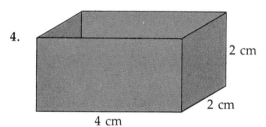

5.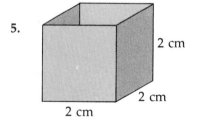

6.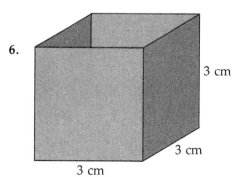

Volume of boxes

What is the volume
of this box?

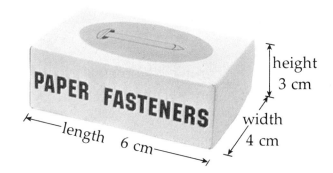

height
3 cm

←——length
6 cm——→

width
4 cm

Finding the answer

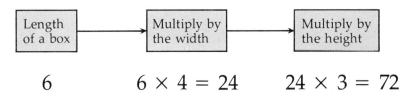

| Length of a box | Multiply by the width | Multiply by the height |

6        $6 \times 4 = 24$ $24 \times 3 = 72$

The volume of the box is 72 cm³.

Find the volume of each box.

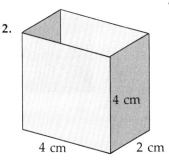

1.

2 cm
3 cm
3 cm

2.

4 cm
4 cm
2 cm

3.

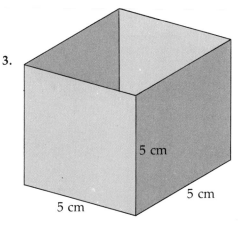

5 cm
5 cm
5 cm

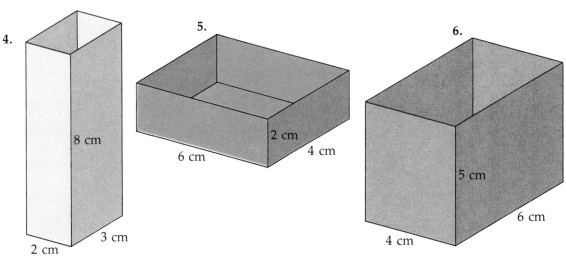

4.

8 cm
3 cm
2 cm

5.

2 cm
6 cm
4 cm

6.

5 cm
6 cm
4 cm

Find the volume.

1. 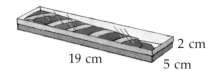 2 cm
19 cm
5 cm

2. 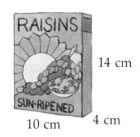 14 cm
10 cm 4 cm

3. 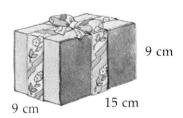 9 cm
9 cm 15 cm

4. 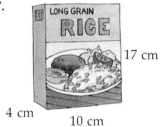 20 cm
10 cm 10 cm

5. 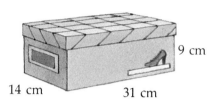 9 cm
14 cm 31 cm

6.  18 cm
14 cm 4 cm

7.  17 cm
4 cm 10 cm

8.  13 cm
6 cm 9 cm

9.  24 cm
17 cm 4 cm

Practicing your skills

Add or subtract.

1. 1642 2187 + 3475	**2.** 5609 5284 + 2168	**3.** 2761 1940 + 9007	**4.** 9763 8315 + 9998	**5.** 7321 8106 + 9490
6. 7241 − 3589	**7.** 8015 − 2743	**8.** 6412 − 5731	**9.** 7005 − 3609	**10.** 8156 − 1929
11. 7.02 12.54 + 3.42	**12.** 8.17 6.25 + 3.59	**13.** 41.5 7.82 + 19.04	**14.** 1.025 7.6 + 25.32	**15.** 78.9 3.461 + 82.754
16. 25.34 − 19.56	**17.** 38.01 − 25.5	**18.** 46.2 − 15.89	**19.** 50.37 − 34.09	**20.** 91.1 − 72.63

Capacity

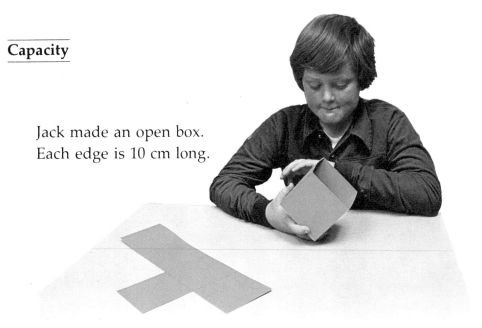

Jack made an open box.
Each edge is 10 cm long.

The volume of this box is 1000 cm³.
The box holds 1 **liter** (L).
One thousandth of a liter is 1 **milliliter** (mL)
One cubic centimeter will hold 1 mL

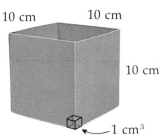

How many milliliters does each object hold?

1.

volume: 20 cm³
answer: 20 mL

2.

volume: 250 cm³

3.

volume: 5 cm³

4.

volume: 340 cm³

5.

volume: 1890 cm³

6.

volume: 170 cm³

How many liters of water are there in the aquarium?

depth of water 20 cm

length 75 cm

width 30 cm

Volume of water:

length   width   depth   volume
  ↓   ↓   ↓   ↓
$75 \times 30 \times 20 = 45\,000 \text{ cm}^3$

There are 45 000 mL or 45 L of water in the aquarium.

Find the number of liters of water in the aquarium for each of these depths.

1. 24 cm

2. 8 cm

3. 28 cm

4. 12 cm

5. 4 cm

6. 16 cm

7. The aquarium is 30 cm in height. How much water will it hold when filled to the top?

☆ 8. Find the amount of water in an aquarium in your school or home.

Practicing your skills

Multiply.

1. 345×48

2. 794×62

3. 805×25

4. 953×71

5. 618×36

6. 9.72×59

7. 11.9×3.7

8. 3.58×6.3

9. 52.8×0.74

10. 6.08×0.42

Divide.

11. $76\overline{)588}$

12. $61\overline{)475}$

13. $94\overline{)924}$

14. $86\overline{)372}$

15. $74\overline{)444}$

16. $17\overline{)689}$

17. $63\overline{)516}$

18. $46\overline{)344}$

19. $45\overline{)325}$

20. $23\overline{)635}$

Units of mass

The basic unit of mass is the **kilogram** (kg).

little league bat—
about 1 kilogram

two footballs—
about 1 kilogram

1 liter of water—
1 kilogram

A gram (g) is 0.001 of a kilogram.

 1 mL of water
has a mass
of 1 gram.

1000 grams = 1 kilogram

new lead pencil—
about 5 grams

small paper clip—
about 1 gram

Chalkboard eraser
about 50 grams

Is the mass given in **grams** or **kilograms?**

1. a sheet of tablet paper
   mass: 5

2. basketball
   mass: 600

3. bowling ball
   mass: 7

4. glass of water
   mass: 275

5. sack of sugar
   mass: 2

6. book
   mass: 450

7. automobile
   mass: 1500

8. orange
   mass: 250

9. box of cereal
   mass: 420

10. scissors
    mass: 192

11. small dog
    mass: 5000

12. table-tennis ball
    mass: 3

Choose the best estimate for the mass of each object.

1. pocket comb	2. medium apple	3. metal teaspoon
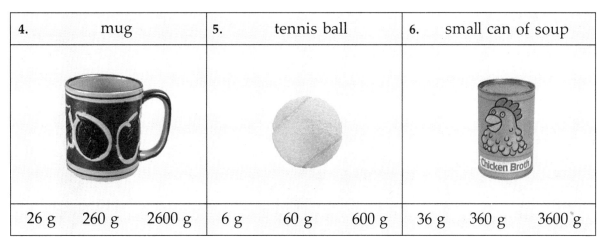		
1 g 7 g 70 g	20 g 200 g 2000 g	5 g 25 g 100 g

4. mug	5. tennis ball	6. small can of soup
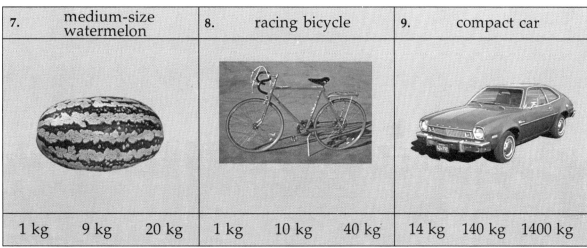		
26 g 260 g 2600 g	6 g 60 g 600 g	36 g 360 g 3600 g

7. medium-size watermelon	8. racing bicycle	9. compact car
1 kg 9 kg 20 kg	1 kg 10 kg 40 kg	14 kg 140 kg 1400 kg

☆ **10.** About how many square centimeters of graph paper are needed to balance a mass of 1 gram?

Temperature

A commonly used unit of temperature is the degree Celsius. A thermometer is used to measure temperature.

The thermometer shown at the right shows some familiar temperatures.

Temperatures can drop below zero. For example, ⁻10° C means "ten degrees below zero."

Use the thermometer at the right to find each temperature.

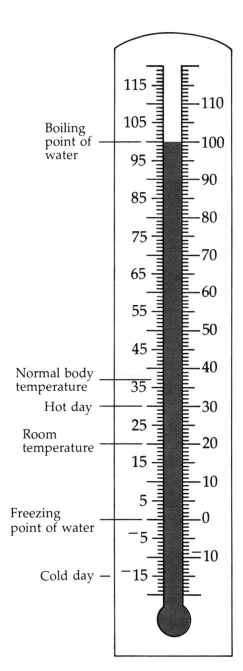

1. boiling point of water

2. freezing point of water

3. normal body temperature

4. room temperature

5. hot day

6. cold day

Read the temperature shown on each thermometer.

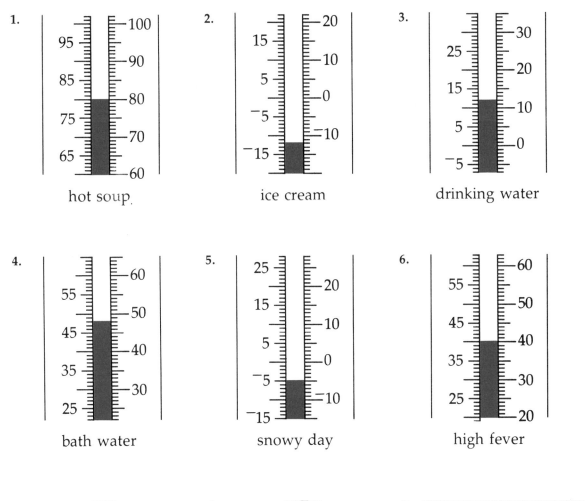

1. hot soup

2. ice cream

3. drinking water

4. bath water

5. snowy day

6. high fever

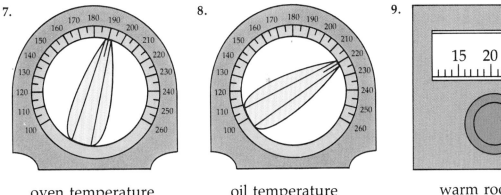

7. oven temperature for baking cookies

8. oil temperature for French-fried potatoes

9. warm room

Answers for Self-check 1. 36 cm³ 2. 64 m³ 3. 36 cm³ 4. 1000 5. 1 6. 50 mL 7. 6 mL
8. 1000 mL 9. 1000 10. 0° C 11. 39° C 12. ⁻5° C 13. 80° C

Self-check

Find the volume.

1. 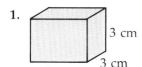 3 cm
3 cm
4 cm

2. 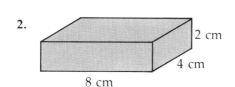 2 cm
4 cm
8 cm

3. 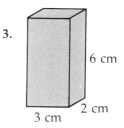 6 cm
2 cm
3 cm

4. 1 liter = ▨ milliliter(s)

5. 1 cm³ holds ▨ mL.

How many milliliters does each hold?

6. 50 cm³

7. 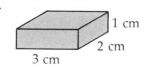 1 cm
2 cm
3 cm

8.  1 liter

9. 1 kilogram = ▨ grams

10. Water freezes at ▨° C.

Which is the best estimate of the temperature?

11. fever temperature
  A 37° C
  B 39° C

12. cold day
  A ⁻5° C
  B 12° C

13. bowl of hot soup
  A 30° C
  B 80° C

Answers for Self-check—page 343

Test

Find the volume.

1. 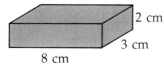 2 cm
3 cm
8 cm

2. 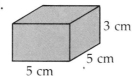 3 cm
5 cm
5 cm

3. 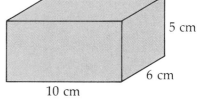 5 cm
6 cm
10 cm

4. 1000 milliliters = ▨ liter(s)

5. 1 mL is the same as ▨ cm³.

How many milliliters does each hold?

6. 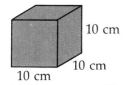 10 cm
10 cm
10 cm

7. 20 cm³

8. 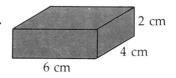 2 cm
4 cm
6 cm

9. 1000 grams = ▨ kilogram(s)

10. Water boils at ▨° C.

Which is the best estimate of the temperature?

11. freezing point of water
  A 0° C
  B 100° C

12. room temperature
  A 20° C
  B 30° C

13. normal body temperature
  A 77° C
  B 37° C

Triangulation

Use 5-by-5 dot paper, graph paper, or a geoboard to play this game.

Make a set of 25 cards with the ordered pairs of numbers from (0,0) to (4,4). That is, make one card for each of the points on the geoboard.

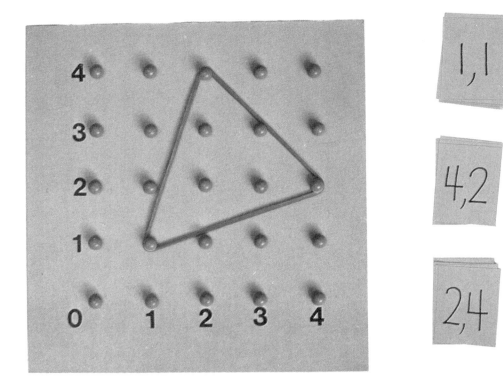

Rules:

1. Shuffle the cards. Each player draws three cards from the deck.

2. Each player makes a triangle, using the three points from the three cards drawn.

3. Find the area of the triangle formed. If the three points are in a line the area is zero.

4. Find the sum of the areas you make in four turns. The highest total wins the game.

Measurement: Other Units

Getting started

Which nail is longer?

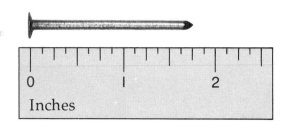 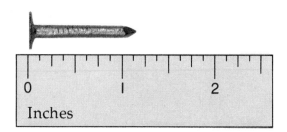

The box nail is about $1\frac{3}{4}$ inches long.
The roofing nail is about $1\frac{1}{8}$ inches long.
The box nail is longer.

Find the length of each segment to the nearest eighth of an inch.

1. |————————————|

2. |————————————————|

3. |——————————————|

4. |——————|

5. |——————————————————————|

6. |————————————————————|

Draw segments that have these lengths.

7. $2\frac{1}{2}$ in.   8. $3\frac{1}{8}$ in.   9. $4\frac{3}{4}$ in.   10. $1\frac{5}{8}$ in.

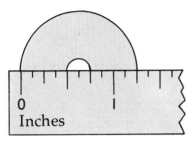

The **diameter** of the
spool is $1\frac{1}{4}$ in.

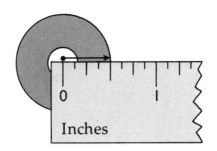

The **radius** of the
washer is $\frac{1}{2}$ in.

Measure the diameter of each circle in inches. Use an inch ruler.

1.

2.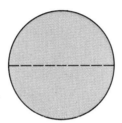

3.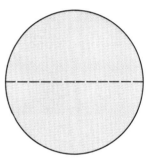

4.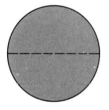

5.

6.

Give the radius of each circle in inches.

7.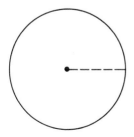

8.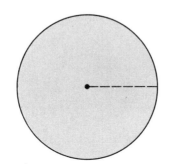

9.

Other units of length

Unit	Abbreviation	Relation
inch	in.	12 in. = 1 ft
foot	ft	3 ft = 1 yd
yard	yd	36 in. = 1 yd
mile	mi	5280 ft = 1 mi 1760 yd = 1 mi

A bicycle rider might travel 1 mile in 3 or 4 minutes.

Choose the correct unit, inches, feet, yards, or miles for each measurement.

1. Judy is 54 ___?___ tall.

2. The door is 7 ___?___ high.

3. In 18 minutes, John ran 2 ___?___ .

4. In a car you might travel 55 ___?___ in one hour.

5. One fourth of a mile is 440 ___?___ .

6. The tall person is 6 ___?___ in height.

7. One yard is 36 ___?___ .

8. A fast runner can run 100 ___?___ in 10 seconds.

9. Mt. Everest is about 5.5 ___?___ in height.

10. It is 90 ___?___ between the bases of a baseball diamond.

Use the table to change these units.

11. Karen jogged 3 miles.
    How many feet is this?
    Hint: 5280 ft in each mile

12. Mike is 60 in. tall.
    What is Mike's height in feet?
    Hint: Each foot is 12 inches.

13. Sue bought material that is 18 ft long.
    How many yards did she buy?

14. Ben ran the 50 yard dash.
    How many feet did he run?

The distance around a region is called the **perimeter** of the region. What is the perimeter of the basketball court?

Since the measurements are given in the same unit, add the lengths of the sides.

$$\begin{array}{r} 94 \\ 50 \\ 94 \\ +\,50 \\ \hline 288 \end{array}$$

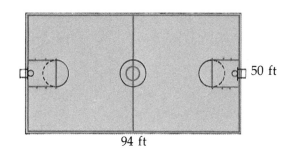

50 ft

94 ft

The perimeter is 288 ft.

Find the perimeter of each.

1.

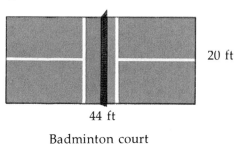

20 ft

44 ft

Badminton court

2.

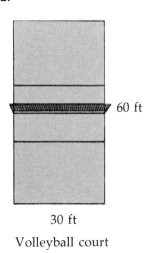

60 ft

30 ft

Volleyball court

3.

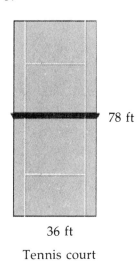

78 ft

36 ft

Tennis court

You will need to change some units first, before you solve these.

4. Find the perimeter in feet.

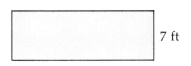

7 ft

6 yd

5. Find the perimeter in yards.

8 ft

13 ft

☆ **6.** Find the perimeter in inches.

16 in

2 ft 7 in

Area of rectangles

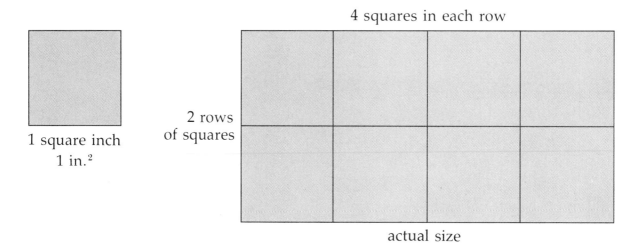

4 squares in each row

2 rows of squares

actual size

1 square inch
1 in.²

How many square inches would it take to cover the large rectangle?

We say: The **area** of the rectangle is 8 square inches.
We write: Area = 8 in.²

What is the area of
this rectangle?

Area = length × width
Area = 8 × 6 = 48
Area = 48 in.²

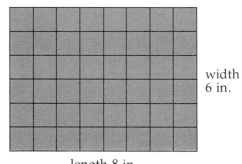

smaller
than
actual
size

width
6 in.

length 8 in.

Give the area of these rectangles in square inches.

1.

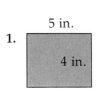

5 in.

4 in.

2.

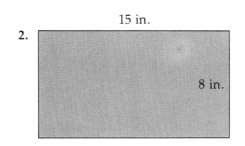

15 in.

8 in.

3.

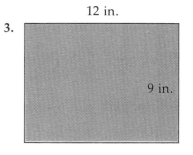

12 in.

9 in.

Find the area of each rectangle in square inches.

1.

7 in.

15 in.

2.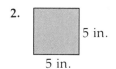

5 in.

5 in.

3.

7 in.

27 in.

4.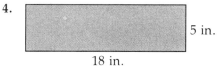

5 in.

18 in.

5.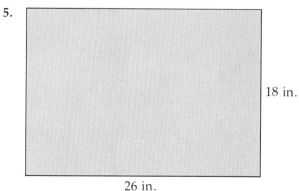

18 in.

26 in.

6.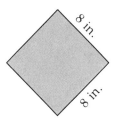

8 in.

8 in.

7. length: 28 in.
width: 11 in.

8. length: 42 in.
width: 33 in.

9. A rug is 12 feet long
and 9 feet wide.
What is the area
in square feet?

10. How many square inches
are there in 1 square foot?

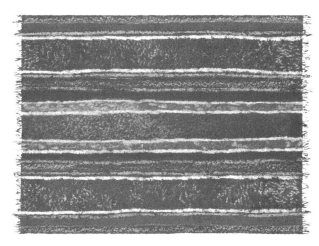

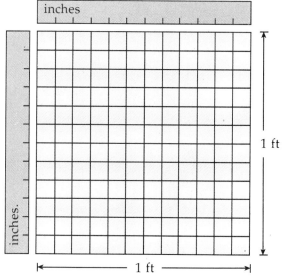

inches

inches.

1 ft

1 ft

Area of a triangle

A triangle has a height of 3 inches and a base of 4 inches. What is the **area** of the triangle?

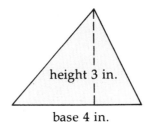

height 3 in.

base 4 in.

Finding the answer

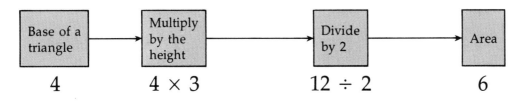

Base of a triangle	Multiply by the height	Divide by 2	Area
4	4 × 3	12 ÷ 2	6

The area is 6 in².

Find the area of each triangle.

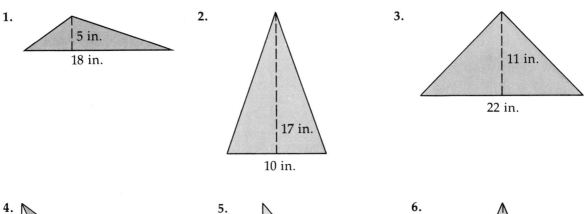

1. 5 in.
    18 in.

2. 17 in.
    10 in.

3. 11 in.
    22 in.

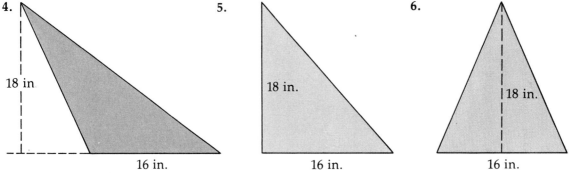

4. 18 in
    16 in.

5. 18 in.
    16 in.

6. 18 in.
    16 in.

1. Find the area of each triangle.

2. Is the sum of the areas of the blue and the yellow triangles equal to the area of the green triangle?

3. Is the area of the green triangle equal to half the area of the whole rectangle?

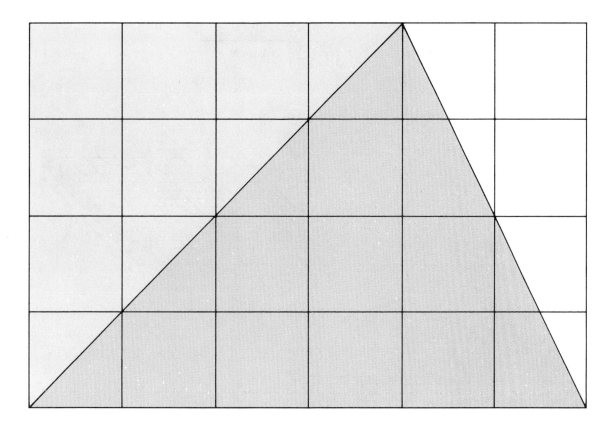

Find the area of each triangle with base b and height h.

4. $b = 14$ in.
   $h = 3$ in.

5. $b = 27$ in.
   $h = 16$ in.

6. $b = 8$ ft
   $h = 3$ ft

7. $b = 15$ ft
   $h = 12$ ft

8. $b = 2$ mi
   $h = 1$ mi

9. $b = 32$ in.
   $h = 24$ in.

10. $b = 10$ yd
    $h = 9$ yd

11. $b = 120$ ft
    $h = 40$ ft

12. $b = 66$ ft
    $h = 50$ ft

13. $b = 26$ mi
    $h = 15$ mi

14. $b = 84$ in.
    $h = 51$ in.

15. $b = 43$ in.
    $h = 44$ in.

Volume

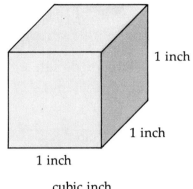

This is a **cubic** inch. Think of the cubes below as **cubic** inches. You can learn how many **cubic** inches are in one cubic foot.

1 inch

1 inch

1 inch

cubic inch

Give the number of cubic inches for each picture.

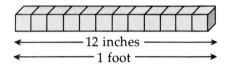

← 12 inches →

← 1 foot →

1. ▥ cubic inches

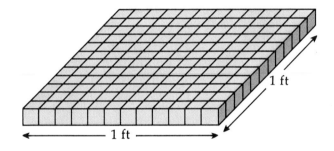

1 ft

1 ft

2. ▥ cubic inches

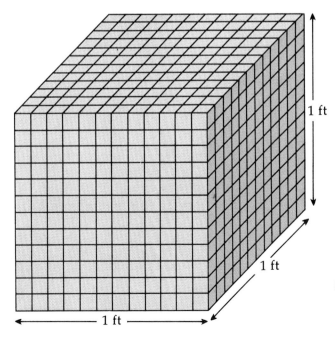

1 ft

1 ft

1 ft

3. ▥ cubic inches

The **volume** of a box is the product of the length times the width times the height.

Volume = length × width × height
Volume = 10 × 6 × 2
Volume = 120 in^3

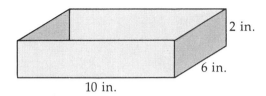
2 in.
6 in.
10 in.

Find the volume of each box.

1.
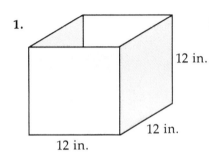
12 in.
12 in.
12 in.

2.
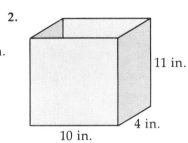
11 in.
4 in.
10 in.

3.
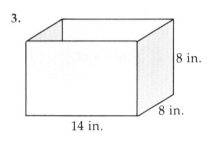
8 in.
8 in.
14 in.

4.

2 in.
8 in.   7 in.

5.
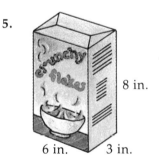
8 in.
6 in.   3 in.

6.
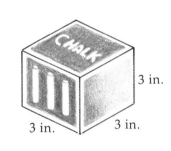
3 in.
3 in.   3 in.

7.
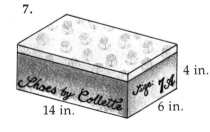
4 in.
14 in.   6 in.

8.
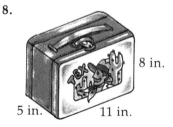
8 in.
5 in.   11 in.

9.

3 in.
18 in.   12 in.

10.
length: 24 in.
width: 20 in.
height: 9 in.

11.
length: 5 ft
width: 5 ft
height: 5 ft

12.
length: 33 in.
width: 26 in.
height: 24 in.

Other units of capacity

1 gallon (gal) will hold 4 quarts (qt).

1 quart will hold 2 pints (pt).

1 pint will hold 2 cups (c).

Use the pictures above to complete the following.

1. 8 qt = ▥ gal

2. 4 c = ▥ qt

3. $\frac{1}{2}$ qt = ▥ pt

4. 4 pt = ▥ qt

5. 16 c = ▥ gal

6. $\frac{1}{2}$ pt = ▥ c

7. 8 pt = ▥ qt

8. 1 qt = ▥ c

9. $\frac{1}{2}$ gal = ▥ qt

10. 8 pt = ▥ gal

11. 1 gal = ▥ pt

12. 3 qt = ▥ pt

1. We need to drink about
   2 qt of water or some
   other liquid each day.
   How many pints is this?

2. Miss Jansen used 1 gallon
   of gasoline to drive 20 miles.
   How far did she drive on
   1 quart of gasoline?

3. A pint jar of peanut butter
   costs 89¢. A quart jar costs
   $1.55. Is it cheaper to
   buy 2 pints or 1 quart jar
   of peanut butter?

4. A gallon of apple cider costs
   $1.60. How much is this
   for 1 quart of cider?

5. A recipe calls for $\frac{1}{2}$ pint
   of whipping cream. How
   many cups is this?

6. Bill bought 6 pints of grape juice.
   How many quarts is this?

7. Milk cost 76¢ a $\frac{1}{2}$ gal.
   At this price, what is the
   cost of 1 quart?

8. John paid 15¢ for $\frac{1}{2}$ pt of milk
   for his lunch. How much
   is this for 1 quart of milk?

Guess which number below is
greatest and which is smallest.

1. number of seconds in an hour
2. number of hours in a year
3. number of minutes in a week

Now find each number to check
your guesses.

1 minute = 60 seconds
1 hour = 60 minutes
1 day = 24 hours
7 days = 1 week
365 days = 1 year
100 years = 1 century

Weight

Some weights of objects are given below.

9 pennies—
about 1 ounce

pint of milk—
about 1 pound

large draft horse—
about 1 ton
or 2000 pounds

16 ounces (oz) = 1 pound (lb)
2000 pounds = 1 ton (T)

Choose the best estimate for the weight of each object.

1. football

A 1 oz
B 1 lb
C 1 T

2. automobile

A 2 oz
B 2 lb
C 2 T

3. paper punch

A 4 oz
B 4 lb
C 4 T

4. book

A 28 oz
B 28 lb
C 28 T

5. bowling ball

A 16 oz
B 16 lb
C 16 T

6. baseball

A 5 oz
B 5 lb
C 5 T

7. blue whale

A 150 oz
B 150 lb
C 150 T

8. 5 nickels

A 1 oz
B 1 lb
C 1 T

9. quart of milk

A 2 oz
B 2 lb
C 2 T

How many ounces?

1.

2.

3.

How many pounds?

4.

5.

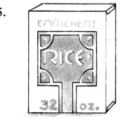

6.

How many tons?

7.

8.

9.

rhinoceros
4000 lb

elephant
10 000 lb

gray whale
80 000 lb

Think !

How many pounds do you weigh?

About how many persons your size
would it take to weigh **one** ton?

Changing Units

Unit Relationships

Length	Capacity	Weight	Time
12 in. = 1 ft 3 ft = 1 yd 36 in. = 1 yd 5280 ft = 1 mi	2 c = 1 pt 2 pt = 1 qt 4 c = 1 qt 4 qt = 1 gal	16 oz = 1 lb 2000 lb = 1 ton	60 sec = 1 min 60 min = 1 hr 24 hr = 1 week 7 d = 1 week

What is the perimeter and area
of the rectangle?

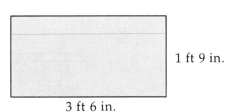

1 ft 9 in.

3 ft 6 in.

Finding the answer

Perimeter

Add the lengths of the sides → Regroup to a larger unit if possible

3 ft 6 in.
1 ft 9 in.
3 ft 6 in.
1 ft 9 in.
―――――
8 ft 30 in.

30 in. = 2 ft 6 in.

8 ft 30 in. = 10 ft 6 in.
The perimeter is 10 ft 6 in.

Area

Change to a single unit → Multiply the length by the width

1 ft 9 in. = 21 in.
3 ft 6 in. = 42 in.

21 in. × 42 in. = 882 in.²
The area is 882 square inches.

Find the perimeter and area of each rectangle.

1.

2 yd 2 ft

4 yd 2 ft

2.

2 ft 6 in.

5 ft 4 in.

3.

2 ft 8 in.

6 ft 5 in.

Give the number for each ||||.

Capacity

1. 3 pt 1 c = |||| c
2. 10 c = |||| pt
3. 13 c = |||| qt |||| c
4. 4 qt 1 pt = |||| pt
5. 12 pt = |||| qt
6. 9 pt = |||| qt |||| pt
7. 3 gal 2 qt = |||| qt
8. 20 qt = |||| gal
9. 11 c = |||| pt |||| c
10. 5 qt 3 c = |||| c
11. 16 c = |||| qt
12. 21 qt = |||| gal |||| qt

Weight

13. 3T = |||| lb
14. 5000 lb = |||| T |||| lb
15. 3 lb 6 oz = |||| oz
16. 4 lb = |||| oz
17. 50 oz = |||| lb |||| oz
18. 7 lb 13 oz = |||| oz

Time

19. 5 min = |||| sec
20. 3 min 20 sec = |||| sec
21. 150 sec = |||| min |||| sec
22. 3 hr = |||| min
23. 5 hr 15 min = |||| min
24. 200 min = |||| hr |||| min
25. 4 d = |||| hr
26. 4 hr 45 min = |||| min
27. 175 min = |||| hr |||| min
28. 6 wk = |||| d
29. 2 d 7 hr = |||| hr
30. 50 hr = |||| d |||| hr

Solve.

31. The game started at 2:30 p.m. It lasted 1 hour and 45 minutes. At what time was it over?

32. Joan bought a package of meat that weighed 3 lb 9 oz. How many ounces of meat did Joan buy?

33. The recipe called for 3 cups of milk. Joe needed to make 4 times the recipe. How many quarts of milk does he need to buy?

34. A fence around a square region was 5 yd 2 ft on each side. What is the total length of the fence?

Answers for Self-check 1. $4\frac{3}{8}$ in. 2. 108 square feet 3. 576 cubic yards
4. 8 cups 5. B 6. 9 ft 4 in. 7. 588 square inches

Self-check

1. Find the length to the nearest eighth of an inch.

   ├────────────────────────────────────┤

2. Give the area of a triangle with base 36 ft and height 6 ft.

3. Give the volume of a box with length 12 yd, width 8 yd, and height 6 yd.

4. How many cups are in 4 pints?

5. Choose the best estimate for the weight of a bicycle.

   A 25 oz

   B 25 lb

   C 25 T

6. Give the perimeter of the rectangle.

7. Give the area of the rectangle.

1 ft 2 in.

3 ft 6 in.

Answers for Self–check—page 353B

Test

1. Find the length to the nearest eighth of an inch.   ├──────────┤

2. Give the area of a triangle with base 16 in. and height 9 in.

3. Give the volume of a box with length 25 ft, width 12 ft, and height 7 ft.

4. How many quarts are in 2 gallons?

5. Choose the best estimate for the weight of a glass of juice.

   A 16 oz

   B 16 lb

   C 16 T

6. Give the perimeter of the rectangle.

7. Give the area of the rectangle.

2 ft

4 yd 2 ft

Temperature Search

1. Give each temperature in Fahrenheit degrees.

2. Put tracing paper over the ice block. Shade the spaces that show each temperature or one close to it.

3. Your shaded regions should show the number of a familiar temperature. Can you tell what it is?

Normal body
temperature

Boiling water

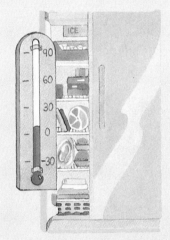

Inside a freezer

Cold day in Alaska

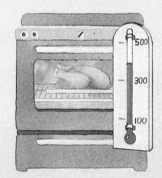

Hot oven

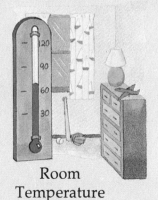

Room
Temperature

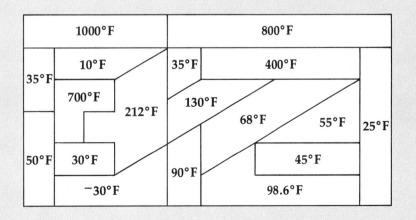

1000°F				800°F		
35°F	10°F		35°F	400°F		
	700°F	212°F	130°F			
				68°F	55°F	25°F
50°F	30°F		90°F		45°F	
	−30°F			98.6°F		

Level 28 review

Multiply.

1. $\frac{5}{8} \times \frac{3}{4}$ 2. $\frac{1}{2} \times \frac{5}{12}$ 3. $\frac{2}{3} \times \frac{5}{6}$ 4. $\frac{7}{8} \times \frac{1}{4}$ 5. $\frac{1}{3} \times \frac{1}{10}$

6. $7 \times \frac{3}{5}$ 7. $\frac{1}{2} \times 8$ 8. $1\frac{1}{2} \times \frac{3}{4}$ 9. $\frac{5}{6} \times 3\frac{1}{3}$ 10. $2\frac{2}{5} \times 1\frac{1}{2}$

11. 3×0.2 12. 5×0.3 13. 0.4×0.2 14. 0.1×0.5 15. 0.06×2

16.
$$\begin{array}{r} 2.3 \\ \times\ \ 4 \\ \hline \end{array}$$
17.
$$\begin{array}{r} 5.7 \\ \times\ \ 6 \\ \hline \end{array}$$
18.
$$\begin{array}{r} 3.14 \\ \times\ \ \ 7 \\ \hline \end{array}$$
19.
$$\begin{array}{r} 4.5 \\ \times\ 0.3 \\ \hline \end{array}$$
20.
$$\begin{array}{r} 7.82 \\ \times\ \ 0.6 \\ \hline \end{array}$$

21.
$$\begin{array}{r} 6.34 \\ \times\ \ 0.5 \\ \hline \end{array}$$
22.
$$\begin{array}{r} 94.8 \\ \times\ \ 6.2 \\ \hline \end{array}$$
23.
$$\begin{array}{r} 1.74 \\ \times\ \ 3.5 \\ \hline \end{array}$$
24.
$$\begin{array}{r} 6.34 \\ \times\ \ 2.6 \\ \hline \end{array}$$
25.
$$\begin{array}{r} 82.4 \\ \times\ 0.48 \\ \hline \end{array}$$

26.
$$\begin{array}{r} 5.022 \\ \times\ \ \ \ 3 \\ \hline \end{array}$$
27.
$$\begin{array}{r} 0.049 \\ \times\ \ \ \ 9 \\ \hline \end{array}$$
28.
$$\begin{array}{r} 3.25 \\ \times\ 0.6 \\ \hline \end{array}$$
29.
$$\begin{array}{r} 7.118 \\ \times\ \ \ \ 5 \\ \hline \end{array}$$
30.
$$\begin{array}{r} 0.06 \\ \times\ 0.4 \\ \hline \end{array}$$

Add.

31.
$$\begin{array}{r} 6\frac{1}{3} \\ +\ 5\frac{2}{3} \\ \hline \end{array}$$
32.
$$\begin{array}{r} 2\frac{1}{2} \\ +\ 3\frac{3}{4} \\ \hline \end{array}$$
33.
$$\begin{array}{r} 7\frac{2}{5} \\ +\ 4\frac{1}{10} \\ \hline \end{array}$$
34.
$$\begin{array}{r} 9\frac{1}{10} \\ +\ 2\frac{3}{10} \\ \hline \end{array}$$
35.
$$\begin{array}{r} 4\frac{1}{6} \\ +\ 5\frac{2}{9} \\ \hline \end{array}$$

36.
$$\begin{array}{r} 14\frac{1}{8} \\ +\ 12\frac{3}{4} \\ \hline \end{array}$$
37.
$$\begin{array}{r} 25\frac{9}{10} \\ +\ 15\frac{3}{10} \\ \hline \end{array}$$
38.
$$\begin{array}{r} 10\frac{7}{12} \\ +\ \ 8\frac{1}{2} \\ \hline \end{array}$$
39.
$$\begin{array}{r} 34\frac{2}{3} \\ +\ 56\frac{5}{12} \\ \hline \end{array}$$
40.
$$\begin{array}{r} 21\frac{7}{10} \\ +\ 37\frac{3}{5} \\ \hline \end{array}$$

Subtract.

41.
$$\begin{array}{r} 6\frac{2}{5} \\ -\ 3\frac{1}{10} \\ \hline \end{array}$$
42.
$$\begin{array}{r} 8\frac{9}{10} \\ -\ 5\frac{2}{5} \\ \hline \end{array}$$
43.
$$\begin{array}{r} 15\frac{1}{3} \\ -\ 7\frac{5}{6} \\ \hline \end{array}$$
44.
$$\begin{array}{r} 12\frac{3}{4} \\ -\ 9\frac{2}{3} \\ \hline \end{array}$$
45.
$$\begin{array}{r} 7\frac{1}{2} \\ -\ 2\frac{3}{4} \\ \hline \end{array}$$

46.
$$\begin{array}{r} 11\frac{1}{3} \\ -\ 7\frac{4}{5} \\ \hline \end{array}$$
47.
$$\begin{array}{r} 17\frac{3}{10} \\ -\ 9\frac{4}{5} \\ \hline \end{array}$$
48.
$$\begin{array}{r} 31\frac{2}{3} \\ -\ 18\frac{3}{4} \\ \hline \end{array}$$
49.
$$\begin{array}{r} 25\frac{1}{4} \\ -\ 16\frac{7}{12} \\ \hline \end{array}$$
50.
$$\begin{array}{r} 29\frac{1}{2} \\ -\ 12\frac{7}{10} \\ \hline \end{array}$$

Appendix

Add.

	A	B	C	D	E	F	G	H	I	J
1.	7 +2	9 +8	8 +1	5 +6	3 +0	6 +7	0 +9	9 +3	1 +7	3 +9
2.	1 +6	8 +2	6 +8	7 +5	0 +8	2 +7	4 +9	3 +5	4 +0	3 +3
3.	4 +5	0 +1	5 +2	6 +1	4 +7	0 +0	7 +6	9 +4	6 +3	9 +0
4.	2 +1	5 +5	6 +5	7 +3	5 +8	7 +1	2 +4	8 +9	6 +2	7 +7
5.	0 +3	1 +1	9 +2	5 +0	4 +4	8 +7	2 +6	4 +2	0 +7	5 +1
6.	2 +8	1 +2	7 +8	1 +8	4 +6	3 +8	0 +4	8 +8	3 +6	1 +5
7.	3 +1	0 +5	9 +5	2 +9	9 +6	4 +3	9 +9	2 +2	0 +6	3 +4
8.	4 +8	9 +7	6 +9	3 +2	4 +1	1 +9	5 +4	7 +9	6 +6	0 +2
9.	1 +4	5 +7	8 +6	8 +0	5 +3	8 +4	2 +0	7 +4	1 +3	8 +5
10.	7 +0	8 +3	9 +1	1 +0	6 +4	5 +9	2 +3	6 +0	2 +5	3 +7

Subtract.

	A	B	C	D	E	F	G	H	I	J
1.	6 −3	17 − 8	15 − 9	8 −7	4 −1	9 −5	12 − 6	10 − 4	5 −5	7 −1
2.	15 − 7	12 − 9	8 −5	9 −9	7 −5	13 − 6	11 − 5	10 − 8	4 −3	9 −3
3.	14 − 8	3 −2	1 −0	17 − 9	11 − 8	5 −2	8 −2	13 − 4	10 − 6	14 − 7
4.	9 −7	6 −6	6 −0	16 − 8	8 −4	12 − 3	7 −7	10 − 1	13 − 9	11 − 2
5.	9 −1	7 −3	5 −4	2 −2	8 −0	9 −2	13 − 7	11 − 3	7 −4	3 −3
6.	5 −3	16 − 9	9 −6	1 −1	14 − 9	12 − 4	4 −4	8 −6	3 −0	13 − 8
7.	18 − 9	6 −4	13 − 5	10 − 7	6 −1	0 −0	14 − 6	6 −2	9 −8	15 − 8
8.	2 −0	15 − 6	4 −2	12 − 8	9 −0	6 −5	11 − 9	10 − 2	2 −1	5 −0
9.	9 −4	8 −3	16 − 7	14 − 5	5 −1	12 − 5	3 −1	10 − 9	4 −0	11 − 7
10.	10 − 3	8 −8	7 −2	12 − 7	7 −0	11 − 6	8 −1	10 − 5	11 − 4	7 −6

Multiply.

	A	B	C	D	E	F	G	H	I	J
1.	3 ×4	5 ×9	2 ×2	9 ×5	7 ×8	1 ×0	0 ×4	9 ×1	3 ×7	6 ×2
2.	2 ×9	7 ×5	9 ×3	0 ×9	6 ×6	2 ×6	8 ×6	1 ×2	9 ×0	1 ×8
3.	5 ×5	2 ×3	1 ×4	5 ×1	9 ×7	3 ×9	3 ×3	9 ×4	8 ×9	1 ×1
4.	2 ×5	0 ×2	6 ×8	2 ×7	7 ×3	4 ×4	8 ×1	2 ×8	9 ×8	4 ×1
5.	1 ×5	5 ×2	0 ×0	7 ×2	3 ×8	8 ×4	8 ×8	4 ×9	3 ×6	1 ×7
6.	4 ×8	1 ×9	6 ×3	0 ×7	7 ×9	5 ×8	3 ×0	5 ×3	9 ×9	4 ×6
7.	4 ×2	3 ×1	9 ×6	0 ×8	6 ×4	8 ×7	2 ×4	6 ×0	3 ×2	4 ×7
8.	0 ×6	4 ×5	7 ×6	9 ×2	2 ×1	5 ×0	7 ×7	3 ×5	5 ×7	2 ×0
9.	0 ×5	4 ×3	6 ×9	8 ×3	6 ×5	8 ×0	5 ×6	0 ×3	7 ×1	5 ×4
10.	1 ×6	0 ×1	6 ×1	8 ×5	7 ×4	7 ×0	1 ×3	6 ×7	8 ×2	4 ×0

Divide.

	A	B	C	D	E	F	G	H	I
1.	8)24	6)42	7)7	1)5	8)56	9)81	7)14	5)25	1)4
2.	5)10	6)18	2)6	9)9	7)42	1)0	7)21	8)16	1)9
3.	2)4	2)2	5)30	3)27	2)10	5)45	2)18	6)6	4)24
4.	4)20	5)40	3)6	1)3	9)18	6)36	6)54	3)9	5)15
5.	5)0	4)4	3)15	6)24	8)32	3)0	7)49	8)40	5)20
6.	4)36	2)12	7)28	6)0	3)24	9)45	7)63	9)0	7)56
7.	8)8	4)16	5)5	4)28	4)32	2)16	1)1	5)35	9)72
8.	1)6	2)14	9)27	9)54	1)8	1)2	3)21	3)3	8)48
9.	6)12	7)0	1)7	9)36	6)48	6)30	3)18	8)64	4)0
10.	7)35	4)12	2)8	8)0	4)8	9)63	8)72	3)12	2)0

Add.

	A	B	C	D	E	F	G	H	I	J
1.	2 + 3	5 + 4	2 + 6	3 + 3	4 + 0	5 + 2	1 + 8	3 + 7	0 + 8	9 + 2
2.	0 + 6	6 + 4	3 + 4	8 + 5	5 + 3	7 + 4	4 + 2	9 + 4	2 + 7	1 + 4
3.	2 + 8	5 + 6	1 + 5	7 + 7	6 + 1	8 + 3	7 + 5	8 + 6	2 + 2	3 + 9
4.	7 + 6	8 + 8	2 + 0	3 + 6	4 + 8	9 + 5	7 + 8	1 + 7	9 + 1	4 + 4
5.	5 + 5	6 + 9	1 + 2	8 + 9	3 + 1	6 + 6	5 + 0	9 + 7	0 + 7	9 + 9

Subtract.

	A	B	C	D	E	F	G	H	I	J
1.	11 − 4	6 − 2	2 − 0	4 − 3	8 − 4	10 − 7	14 − 6	5 − 3	1 − 1	12 − 8
2.	10 − 2	3 − 1	7 − 4	9 − 4	11 − 5	6 − 4	5 − 1	14 − 9	8 − 2	4 − 2
3.	9 − 6	6 − 1	10 − 4	2 − 2	7 − 6	13 − 7	12 − 4	5 − 2	7 − 1	9 − 2
4.	11 − 7	15 − 7	18 − 9	10 − 5	6 − 6	8 − 6	9 − 3	12 − 5	10 − 6	11 − 3
5.	13 − 6	4 − 1	7 − 5	12 − 6	13 − 4	10 − 3	3 − 2	17 − 8	9 − 5	14 − 8

Add.

1. $\begin{array}{r} 38 \\ + 46 \end{array}$	2. $\begin{array}{r} 52 \\ + 68 \end{array}$	3. $\begin{array}{r} 27 \\ + 16 \end{array}$	4. $\begin{array}{r} 65 \\ + 39 \end{array}$	5. $\begin{array}{r} 72 \\ + 44 \end{array}$	6. $\begin{array}{r} 36 \\ + 85 \end{array}$
7. $\begin{array}{r} 59 \\ + 21 \end{array}$	8. $\begin{array}{r} 64 \\ + 47 \end{array}$	9. $\begin{array}{r} 33 \\ + 79 \end{array}$	10. $\begin{array}{r} 75 \\ + 26 \end{array}$	11. $\begin{array}{r} 25 \\ + 65 \end{array}$	12. $\begin{array}{r} 93 \\ + 18 \end{array}$
13. $\begin{array}{r} 43 \\ + 17 \end{array}$	14. $\begin{array}{r} 37 \\ + 54 \end{array}$	15. $\begin{array}{r} 84 \\ + 28 \end{array}$	16. $\begin{array}{r} 66 \\ + 87 \end{array}$	17. $\begin{array}{r} 58 \\ + 47 \end{array}$	18. $\begin{array}{r} 95 \\ + 38 \end{array}$
19. $\begin{array}{r} 76 \\ + 59 \end{array}$	20. $\begin{array}{r} 45 \\ + 97 \end{array}$	21. $\begin{array}{r} 67 \\ + 87 \end{array}$	22. $\begin{array}{r} 29 \\ + 74 \end{array}$	23. $\begin{array}{r} 86 \\ + 44 \end{array}$	24. $\begin{array}{r} 56 \\ + 59 \end{array}$
25. $\begin{array}{r} 324 \\ + 468 \end{array}$	26. $\begin{array}{r} 543 \\ + 267 \end{array}$	27. $\begin{array}{r} 651 \\ + 139 \end{array}$	28. $\begin{array}{r} 285 \\ + 736 \end{array}$	29. $\begin{array}{r} 452 \\ + 569 \end{array}$	30. $\begin{array}{r} 376 \\ + 678 \end{array}$
31. $\begin{array}{r} 435 \\ + 687 \end{array}$	32. $\begin{array}{r} 729 \\ + 594 \end{array}$	33. $\begin{array}{r} 317 \\ + 846 \end{array}$	34. $\begin{array}{r} 473 \\ + 986 \end{array}$	35. $\begin{array}{r} 528 \\ + 698 \end{array}$	36. $\begin{array}{r} 739 \\ + 95 \end{array}$
37. $\begin{array}{r} 574 \\ + 587 \end{array}$	38. $\begin{array}{r} 642 \\ + 797 \end{array}$	39. $\begin{array}{r} 489 \\ + 68 \end{array}$	40. $\begin{array}{r} 837 \\ + 89 \end{array}$	41. $\begin{array}{r} 375 \\ + 748 \end{array}$	42. $\begin{array}{r} 506 \\ + 875 \end{array}$
43. $\begin{array}{r} 753 \\ + 579 \end{array}$	44. $\begin{array}{r} 826 \\ + 397 \end{array}$	45. $\begin{array}{r} 952 \\ + 468 \end{array}$	46. $\begin{array}{r} 687 \\ + 104 \end{array}$	47. $\begin{array}{r} 859 \\ + 287 \end{array}$	48. $\begin{array}{r} 489 \\ + 362 \end{array}$
49. $\begin{array}{r} 3257 \\ + 489 \end{array}$	50. $\begin{array}{r} 2761 \\ + 9857 \end{array}$	51. $\begin{array}{r} 4638 \\ + 2794 \end{array}$	52. $\begin{array}{r} 6509 \\ + 3872 \end{array}$	53. $\begin{array}{r} 5367 \\ + 2636 \end{array}$	54. $\begin{array}{r} 7482 \\ + 2648 \end{array}$
55. $\begin{array}{r} 5024 \\ + 3698 \end{array}$	56. $\begin{array}{r} 9546 \\ + 489 \end{array}$	57. $\begin{array}{r} 8274 \\ + 5967 \end{array}$	58. $\begin{array}{r} 7088 \\ + 3786 \end{array}$	59. $\begin{array}{r} 4963 \\ + 8589 \end{array}$	60. $\begin{array}{r} 6257 \\ + 7983 \end{array}$

Add.

| 1. | 83 + 38 | 2. | 46 + 57 | 3. | 75 + 49 | 4. | 364 + 287 | 5. | 628 + 495 | 6. | 961 + 339 |

| 7. | 3602 + 4857 | 8. | 7534 + 2486 | 9. | 6483 + 1529 | 10. | 5796 + 3687 | 11. | 4078 + 7993 | 12. | 2806 + 3884 |

| 13. | 5381 + 2968 | 14. | 6537 + 4685 | 15. | 7285 + 3496 | 16. | 3198 + 9465 | 17. | 8462 + 739 | 18. | 4893 + 9657 |

19.
326
483
+ 261

20.
205
783
+ 275

21.
36
472
+ 564

22.
645
79
+ 321

23.
407
628
+ 741

24.
822
364
+ 874

25.
427
369
+ 74

26.
638
205
+ 481

27.
815
32
+ 673

28.
436
571
+ 725

29.
52
836
+ 428

30.
618
321
+ 563

31.
310
426
45
+ 521

32.
4615
321
7646
+ 15

33.
7613
2511
384
+ 21

34.
5326
2148
79
+ 304

35.
361
752
4305
+ 2943

36.
8064
244
368
+ 2644

37.
32
243
1576
+ 5662

38.
5622
3278
4311
+ 75

39.
1842
361
28
+ 539

40.
4064
72
364
+ 420

41.
7161
1389
421
+ 756

42.
9203
1365
249
+ 3666

43. 354 + 1482 + 71 + 288

44. 1909 + 364 + 2656 + 19

45. 18 + 3261 + 408 + 324

46. 7257 + 3621 + 27 + 1840

47. 4037 + 2615 + 1382 + 420

48. 38 + 8421 + 3611 + 1020

Add.

1. 15 38 + 72	**2.** 46 52 + 21	**3.** 99 32 + 65	**4.** 47 53 + 39	**5.** 12 85 + 46	**6.** 42 49 + 76
7. 736 819 + 257	**8.** 441 69 + 525	**9.** 954 370 + 123	**10.** 16 875 + 237	**11.** 882 419 + 533	**12.** 702 611 + 299
13. 7269 3815 + 2262	**14.** 1531 6992 + 7846	**15.** 4431 5268 + 7796	**16.** 3457 7814 + 9266	**17.** 2201 7557 + 3985	**18.** 9806 3721 + 8169
19. 7265 3817 4404 + 3724	**20.** 38 175 2216 + 3993	**21.** 4692 38 655 + 3169	**22.** 361 22 4535 + 227	**23.** 6977 3251 7869 + 114	**24.** 3818 469 2312 + 6654
25. 152 68 5922 + 384	**26.** 6132 5877 96 + 390	**27.** 7214 365 72 + 9191	**28.** 330 785 6422 + 740	**29.** 9832 6115 2959 + 388	**30.** 714 3602 5601 + 311
31. 4951 7811 3666 + 7257	**32.** 9867 4359 3112 + 8476	**33.** 3581 7664 4822 + 9255	**34.** 3076 8914 2603 + 9115	**35.** 4581 6972 2424 + 6879	**36.** 7381 4952 3466 + 8923

37. 68 + 3131 + 544

38. 796 + 9414 + 12

39. 38 + 469 + 2217

40. 896 + 3447 + 919

41. 6964 + 1152 + 3516 + 73

42. 921 + 3657 + 786 + 2152

43. 3865 + 4994 + 72 + 818

44. 558 + 42 + 735 + 9441

Subtract.

1. 616 − 378	2. 424 − 166	3. 318 − 129	4. 944 − 367	5. 230 − 175	6. 776 − 278
7. 311 − 256	8. 863 − 195	9. 540 − 267	10. 913 − 254	11. 722 − 258	12. 440 − 145
13. 612 − 423	14. 336 − 277	15. 545 − 178	16. 484 − 198	17. 265 − 197	18. 383 − 297
19. 720 − 266	20. 823 − 176	21. 236 − 157	22. 451 − 183	23. 717 − 269	24. 932 − 568
25. 2129 − 1631	26. 5540 − 2690	27. 1783 − 1499	28. 8126 − 5342	29. 9145 − 2518	30. 6811 − 1930
31. 4352 − 1627	32. 3521 − 1255	33. 8843 − 3951	34. 5619 − 2734	35. 9631 − 3278	36. 7135 − 2617
37. 2163 − 1577	38. 8632 − 4956	39. 7324 − 1888	40. 4652 − 2996	41. 3485 − 2696	42. 7255 − 2477
43. 6636 − 1887	44. 5431 − 2758	45. 3263 − 1579	46. 2468 − 1789	47. 9362 − 4794	48. 7516 − 4849
49. 2286 − 1598	50. 3134 − 1677	51. 2782 − 1993	52. 9110 − 3265	53. 7817 − 4969	54. 5560 − 2982
55. 4137 − 2659	56. 3120 − 1454	57. 2767 − 1989	58. 5610 − 1933	59. 6220 − 1941	60. 8313 − 5644

360B   More practice

Set A   For use after page 23

Subtract.

1.	23 − 16	2.	42 − 27	3.	51 − 15	4.	60 − 38	5.	34 − 17	6.	85 − 48
7.	76 − 49	8.	33 − 27	9.	64 − 26	10.	52 − 38	11.	41 − 23	12.	90 − 54
13.	53 − 25	14.	66 − 38	15.	72 − 24	16.	84 − 58	17.	65 − 49	18.	43 − 18
19.	131 − 34	20.	140 − 61	21.	183 − 79	22.	170 − 96	23.	162 − 65	24.	154 − 79
25.	182 − 89	26.	173 − 44	27.	161 − 87	28.	137 − 69	29.	191 − 78	30.	146 − 86

Set B   For use after page 25

Subtract.

1.	326 − 178	2.	719 − 463	3.	560 − 295	4.	215 − 187	5.	473 − 286	6.	837 − 359
7.	943 − 587	8.	352 − 168	9.	431 − 176	10.	824 − 456	11.	762 − 379	12.	515 − 158
13.	639 − 262	14.	527 − 138	15.	740 − 376	16.	418 − 273	17.	356 − 177	18.	842 − 367
19.	4561 − 2793	20.	7211 − 1476	21.	8432 − 3657	22.	9234 − 2386	23.	3474 − 1398	24.	5673 − 2685
25.	8135 − 3279	26.	6426 − 1748	27.	4653 − 2987	28.	7440 − 3786	29.	9126 − 4437	30.	6325 − 2347

Subtract.

1.	603 − 236	2.	205 − 148	3.	708 − 319	4.	300 − 158	5.	502 − 268
6.	900 − 343	7.	801 − 256	8.	304 − 177	9.	706 − 389	10.	207 − 129
11.	702 − 275	12.	903 − 437	13.	605 − 346	14.	804 − 525	15.	401 − 183
16.	2063 − 1155	17.	5701 − 3967	18.	8000 − 6523	19.	4006 − 1129	20.	2302 − 1635
21.	3054 − 1286	22.	6005 − 3238	23.	7306 − 4823	24.	9050 − 1932	25.	4000 − 1465
26.	8007 − 3749	27.	7022 − 2657	28.	6031 − 4485	29.	5604 − 1739	30.	9003 − 5614

Find the total amounts or differences.

1.	$ 3.85 + 4.69	2.	$ 7.63 + 2.48	3.	$ 5.26 + 9.38	4.	$ 8.54 + 7.62	5.	$ 6.97 + 4.36
6.	$ 9.40 − 3.26	7.	$ 12.51 − 4.83	8.	$ 11.72 − 6.35	9.	$ 28.51 − 14.76	10.	$ 64.23 − 28.47
11.	$ 56.43 + 28.72	12.	$ 39.58 + 76.45	13.	$ 45.82 + 63.29	14.	$ 126.15 + 25.38	15.	$ 264.72 + 137.49
16.	$ 10.00 − 2.54	17.	$ 25.65 − 9.87	18.	$ 5.00 − 2.38	19.	$ 76.21 − 15.75	20.	$ 47.06 − 21.38
21.	$ 3.75 2.25 + 9.00	22.	$ 12.52 8.73 + 11.50	23.	$ 26.38 15.71 + 42.07	24.	$ 36.49 0.59 + 2.88	25.	$ 0.75 1.10 + 52.15

Set A   For use after page 69

Add.

1.	5.2 + 3.9	2.	6.8 + 5.7	3.	0.7 + 0.6	4.	2.8 + 9.6	5.	8.4 + 3.7	6.	2.9 + 0.8
7.	6.32 + 4.07	8.	24.6 + 15.59	9.	9.76 + 14.3	10.	8.51 + 3.49	11.	37.82 + 24.67	12.	4.38 + 17.6
13.	46.81 + 27.3	14.	72.64 + 58.37	15.	86.5 + 38.76	16.	48.327 + 62.783	17.	52.159 + 48.678	18.	31.982 + 46.089
19.	3.6 4.7 + 5.9	20.	0.8 0.9 + 0.7	21.	26.5 38.4 + 72.8	22.	3.258 6.42 + 7.1	23.	5.79 3.882 + 4.6	24.	46.12 521.83 + 57.35

25. $3.612 + 5.783 + 6.215$

26. $7.46 + 18.2 + 21.764$

27. $4.71 + 5.82 + 6.015$

28. $12.71 + 13.6 + 24.55$

Set B   For use after page 73

Subtract.

1.	4.2 − 3.6	2.	0.6 − 0.5	3.	12.5 − 3.7	4.	25.3 − 7.8	5.	36.4 − 21.9	6.	38.2 − 17.5
7.	43.7 − 26.85	8.	82.41 − 36.74	9.	78.5 − 49.87	10.	91.76 − 54.38	11.	84.54 − 47.36	12.	46.5 − 32.78
13.	13.6 − 6.52	14.	32.06 − 18.78	15.	26.061 − 15.507	16.	0.56 − 0.382	17.	6.504 − 0.007	18.	0.48 − 0.09
19.	5.704 − 0.368	20.	32.00 − 4.76	21.	7.93 − 2.765	22.	8.302 − 6.548	23.	13.72 − 4.891	24.	5.203 − 1.766

25. $6.53 − 2.78$

26. $0.65 − 0.283$

27. $7.502 − 3.768$

28. $36.201 − 12.843$

29. $52.005 − 9.336$

30. $7.02 − 2.643$

Multiply.

	A	B	C	D	E	F	G	H	I	J
1.	2 × 3	3 × 5	4 × 4	6 × 2	1 × 5	0 × 6	5 × 2	7 × 3	2 × 4	3 × 6
2.	5 × 0	2 × 2	1 × 7	4 × 8	6 × 5	8 × 1	9 × 4	8 × 5	4 × 3	2 × 8
3.	9 × 6	1 × 4	3 × 3	5 × 8	3 × 7	4 × 6	6 × 1	3 × 2	7 × 0	6 × 6

4. 8×2 5. 4×5 6. 6×3 7. 9×7 8. 8×6 9. 7×7

10. 5×6 11. 4×7 12. 3×8 13. 2×9 14. 7×8 15. 3×9

16. 9×9 17. 7×5 18. 5×5 19. 6×7 20. 2×7 21. 8×8

22. 9×8 23. 5×9 24. 4×2 25. 5×4 26. 2×6 27. 6×4

Divide.

1. $16 \div 4$ 2. $4 \div 2$ 3. $18 \div 3$ 4. $12 \div 6$ 5. $35 \div 5$ 6. $28 \div 7$

7. $15 \div 5$ 8. $16 \div 2$ 9. $24 \div 4$ 10. $32 \div 8$ 11. $21 \div 7$ 12. $27 \div 3$

13. $14 \div 2$ 14. $9 \div 1$ 15. $81 \div 9$ 16. $0 \div 6$ 17. $20 \div 5$ 18. $24 \div 8$

19. $24 \div 6$ 20. $56 \div 8$ 21. $15 \div 3$ 22. $30 \div 5$ 23. $48 \div 6$ 24. $12 \div 3$

25. $45 \div 9$ 26. $36 \div 6$ 27. $40 \div 5$ 28. $42 \div 7$ 29. $28 \div 4$ 30. $36 \div 9$

31. $5\overline{)25}$ 32. $7\overline{)49}$ 33. $4\overline{)20}$ 34. $8\overline{)16}$ 35. $2\overline{)18}$ 36. $8\overline{)48}$

37. $3\overline{)9}$ 38. $4\overline{)32}$ 39. $6\overline{)30}$ 40. $5\overline{)45}$ 41. $7\overline{)14}$ 42. $9\overline{)27}$

43. $7\overline{)35}$ 44. $9\overline{)54}$ 45. $8\overline{)64}$ 46. $7\overline{)63}$ 47. $9\overline{)72}$ 48. $2\overline{)10}$

49. $4\overline{)36}$ 50. $2\overline{)12}$ 51. $7\overline{)56}$ 52. $8\overline{)40}$ 53. $3\overline{)21}$ 54. $9\overline{)0}$

Set A   For use after page 129

Multiply.

1. 30×20 2. 70×40 3. 5×30 4. 6×20 5. 3×800 6. 20×90

7. 2×7000 8. 10×50 9. 4×3000 10. 5×600 11. 3000×7 12. 80×10

13. 100×3 14. 2×40 15. 8×200 16. 40×50 17. 6×300 18. 7×1000

19. 3×90 20. 60×40 21. 7×50 22. 6×7000 23. 80×4 24. 50×20

25. 50×80 26. 600×6 27. 40×9 28. 50×50 29. 10×60 30. 9×5000

31. 30×10 32. 7×30 33. 4×200 34. 2000×6 35. 8×100 36. 4000×6

37. 50×60 38. 700×2 39. 80×20 40. 3×500 41. 6×800 42. 80×40

43. 70×90 44. 5×7000 45. 60×9 46. 9×900 47. 3×300 48. 70×70

Set B   For use after page 133

Divide.

1. $1800 \div 3$ 2. $2400 \div 80$ 3. $1200 \div 20$ 4. $3600 \div 9$ 5. $2100 \div 30$

6. $16\,000 \div 2$ 7. $3500 \div 70$ 8. $1500 \div 5$ 9. $32\,000 \div 8$ 10. $300 \div 10$

11. $2500 \div 50$ 12. $20\,000 \div 4$ 13. $2800 \div 7$ 14. $2700 \div 3$ 15. $3000 \div 60$

16. $64\,000 \div 8$ 17. $42\,000 \div 7$ 18. $3500 \div 50$ 19. $4800 \div 80$ 20. $5600 \div 7$

21. $700 \div 10$ 22. $4900 \div 7$ 23. $5400 \div 6$ 24. $40\,000 \div 8$ 25. $1800 \div 20$

26. $1400 \div 20$ 27. $3600 \div 60$ 28. $8100 \div 90$ 29. $2400 \div 8$ 30. $3200 \div 40$

31. $27\,000 \div 3$ 32. $72\,000 \div 9$ 33. $4800 \div 6$ 34. $1600 \div 40$ 35. $4500 \div 50$

Multiply.

1. 32
    × 26

2. 44
    × 52

3. 64
    × 28

4. 35
    × 73

5. 56
    × 62

6. 71
    × 49

7. 46
    × 38

8. 82
    × 57

9. 37
    × 66

10. 29
    × 46

11. 93
    × 37

12. 65
    × 56

13. 234
    × 45

14. 791
    × 36

15. 814
    × 29

16. 375
    × 25

17. 462
    × 54

18. 543
    × 67

Multiply.

1. 234
    × 331

2. 567
    × 423

3. 821
    × 245

4. 378
    × 524

5. 715
    × 363

6. 456
    × 832

7. 943
    × 426

8. 782
    × 237

9. 574
    × 526

10. 291
    × 647

11. 439
    × 726

12. 625
    × 349

13. 538
    × 295

14. 846
    × 376

15. 921
    × 518

16. 457
    × 632

17. 764
    × 485

18. 367
    × 924

Multiply.

1. $ 1.85
    ×   6

2. $ 1.20
    ×   9

3. $ 7.03
    ×   8

4. $ 6.22
    ×   34

5. $ 9.07
    ×   28

6. $ 8.40
    ×   6

7. $ 0.38
    ×   42

8. $ 0.75
    ×   25

9. $ 9.00
    ×   45

10. $ 8.45
    ×   26

11. $ 15.29
    ×   55

12. $ 0.82
    ×   75

13. $ 22.43
    ×   17

14. $ 36.18
    ×   29

15. $ 74.51
    ×   31

16. $ 9.84
    ×   72

17. $ 5.68
    ×   38

18. $ 7.50
    × 463

19. $ 9.03
    × 724

20. $ 7.62
    × 481

21. $ 0.86
    ×   93

22. $ 4.80
    × 379

23. $ 8.04
    × 265

24. $ 6.42
    × 705

Multiply.

1. $\begin{array}{r} 25 \\ \times\ 17 \end{array}$
2. $\begin{array}{r} 43 \\ \times\ 62 \end{array}$
3. $\begin{array}{r} 74 \\ \times\ 31 \end{array}$
4. $\begin{array}{r} 92 \\ \times\ 34 \end{array}$
5. $\begin{array}{r} 58 \\ \times\ 52 \end{array}$
6. $\begin{array}{r} 19 \\ \times\ 77 \end{array}$

7. $\begin{array}{r} 39 \\ \times\ 82 \end{array}$
8. $\begin{array}{r} 51 \\ \times\ 68 \end{array}$
9. $\begin{array}{r} 42 \\ \times\ 29 \end{array}$
10. $\begin{array}{r} 69 \\ \times\ 73 \end{array}$
11. $\begin{array}{r} 34 \\ \times\ 22 \end{array}$
12. $\begin{array}{r} 99 \\ \times\ 13 \end{array}$

13. $\begin{array}{r} 16 \\ \times\ 44 \end{array}$
14. $\begin{array}{r} 61 \\ \times\ 28 \end{array}$
15. $\begin{array}{r} 79 \\ \times\ 42 \end{array}$
16. $\begin{array}{r} 53 \\ \times\ 36 \end{array}$
17. $\begin{array}{r} 85 \\ \times\ 54 \end{array}$
18. $\begin{array}{r} 47 \\ \times\ 27 \end{array}$

19. $\begin{array}{r} 126 \\ \times\ 32 \end{array}$
20. $\begin{array}{r} 83 \\ \times\ 95 \end{array}$
21. $\begin{array}{r} 357 \\ \times\ 55 \end{array}$
22. $\begin{array}{r} 67 \\ \times\ 24 \end{array}$
23. $\begin{array}{r} 711 \\ \times\ 38 \end{array}$
24. $\begin{array}{r} 28 \\ \times\ 87 \end{array}$

25. $\begin{array}{r} 642 \\ \times\ 23 \end{array}$
26. $\begin{array}{r} 36 \\ \times\ 73 \end{array}$
27. $\begin{array}{r} 391 \\ \times\ 65 \end{array}$
28. $\begin{array}{r} 62 \\ \times\ 26 \end{array}$
29. $\begin{array}{r} 894 \\ \times\ 42 \end{array}$
30. $\begin{array}{r} 86 \\ \times\ 55 \end{array}$

31. $\begin{array}{r} 274 \\ \times\ 69 \end{array}$
32. $\begin{array}{r} 98 \\ \times\ 24 \end{array}$
33. $\begin{array}{r} 825 \\ \times\ 37 \end{array}$
34. $\begin{array}{r} 76 \\ \times\ 87 \end{array}$
35. $\begin{array}{r} 558 \\ \times\ 73 \end{array}$
36. $\begin{array}{r} 38 \\ \times\ 44 \end{array}$

37. $\begin{array}{r} 489 \\ \times\ 75 \end{array}$
38. $\begin{array}{r} 94 \\ \times\ 72 \end{array}$
39. $\begin{array}{r} 518 \\ \times\ 57 \end{array}$
40. $\begin{array}{r} 42 \\ \times\ 55 \end{array}$
41. $\begin{array}{r} 163 \\ \times\ 49 \end{array}$
42. $\begin{array}{r} 78 \\ \times\ 59 \end{array}$

43. $\begin{array}{r} 296 \\ \times\ 72 \end{array}$
44. $\begin{array}{r} 727 \\ \times\ 33 \end{array}$
45. $\begin{array}{r} 444 \\ \times\ 59 \end{array}$
46. $\begin{array}{r} 343 \\ \times\ 91 \end{array}$
47. $\begin{array}{r} 592 \\ \times\ 85 \end{array}$
48. $\begin{array}{r} 754 \\ \times\ 36 \end{array}$

49. $\begin{array}{r} 653 \\ \times\ 45 \end{array}$
50. $\begin{array}{r} 995 \\ \times\ 26 \end{array}$
51. $\begin{array}{r} 277 \\ \times\ 38 \end{array}$
52. $\begin{array}{r} 318 \\ \times\ 49 \end{array}$
53. $\begin{array}{r} 425 \\ \times\ 75 \end{array}$
54. $\begin{array}{r} 515 \\ \times\ 68 \end{array}$

55. $\begin{array}{r} 785 \\ \times\ 43 \end{array}$
56. $\begin{array}{r} 859 \\ \times\ 92 \end{array}$
57. $\begin{array}{r} 346 \\ \times\ 51 \end{array}$
58. $\begin{array}{r} 432 \\ \times\ 76 \end{array}$
59. $\begin{array}{r} 917 \\ \times\ 25 \end{array}$
60. $\begin{array}{r} 562 \\ \times\ 39 \end{array}$

Divide.

1. 3)137   2. 5)131   3. 7)108   4. 6)505   5. 4)210

6. 4)254   7. 5)231   8. 8)434   9. 7)186   10. 2)187

11. 7)4216   12. 8)2602   13. 4)2937   14. 9)1149   15. 5)2307

16. 2)1507   17. 4)834   18. 9)3369   19. 3)1877   20. 6)2840

Divide.

1. 4)5622   2. 5)35 318   3. 8)25 692   4. 6)25 929   5. 2)7091

6. 3)19 263   7. 7)36 473   8. 5)19 123   9. 4)28 414   10. 6)31 886

11. 6)48 682   12. 2)18 429   13. 7)32 788   14. 3)22 568   15. 5)32 067

16. 7)58 887   17. 3)13 841   18. 6)30 087   19. 8)33 897   20. 9)34 420

Divide.

1. 30)1452   2. 50)3117   3. 20)1128   4. 70)2195   5. 60)1411

6. 40)1495   7. 80)2133   8. 90)3811   9. 30)1647   10. 20)1318

11. 60)12 920   12. 30)19 251   13. 20)15 695   14. 80)25 972   15. 40)21 455

16. 70)26 922   17. 60)28 432   18. 90)23 618   19. 30)24 732   20. 20)13 091

Set A   For use after page 189

Divide.

1. $22\overline{)144}$ 2. $34\overline{)191}$ 3. $17\overline{)145}$ 4. $68\overline{)518}$ 5. $52\overline{)230}$

6. $92\overline{)330}$ 7. $46\overline{)437}$ 8. $73\overline{)328}$ 9. $82\overline{)461}$ 10. $67\overline{)426}$

11. $74\overline{)407}$ 12. $28\overline{)211}$ 13. $39\overline{)256}$ 14. $45\overline{)377}$ 15. $81\overline{)397}$

16. $64\overline{)238}$ 17. $53\overline{)302}$ 18. $47\overline{)318}$ 19. $32\overline{)156}$ 20. $26\overline{)239}$

Set B   For use after page 191

Divide.

1. $41\overline{)207}$ 2. $53\overline{)248}$ 3. $62\overline{)389}$ 4. $28\overline{)210}$ 5. $91\overline{)346}$

6. $76\overline{)351}$ 7. $85\overline{)552}$ 8. $34\overline{)328}$ 9. $52\overline{)348}$ 10. $63\overline{)547}$

11. $53\overline{)1703}$ 12. $65\overline{)1916}$ 13. $48\overline{)3653}$ 14. $39\overline{)2340}$ 15. $27\overline{)2465}$

16. $74\overline{)3884}$ 17. $82\overline{)6241}$ 18. $94\overline{)2541}$ 19. $26\overline{)950}$ 20. $42\overline{)3464}$

21. $35\overline{)1692}$ 22. $76\overline{)2746}$ 23. $83\overline{)6665}$ 24. $54\overline{)3468}$ 25. $61\overline{)4398}$

Set C   For use after page 193

Divide.

1. $63\overline{)3414}$ 2. $33\overline{)1263}$ 3. $98\overline{)7061}$ 4. $29\overline{)1633}$ 5. $46\overline{)2208}$

6. $79\overline{)5956}$ 7. $67\overline{)4162}$ 8. $72\overline{)6348}$ 9. $32\overline{)1666}$ 10. $55\overline{)1547}$

11. $66\overline{)5512}$ 12. $89\overline{)3478}$ 13. $41\overline{)1151}$ 14. $93\overline{)7537}$ 15. $28\overline{)1330}$

16. $71\overline{)2272}$ 17. $34\overline{)3263}$ 18. $96\overline{)2026}$ 19. $28\overline{)1528}$ 20. $47\overline{)3666}$

21. $52\overline{)2450}$ 22. $86\overline{)4867}$ 23. $65\overline{)1878}$ 24. $38\overline{)2964}$ 25. $72\overline{)4695}$

Give the missing numerator or denominator.

1. $\frac{1}{4} = \frac{n}{24}$ 2. $\frac{3}{12} = \frac{n}{36}$ 3. $\frac{3}{7} = \frac{9}{n}$ 4. $\frac{5}{6} = \frac{30}{n}$ 5. $\frac{4}{9} = \frac{n}{27}$

6. $\frac{3}{8} = \frac{12}{n}$ 7. $\frac{2}{6} = \frac{10}{n}$ 8. $\frac{3}{4} = \frac{15}{n}$ 9. $\frac{5}{12} = \frac{10}{n}$ 10. $\frac{1}{2} = \frac{4}{n}$

11. $\frac{2}{3} = \frac{n}{18}$ 12. $\frac{2}{4} = \frac{n}{20}$ 13. $\frac{2}{5} = \frac{n}{15}$ 14. $\frac{3}{6} = \frac{12}{n}$ 15. $\frac{5}{7} = \frac{25}{n}$

16. $\frac{5}{8} = \frac{10}{n}$ 17. $\frac{2}{9} = \frac{6}{n}$ 18. $\frac{5}{10} = \frac{n}{20}$ 19. $\frac{4}{12} = \frac{n}{36}$ 20. $\frac{6}{15} = \frac{n}{30}$

21. $\frac{1}{8} = \frac{3}{n}$ 22. $\frac{3}{4} = \frac{18}{n}$ 23. $\frac{2}{7} = \frac{n}{21}$ 24. $\frac{1}{5} = \frac{n}{15}$ 25. $\frac{7}{12} = \frac{21}{n}$

26. $\frac{3}{10} = \frac{n}{30}$ 27. $\frac{3}{15} = \frac{6}{n}$ 28. $\frac{3}{9} = \frac{9}{n}$ 29. $\frac{3}{4} = \frac{9}{n}$ 30. $\frac{7}{10} = \frac{14}{n}$

31. $\frac{1}{3} = \frac{n}{24}$ 32. $\frac{4}{5} = \frac{16}{n}$ 33. $\frac{2}{8} = \frac{n}{16}$ 34. $\frac{6}{9} = \frac{18}{n}$ 35. $\frac{1}{9} = \frac{2}{n}$

36. $\frac{9}{12} = \frac{n}{24}$ 37. $\frac{1}{2} = \frac{5}{n}$ 38. $\frac{8}{12} = \frac{16}{n}$ 39. $\frac{2}{3} = \frac{n}{21}$ 40. $\frac{5}{9} = \frac{15}{n}$

41. $\frac{4}{8} = \frac{16}{n}$ 42. $\frac{3}{5} = \frac{n}{20}$ 43. $\frac{1}{7} = \frac{n}{14}$ 44. $\frac{9}{10} = \frac{18}{n}$ 45. $\frac{8}{15} = \frac{n}{30}$

Give the lowest terms fraction.

1. $\frac{4}{10}$ 2. $\frac{6}{12}$ 3. $\frac{3}{15}$ 4. $\frac{8}{16}$ 5. $\frac{4}{18}$

6. $\frac{20}{40}$ 7. $\frac{9}{18}$ 8. $\frac{28}{70}$ 9. $\frac{18}{21}$ 10. $\frac{20}{36}$

11. $\frac{10}{15}$ 12. $\frac{18}{60}$ 13. $\frac{12}{14}$ 14. $\frac{14}{28}$ 15. $\frac{36}{40}$

16. $\frac{16}{24}$ 17. $\frac{15}{20}$ 18. $\frac{48}{80}$ 19. $\frac{27}{30}$ 20. $\frac{50}{100}$

21. $\frac{10}{12}$ 22. $\frac{24}{56}$ 23. $\frac{12}{18}$ 24. $\frac{4}{16}$ 25. $\frac{12}{15}$

26. $\frac{6}{14}$ 27. $\frac{2}{10}$ 28. $\frac{18}{36}$ 29. $\frac{18}{24}$ 30. $\frac{36}{45}$

31. $\frac{15}{21}$ 32. $\frac{14}{16}$ 33. $\frac{20}{30}$ 34. $\frac{4}{12}$ 35. $\frac{14}{20}$

36. $\frac{36}{80}$ 37. $\frac{10}{14}$ 38. $\frac{750}{1000}$ 39. $\frac{56}{70}$ 40. $\frac{48}{64}$

41. $\frac{70}{100}$ 42. $\frac{16}{20}$ 43. $\frac{27}{60}$ 44. $\frac{8}{14}$ 45. $\frac{20}{25}$

Set A   For use after page 195

Divide.

1. $32\overline{)16\,519}$ 2. $45\overline{)13\,912}$ 3. $63\overline{)25\,963}$ 4. $72\overline{)46\,085}$

5. $84\overline{)27\,141}$ 6. $29\overline{)17\,612}$ 7. $95\overline{)21\,470}$ 8. $64\overline{)25\,096}$

9. $48\overline{)21\,702}$ 10. $33\overline{)24\,027}$ 11. $76\overline{)26\,374}$ 12. $81\overline{)52\,415}$

13. $97\overline{)69\,746}$ 14. $54\overline{)34\,240}$ 15. $35\overline{)10\,120}$ 16. $27\overline{)22\,530}$

Set B   For use after page 263

Add or subtract.

1. $\begin{array}{r} \frac{1}{3} \\ + \frac{2}{3} \\ \hline \end{array}$ 2. $\begin{array}{r} \frac{2}{5} \\ + \frac{4}{5} \\ \hline \end{array}$ 3. $\begin{array}{r} \frac{1}{2} \\ + \frac{3}{2} \\ \hline \end{array}$ 4. $\begin{array}{r} \frac{5}{6} \\ + \frac{2}{6} \\ \hline \end{array}$ 5. $\begin{array}{r} \frac{1}{8} \\ + \frac{3}{8} \\ \hline \end{array}$

6. $\begin{array}{r} \frac{4}{5} \\ - \frac{3}{5} \\ \hline \end{array}$ 7. $\begin{array}{r} \frac{7}{8} \\ - \frac{3}{8} \\ \hline \end{array}$ 8. $\begin{array}{r} \frac{5}{10} \\ - \frac{3}{10} \\ \hline \end{array}$ 9. $\begin{array}{r} \frac{7}{15} \\ - \frac{3}{15} \\ \hline \end{array}$ 10. $\begin{array}{r} \frac{9}{12} \\ - \frac{2}{12} \\ \hline \end{array}$

11. $\begin{array}{r} 7\frac{3}{10} \\ + 9\frac{7}{10} \\ \hline \end{array}$ 12. $\begin{array}{r} 32\frac{7}{100} \\ - 15\frac{3}{100} \\ \hline \end{array}$ 13. $\begin{array}{r} 72\frac{28}{100} \\ + 16\frac{35}{100} \\ \hline \end{array}$ 14. $\begin{array}{r} 136\frac{7}{9} \\ - 49\frac{2}{9} \\ \hline \end{array}$ 15. $\begin{array}{r} 232\frac{7}{10} \\ - 141\frac{3}{10} \\ \hline \end{array}$

16. $\frac{5}{8} + \frac{3}{8}$ 17. $\frac{5}{12} + \frac{9}{12}$ 18. $\frac{5}{16} + \frac{3}{16}$ 19. $\frac{1}{24} + \frac{9}{24}$

20. $\frac{9}{10} + \frac{3}{10}$ 21. $\frac{2}{15} + \frac{5}{15}$ 22. $\frac{1}{17} + \frac{5}{17}$ 23. $\frac{1}{5} + \frac{3}{5}$

24. $\frac{7}{9} - \frac{3}{9}$ 25. $\frac{8}{10} - \frac{5}{10}$ 26. $\frac{14}{15} - \frac{6}{15}$ 27. $\frac{8}{12} - \frac{2}{12}$

28. $\frac{5}{10} - \frac{1}{10}$ 29. $\frac{10}{24} - \frac{6}{24}$ 30. $\frac{7}{12} - \frac{2}{12}$ 31. $\frac{6}{8} - \frac{3}{8}$

Add or subtract.

1. $\frac{2}{3}$
  $+\frac{3}{4}$

2. $\frac{1}{8}$
  $+\frac{1}{16}$

3. $\frac{7}{10}$
  $+\frac{2}{5}$

4. $\frac{3}{5}$
  $+\frac{1}{2}$

5. $\frac{1}{2}$
  $+\frac{1}{4}$

6. $\frac{3}{16}$
  $+\frac{1}{4}$

7. $\frac{7}{10}$
  $+\frac{1}{100}$

8. $\frac{2}{15}$
  $+\frac{2}{3}$

9. $\frac{1}{2}$
  $+\frac{3}{10}$

10. $\frac{2}{5}$
  $+\frac{3}{4}$

11. $\frac{3}{5}$
  $-\frac{1}{2}$

12. $\frac{5}{8}$
  $-\frac{1}{4}$

13. $\frac{5}{6}$
  $-\frac{2}{3}$

14. $\frac{6}{10}$
  $-\frac{1}{2}$

15. $\frac{1}{2}$
  $-\frac{2}{8}$

16. $\frac{2}{3}$
  $-\frac{1}{12}$

17. $\frac{7}{10}$
  $-\frac{1}{5}$

18. $\frac{14}{16}$
  $-\frac{3}{4}$

19. $\frac{7}{10}$
  $-\frac{3}{100}$

20. $\frac{38}{100}$
  $-\frac{1}{4}$

21. $\frac{7}{8}$
  $+\frac{3}{4}$

22. $\frac{3}{4}$
  $-\frac{1}{5}$

23. $\frac{15}{16}$
  $-\frac{3}{8}$

24. $\frac{2}{3}$
  $-\frac{1}{4}$

25. $\frac{2}{9}$
  $+\frac{5}{18}$

Multiply.

1. $\frac{2}{3} \times \frac{1}{4}$

2. $\frac{5}{8} \times \frac{1}{2}$

3. $\frac{3}{5} \times \frac{2}{3}$

4. $\frac{7}{9} \times \frac{1}{3}$

5. $\frac{1}{10} \times \frac{4}{5}$

6. $\frac{2}{10} \times \frac{1}{10}$

7. $\frac{7}{8} \times \frac{1}{4}$

8. $\frac{1}{6} \times \frac{3}{2}$

9. $\frac{1}{3} \times \frac{3}{8}$

10. $\frac{3}{2} \times \frac{2}{5}$

11. $\frac{8}{10} \times \frac{7}{10}$

12. $\frac{6}{7} \times \frac{2}{3}$

13. $\frac{5}{4} \times \frac{1}{5}$

14. $\frac{3}{9} \times \frac{3}{4}$

15. $\frac{4}{7} \times \frac{2}{5}$

16. $\frac{2}{10} \times \frac{2}{1000}$

17. $3\frac{1}{2} \times \frac{1}{4}$

18. $\frac{1}{5} \times 2\frac{1}{3}$

19. $1\frac{1}{5} \times 1\frac{1}{4}$

20. $6 \times \frac{2}{3}$

21. $\frac{1}{8} \times 9$

22. $7 \times \frac{1}{5}$

23. $5 \times \frac{3}{5}$

24. $10 \times \frac{3}{2}$

25. $4 \times 3\frac{1}{2}$

26. $2\frac{5}{6} \times 7$

27. $1\frac{8}{9} \times 3$

28. $5 \times 2\frac{1}{3}$

29. $2\frac{1}{3} \times 2\frac{1}{5}$

30. $3\frac{1}{4} \times 4\frac{1}{2}$

31. $\frac{5}{6} \times 3\frac{1}{3}$

32. $\frac{1}{2} \times 4\frac{1}{8}$

33. $3 \times 4\frac{1}{9}$

34. $6\frac{1}{2} \times \frac{1}{4}$

35. $2\frac{1}{5} \times 3\frac{1}{7}$

36. $4\frac{1}{6} \times 10$

Multiply.

1. 4.6
    × 7

2. 8.2
    × 6

3. 0.5
    × 0.9

4. 0.6
    × 3.8

5. 5.9
    × 0.7

6. 7.8
    × 0.3

7. 0.62
    × 0.5

8. 0.2
    × 0.93

9. 32
    × 0.4

10. 48
    × 0.7

11. 0.521
    × 6

12. 0.391
    × 7

13. 5.73
    × 6

14. 0.74
    × 3.1

15. 6.5
    × 9.2

16. 346
    × 0.7

17. 281
    × 0.5

18. 22.6
    × 7

19. 0.74
    × 3.3

20. 1.55
    × 0.2

21. 38.2
    × 0.9

22. 7.28
    × 0.4

23. 64.7
    × 0.5

24. 0.4
    × 0.8

25. 0.02
    × 0.7

26. 3.2
    × 0.6

27. 0.05
    × 0.9

28. 9.3
    × 0.04

29. 0.08
    × 2.6

30. 0.008
    × 0.7

31. 68
    × 0.03

32. 0.003
    × 0.5

33. 0.05
    × 39

34. 2.68
    × 9

35. 0.041
    × 3

36. 2.04
    × 5

37. 0.063
    × 9

38. 9.31
    × 0.5

39. 6.05
    × 0.3

40. 0.05
    × 0.4

41. 51.3
    × 0.2

42. 0.7
    × 36.5

43. 0.47
    × 0.7

44. 327
    × 0.05

45. 0.08
    × 418

46. 52.6
    × 3.7

47. 8.53
    × 2.7

48. 28.6
    × 5.2

49. 72.7
    × 3.8

50. 44.7
    × 4.8

51. 2.49 × 0.3

52. 0.05 × 0.7

53. 42.3 × 0.1

54. 9.31 × 0.5

55. 0.061 × 5

56. 2.56 × 0.7

57. 68.2 × 0.5

58. 0.521 × 36

Add or subtract.

1. $8\frac{2}{3}$
   $+ 7\frac{1}{3}$

2. $9\frac{2}{5}$
   $+ 4\frac{2}{3}$

3. $26\frac{1}{2}$
   $+ 3\frac{2}{4}$

4. $5\frac{1}{12}$
   $+ 8\frac{2}{3}$

5. $11\frac{2}{10}$
   $+ 7\frac{3}{5}$

6. $4\frac{7}{16}$
   $+ 12\frac{1}{2}$

7. $25\frac{3}{4}$
   $+ 9\frac{1}{2}$

8. $17\frac{7}{8}$
   $+ 12\frac{3}{4}$

9. $31\frac{5}{6}$
   $+ 15\frac{2}{3}$

10. $8\frac{3}{4}$
    $+ 41\frac{3}{4}$

11. $9\frac{1}{5}$
    $+ 7\frac{4}{5}$

12. $15\frac{1}{6}$
    $+ 61\frac{5}{12}$

13. $74\frac{3}{10}$
    $+ 29\frac{1}{2}$

14. $9\frac{3}{8}$
    $+ 37\frac{1}{16}$

15. $31\frac{1}{2}$
    $+ 7\frac{3}{5}$

16. $10\frac{1}{2}$
    $- 2\frac{3}{8}$

17. $26\frac{2}{3}$
    $- 15\frac{5}{6}$

18. 19
    $- 9\frac{2}{3}$

19. $65\frac{3}{4}$
    $- 27\frac{5}{16}$

20. $52\frac{1}{2}$
    $- 28\frac{2}{3}$

21. $19\frac{5}{12}$
    $- 8\frac{1}{2}$

22. $32\frac{3}{4}$
    $- 8$

23. 71
    $- 18\frac{1}{2}$

24. $21\frac{1}{2}$
    $- 17\frac{5}{6}$

25. $92\frac{3}{4}$
    $- 74\frac{5}{8}$

26. $37\frac{3}{10}$
    $- 15\frac{1}{2}$

27. 26
    $- 24\frac{3}{8}$

28. $71\frac{2}{5}$
    $- 38\frac{3}{5}$

29. $46\frac{1}{5}$
    $- 39\frac{9}{10}$

30. $27\frac{2}{4}$
    $- 15\frac{3}{4}$

31. $135\frac{7}{8}$
    $- 48\frac{3}{8}$

32. $257\frac{1}{2}$
    $- 189\frac{7}{10}$

33. $358\frac{72}{100}$
    $- 29\frac{1}{2}$

34. $74\frac{2}{3}$
    $- 8\frac{1}{4}$

35. $119\frac{7}{20}$
    $- 20\frac{3}{4}$

36. $29\frac{1}{4}$
    $37\frac{3}{4}$
    $+ 66\frac{2}{4}$

37. $73\frac{2}{3}$
    $92\frac{1}{3}$
    $+ 65\frac{2}{3}$

38. $28\frac{1}{2}$
    $86\frac{3}{4}$
    $+ 74\frac{1}{4}$

39. $36\frac{3}{5}$
    $75\frac{1}{2}$
    $+ 28\frac{7}{10}$

40. $159\frac{2}{3}$
    $127\frac{1}{2}$
    $+ 186\frac{1}{3}$

Table of Measures

Metric System		English System	

Length

1 millimeter (mm)	$\left\{\begin{array}{l}\frac{1}{10}\text{ centimeter (cm)}\\\frac{1}{1000}\text{ meter (m)}\end{array}\right.$	1 foot (ft)	{12 inches (in.)
1 centimeter (cm)	{10 millimeters (mm)	1 yard (yd)	$\left\{\begin{array}{l}36\text{ inches (in.)}\\3\text{ feet (ft)}\end{array}\right.$
1 decimeter (dm)	$\left\{\begin{array}{l}100\text{ millimeters (mm)}\\10\text{ centimeters (cm)}\end{array}\right.$	1 mile (mi)	$\left\{\begin{array}{l}5280\text{ feet (ft)}\\1760\text{ yards (yd)}\end{array}\right.$
1 meter (m)	$\left\{\begin{array}{l}1000\text{ millimeters (mm)}\\100\text{ centimeters (cm)}\\10\text{ decimeters (dm)}\end{array}\right.$	1 nautical mile	$\left\{\begin{array}{l}6076\text{ feet (ft)}\\1852\text{ meters (m)}\end{array}\right.$
1 kilometer (km)	{1000 meters (m)		

Area

1 square meter (m²)	$\left\{\begin{array}{l}100\text{ square decimeters (dm}^2)\\10\ 000\text{ square centimeters cm}^2)\end{array}\right.$	1 square foot	{144 square inches (in.²)
1 hectare (ha)	$\left\{\begin{array}{l}\frac{1}{100}\text{ square kilometer (km}^2)\\10\ 000\text{ square meters (m}^2)\end{array}\right.$	1 square yard (yd²)	$\left\{\begin{array}{l}9\text{ square feet (ft}^2)\\1296\text{ square inches (in.}^2)\end{array}\right.$
1 square kilometer (km²)	$\left\{\begin{array}{l}1\ 000\ 000\text{ square meters (m}^2)\\100\text{ hectares (ha)}\end{array}\right.$	1 acre (A)	$\left\{\begin{array}{l}43\ 560\text{ square feet (ft}^2)\\4\ 840\text{ square yards (yd}^2)\end{array}\right.$
		1 square mile (mi²)	{640 acres (A)

Volume

| 1 cubic decimeter (dm³) | $\left\{\begin{array}{l}\frac{1}{1000}\text{ cubic meter (m}^3)\\1000\text{ cubic centimeters (cm}^3)\\1\text{ liter (L)}\end{array}\right.$ | 1 cubic foot (ft³) | {1728 cubic inches (in.³) |
| 1 cubic meter (m³) | $\left\{\begin{array}{l}1\ 000\ 000\text{ cubic centimeters (cm}^3)\\1\ 000\text{ cubic decimeters (dm}^3)\end{array}\right.$ | 1 cubic yard (yd³) | $\left\{\begin{array}{l}27\text{ cubic feet (ft}^3)\\46\ 656\text{ cubic inches (in.}^3)\end{array}\right.$ |

Capacity

1 teaspoon	{5 milliliters (mL)	1 cup (c)	{8 fluid ounces (fl oz)
1 tablespoon	{12.5 milliliters (mL)	1 pint (pt)	$\left\{\begin{array}{l}16\text{ fluid ounces (fl oz)}\\2\text{ cups (c)}\end{array}\right.$
1 liter (L)	$\left\{\begin{array}{l}1000\text{ milliliters (mL)}\\1000\text{ cubic centimeters (cm}^3)\\1\text{ cubic decimeter (dm}^3)\\4\text{ metric cups}\end{array}\right.$	1 quart (qt)	$\left\{\begin{array}{l}32\text{ fluid ounces (fl oz)}\\4\text{ cups (c)}\\2\text{ pints (pt)}\end{array}\right.$
1 kiloliter (kL)	{1000 liters (L)	1 gallon (gal)	$\left\{\begin{array}{l}128\text{ fluid ounces (fl oz)}\\16\text{ cups (c)}\\8\text{ pints (pt)}\\4\text{ quarts (qt)}\end{array}\right.$

Mass

1 gram (g)	{1000 milligrams (mg)	1 pound (lb)	{16 ounces (oz)
1 kilogram (kg)	{1000 grams (g)	1 ton (T)	{2000 pounds (lbs)
1 metric ton (t)	{1000 kilograms (kg)		

Glossary

addend Any one of a set of numbers to be added. In the equation $4 + 5 = 9$, the numbers 4 and 5 are addends.

addition An operation that combines a first number and a second number to give exactly one number. The two numbers are called addends, and the result is called the sum of the addends.

angle Two rays from a single point.

approximation One number is an approximation of another number if the first number is suitably "close" (according to context) to the other number.

area The area of a closed figure or region is the measure of that region as compared to a given selected region called the unit, usually a square region in the case of area.

associative (grouping) principle When adding (or multiplying) three numbers, you can change the grouping and the sum (or product) is the same.

Examples: $2 + (8 + 6) = (2 + 8) + 6$
$3 \times (4 \times 2) = (3 \times 4) \times 2$

average The average of a set of numbers is the quotient resulting when the sum of the numbers in the set is divided by the number of addends.

bisect To divide in half or find the midpoint.

centimeter A unit of length. One centimeter is 0.01 meter.

circle The set of all points in a plane which are a specified distance from a given point called the center or center point.

circumference The distance around a circle.

common factor When a number is a factor of two different numbers, it is said to be a common factor of the two numbers.

common multiple A number is a common multiple of two numbers if it is a multiple of each of the numbers.

commutative (order) principle When adding (or multiplying) two numbers, the order of the addends (or factors) does not affect the sum (or product).

Examples: $4 + 5 = 5 + 4$
$3 \times 6 = 6 \times 3$

composite number Any whole number greater than 1 that is not prime.

congruent figures Geometric figures that have the same size and shape.

congruent triangles

coordinates Number pair used in graphing.

coordinate axes Two number lines intersecting at right angles at 0.

cube A rectangular prism (box) such that all faces are squares.

decimal Any base-ten numeral that uses place value to represent a number.

degree A unit of angle measure.

denominator The number indicated by the numeral below the line in a fraction symbol.

diagonal A segment joining two nonadjacent vertices of a polygon. In the figure, the diagonal is segment AB.

diameter A chord that passes through the center point of the circle. The diameter is segment AB.

distributive (multiplication-addition) principle
This principle is sometimes described in terms of "breaking apart" a number before multiplying.

Example: $6 \times (20 + 4) = (6 \times 20) + (6 \times 4)$

dividend In the problem $33 \div 7$, 33 is called the dividend.

Example:
$$4 \leftarrow \text{quotient}$$
$$7\overline{)33} \leftarrow \text{dividend}$$
$$\text{divisor} \nearrow$$
$$\underline{28}$$
$$5 \leftarrow \text{remainder}$$

division An operation related to multiplication as illustrated:

$3 \times 4 = 12$
$12 \div 4 = 3$
$12 \div 3 = 4$

divisor In the problem $33 \div 7$, 7 is called the divisor.

edge An edge of a space figure is one of the segments making up any one of the faces of a space figure.

equality (equals; or =) A mathematical relation of being exactly the same.

equally likely outcomes Outcomes that have the same chance of occurring.

equation A mathematical sentence involving the use of the equality symbol.

Examples: $5 + 4 = 9$; $7 + \square = 8$; $n + 3 = 7$.

equivalent fractions Two fractions are equivalent when it can be shown that they each can be used to represent the same amount of a given object. Also, two fractions are equivalent if these two products are the same:

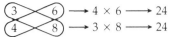

equivalent sets   Two sets that may be placed in a one-to-one correspondence.

estimate   To find an approximation for a given number. (Sometimes a sum, a product, etc.)

even numbers   The whole-number multiples of 2 (0, 2, 4, 6, 8, 10, 12, . . .).

exponent   In the symbol 10^3, the "3" is the exponent. It indicates that 10 is used as a factor three times. Thus: $10^3 = 10 \times 10 \times 10 = 1000$
$$5^4 = 5 \times 5 \times 5 \times 5 = 625$$

face   The face of a given space figure is any one of the plane geometric figures (regions) making up the space figure. *See* edge.

factor   In the equation $6 \times 7 = 42$, 6 and 7 are factors of 42. *See* multiplication.

fraction   A symbol for a fractional number, such as $\frac{2}{3}, \frac{3}{4}, \frac{1}{2},$ and so on.

fractional number   The one number we think about for each set of equivalent fractions.

graph   (1) A set of points associated with a given set of numbers or set of number pairs. (2) A picture used to illustrate a given collection of data. The data might be pictured in the form of a bar graph, a circle graph, a line graph, or a pictograph. (3) To draw the graph of.

greater than ($>$)   One of the two basic inequality relations.

Example: $8 > 5$, read 8 is greater than 5.

greatest common factor   The largest, or greatest, number that is a factor of each of two numbers.

height of a triangle   The height of a triangle from any vertex is the perpendicular distance from that vertex to the opposite side (usually called the base). In the figure, the length of $\overline{CD}$ is the height of the triangle from vertex C to base $\overline{AB}$.

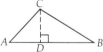

hexagon   A six-sided polygon.

hypotenuse   The side opposite the right angle in a right triangle.

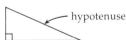

improper fraction   A fraction in which the numerator is greater than or equal to the denominator.

Examples: $\frac{8}{5}, \frac{6}{6}, \frac{12}{3}, \frac{7}{7}$

inequality ($<$, $\neq$, $>$)   In arithmetic, a relation indicating that the two numbers are not the same.

integers   The whole numbers together with their negatives: $\{\ldots, {}^-3, {}^-2, {}^-1, 0, 1, 2, 3, \ldots\}$

least common denominator   The least common multiple of two denominators. The least common denominator for $\frac{3}{4}$ and $\frac{5}{6}$ is 12.

least common multiple   The smallest non-zero number that is a multiple of each of two given numbers. The least common multiple of 4 and 6 is 12.

legs of a right triangle   The two sides of a right triangle other than the hypotenuse.

length   (1) A number indicating the measure of one line segment with respect to another line segment, called the unit. (2) Sometimes used to denote one dimension (usually the greater) of a rectangle.

less than ($<$)   One of the two basic inequality relations. Example: $5 < 8$, read 5 is less than 8.

lowest terms   A fraction is in lowest terms if the numerator and denominator of the fraction have no common factor greater than 1.

meter   The basic unit of length in the Metric System.

midpoint   A point that divides a line segment into two parts of the same size.

mixed-decimal numeral   Numerals such as $0.7\frac{1}{2}$ and $0.33\frac{1}{3}$.

mixed numeral   Symbols such as $2\frac{1}{2}$ and $5\frac{1}{4}$.

multiple   A first number is a multiple of a second number if there is a whole number that multiplies by the second number to give the first number.

Example: 24 is a multiple of 6 since $4 \times 6 = 24$.

multiplication   An operation that combines two numbers, called factors, to give one number called the product.

negative number   A number which will add to a positive number to give a sum of zero.

For example: $5 + {}^-5 = 0$, $19 + {}^-19 = 0$

number pair   Any pair of numbers. Each pair of numbers can be matched with a unique point in the coordinate plane.

numeral   A symbol for a number.

numerator   The number indicated by the numeral above the line in a fraction symbol.

odd number   Any whole number that is not even.

Examples: 1, 3, 5, 7, . . .

one principle   Any number multiplied by 1 is that same number. Sometimes called the identity principle for multiplication.

parallel lines   Two lines which lie in the same plane and do not intersect.

parallelogram   A quadrilateral with its opposite sides parallel.

pentagon   A five-sided polygon.

percent (%)   Per 100; for each; $\frac{1}{100}$.

perimeter   The sum of the lengths of the sides of a given polygon.

period In arithmetic, each set of three digits indicated by spaces when writing a numeral is called a period.

Example:

$$3\ 4\ 2 \qquad 6\ 7\ 4 \qquad 2\ 0\ 8$$

millions' period   thousands' period   units' period

perpendicular lines Two lines that intersect in right angles are perpendicular to each other.

pi (π) The ratio of the circumference to the diameter of a circle; approximately 3.14.

place value A system used for writing numerals for numbers, using only a definite number of symbols or digits. In the numeral 3257 the 5 stands for 50; in the numeral 36 289 the 6 stands for 6000.

polygon A closed geometric figure made up of line segments. A regular polygon has congruent sides and congruent angles.

prime number A number greater than 1 whose only factors are itself and 1. Examples: 2, 3, 5, 7

probability The probability that an event will occur in a set of equally likely outcomes is the number of ways the event can occur divided by the total number of possible outcomes. For example, the probability that a 3 or a 4 will turn up in a single toss of a die is $\frac{2}{6}$ since there are 2 ways the event can occur and there are 6 possible equally likely outcomes.

product The result of the multiplication operation. In $6 \times 7 = 42$, 42 is the product of 6 and 7.

protractor An instrument used for measuring angles.

quadrilateral A four-sided polygon.

quotient The number (other than the remainder) that is the result of the division operation. It may be thought of as a factor in a multiplication equation.

radius (1) Any segment from the center point to a point on the circle. (2) The distance from the center point to any point on the circle.

radius

ratio A pair of numbers used in making certain comparisons. The ratio of 3 to 4 is written $3:4$ or $\frac{3}{4}$.

ray A ray is a certain part of a line.

line   ray

reciprocal Two numbers are reciprocals of one another if their product is 1. Example: $\frac{4}{7}$ and $\frac{7}{4}$ are reciprocals of each other.

rectangle A quadrilateral that has four right angles.

rhombus A parallelogram with 4 congruent sides.

right angle An angle that has the measure of 90 degrees.

right triangle A triangle that has one right angle.

Roman numerals Numerals used by the Romans. Used primarily to record numbers rather than for computing. Examples: IV, IX, XIV, L, C, M.

rotation A motion in which a given figure is turned about a fixed point.

scale drawing A drawing constructed so the ratio of all the dimensions in the drawing to those of the actual object is the same.

segment Two points on a line and all the points on that line that are between the two points.

sequence A collection or set of numbers given in a specific order. Such numbers are commonly given according to some rule or pattern.

set undefined; usually thought of as a group or collection.

similar figures Two figures that have the same shape. △ △ similar figures

skew lines Two lines that are not in the same plane.

solution The number or numbers which result from solving an equation or a given problem.

square A quadrilateral that has four right angles and four sides that are the same length.

subtraction An operation related to addition as illustrated:

$$7 + 8 = 15 \begin{cases} 15 - 8 = 7 \\ 15 - 7 = 8 \end{cases}$$

sum The result obtained by adding any set of numbers.

symmetric figure A plane figure which can be folded in half so that the two halves match.

tangent A line is tangent to a circle if the two figures are in one plane and have exactly one point in common.

tessellation A repeated pattern of regions that can cover a plane.

translation A motion in which each point of a figure is moved the same distance and in the same direction.

trapezoid A quadrilateral with at least one pair of parallel sides.

triangle A three-sided polygon.

unit An amount or quantity adopted as a standard of measurement.

vertex The point that the two rays of an angle have in common.

vertex →

volume The measure, obtained using an appropriate unit (usually a cube), of the interior region of a space figure.

whole number Any number in the set {0, 1, 2, 3, 4, 5, 6, 7, 8, 9, 10, 11, 12, 13, 14, . . .}

zero principle Any number added to zero is that same number. (Also called the identity principle for addition.)

Index

A

Abacus, 5
Acute angle, 45
Addition
    column, 16–17, 68–69, 73
    decimals, 66–69, 73
    estimation, 38–39
    of even and odd numbers, 37
    fractions with like denominators, 260–261
    fractions with unlike denominators, 264–265
    mixed numerals, 260–261, 328–329
    money, 36–37, 72–73
    and place value, 12–13
    of tenths, 259
    2-, 3-, and 4-digit numbers (with regrouping), 14–15
Angles
    acute, obtuse, right, 45
    congruent, 47
    measuring, 46–47
    naming, 44
    of quadrilaterals, 50–51
    of triangles, 48–49
    vertex, 44
Area
    counting unit squares, 166–167, 348A
    using decimals, 320–321
    estimating, 173
    of rectangles, 168–169, 348A–348B
    square centimeter, 167
    square inch, 348A
    of triangles, 170–171, 349A–349B
Associative principle, 13
Average, 200–201

B

Bar graph, 201, 282–283

C

Capacity
    gallons, quarts, pints, cups 351A–351B
    liter and milliliter, 338–339
    milliliter and cubic centimeter, 338–339
Centimeter
    cubic, 335, 338–339
    and millimeters, 88–91
    square, 167
Century, 209
Circle
    graph, 285
    radius and diameter, 90–91, 346B
Column addition
    decimals, 68–69, 73
    2-, 3-, and 4-digit numbers, 16–17

Commutative principle, 13
Comparing
    decimals, 62–63
    line segments, 100–101
    polygons, 102–103
    size of objects, 211
Composite number, 162–163
Congruent
    angles, 47
    figures (graphing), 226–227
    polygons, 102–103
    segments, 100–101
Coordinate geometry
    graph congruent figures, 226–227
    graph points and pictures, 222–223
    graph symmetric figures, 224–225
    secret message, 231
    write coordinate of given point, 221
Cross product, 242–243
Cube, 214
Cubic centimeter, 335, 338–339
Cubic inch, 350A–350B

D

Decade, 209
Decimals
    adding, 66–69, 73
    column addition, 68–69, 73
    comparing, 62–63
    hundredths, 58–59
    multiplication, 302–307
    number line, 63
    reading, 60–61
    subtracting, 70–71
    writing, 57–59, 61
Degree, 46
Denominator, 235
Diameter, 90–91, 346B
Dividend, 177
Division
    estimating quotients, 187
    facts, 118–121
    larger quotients, 194–195
    missing factor, 118
    of money, 202–203
    by multiples of 10, 132–133, 182–183
    of multiples of 10, 100, and 1000, 130–131
    quotient, 118, 177
    remainder, 177
    rounding divisors, 192–193
    short division, 180–181
    and subtraction, 176–177